JOANA KRUSE

HOW VERY BRITISH!

A JOLLY GOOD CULTURE CLASH ROAD TRIP

WWW.JOANAIMAGES.COM
WWW.STORYTELLERSPHOTOGUIDE.COM

Copyright © 2025 Joana Kruse
All rights reserved
The characters and events portrayed in this book are fictitious. Any similarity to real persons, living or dead, is coincidental and not intended by the author.
No part of this book may be reproduced, or stored in a retrieval system, or transmitted in any form or by any means, electronic, mechanical, photocopying, recording, or otherwise, without express written permission of the publisher.

Book cover design & photos: Joana Kruse
www.joanaimages.com

ISBN 978-1-0682970-8-3

CONTENTS

ON BECOMING ACCIDENTALLY BRITISH 4

LONDON IS CALLING 7

AN ITALIAN IN SOUTH WEST ENGLAND 19

A GERMAN IN SOUTH CENTRAL ENGLAND 101

A FRENCH IN SOUTH EAST ENGLAND 173

AN AMERICAN IN EAST ENGLAND 239

A SWEDE IN NORTH ENGLAND 299

BRITISH OR ENGLISH? 361

ABOUT THE AUTHOR 372

DISCOVER MORE BOOKS FROM THE AUTHOR 374

ON BECOMING ACCIDENTALLY BRITISH

Dear Reader,

British culture is a bit like Marmite or warm beer – you get used to it over time. It doesn't happen all at once. Instead, it sneaks up on you, one quirky habit after another, until you feel a flicker of shame seeing someone jump a queue. By then, there's no going back. You're in. You're 'Britainised'.

I arrived one Tuesday in summer many years ago, stepping into the unknown journey of becoming 'an islander'. Heathrow was congested, clouds like tin foil. I'd lived in Italy, Switzerland, and clean Germanic cities. My idea of England was stitched together from boarding-school novels and the odd episode of 'Midsomer Murders'. The country itself was a mystery parcel: I recognised the wrapping, but had no idea what was inside.

My first British house gave me a classic initiation: a charming late Victorian semi in the New Forest with dubious plumbing and separate hot and cold taps. Now, I live in Scotland; the plumbing is still dubious, though I changed the tap.

What fascinated me, and still surprises my visitors, was the wiring. Why are bathroom light switches always outside? Do Brits really think Europeans get electrocuted every day just because they have switches inside the bathroom? This phenomenon also extends to sockets. In mainland Europe, you plug in a device and it immediately works. In Britain, you must flip an extra switch on the socket, as if to declare, "Yes, I am fully committed to this toast." The system is so counterintuitive that my Swiss and Italian friends still call in despair when visiting, convinced that the entire power grid has failed because their phone charger remains inert.

Over time, these peculiarities became invisible. I learned to blow-dry my hair squeezed between my bed and wardrobe without a mirror - no sockets allowed in the bathroom, as you might have guessed. I also learned to say "sorry" when someone stepped on my foot. I joined queues automatically, even when I wasn't sure what they were for. I began to detect the subtlety of British small talk. A simple "Not too bad" can mask anything, from existential despair to uncontainable delight, depending on the lift of an eyebrow.

Sometimes a foreign friend visits, and I see it all again through their eyes: the strange bottle of brown sauce on the table, the misery of Sunday train timetables, the national sport of apologising to inanimate objects, or the medical system that cheerfully puts you on a waiting list but never charges you for a bandage.

But it's exactly this strange, glorious jumble I've come to love. Not as a tourist with chocolate box villages and Colin Firth diving into ponds, but as someone who loves a home lived in long enough to be untidy, yet always welcoming and cosy.

And so, despite all the daily peculiarities and challenges, this book is a love letter to the UK, written by someone who's long stopped trying to understand what's going on here, but has decided to enjoy it anyway. Britain might be a land of baffling politics, low salaries, high costs, and potholes as deep as Scotland's lochs. Yet, it's also a land of kindness and tolerance, where people help you battle through life each day.

What follows are tales of cultural collision. Yes, I use stereotypes. I know full well that not every German is punctual, not every French person a wine snob, and some Brits can express emotion without requiring medical attention afterwards. Consider these gentle caricatures as shorthand – useful fictions that reveal real differences. This isn't anthropology; it's a collection of mishaps and misunderstandings that make cross-cultural living both maddening and delightful. And no, I don't think British culture is superior to any other. (At least I wouldn't admit it when anyone's listening.)

But there is a great deal more to Britain than cryptic conversation and peculiar social codes. There are the festivals, for a start: weird, wild affairs that make no sense. There is history, layered deep, sometimes painted bloody red, sometimes played for laughs. There are places you could not replicate if you tried, and a national knack for stubbornly hanging on to what has gone before.

We will set off on a jolly good culture clash road trip, but rather than providing a tidy list of tourist spots, I plan to show you the England you might bypass in a guidebook. After all, this was never meant to be a tourist tour. The point is to get under England's skin – to dig out its stories, its oddities, its glorious muddle. Imagine: a village whose nationality changed fourteen times, a pie that can fend off poison, an entire lighthouse up and trundled on rails to safety, flaming barrels, plates full of nettles to eat, the smuggling grandma, the New Forest Cowgirl. These are the sorts of stories you remember. Let me, then, introduce you to my England.

If you want insights into a culture that may be the weirdest in Europe, treat this as a crash course in exploring the world's most idiosyncratic island. You won't learn how to make a perfect cup of tea (that's genetic) or decode the property market (no one can). But you'll see that beneath polite reserve and eccentric habits is a nation that is, in its own way, warm, supportive, surprisingly chatty – far less reserved than you might think – tolerant, and wonderfully unique. And even the weather is not as bad as some say! I wouldn't trade my adopted home, including potholes and brown sauce, for a lifetime of sensible plumbing.

One final note: **what follows is fiction** – but fiction stitched from a patchwork of very real encounters, misunderstandings, and adventures gathered over the years. The festivals you'll meet don't always appear in the right season; I've bent time a little to weave them into the journey. Think of it less as a strict calendar, more as a storyteller's licence.

So, welcome. Make yourself a cup of tea. If the kettle doesn't work, check the socket switch. And enjoy this road trip with some continental and American friends who are just as baffled by the Brits.

Warmly, Joana

P.S.: In case you dare to put foot on this odd island after reading the book, how about some inspirational ideas on what to see? You can get my book "Travel Sparks: England" on AMAZON, photographed and written by me.

LONDON IS CALLING

There's a particular shade of grey that only reveals itself in London after three consecutive days of drizzle. Every surface, from the bin lorries to the cobblestones, is mattified.

Today's project was particularly demanding. Six hours. That's how long I'd been hunched over my screen, painstakingly nudging pixels and smoothing out the digital blood spatter from the armpit of a man in a finely tailored suit. Not real blood, of course – just a photo destined for a book cover. The publisher claimed this new thriller author was "the next big thing," but I was sceptical. His bio described him as "mysterious," which behind the desk meant "nobody's met him and there's a persistent rumour he's AI." My assignment: "make it bleaker, but sexy."

I was in the process of adding a final, faint reflection of a raven to the office window behind the murder victim when my phone vibrated. The abrupt buzz of an unknown caller cut through my focus. I let it ring twice more. Spambots are endemic.

"Brianna here," I answered, irritation lacing my voice as I glanced at the clock. The interruption felt unwelcome, a jarring note in the symphony of my meticulously crafted crime chaos. The last thing I needed was a phone call.

"Brianna, good afternoon! I hope I'm not catching you at a bad time," said a woman's voice, professionally cheerful. A familiar undertone – either an agent, or someone trying to sell me a subscription to photographic insurance.

"Is there a good time?" I replied, then immediately regretted it.

The voice persisted, undaunted. "My name's Elaine from the British International Exchange. I'm the programme director. We've been following your portfolio with great interest. Your Faroe and Scottish Highlands series, in particular, is exquisite."

I swivelled my chair until I could see the aforementioned series. My proudest landscape from the Azores hung slightly askew. Ryan – my erstwhile assistant and platonic lodestar – had attempted to "eyeball it" while standing on a kitchen stool.

Next to it, the Swiss Alps, or as Ryan had called it, "Lord of the Rings with better cheese." The Morocco trip, still unframed, lurked by the bookcase, awaiting its moment of glory. I'd spent years on the road chasing the light with my camera, usually with Ryan in tow. The images did look good together, but compliments from strangers rarely set me at ease.

Elaine pressed on. "We're launching a cross-country initiative to showcase the diversity of England's landscapes. And it's an entirely rural project – no cities, as I gather you're not a fan. Photographers from across Europe, paired with you as a local photographic guide. A little bit of cultural exchange, a little bit of adventure. All expenses covered, naturally."

This was where my personality always split in two. Part of me – the hermit, the control freak, the person who once wore noise-cancelling headphones to a dinner party – screamed in terror. But the other part, the one with a world map tacked above the kettle and a passport always within arm's reach, leaned forward, senses sharp with curiosity.

"Is it strictly landscape, or are you looking for more... editorial stuff?" I asked, already picturing my calendar.

"Whatever inspires you," Elaine said. "Your eye for composition is exactly what we want. And, if I'm not mistaken, you've worked with international students before?"

I had, briefly, during a poorly funded university outreach where I'd tried to teach a group of Erasmus students how to use darkroom chemicals without giving themselves facial tattoos. The memory was both terrifying and hilarious, but it did mean I wasn't wholly unqualified.

"And I'd be paired with...?"

"We can match you with an assistant of your choice, if you have someone in mind. You'd be leading the project, Brianna. You'd have creative control. Are you interested?"

It took all of three seconds for the words "creative control" and "expenses covered" to overpower my instincts. Still, I made a show of deliberation. "Could you send the details over by email?"

"They're on their way," Elaine chirped. "We'd need an answer by the end of the week. Let me know if you have any questions!"

The line went dead. I stared at the phone for a moment, then at my unfinished cover art, then at the plants in my room. I picked up my favourite mug (green, chipped, with a Highland cow dressed in a kilt) and flicked the kettle on. This was a decision that required green tea.

As I waited for the water to boil, I did a mental inventory of what would be required to survive several weeks shepherding foreign photographers across England. Endless patience. Wellies. Ryan, definitely – nobody else would be mad enough to work with me that long with the promise of "scenic vistas" and "character-building weather." I pictured him now: in his flat in Camden, surrounded by Bluetooth speakers and vegan energy bars, possibly deep in an argument with an Amazon delivery man, passionately debating how to improve the delivery route using one of his latest app creations.

The kettle clicked off. I poured the water over a bag that claimed, optimistically, to contain "artisan whole-leaf sencha," and watched as the green liquor bled into the mug. Routine is a funny thing; it can feel like a shackle until someone threatens to take it away, at which point you cling to it like a life raft. I spent the next ten minutes slowly sipping the tea, weighing the merits of travel against the horrors of explaining this unexplainable country to completely clueless foreigners.

Just then, my phone buzzed again. This time it was a message, with a subject line that read: "INTERNATIONAL PHOTOGRAPHY PROJECT: FULL DETAILS."

I scanned the attachment, noting the travel schedule (ambitious but not impossible), the list of participating English regions, and a brief bio of my prospective students. Nothing looked particularly fatal.

I was halfway through composing a reply ("Happy to discuss further, please see my attached portfolio and a list of allergies and dietary requirements") when my thumb hovered over Ryan's contact. There's a kind of giddy, anticipatory thrill that comes from knowing you're about to disrupt someone else's perfectly ordinary day. I pressed the dial and waited.

He picked up on the fourth ring, sounding as if he'd just

awoken from a hibernation. "Jo? That you? Is it urgent?"

"Only if you consider the British International Exchange urgent. They want to pay me to lead a photography project with students from around the world. They said I can bring an assistant."

There was a long pause, filled with the subtle noises of someone trying to sit up without actually leaving their bed. "That's... brilliant. Wait, is this the thing you mentioned last month, or is this new?"

"New. And they're offering full travel, decent accommodation, and you get to eat your way through the vegan cafés of the UK at someone else's expense."

"Brilliant!" he said again, voice rising an octave. "When do we start? I've been dying to try that new vegan café in Cornwall anyway! They do a seaweed latte that's supposed to taste like the Atlantic, in a good way."

I smiled, in spite of myself. "You realise this will involve actual work, not just Instagramming your breakfast."

"Please. I'm an old pro. Besides, I've been practising my outdoorsy look. Got the waterproofs, and even a new drone."

We ran through the logistics, both feigning professionalism but mostly just making up for lost time. Ryan's excitement was infectious, and I found myself already plotting camera angles and potential disasters (a few involving students, several involving Ryan, and one elaborate scenario with a runaway sheep in the Cotswolds). I hadn't realised how much I missed the anticipation of travel – the electric, restless energy of not knowing what could happen next.

By the time I hung up, dusk had crept over Islington, and the room had turned from silver to pewter. My tea was cold, forgotten in the excitement. I poured myself a new cup and surveyed the wall of landscapes. Switzerland, Scotland, Morocco, and now... who knows?

I opened the laptop and started a packing list. Number one: Ryan. Number two: green tea. Everything else would sort itself out.

The café had the air of a place that had once been a launderette and still hadn't quite lost the scent of detergent. I'd chosen it for two reasons: proximity (I could see my own bedroom window if I craned my neck), and a green tea that didn't taste like the aftermath of a lawnmower accident. I claimed my usual seat – back to the wall, optimal view of the door – and spent a solid twenty minutes arranging maps and notepads to look as if I'd been productive since sunrise.

Ryan arrived at 10:18, more than one hour late. A record even by his standards. I watched as he ricocheted through the door, nearly decapitating a barista with his overstuffed backpack. Cables, chargers, and the occasional protein bar protruded from every available pocket. He caught sight of me, tripped over a footstool, and landed in the adjacent chair with the grace of a sack of compost.

"Sorry, sorry!" he said, already pawing through his rucksack. "Bus was late, then my GPS sent me to the wrong street, and my battery's at two percent. Disaster. Absolute disaster."

"You live only three tube stops away," I reminded him.

He grinned, undeterred. "Don't underestimate TFL's ability to ruin a man before noon." He flagged down the waiter – a woman with a geometric buzzcut and a line of tiny silver hoops marching up her ear – and ordered an oat flat white and two vegan pain au chocolat, the second of which he reluctantly offered me. I declined and watched as he inhaled both pastries in a display of single-mindedness I'd always found oddly impressive.

"Right!" He wiped his hands on the inside of his sleeve, then yanked a battered tablet from his bag. "Let's talk itinerary."

I had already unrolled my maps and annotated them in four colours: blue for rural roads, green for EV charging points, orange for "potentially photogenic, pending weather," and red for "places Brianna never wishes to see again." Ryan ignored all of this and launched straight into his own presentation, which consisted of a Pinterest board entitled "ENGLAND MADNESS – RYAN'S PICKS."

"Did you know there's a town that does competitive worm charming?" he began, swiping enthusiastically. "And up

North, they have a festival where people dress up as mobile phones and chase each other through the high street. Also, I've already mapped every top-rated vegan establishment between here and Sheffield. That's dedication."

I did my best to ignore him, something I had become quite skilled at over the years, and tried to keep our planning on track. "The plan is to drive west, hit the coast at Dorset and Cornwall, then work our way up through the Cotswolds, the east, and into the north of England." I traced the route with my finger.

He chewed thoughtfully on his (third) pain au chocolat. "And we're doing this in your electric car?"

"I've already checked the charging points. We'll never be more than 35 miles from salvation."

"Unless we get stuck behind a Morris Minor rally in Dorset again. I thought we'd die out there." He leaned in conspiratorially. "Did you know some places don't even have Wi-Fi?"

I sipped my Matcha, letting the silence do the heavy lifting. Ryan had a horror of disconnection that bordered on the spiritual; he'd once threatened to start a Change.org petition when I had booked us a hotel in the Outer Hebrides that had just started offering 'digital detox weekends.'

I laid out the schedule in full view. This wasn't the usual approach – the business of ticking off the big, photogenic crowd-pleasers – but rather a mission to ferret out the quirkiest places on offer. The logic was plain: if you were going to show foreigners around who want to get to know the Brits, you ought to dazzle them, not with stately piles or sombre grandeur, but with the unmistakable stamp of British madness.

"If we stick to this, we'll have time for detours. But not if you insist on reviewing every vegan bakery from here to John o' Groats."

He looked genuinely hurt. "You can't rush art, Jo. Or pastry."

A nearby table snorted with laughter, and I realised we'd drawn the attention of the café's entire student population.

I pretended not to notice. "Have you sorted your equipment yet?"

He nodded, swallowing. "Three camera bodies, two drones,

new tripod. I've got backup SD cards, and I even labelled the cables."

"Impressive," I conceded.

He looked pleased. "I also ordered matching jackets for us. Ethically sourced, obviously."

"Are they also hideous?" I asked, picturing the highlighter-yellow monstrosity he'd once worn on the Yorkshire moors.

"Only a little. But safety first."

We spent the next hour reconciling our visions for the trip. Ryan lobbied hard for "maximum serendipity," which I interpreted as "allow time for unplanned snacks and catastrophic weather." I insisted on daily backups and a rigid travel log, though I knew full well the system would be abandoned by Day 3 in favour of hastily scrawled notes on napkins. Our negotiation style hadn't changed in a decade; it was less "give and take" and more "gently wear down the other party until all that's left is a mutual respect for each other's stubbornness."

We left the café together, the door's little bell marking our exit. Outside, the rain had stopped and the city shimmered with that peculiar London optimism – a promise that, at least for the next twenty minutes, things might go according to plan.

My phone buzzed as we reached the street. "Ooh, new message from the Exchange," I announced, squinting at the screen. "Apparently, our first international student is arriving tomorrow. Italian. Wants to do a pre-trip talk. You in?"

Ryan considered the implications. "Sure. But you're handling the logistics."

I winked, already typing 'yes' as an answer. What could possibly go wrong?

There's a ritual to the beginnings of any expedition, no matter how small-scale or domesticated. For me, it was always about lists. I'd spent the morning revising our itinerary, checking photo stops against weather forecasts, and double-checking which charging stations had been recently reviewed as "actually functioning" by similarly afflicted EV drivers.

After updating my list, I messaged Ryan the latest update and suggested we reconvene at the café to finalise everything. He responded with a thumbs-up emoji and a GIF of a dancing sheep, which I took to mean "I'm already on my way." By the time I arrived, he'd claimed our usual table and was attempting to print out the route via a portable, battery-powered printer. It coughed out a single page, smeared and unreadable, then expired with a noise that was half defeat, half defiance.

"Technology is a cruel mistress," he declared, stuffing the printer back into his backpack. "Anyway, did you see? Our Italian is joining us here soon. Elaine says we should show him 'proper British hospitality.' Do you think that means warm beer or just pretending to enjoy drizzle?"

"Probably both," I said, shaking out the maps. "His name's Marco Ricci from Florence. Apparently won some awards for conceptual portraiture."

Ryan whistled. "Impressive. Is he the moody type, or the espresso-fuelled, shouty sort?"

As if on cue, the café's door burst open. In strode a man in his mid twenties, dressed as if he'd taken an aggressive stance against neutrals: lemon yellow trousers, a turquoise puffer, and a scarf patterned like a migraine. Around his neck dangled a camera, plus a pair of sunglasses that looked positively defiant in the ambient London gloom. He scanned the room, eyes alighting on our table, and with a flourish, strode over.

"Buongiorno!" he announced, volume pitched somewhere between a street preacher and a football manager on match day. "You must be my photography maestri!"

A clatter as he deposited his gear – and himself – at our table, immediately scattering the careful arrangement of maps and blocking out most of my view. The nearest patrons looked up, disconcerted, then buried themselves in their laptops with the universal British expression of "If I ignore this, perhaps it will stop."

I offered a hand. "Brianna. This is Ryan. Welcome to... well, London."

Marco shook both our hands at once, then produced a battered Moleskine and a box of coloured pencils. "Thank you! I am very much excited to discover your England. It is so... what is the word... moody. Yes! Moody."

I slid my colour-coded itinerary across the table, tapping a highlighted section with my pen. "You're our South West companion - cream teas and mysterious stone circles."

Marco began sketching something – our faces, the room, it was hard to tell – all while talking at the same time. "In Italia, the light is always warm, like honey. Here it is more... mysterious. Melancholy!"

He looked up, eyes shining. "I wish to see all of it. The cliffs, the cottages, the strange little villages. And I hear there are very good pasties in Cornwall?" He winked at Ryan, who visibly melted.

"Best in the world, apparently," Ryan confirmed.

"Perfect!" Marco said. "My Mamma says, if you wish to know a place, first you must eat its food and then talk to its nonnas. Maybe we will do both, si?"

He spread his portfolio across our remaining surface area, each photograph more dramatic than the last. Storm clouds over Milan, an old man's face in chiaroscuro, a street dog silhouetted by fireworks. There was a certain fever to his work: not content to observe, it seemed to want to possess every shade of emotion. I found myself both impressed and faintly exhausted just looking at them.

Ryan, however, was utterly besotted. "These are incredible! Did you shoot the fireworks with a tripod?"

"No, no, no. Always handheld. More... how you say... authentic." He pantomimed holding a camera and lurching side to side, nearly knocking over my green tea. I rescued it at the last second.

He grinned. "Sorry! I am too much sometimes, I know. My father says my heart is too big for my body, but what can I do?"

I shot a look at Ryan, who was now busy showing Marco the digital version of our route. The two were already thick as thieves, swapping lens recommendations and debating the merits of mirrorless over DSLR. I sipped my tea and resigned myself to playing responsible adult – the only grown-up in a travelling circus of veganised chaos.

"So," Marco said, "what is our first destination?"

"Wiltshire and Dorset," I said. "And then the rest of the South West. Devon, Cornwall…"

He clapped his hands, nearly decapitating a pain au chocolat with his elbow. "Ah! The coast. The moors. The endless sky! It will be magnificent. When do we go?"

I checked the time. "We'll pick you up from your hotel at 7am tomorrow. Hope you packed light. My EV is small."

"Excellent," he said, then, more quietly, "I hope I do not disappoint."

As we gathered our things and headed out, Marco lingered by the café window, looking up at the sooty clouds. "In Italy, we say that a trip should start with a little bit of rain. It is good luck."

Ryan, shouldering his pack, said, "You're going to have the luckiest journey on record, then."

Marco beamed. "I very much hope so."

I smiled, too. Maybe it was the company, or maybe it was the elevating effect of green tea, but for once, I was looking forward to whatever storm we were heading into.

AN ITALIAN IN SOUTH WEST ENGLAND

Marco's packing approach put me in mind of some odd hybrid between a Verdi opera and the preview for a Sotheby's auction – brisk, faintly feverish, and not without a certain dramatic flair. He wasn't simply standing in front of the hotel entrance; he was posed there, as if the whole event might be captured for posterity and, who knows, possibly even hung in a museum someday. On either side of him, arrayed with an engineer's exactitude, stood a defensive wall of luggage. The arrangement bordered on choreography: suitcases by size, each topped off with its matching tote, their colours fading in a stately gradient from camel brown through midnight blue before the whole thing was interrupted by a single, almost indecently red duffel. He dressed like he expected a passing photographer at any moment, or perhaps a call from Milan about a yacht party hosted by a lesser prince: navy shirt tailored to within an inch of its life, white linen trousers with creases so sharp you could cut a peach on them, and brown loafers. Marco scanned the pavement, and for a moment I thought he was waiting for a red carpet to roll out before him, maybe by magic or by decree.

I edged my electric car to the kerb and gave the horn a brisk, decisive tap. Marco's face, already lively, seemed to light up even further. It was as though the sound itself had thrown a switch.

"Ciao!" He waved, one hand holding up his phone for a quick selfie.

Behind me, Ryan had already unbuckled and was leaping out, displaying the boundless enthusiasm only found in Labrador puppies or people who've had three oat milk lattes before 10 am. Grinning at Marco and pointing at the luggage fortress, he said, "Blimey, mate, moving in or just the spring collection?"

Marco's English was excellent, but he blinked for a moment, calculating whether Ryan was genuinely curious or just being British. He went for earnest. "You never know what the countryside will require! My Nonna always said, better to arrive over-dressed than under-fed. But I also read it will be cold?"

I glanced at the expanse of cream silk shirts draped over his arm. "Not really. We are travelling to the sunniest part of England, the South West. We might even get 15 °C!"

He shuddered for effect, then switched to Italian to check his phone. "Mamma mia," he declared, genuinely dismayed. "Gale-force winds? Fourteen degrees, in summer? At home, even in winter, it's warmer!"

Ryan took this as his cue. "You'll want wellies. None of that will last five minutes in Dorset mud." He gestured at Marco's shoes, retreated to the boot, rummaged, and returned with ancient, violently green rubber boots and an anorak that looked like it had seen service at Dunkirk.

Marco eyed the boots like boiled cabbage. "No, grazie."

I arched an eyebrow. "Your choice: these, or cold and muddy. The Wellies are proper English kit." It hardly seemed necessary to say more; this was England, after all, and in England, mud has a way of finding its way into everything. You simply wore Wellies, or you didn't, and then you saw how you liked the consequences.

The moment stretched. Marco's eyes lingered on the anorak, then flickered back to his own chic blazer with something like longing. "Okay," he said, "but if my Mamma asks, you tell her I looked fantastic."

"She'll hear you ranked best-dressed at the National Trust gift shop."

"Perfetto!" He beamed, undeterred, and began rearranging his luggage. Half went into the boot, half reluctantly zipped into the "city only" suitcase for return to the hotel's storage. Ryan passed him the Wellies, which Marco took between thumb and forefinger, as if they might leak toxins through the air. He offered an exaggerated sigh for effect, then began folding his linen and silk with military precision. All the while, he cast pained glances at every rejected shirt.

I watched, partly for amusement and partly out of anthropological curiosity, as he laid a cashmere scarf on top of the pile, stroked it once for luck, and zipped the suitcase shut with a sound that could only be described as tragic.

Ryan donned his parka and produced orange-teal striped socks. "Unisex, size 10-13. Go mad."

Marco accepted them with a look of polite horror, but gamely jammed them into the boots. "Bellissimo," he muttered, though it sounded more like a curse.

Once everything was loaded - or back at the hotel's storage room - Marco slid into the back seat. Ryan plopped into the passenger seat and immediately opened a packet of vegan sausage rolls. He offered one to Marco, who declined with a tragic shake of the head and a mournful "I cannot eat this before eleven." I started the engine, and we eased away from the hotel. We left behind only the faint smell of expensive cologne.

As we navigated through morning traffic, Marco took in the city with wide eyes, snapping a few photos out the window. "London is... how you say, very grey?"

"Wait till we hit the Dorset border," I said. "You'll be begging for a cloud." Not that I was entirely sure irony translated. Our Italian companion only blinked, inscrutable. And with that, we set off – just the three of us and the long, hissing road ahead.

The electric car's only concession to sound was a faint, expectant whine – a noise somewhere between an anxious mosquito and a distant dentist's drill. We carved our way southwest from London, trading city for open fields. I drove with the window slightly open, savouring the rare sensation of absolute quiet on the motorway. This was rapidly eclipsed by Marco's running commentary and the irregular gunshots of his camera's shutter.

The moment we hit the green, rolling Dorset hills, Marco's nose was glued to the glass, an effect only mildly compromised by his having managed to fog the entire pane with his breath. "Ragazzi, look! The green! It is everywhere! How can it be so green? In Italia everything is brown in summer. And the sheep, mamma mia, they are like clouds with legs!" He pressed his phone against the window, camera app primed, and took a burst of photos before switching to his proper camera, then a GoPro for good measure.

"It is always green," I replied, not unkindly. "Even in winter. And in summer, somehow, we manage not to scorch our grass to straw under an Italian sun."

"Our little, wet, fertile island," Ryan chimed in from the back, sounding oddly proud as if staying lush and damp was a cause for national pride.

We sped through villages with names like Witchampton and Stoney Cross. Their houses, built from centuries-old stone, were trimmed with impossibly neat roses. Marco photographed each one as if he might be the last to see them. I half-expected the police to be alerted to a stranger snapping photos in every rural parish west of Southampton.

After an hour or so, Marco turned serious. "How do people live here? It is so empty. In Florence, you cannot drive five minutes without a Vespa and a woman shouting at you from the pavement."

"We have sheep," Ryan offered, finishing his snack and already rummaging for the next packet. "And wind. Lots of wind. Sometimes both at once."

Marco looked thoughtful, snapping a series of rapid-fire shots at a distant hill where a single tree was being stoically battered by the wind. "This is real England, yes? The old stones and the big sky?"

I nodded. "That's the myth, anyway. But most of us live in two-up two-downs with wheelie bins and neighbours we pretend not to recognise at the supermarket."

"I like your myth," Marco said more softly. "It is peaceful. Even with the cold."

The miles ticked by. The motorway faded into a patchwork of rural roads, each narrower than the last, flanked by hedgerows so tall they gave the impression of driving through a leafy trench. Occasionally, a suicidal pheasant would vault across our path, prompting a yelp from Ryan and a volley of furious Italian from Marco, who by now had amassed enough wildlife photos for a niche but comprehensive coffee table book.

We reached the heart of Dorset and began threading our way through hamlets that looked as though they had been lifted straight from a BBC period drama. Each turn revealed another postcard: a church steeple rising out of the mist, a thatched-roof pub, children in hi-vis vests collecting litter for a Duke of Edinburgh badge. Marco clicked and whirred, each shot accompanied by a whispered reverence. "Incredible. This is like a film. But better, because it is real."

We drove on. The sky remained stubbornly blue, as if performing for our guest. Marco's "magnifico"s began to taper, replaced by quiet awe. Occasionally, he would simply rest his head against the window. Boots planted firm, camera on his lap, he just watched the world go by.

I let the road do the talking. Hedge and field, wall and sheep, all rolling past in the relentless order of the English countryside. It was easy to see how someone could fall in love with the place, despite – or perhaps because of – its refusal to ever be as dramatic as Marco's home.

Somewhere outside of Wimborne Minster, we passed a sign for a country pub with a beer garden. Marco perked up instantly, boots squeaking with renewed purpose. "Can we stop? I want to see inside. Maybe there is a ghost."

"There's always a ghost," I quipped. "It is part of the British marketing strategy."

We pulled into the gravel lot, our little electric car the only thing within fifty miles not caked in mud or moss. As we stepped out, Marco took one last photo, this time of his own boots. He turned to me and grinned, the city-dweller finally at peace with his Wellies. "I am ready for the sheep," he said, with a wink.

I couldn't argue.

The pub was probably called The Hare & Sprocket, but I wasn't sure. The sign had lost its ampersand to the elements decades ago. Now, the animal and the mechanical hardware gazed across the paintwork like estranged relatives at a bad wedding. Outside, the beer garden was filled with the usual off-duty farmers, sun-punished ramblers, and some dog walkers in reasonable clothing. They gathered around battered picnic tables under umbrellas the size of small satellites.

We'd barely crossed the threshold when Marco, evidently overcome by the urge to share his adventure with his homeland, whipped out his phone and placed a video call right in the entryway. His mother answered before the first ring finished, appearing on screen in full kitchen regalia, hair up, and brandishing a wooden spoon with the authority of the Pope's sceptre.

"Mamma!" Marco bellowed, raising the phone and gesturing with such force that he nearly knocked down a passing barmaid. "Guarda! I am in the real English countryside! It is amazing!"

From behind the bar, the landlord looked up, then resumed polishing a glass with the vigour of someone hoping to erase the memory of every tourist he'd ever served.

I tried to steer Marco toward a quiet corner. But he was already halfway across the pub, narrating his journey in rapid-fire Italian to an audience of one. The rest of the room became unintentional extras. "Piccole pecore bianche, sheep, Mamma, everywhere!" And the hills, le colline verdi, sono incredibili!"

At the next table, a group of locals shifted in unison, performing that uniquely British manoeuvre where a person both turns away and grows stiller, as if by out-freezing the disruption they can render it invisible. The dog under their feet was less concerned, perking up in anticipation of some snack-based windfall.

Ryan, meanwhile, had procured a pint of local cider and a family bag of vegetable crisps, and was already halfway through both. He popped a crisp into his mouth, chewed thoughtfully, and said, "He's enthusiastic, isn't he? Can't blame him."

"He might actually get himself into trouble," I replied, eyeing Marco, who had taken to gesturing at the contents of the pub, panning his phone camera across the room with the gravity of a man live-streaming the fall of the Berlin Wall. Several faces disappeared behind newspapers. One man retreated to the toilets and may still be there.

I made the international gesture for "lower your voice, please" – holding my palm flat and giving Marco a meaningful glare – but Marco was operating at a frequency not yet mapped by conventional etiquette. He plonked himself down at our table, set his phone against a ketchup bottle to prop it up, and continued the play-by-play.

There is this iron law, a commandment implicit in every British soul, drilled into children the minute they could clutch a packet of Rowntree's Fruit Pastilles: DO NOT RAISE YOUR VOICE IN PUBLIC. To break it would be more than bad manners – it was, in a way, a crisis in the order of things. So it came as something of a quiet shock for the other patrons to discover that this was not gospel everywhere. In Italy, it seems, no one has ever heard of this law.

"Mamma, look! These are my friends. Brianna is the driver, she is very British, she doesn't even talk with her hands!" He then turned the phone to Ryan, who waved cheerfully.

"Ciao, Mrs Ricci," Ryan said, mouth full of crisps.

Marco's mother responded with a brief, appraising look. Then she launched into a barrage of advice that Marco relayed in real time. "She says, don't trust the food. Also, remember to call Nonna tonight, or she will be sad. Also, she wants to know if you have family, bambini." This last was delivered directly to me.

I escaped the family business talk and went up to the bar, placing our order with an apologetic smile. "Sorry about us being so noisy," I said to the barman, who gave a long-suffering nod and set about pulling three pints with stoic efficiency.

"Where's he from, then?" the barman asked, nodding to Marco.

"Italy," I said.

"Ah," he replied, as if that explained both the volume and the hand gestures. "They don't really do quiet, do they?"

"Not really," I agreed.

Drinks in hand, I returned to find Marco still mid-monologue, now narrating the contents of the beer garden for his mother's benefit: "There is a man with a dog! And so many umbrellas, even when it is not raining. Also, the beer is warm, but they say it is normal."

Ryan offered Marco a crisp, which was refused with a tragic sigh and a hand over the heart. "It's almost healthy," Ryan assured him, as if this might tip the scales. "Practically vegetables. Just with a little fat and salt to keep things interesting."

Marco looked unimpressed but took one anyway, crunching it for the camera. "Molto bene!" he lied, a consummate diplomat.

By the time we'd finished our drinks, Marco's call had ended, but his energy had not. He bounced from table to table, pausing at each spot to line up shots and snap photos of the ancient dartboard, the mounted deer head, and the hand-painted menu offering Steak & Ale Pie. At the menu, he stopped, pulled out his phone, filmed it and said clearly, "Pie is important to English culture." The locals pretended to be irritated by his antics, but I caught at least two of them subtly adjusting their hair and clothes, preening for the camera when they thought no one was looking.

Afterwards, back in the car park, Marco turned to us and said, "My Mamma thinks you are both wonderful. She says next time you must visit Florence and eat real food."

There's something deeply unsettling about a 4 a.m. alarm, especially after a day spent navigating country lanes with an Italian photographer who treats every sheep like it's the Second Coming. I fumbled for my phone in the dark of our rented cottage, silencing it before it could wake Ryan in the next room. Given his brass band of snores, though, this seemed unlikely. The sunrise tour at Stonehenge had seemed a brilliant idea when I'd booked it. Now, with sleep clinging to me like a needy cat, I wondered if seeing ancient stones in slightly better lighting was worth sacrificing what little remained of the night.

I dressed in the dark, layering jumpers under my raincoat. By the time I'd made a flask of green tea – my personal insurance against calamity in all its forms – I could hear Marco already moving about in his room.

Ryan, predictably, required extraction. I rapped sharply on his door.

"I'm awake," he lied, in a voice that suggested consciousness was at best a distant relative.

"We leave in fifteen minutes," I said firmly. "With or without you."

There was a thud that I interpreted as his body finally achieving vertical status. "Tea?" he croaked, the word floating out as if on a life raft.

"Already made. In the kitchen."

"You're a saint," he mumbled. "A horrible morning person, but a saint."

We left in darkness, our little electric car silent except for the occasional beep of the sat-nav and Ryan's sighs, which emerged at mathematically precise two-minute intervals.

"It's still night," he observed mournfully, as if this were a personal betrayal on my part. "The birds aren't even up yet."

From the back seat, Marco was already a whirlwind of activity, checking camera settings and arranging lenses in a padded bag. "This will be magnifico! The ancient stones in the first light – just think of the magic!"

"Just think of the breakfast we could be having instead," Ryan countered, but even he couldn't maintain total grumpiness in the face of Marco's unbridled excitement.

We arrived at the visitor centre with time to spare. In the pale dawn, it looked oddly futuristic – glass and sweeping curves – a clear contrast to the ancient monument it served. A small group of similarly bleary-eyed tourists huddled near the shuttle stop, clutching cameras or coffee, sometimes both.

Marco was practically vibrating with anticipation. "Will we really be able to walk among them?" he asked, for perhaps the fifth time since we left our accommodation. "Not just look from behind barriers?"

"Yes, Marco. Special access. Right up close to the stones. You can smell them if you want."

"They have a smell?" His eyes widened.

"Mostly wet moss and time," I said, feeling slightly guilty for teasing him, but not enough to stop.

The shuttle arrived – a squat, practical vehicle that looked as if it had been designed specifically for ferrying tourists to see rocks. We boarded in silence, the early hour enforcing a kind of reverence among even the chattiest visitors. The driver gave a perfunctory nod as we showed our tickets, then set off down the access road, the engine humming softly in the stillness.

And then, suddenly, they were there. Emerging from the mist like something from an album cover of an indie band – Stonehenge.

We disembarked, the cold morning air hit me like a slap. The sparkling grass and our breath formed clouds that hung in the stillness. Above us, the sky shifted from charcoal to pale blue, with streaks of pink on the eastern horizon.

Marco had gone utterly still, his camera forgotten in his hands. For once, he seemed unable to find the words, even in Italian.

"Come on," I said softly. "Let's go in."

Our small group approached the stone circle in silence, led by a guide who spoke in hushed tones about respecting the site. Inside the ring of monoliths, I felt that familiar tingle – part awe, part something harder to name. The last time I'd been here was as a child, back when you could still walk right to the stones without all the infrastructure, tickets, or shuttles.

"I came here when I was ten," I told Marco and Ryan as we stood in the centre of the circle. "You could just park on the road and walk straight up to the stones. Completely different experience then – no visitor centre, no fences. Just the stones and the sky."

"Better?" Ryan asked, his hands stuffed deep in his pockets against the chill.

I considered this. "It felt more immediate then – less managed, but also more damaged. People chipped off bits as souvenirs and carved their initials. That's why preservation matters."

"But now it's like Piccadilly Circus with tour buses," Ryan observed.

"Later it will be." I agreed. "By nine, there'll be crowds five deep behind the ropes, all taking the same photo. That's why this early access is worth it – for moments like this."

The first proper sunlight was beginning to touch the tops of the tallest stones, turning the grey surface golden. The few of us inside the circle were scattered around, each finding our own space among the ancient megaliths. It was quiet enough to hear the distant call of birds and the soft click of camera shutters.

Marco had finally recovered his voice. He approached the nearest stone with caution. "Can we touch them?" he whispered, his fingers hovering inches from the lichen-spotted surface.

"Yes, but carefully," I said. "No scratching or–"

"What if I travel through time?" he interrupted, his expression deadly serious.

I blinked. "I'm sorry?"

"Like in Outlander. The stones, they make people travel through time. What if I touch them and disappear to ancient Britain with no pasta?"

I couldn't help smiling. "Marco, this is England, not Scotland. Different stones entirely. Our stones are much more sensible – they just sit here looking impressive, not sending people through time warps."

"Are you certain?" He eyed the nearest monolith suspiciously. "How do you know they don't work the same way?"

"Because if they did, we'd have lost half of Wiltshire's tourists by now. Think of the TripAdvisor reviews: 'Great stones, accidentally sent my husband to the Bronze Age, two stars.'"

Marco laughed, but he still approached the stone with exaggerated caution, extending one finger to touch it as if testing a hot iron. When nothing happened – no swirling vortex, no sudden displacement – he placed his whole palm against the cool surface and closed his eyes.

The moment was shattered by the arrival of what could only be described as a walking anachronism.

He appeared from behind one of the larger stones as if he'd materialised there – a man of indeterminate age, with a white beard halfway down his chest. On his head sat a crown of oak leaves, and he wore robes of undyed wool, rippling in the breeze. The effect was somewhere between 'Gandalf on holiday' and 'history professor who's taken method teaching too far.'

The druid – for what else could he be? – made a beeline for Marco, moving with surprising speed for someone dressed in what appeared to be several blankets. Before I could intervene, he had placed a hand on Marco's shoulder, causing our Italian friend to yelp and spin around.

"You feel it, don't you?" the druid said in a surprisingly normal Home Counties accent. "The energy lines. They run right through here, you know. Invisible to most, but clearly not to you."

Marco's eyes were as big as saucers. "Are you... are you real?"

The druid laughed, the sound unexpectedly down-to-earth and at odds with his appearance. "As real as these stones, young man."

Ryan, who had been watching this exchange with undisguised fascination, stepped forward. "Excuse me, but are you an actual druid? Like, officially?"

The man turned to Ryan, eyes twinkling beneath bushy brows. "I am indeed. Order of Bards, Ovates and Druids. I've been coming to these stones for forty years."

"Brilliant." Ryan's tiredness seemed to have evaporated entirely. "I've always wondered – what do druids actually do on a day-to-day basis? I mean, when you're not at stone circles or conducting ceremonies."

The druid – who introduced himself as Arthur, fittingly – began explaining modern druidry: mostly community service and environmental activism, and, to Ryan's disappointment, very little human sacrifice.

I left them to it and wandered around the perimeter of the stone circle, watching the sun rise fully above the horizon. The stones cast long shadows across the grass, creating patterns that seemed almost deliberate, though whether by design or happy accident, no one could say for certain.

"Beautiful, isn't it?" Arthur had appeared beside me.

"It is," I agreed. "You must have seen a lot of sunrises here."

"More than I can count. The summer solstice is the real spectacle. The sun rises directly over the Heel Stone, shining its first ray into the centre. Thousands come to see it."

"I've always wanted to attend," I admitted. "But the crowds put me off."

"Ah, yes, it does get rather packed. But there's something

31

special about being part of that human chain, stretching back thousands of years. All those people, gathered for the same purpose as their ancestors. Makes you think, doesn't it?"

I nodded, watching as the light shifted across the stones. "Do you think we'll ever know what it was really for? Stonehenge, I mean."

Arthur chuckled. "Oh, there are theories aplenty. Calendar, temple, healing centre, burial ground. Probably served many purposes over the years. That's the thing about these old places – they keep their secrets well. We can only guess, but we'll never know for certain."

"I prefer it that way," I said. "Some mystery is good for the soul."

He nodded approvingly. "A woman after my own heart. Now, where's your Italian friend got to? The sensitive one."

I looked around, suddenly realising I hadn't seen Marco for some time. "Good question."

We found him on the far side of the circle, sitting cross-legged with his back against one of the larger stones, eyes closed, hands resting on his knees. His camera lay forgotten on the grass beside him.

"Marco?" I approached cautiously. "Are you all right?"

His eyes fluttered open, and for a moment, he seemed confused, as if waking from a deep sleep. "Brianna," he said softly. "I can feel the energy. It's... incredible."

"The energy?" I exchanged glances with Ryan, who had joined us.

"Yes, like... electricity, but not painful. Warm. And I saw things, in my mind. Men, hundreds of them, working together. Building this place."

Arthur crouched down beside him, surprisingly spry for a man of his apparent years. "A vision, perhaps. It happens sometimes, to those who are receptive."

Marco nodded earnestly. "I saw them bringing the stones. So many people, pulling together."

Arthur smiled. "It was indeed a massive undertaking. The bluestones – those smaller ones, with the bluish tint when wet – they came from the Preseli Hills in Wales. That's over 150 miles away. Imagine that journey, some 4,500 years ago."

"How did they move them?" Ryan asked.

"Most likely dragged on wooden sledges over land, then floated on rafts along the rivers and coast. Each one weighs between two and five tons. But the really impressive feat was moving the sarsen stones – these larger ones." He patted the massive monolith Marco was leaning against. "They came from Marlborough Downs, about twenty miles from here. Some weigh up to forty tons."

"Forty tons?" Marco looked up at the stone towering above him.

"Indeed. Likely dragged on sledges too, possibly made slippery with animal fat. Then they had to erect them, which meant digging deep holes, tipping the stones in, then pulling them upright with ropes and wooden frames. And remember, this was around 2500 BCE – no modern machinery, no metal tools as we know them. Just stone, bone, antler, and wood."

We all fell silent, contemplating the sheer scale of human effort represented by the circle surrounding us.

"It is amazing," Marco finally said, "how well they must have worked together. Hundreds of people, all moving as one, just to position a single stone."

Arthur nodded. "Absolute cooperation was essential. One person out of step could mean disaster."

"I think," Marco said thoughtfully, "this was perhaps the beginning of British orderliness."

"How do you mean?" I asked.

"In Rome, the city just... happened. It grew in layers, one on top of another, chaotic and beautiful. But this – " he gestured around the stone circle – "this required planning, precision. The kind of discipline that says 'everyone must queue properly or the forty-ton stone falls on your foot.'"

Arthur threw back his head and laughed, a sound so incongruously modern that it momentarily shattered his mystic persona. "I've never heard it put quite that way before, but you might be onto something there, young man. The British love of order does run rather deep."

Our tour guide was now making the rounds, gently herding

people back toward the shuttle bus. Our time inside the circle was coming to an end.

"The masses will be arriving soon," Arthur sighed, helping Marco to his feet. "Back behind the ropes they go, these old friends of mine."

As we walked to the waiting shuttle, I glanced over my shoulder for one last look at the stones, now fully illuminated in the morning light. Despite the visitor centre, despite the managed access and the gift shop that would soon be selling Stonehenge pencil sharpeners and tea towels, there was still something profoundly moving about this place. Something that transcended tourism and ticked boxes on travel itineraries.

As we returned to the visitor centre, where coaches were already beginning to arrive with their cargo of daytime tourists, I felt oddly grateful for our early start. For the brief time we'd spent inside the circle, with only the stones and the sunrise and a druid named Arthur for company. It had been worth the 4 a.m. alarm after all.

By the time we reached Abbotsbury, the sky had sorted itself out into a pale, washed blue, and the sun was hanging at that precise angle that makes the hillside and the chapel perched above it look as though they'd been plugged in from behind. St Catherine's Chapel – which I'd assumed would be a demure, churchy affair – turned out to be more of a squat stone barn with definite ideas about its own indestructibility, stuck up there in the wind, with the sort of exposure that could, I'm told, corrode a bicycle to powder in a matter of days.

We clambered up the last bit of the track, Marco some paces behind. "Why is it always uphill?" he called, or possibly shouted; the wind had opinions of its own and carried voices wherever it fancied.

The chapel door was open, and no one was home. There was a stone altar, which was about as welcoming as a bus station bench, and the windows were more reminiscent of wartime gun slits than anything intended to let in the light. The best part of the place was the view: Chesil Beach rolling itself out along the horizon, a stripe of gold between the green and the Channel. Very nearly cinematic – and I don't mean that sarcastically.

Marco shrugged off his rucksack and circled the chapel, taking photos from every angle. As if on cue, a local couple with dogs joined us. At this stage, I was blissfully unaware that my romantic prospects were about to be discussed like a case of potatoes at the market.

She was the sort of woman you expect to find haunting English churchyards – floral scarf knotted with conviction, Barbour jacket, boots that had clearly enjoyed a long and meaningful relationship with mud. Two spaniels trotted at her heels, and there was a husband, whose slightly miserable face suggested he'd lost a bet. The spaniels made a beeline for Ryan, who greeted them with a customary British dog speech: "Hello," pitched at an animal level.

The woman herself approached, and with a "Morning!" that brooked no delays, inserted herself into the scene. "Are you here for the view, or are you one of the walkers?" she asked, accent so thick you could have spread it on toast. "Photographers," I said. "Travel guide. He's Italian." I felt obliged to add that last bit for context, though I'm not sure it helped.

She seemed to find this hilarious. Then, after some expert up-and-downing, she fixed me with a look of the type that usually precedes a formal inquisition. "Have you been up here before?"

"No, but I've read about the wishing holes," I said, hoping she'd be impressed and possibly diverted.

She was – but more than I'd intended. "Oh, you must try them! Unmarried women make pilgrimages just to wish for a good husband." She beamed at me, looking as if she might start measuring me for a wedding veil on the spot. There was a little pause as she considered the three of us. Then she lowered her voice to a stage whisper. "Are you single, dear? Or is one of them yours? Or... both?"

Not wanting to give her the satisfaction, I said, "Technically yes, I am single, but I'm in a steady relationship with my camera." A line that has never once worked as an escape route.

She cackled, then gave me the sort of look that says, "We'll see about that." Next moment, her hand was on my elbow, and before I knew it, I was being frog-marched towards the ancient stonework, the spaniels weaving around our ankles as if they'd been paid.

"Really, I'm quite content as I am," I tried, but she was having none of it.

"Don't be silly, dear. St Catherine never fails," she said, and before I'd even worked out which way was up, I was positioned in front of a pair of worn columns under a low arch.

Ryan and Marco appeared behind us. Ryan had his phone out, filming while narrating, "Observe the local custom, ancient and mysterious, possibly dangerous if mispronounced."

The woman ignored this, concentrating instead on my posture. "Kneel, love. That's it. Hands in the holes. You must say the prayer out loud."

"What's the prayer?" I managed, stalling.

Eyes shut, she incanted: "St Catherine, St Catherine, oh lend me thy aid, and grant that I never may die an old maid." She opened her eyes and looked at me. "Your turn, dear. Say it nice and clear."

Ryan was vibrating with anticipation, Marco grinning, and I, wishing the wind would sweep me into the Channel, complied. Stone cold under my knees, I slid my hands into the holes. "St Catherine, St Catherine, please lend me your aid... and grant that I never may marry an old mate." I shot Ryan a look, who was finding this deeply entertaining.

"Louder!" barked the woman, the spaniels now adding their own canine counterpoint.

So I repeated it, correct words this time, feeling faintly ridiculous. The wind took the words and sent them out to sea; the spaniels howled in response.

"Lovely!" said the woman, clapping as if I'd just finished a sonata. "You're all set, now."

I got up, brushed the grit off my knees. "So how soon does it work?" I asked, hoping she'd say 'never'.

"Oh, sometimes straight away! Sometimes it takes a bit. But

it always works. My neighbour's cousin did it twice, and she got two husbands." There was a note of warning in her voice.

Ryan, nearly in hysterics, said, "Mind you don't overdo it, Jo."

I replied, "I'd be lucky to get a dog," as I watched the spaniels, who promptly turned to sniff each other's nether regions with focused attention.

The woman gave me a final reassuring pat and turned to Ryan and Marco. "Now, which of you gentlemen is next? Works for men, too."

Marco raised his hands. "No, no, I have already someone cooking for me – my Mamma!" He knew when not to get involved, but she looked at him as if she suspected he was hiding a secret fiancée.

Ryan said, "Actually, I'm quite happy single. Also, I don't think anyone's ready for me."

The husband, who had so far contributed nothing beyond a noble silence, cleared his throat and said, "Didn't work for our daughter. She's living in Brighton. With a cat."

The woman shot him a look that could wither a hedge. "That's because she didn't do it properly," she said, prim as ever. "You have to believe." She whistled to the spaniels and marched off, husband trailing in her wake.

I sagged against the wall, only just recovering from being conscripted to vintage matchmaking. "That was intense," I said, wind tugging at my jacket like an eager conspirator.

Marco, still processing, said, "In Italia, we do the same. Desperate spinsters praying in churches for husbands."

I couldn't help laughing. "Oh, thank you for calling me a 'desperate spinster'!" The wind, my bruised pride, all of it seemed suddenly quite funny. "Well," I said, "I suppose now I wait to see if St Catherine delivers."

I'd visited Knowlton Church dozens of times, but dusk transforms even the familiar places. The church – little more than ruins – stood in the centre of a Neolithic henge. Some claimed the veil between worlds was thin here. Not that I

37

believed in such things, but it made for excellent photography. That was precisely why we were here.

I set up my tripod with the practice of someone who could probably do it blindfolded after a bottle of wine. The light was perfect – this special golden hour glow. The ruins caught the last rays of sun, the stone turning amber as the sky darkened.

"This is magnifico!" Marco circled the perimeter of the church, camera already clicking away at machine-gun pace. "It looks like a painting, no?"

"Looks bloody creepy to me," Ryan muttered, hands thrust deep into his pockets. "Remind me again why we couldn't do this at, I don't know, midday?"

"Because midday light is flat and boring," I said, adjusting my aperture. "And because this place is rather special at sunset."

"Special how?" Marco asked, crouching to frame a shot through one of the gaps in the walls.

I finished setting up before answering. "Well, Knowlton Church is considered one of the most haunted places in England. It's inside a Neolithic henge – the circular bank around us. Christians built this church here in the twelfth century, probably to claim the pagan site."

Marco looked up, suddenly more interested. "Haunted? Like, with real ghosts?"

"So they say." I checked my light meter. "The village that once surrounded it was abandoned after the Black Death. Plague victims were brought here, which might explain why people claim to see... things."

"What kind of things?" Ryan asked, despite clearly not wanting to know the answer.

I shrugged, pretending to focus on my camera settings. "Oh, you know. The usual ghostly repertoire. A weeping nun. A phantom horseman. Voices. Cold spots. Mists that form and dissipate without explanation."

"Mamma mia," Marco whispered, his face lighting up with ghoulish delight. "This is better than Stonehenge!"

"Please don't encourage her," Ryan said, looking nervously at the deepening shadows. "Bree loves this spooky stuff. She once made me spend the night in a haunted castle in Scotland. I didn't sleep for three days afterwards."

"You claimed you saw a headless monk," I reminded him.

"It was the hotel manager carrying towels!"

I smiled and returned to my work, lining up a shot of the arched window. Evening settled around us in a very peculiar stillness. No birds. No breeze. Just fading light and three humans with their technology.

"Have you ever seen anything here?" Marco asked, sidling up beside me.

"Not really," I admitted. "Though there was one time I was photographing at dusk, and I could have sworn I heard a bell."

"There's no bell," Ryan pointed out, gesturing at the ruined tower.

"Exactly."

Marco looked delighted. Ryan looked as if he might be calculating the distance back to the car.

The sun dipped lower, and I suggested we move inside what remained of the nave. The ruins were open to the sky, but the walls still stood, creating perfect frames for the fading light. We positioned ourselves near the eastern end, where the altar once stood.

"Stand over there," I directed them. "Your shadows will fall on that wall."

They obliged. Marco struck an exaggerated pose; Ryan stood with the rigid posture of someone trying hard not to touch anything that might be cursed. I joined them, setting my camera to timer mode so I could be in the shot too. We formed a line, our elongated shadows stretching across the ancient stonework like strange, attenuated versions of ourselves.

And then there were four.

I noticed it first – a fourth shadow, slightly apart from ours, standing to the right. A tall, slender silhouette that didn't belong to any of us.

"Um," I said, my voice oddly tight. "Is anyone else seeing that?"

Marco followed my gaze. His intake of breath was audible.

"What?" Ryan asked, then, "Oh. Oh no. No, no, no."

We turned, almost in unison, to look behind us. The space was empty. Just the open ruins and the deepening twilight.

"That's...odd," I said, forcing a calm tone. "Probably just the light playing tricks."

"Light doesn't do that," Ryan said, his voice an octave higher than usual. "Light follows rules. That – " he gestured wildly at the wall – "is not following rules."

The shadow remained for a few seconds more, then seemed to melt into the stonework, leaving only our three silhouettes once again.

"I need to google this," Ryan declared, fumbling for his phone. His face, illuminated by the screen, looked ghostly in the gathering darkness. He tapped frantically, then frowned. "That's weird. I had full battery when we got here, and now it's dead."

"Maybe the cold?" I suggested, though the evening was mild.

"Let me try mine," Marco offered, retrieving his phone from his pocket. He pressed the power button several times, looking increasingly confused. "Nothing. It was working fine earlier."

A creeping unease settled over me, but I maintained my composure. Technology fails; that's what it does. I reached for my own phone, confident that at least one of our devices would cooperate.

The screen lit up, showing a healthy 82% battery. "See? Mine's fine – "

The numbers changed before my eyes: 82%. 57%. 23%. 0%. The screen went black.

"That's... not normal," I admitted, staring at the dead phone in my hand.

"Can we leave now?" Ryan asked, his voice barely above a whisper.

"Not yet," I said, trying to sound confident. "I still need some shots. There must be a rational explanation."

I returned to my camera, grateful for its mechanical reliability. Phone might fail, but good old optics and physics wouldn't let me down. I peered through the viewfinder, focused on the arched window, and caught the last light streaming through.

"Jo," Marco said quietly. "There is someone in the church."

"We're in the church," I replied without looking up.

"No. A woman. By the wall. In... how do you say... nun clothes?"

I sighed and straightened. "Marco, there's no – "

The words died in my throat. Through my viewfinder, I caught a coil of mist rising near the wall where Marco pointed. It wasn't quite human-shaped, but it was... something. An eddy in the air, twisting against the breeze.

"Do you see her?" Marco pressed.

"I see... something," I admitted, adjusting my focus. "But it's probably just condensation. The temperature's dropping, and old stones like these hold the day's heat. When it meets the cooler air – "

"She's praying," Ryan interrupted, his voice strangled. He had backed against the opposite wall, eyes wide. "I can see her. She's kneeling."

I looked again. The mist had thickened, coalescing into a vaguely human-shaped form. But a nun? My rational mind rejected the idea even as my eyes struggled to make sense of what they were seeing.

"It's just mist," I insisted, though with less conviction than before. "Our brains are pattern-recognition machines. We see faces in clouds, figures in random shapes. It's called pareidolia."

"Tell that to her!" Ryan hissed, pointing.

I turned my head, following his gesture, but saw nothing except stone and shadow. When I looked back through my viewfinder, the mist had dispersed.

"See? It's gone. Just an atmospheric effect." I tried to sound confident, though a small part of me was relieved the phenomenon had vanished.

Marco had gone very still. "Something just touched me," he whispered.

"What?" I lowered my camera.

"Here." He pointed to his sleeve. "I felt a tug. Like someone pulled it."

"It was probably a branch, or your jacket caught on something," I said, but even to my ears, the explanation sounded thin.

"There are no branches here, Brianna." Marco's voice had lost its usual exuberance. "And I was standing still."

Ryan had edged towards the entrance. "I feel like we're being watched," he said, scanning the ruins. "Like there are eyes, everywhere. Can we please go now?"

I hesitated, torn between my professional desire to finish the shoot and an increasingly insistent voice in my head suggesting that perhaps Ryan had a point. The light was nearly gone anyway, and the atmosphere had shifted from atmospheric to downright unnerving.

"All right," I conceded, beginning to pack up my equipment.

I had barely finished dismantling my tripod when Marco let out a yelp.

"What now?" I asked, more sharply than intended.

"Cold," he said, rubbing his arms. "It suddenly got very cold. Right here, like walking through a freezer."

I was about to dismiss this as imagination when I felt it too. A pocket of air so cold it seemed to seep through my clothes and settle directly on my skin. This wasn't simply cool. It was a bone-deep chill that had no place on a mild summer evening.

Ryan didn't wait for confirmation. "Car. Now," he said, already moving.

For once, I didn't argue. I hurriedly zipped my camera bag, slung it over my shoulder, and followed, Marco close behind me.

We walked quickly at first, then faster, until we were nearly running toward where we'd parked. The cold air seemed to follow us, a bubble of winter in the midst of summer. I told myself it was just a thermal anomaly, a quirk of topography and air pressure. Still, the explanation felt hollow.

Ryan reached the car first, yanking at the handle with such force I feared he might tear it off. "Unlock it!" he shouted.

I fumbled with the key fob, pressing the button with shaking fingers. The car's lights flashed, and Ryan practically dove inside. Marco was only a step behind, clambering into the back seat with none of his usual grace. I tossed my camera bag in after him and slid into the driver's seat, slamming the door.

The moment we were all inside, Ryan hit the central locking button. The sound of all four locks engaging was oddly comforting.

We sat in silence for a moment, our breathing loud in the confined space. Outside, the ruins stood silhouetted against the darkening sky, looking perfectly ordinary and harmless.

"Well," I said at last, trying to sound casual, "that was... interesting."

"Interesting?" Ryan echoed. "Jo, our phones died simultaneously, we saw a ghost nun, and we were chased by Arctic air in the middle of June. That's not interesting, that's the beginning of a horror film!"

"We don't know that we saw a ghost," I said, though my usual scepticism felt performative now. "It could have been a trick of the light, or mist, or – "

"Someone pulled my sleeve," Marco interjected. He'd gone unusually quiet, his usual exuberance dimmed. "I felt it. Fingers."

I had no rational explanation for that one. Instead, I switched on the electric car, comforted by the familiar hum. The dashboard lit up, and with it, my phone suddenly chimed from my pocket. I pulled it out – 53% battery, perfectly functional.

"My phone's working again," I said.

Marco checked his. "Mine too! Half battery, like nothing happened."

Ryan was staring out the rear window, his face pale in the reflection. "She's there," he whispered.

"Who?" I asked, though I knew the answer.

"The nun. Standing by the entrance. Watching us."

I turned, following his gaze. All I could see was the dust our car had kicked up, red in the rear lights. It was just dust, just particles caught in the light.

Wasn't it?

The drive from Knowlton to Marshwood passed in silence. It seemed as if speaking might summon whatever had followed us from the church. By the time we reached the village, Ryan had regained enough composure to demand sustenance. "Food," he announced, as we crawled past a row of cottages so picture-perfect they looked as if they might dissolve in the rain. "Something normal. And not haunted. Proper vegan dinner."

"I think we deserve some culinary," I agreed, navigating Marshwood's narrow main lane.

Ryan squinted through the window at Marshwood's centre. "Is that a pub? It is! The Bottle Inn. Let's go there immediately. I need something warm and solid and preferably containing chips."

I parked in a small gravel area next to the pub, a whitewashed building with a thatched roof that sagged slightly in the middle like an old mattress. A wooden sign creaked gently in the evening breeze.

"Looks proper," Ryan said approvingly, already halfway out of the car. "The more ancient the pub, the better the chips. It's a law of physics."

We entered to find the place unexpectedly lively for a weeknight in a village barely qualifying for a spot on the map. A crowd had gathered around several tables pushed together at the centre of the room, creating a makeshift arena. The air held an odd mix of scents: the yeasty sweetness of beer, the earthy tang of wood smoke, and something green and sharp – like freshly mown grass, edged with a bitter, almost medicinal note that caught at the back of my throat.

"What's that smell?" Marco muttered, nose wrinkling.

Before I could hazard a guess, our attention was drawn to the activity at the central tables. A woman with arms like coiled rope and hair ruthlessly corralled into a ponytail was methodically stripping leaves from a stalk of what appeared to be –

"Are those nettles?" Ryan blurted, blinking in disbelief.

Indeed they were. The tables were covered with piles of the stinging plants, their distinctive serrated leaves sharp and bright even in the pub's dim lighting, giving off a faint, earthy smell. The woman wasn't alone in her task. A half-dozen others were similarly engaged, each with a pint next to them and a determined set to their jaws.

"Is this some sort of craft activity?" Marco suggested hopefully. "Maybe they make... how do you say... baskets?"

A broad-shouldered man at the bar overheard us and let out a laugh that seemed to originate somewhere around his knees. "Baskets? Nah, mate. Training, in'it?" He gestured to the nettle-strippers with a certain pride, as if they were elite athletes under his personal supervision. "Championship's coming up."

We approached the bar with the cautious step of outsiders who have clearly walked into something they don't understand. The barman – a fellow with forearms marked by what looked suspiciously like nettle stings – greeted us.

"You'll be wanting to know about the nettles, then?" he said, not waiting for confirmation. "World Nettle Eating Championship. Takes place right here every summer. This lot," he nodded toward the tables, "are local hopefuls. Getting in some practice."

Ryan gawked at him. "Nettle eating? Consuming stinging nettles – the plants that cause painful welts if you brush against them?"

"The very same," the barman confirmed cheerfully. "Been going since the '80s. Started as a bet about who could grow the tallest nettle, if you can believe it. Then some bright spark wondered what they'd taste like. Now we get competitors from all over."

I glanced at the walls, which I now noticed were covered with framed photographs of men and women holding bundles of nettles. Their faces displayed varying combinations of triumph, agony, and what could only be described as nettle-induced delirium. In one particularly prominent photo, a man with lips swollen to cartoon proportions grinned through tears, holding a measuring tape against a mountain of stripped nettle stalks.

"That's last year's champion," the barman said, following my gaze. "Seventy-four feet of nettles, he put away."

Marco had gone slightly pale. "But why?" he breathed, a man doubting not only nettle consumption but British culture itself.

"Why not?" the barman replied, with the perfect logic of rural England. "Now, what can I get you? We've got a special nettle menu on tonight."

Ryan, who had been watching the proceedings with growing fascination, turned to us with an unsettling glint in his eye. "We have to try this," he declared. "When in Rome, and all that."

"We are not in Rome," Marco insisted. "In Rome, we eat pasta, not plants that fight back. My Mamma would have a heart attack if she saw this. In Italy, nettles are for keeping the slugs away from the tomatoes, not for... this culinary madness."

I sympathised with Marco's horror, but there was something about the absurdity of it all. The earnest competitors, the village pride, the sheer eccentricity – after our uncanny experience at the church, this appealed to me. This was weird, yes, but weird in a comprehensibly human way.

"What's on the nettle menu?" I asked, earning a betrayed look from Marco and an approving nod from Ryan.

The barman slid a handwritten menu across the counter. "Nettle soup's the most popular. We also have nettle pesto with pasta. There's nettle pie – vegan version available – and nettle tea, of course. Supposed to be very healthy."

"Is there anything without nettles?" Marco asked hopefully.

"Chips," the barman offered. "Though we do fry them in a nettle-infused oil."

In the end, we decided on a strategic approach: nettle soup for all (the least threatening option), a plate of chips for Marco's peace of mind, and nettle tea to complete the experience. Ryan also ordered a pint of local cider, citing historical precedent. "It's traditional," he insisted. "The cider helps with the sting. It's practically medicinal."

As we waited for our food, I observed the training session with growing interest. The techniques varied: some competitors folded the leaves carefully before eating them, others simply tossed them back like shots, and still others employed a methodical chewing strategy that seemed designed to minimise contact with lips and gums.

"They're all in pain," Marco observed, watching a woman wince as she stripped another stalk. "Why do it?"

A wiry man at the next table overheard and leaned over. "It's not so bad once you get going," he said. "The first few are the worst. After that, your mouth goes a bit numb. It's the hands that suffer most." He held up fingers dotted with angry red welts. "Worth it though, for the glory."

"The glory," Marco echoed faintly.

Our food arrived – three bowls of vibrant green soup that steamed innocently. The aroma was surprisingly pleasant, herbaceous with a hint of garlic.

"Bottoms up," I said, lifting my spoon. The taste was milder than expected – rather like a robust spinach soup with a peppery kick. There was a slight tingling on my tongue, but nothing unbearable.

Ryan attacked his bowl with enthusiasm. "This is actually quite good," he declared after several spoonfuls. "Earthy. Complex. I can see why they made a competition out of it."

Marco approached his bowl as one might a suspicious package, taking the smallest possible spoonful and letting it hover near his lips for a long moment before committing. His expression cycled through wariness, surprise, and reluctant appreciation.

"It's... not terrible," he conceded. "But in Italy, we would make this with basil, not plants that hate you."

As we ate, the training session at the central tables intensified. The woman with the rope-like arms was now demonstrating what appeared to be speed techniques, plucking leaves with practised efficiency and consuming them at a rate that bordered on alarming.

"That's Maggie," the barman informed us, appearing with our nettle tea. "Last year's women's champion. Sixty-eight feet of nettles. New world record." He spoke with the reverence usually reserved for war heroes.

Maggie, hearing her name, looked up and nodded in our direction. Her gaze lingered on Ryan, who was now enthusiastically finishing his soup and eying the nettle tea with interest.

"You've got good technique," she called over. "You've done this before, haven't you?"

Ryan paused, spoon halfway to his mouth. "Me? No, this is my first nettle... anything, really."

Maggie squinted at him appraisingly. "You sure? You eat like a pro. No hesitation."

Before Ryan could clarify that he eats anything, as long as it is vegan, like a pro, a man leaned forward. "Hang on, I know you," he said, snapping his fingers. "You competed in Llandrindod Wells last year, didn't you? The Welsh championship?"

"No, I really didn't," Ryan protested, but a murmur had already gone through the group. Several competitors were now looking in our direction with newfound interest.

"It is him," someone else chimed in. "The vegan champion from Cardiff. Set a record for the speed round."

I shot Ryan a questioning look. He shook his head minutely, eyes wide with panic.

"You must be mistaken," I began, but it was too late. Chairs scraped as several nettle enthusiasts migrated to our table, bearing fresh stalks like green offerings.

"Show us your technique," Maggie said, placing a particularly robust nettle plant in front of Ryan. "The Welsh method's different from ours, I hear."

Ryan looked at the nettle, then at me, then at Marco, who was watching the proceedings with the horrified fascination of someone witnessing an elaborate form of British self-torture.

"I'm not actually – " Ryan tried again.

"Don't be modest," the man interrupted. "We're all friends here. Just a quick demonstration."

Trapped in a web of British politeness and a sudden urge to pull a prank, Ryan did what any Ryan person would do: he decided to bluff. Reaching for his cider, he took a fortifying gulp, then addressed his audience with the confidence of a man who has just made a terrible decision but is committed to seeing it through.

"Well, the thing about nettles," he began, adopting what he clearly thought was a knowledgeable tone, "is that they're all about mind over matter. Vegan power, you know? The plant... communicates with you. You have to listen to it."

I nearly choked on my tea. Marco was staring at Ryan as if he'd grown a second head.

"That's deep," someone murmured appreciatively.

Emboldened, Ryan reached for the nettle stalk, carefully

avoiding the leaves as he'd observed the others doing. With deliberate ceremony, he plucked a single leaf and held it aloft.

"The key," he said, stalling, "is to respect the nettle. Thank it for its sacrifice."

He locked eyes with the leaf, as if engaged in silent communion, then quickly popped it into his mouth. For one triumphant moment, he chewed with what appeared to be thoughtful consideration. Then his expression shifted, cycling through surprise, dismay, and finally undisguised horror as the full impact of raw nettle made contact with his unprepared taste buds.

"Mmm," he managed, eyes watering. "Interesting... texture. Different to the Welsh ones."

Ryan's face had taken on a peculiar hue – a sort of greyish pink that suggested internal conflict of the highest order. He reached for his cider with a hand that trembled slightly, took another gulp, and then frowned at the nettle stalk as if it had personally betrayed him.

"Actually," he said, voice strained, "I've just noticed something concerning about these particular nettles. There's... er... evidence of caterpillars. Very small ones. Almost invisible, really, but as a vegan, I couldn't possibly consume them. It would be against my principles."

There was a puzzled silence.

"Caterpillars?" Maggie repeated, examining the nettle stalk. "I don't see any."

"Microscopic," Ryan insisted. "Vegan special training, we can spot them. Very advanced technique."

The Yorkshire man leaned in, squinting at the plant with sudden suspicion. "Hold on. You're not the Cardiff champion at all, are you?"

Ryan's nettle-induced flush deepened. "I, er, might have been mistaken for someone else. Happens all the time. I have one of those faces."

The mood around the table shifted perceptibly. Maggie's encouraging smile transformed into something less welcoming.

"You were having us on," she said flatly.

"Not intentionally," Ryan protested, reaching for his cider again. "It was a misunderstanding. I genuinely wanted to try

49

the nettles. And the soup was delicious! Really... stingy. In a good way."

I decided it was time to intervene before Ryan dug himself any deeper. "We should probably be going," I said, reaching for my wallet. "Long day tomorrow. More Dorset sights to see."

Marco, who had been watching the proceedings with increasing alarm, was already halfway to his feet. "Yes, very early. Sunrise photographs. Very important for the travel guide."

We paid our bill with the speed of people fleeing a crime scene, adding a generous tip that I hoped might compensate for Ryan's unintentional deception. As we edged toward the door, the nettle enthusiasts returned to their training, though I noticed several glances that suggested we would not be welcomed back as nettle-eating apprentices anytime soon.

Outside, the night air felt blissfully cool against my still-tingling lips. Ryan was frantically wiping his tongue with a tissue, making sounds that evoked the image of a cat with a hairball.

"That was the worst thing I've ever voluntarily put in my mouth," he declared, once his powers of speech returned. "And I once ate a vegan cheese that was actually just yellowed coconut oil."

"You brought it on yourself," I pointed out, unlocking the car. "Nobody asked you to impersonate a Welsh nettle champion."

"I didn't impersonate anyone! They decided I was some Welshman, and things just... escalated."

Marco was still shaking his head in disbelief. "In my country, if you eat something that hurts you, it's called 'poison,' not 'championship.' My Mamma wouldn't approve if she knew what I am doing here on this island."

"Well," I said, as we drove toward our accommodation, "at least there was no nun."

T he military had promised they could return. That thought lingered as we paused en route to Lyme Regis at a place I remembered, thinking Marco might find it interesting.

We arrived to find the skeletal remains of what had once been a perfectly ordinary Dorset village, its stone cottages now roofless and hollow-eyed, watching us with the patient indifference of the long-abandoned.

"What is this place?" Marco asked, already halfway out before I'd fully switched off the car.

"Tyneham," I replied. "Ghost village. But not the supernatural kind – just the sad, human kind."

At the entrance, a worn sign read: "TYNEHAM VILLAGE – EVACUATED DECEMBER 1943." Nearby, a noticeboard stated the villagers had only a month to abandon their homes and memories, so the War Office could use the land for tank training before D-Day.

We strolled through the village remains. "They left... everything?" Marco asked, pointing at a possible school, old desks visible inside.

"They thought they were coming back," I said. "The military promised the village would be returned after the war."

"But they never came back," Ryan finished, gazing at the abandoned homes.

"No. Once the military had it, they kept it. Said it was too important for training."

Marco was quiet. "In Italy, after the war, people went home, even if there was nothing left. They rebuilt. Here..." He looked around. "It's like time stopped."

That was precisely it, I thought. Tyneham existed in a peculiar limbo – not destroyed completely like so many villages during the war, but not allowed to continue either.

After a few more minutes of quiet exploration, I gathered us together. "We should get going," I said. "Lyme Regis awaits." We made our way back to the car, leaving Tyneham behind.

We drove toward Lyme Regis, passing fields and woods until the road finally reached the sea. I could feel the shift in the air through my partially opened window – that distinctive briny quality that signals the coast long before you actually see water. Ryan, evidently recovered from his nettle-eating fiasco the night before, had been methodically working his way through a packet of vegan seaweed crisps while providing an increasingly fervent monologue about Meryl Streep's windswept hair.

"You're going to love The Cobb," he announced to Marco for perhaps the fifth time. "It's iconic. Literary. Cinematic. The bit where she stands at the end, looking out to sea, her cape billowing dramatically – pure cinema."

Marco glanced up with polite confusion. "The cob? Like corn?"

"No, The Cobb – C-O-B-B. It's a stone pier. Very famous. It's in 'The French Lieutenant's Woman' and Jane Austen's 'Persuasion.' Absolute cultural landmarks."

The road eventually levelled out. Lyme Regis unfurled before us – a tumble of buildings clinging to the hillside as it sloped toward the sea. We pulled into a car park near the harbour. Our electric car settled between a camper van plastered with surf stickers and an ancient Volvo that appeared to be hibernating under a layer of seagull contributions.

As we walked toward the seafront, Ryan's enthusiasm reached a fever pitch. He strode ahead, arms windmilling as he pointed out landmarks that meant nothing to anyone who hadn't memorised the town's cinematic CV. "That's where they filmed the market scene in the 1995 adaptation of 'Persuasion'! And down there – that's where Captain Wentworth helped Anne into the carriage!"

Marco nodded politely, clearly having no idea who Captain Wentworth might be, but already raising his camera to capture the harbour's gentle curve.

The Cobb itself came into view as we rounded the corner – a massive stone pier arcing gracefully into the sea like a crooked finger beckoning ships to safety. It was an impressive feat of engineering, disguised as something organic. It seemed as if the coastline had decided to extend itself in a perfect curve.

"There it is," Ryan breathed. "The most famous jetty in English literature."

I watched Marco frame his first shot, capturing the sprawl of stone against restless, grey-blue water. Clouds thickened, casting a pewter tint over the waves – a shifting, unsettled colour, neither green nor grey, as if the sea couldn't decide what to become.

"It is very... solid," Marco observed, squinting through his viewfinder. "In Italy, we would have added more statues. Perhaps a saint to bless the fishermen."

Ryan was already halfway down the promenade, waving frantically for us to catch up. "Come on! You have to see the exact spot where Meryl Streep stood in 'The French Lieutenant's Woman'! It's cinema history!"

We followed at a more reasonable pace. Marco paused every few steps, quick to capture the changing perspective of The Cobb as we approached. Overhead, the wind picked up. Gulls wheeled above, and the water ruffled into small, frothing peaks.

When we reached Ryan, he was standing at the base of the stone pier, his expression bordering on religious ecstasy. "This is it. This is where it all happened. The most iconic scene in British drama."

Marco looked around, confused. "What happened here? A battle?"

"Better," Ryan said, his voice dropping to a dramatic whisper. "Meryl Streep, 1981, standing at the end of The Cobb in a black cloak, staring out to sea while the waves crashed around her. It's the poster image. It's everything."

Without warning, Ryan began to climb the stone steps, making his way onto the high ridge of The Cobb itself. The structure was massive up close. Blocks of Portland stone were fitted together with such precision that even centuries of battering by the sea hadn't dislodged them.

"Be careful," I noted the slick patches where spray had made the surface treacherous. "It's not worth breaking an ankle for a recreation shot."

Ryan ignored me. He reached a point near the end where the structure widened slightly, climbed the stone steps, and made his way onto the high ridge of The Cobb. Facing us, he dramatically wrapped his arms around himself, pulled an imaginary hood over his head, and stared out to sea with what he clearly believed was a perfect imitation of tormented Victorian longing.

"This is the exact spot!" Ryan shouted over the wind. "She

stood right here, looking for the French lieutenant who would never return! It's cinema gold!"

I rolled my eyes so hard I nearly gave myself a headache. Marco, to his credit, dutifully photographed Ryan's performance, though I noticed he was struggling to keep a straight face.

He ran his hand along the weathered stone. "How old is this place?"

"Parts of it date back to the 13th century," I said, "though it's been rebuilt and extended many times. It's one of the oldest working harbours in the country."

Ryan had finally exhausted his Meryl Streep impressions and was now excitedly pointing to another section of the harbour. "And over there – that's where Louisa Musgrove fell in 'Persuasion'! Jane Austen actually set a pivotal scene right here. She visited Lyme Regis herself in 1804."

Marco frowned. "Fell? Was she pushed?"

Ryan waved dismissively. "No, no. She jumped down from the steps, expecting Captain Wentworth to catch her, but he wasn't ready, and she knocked herself unconscious. Very dramatic. Changed the whole course of the novel."

I watched as Marco digested this information, brow furrowed in patient confusion, as if following the plot of a soap opera he'd never seen. He nodded politely. Then, he lifted his camera again and photographed The Cobb itself. He moved slowly, capturing the way the stone changed colour where the sea had washed it, the perfect curve of its construction against the horizon, and the gulls that used its highest points as lookout posts.

As he took his photos, I realised The Cobb had finally spoken to him in its own, silent language – one he understood far better than Victorian heartbreak or literary trivia. Sometimes, the salt-stained curve of weathered stone or a rush of briny sea air reveals more than a thousand English novels about the true spirit of Britain.

The moment we crossed the county line, Devon made its intentions clear. The lanes were scarcely wider than a decent bookshelf, evidently mapped out for horse-drawn transport and less for modern cars. Our little electric car wheezed up inclines and squeezed between hedgerows that scraped both wing mirrors. The green tunnel only occasionally broke to reveal patchwork fields and granite-speckled farmhouses.

"Brianna, slow down! I must photograph these – what do you call them? The stone walls with no cement?" Marco pressed his face to the window, fogging the glass with his breath and enthusiasm.

"Dry stone walls," I replied, easing off the accelerator as we rounded yet another blind corner. "They're built by hand, each stone balanced perfectly on the others. No mortar needed."

The navigation system announced our imminent arrival with its customary lack of inflexion, and I steered the car into a small gravel car park beside what could only be described as the perfect picture of a Devon tea room. The building was a stone cottage, walls partially obscured by roses climbing with wild determination toward the slate roof. A hand-painted wooden sign swung gently in the breeze: "Primrose Cottage Tea Room – Est. 1932."

"This is perfect," Marco breathed, already framing the cottage through his viewfinder. "Like from a film about the English countryside."

Ryan finally looked up from his phone. "They have vegan options. Four-point-eight stars on Happy Cow. The reviewer says the vegan clotted cream is, and I quote, 'Indistinguishable from the artery-clogging original.'"

We walked through the garden leading to the tea room, the three of us pausing as lavender bushes hummed with bees. A tabby cat perched on a stone bench watched our progress with aristocratic disdain. I pushed open the door, which jingled gently, and we stepped inside, immediately wrapped in warmth scented with butter, sugar, and bergamot.

Inside, the low ceiling made Ryan duck under wooden beams. Tables of worn oak were set with tiny vases of fresh flowers and mismatched china, collected over the course of decades. Lace-trimmed napkins and shiny silver teaspoons waited at each place.

The room was half-full, mostly with patrons who looked as if they might have been there since opening day. Two women with identical perms shared a pot of tea. A man in tweed read his newspaper with intense focus. In the corner, a younger couple of tourists in matching anoraks consulted a map with puzzled brows.

Every head turned, almost imperceptibly, as we entered – the subtle radar of a small community registering new arrivals.

"Sit anywhere you fancy, loves." The voice belonged to a woman emerging from what I presumed was the kitchen, bearing a tea trolley before her like a votive offering. She was of indeterminate age – somewhere between sixty and eternal – with silver hair swept into a loose bun and an apron that bore the battle scars of flour, jam, and butter. Her smile was genuine.

We chose a table near the window so Marco could have the best light for his inevitable photography. The proprietress wheeled her trolley to our table with the fluid grace of someone who had performed this ritual thousands of times.

"Now then," she said, as if continuing a conversation we'd been having for years, "we've got Assam, Darjeeling, Earl Grey, or a nice local blend with a hint of Dartmoor honey."

I hesitated, scanning for options beyond the traditional black teas. "Do you have any green tea, by chance? No milk or honey, please."

The woman nodded and brought over a trolley for us to choose from. It was loaded with scones, stacked high and still warm. Their golden tops were golden, slightly cracked, showing the soft inside. Next to them was a bowl of clotted cream, thick and yellow at the edges, and a pot of strawberry jam, bright and clear.

Marco stared at the display with the reverence of a man witnessing a miracle. "What is this cream? It looks like... like cloud made solid."

"That's Devonshire clotted cream, love," the proprietress

said with evident pride. "Made just down the road at Hillside Farm. Been using them for thirty years."

Ryan leaned forward, his expression hovering between hope and trepidation. "I read online that you offer vegan options?"

"Oh yes, we do indeed. My granddaughter's vegan, showed me how to make the cream with coconut and a bit of this and that. We have vegan scones too, if you want them. Just as good, if you ask me."

"That would be perfect," Ryan said, visibly relieved.

"And you, dear?" She turned to Marco, who was still transfixed by the clotted cream.

"I will have the traditional, please. Everything as it should be. I want the full English experience."

"Devonshire experience," she corrected gently.

As she bustled away to prepare our tea, I noticed the two women by the window observing us with undisguised interest. One whispered to the other behind her hand, then both nodded in our direction with the cautious approval of locals assessing whether newcomers might be worth adding to their conversational repertoire.

"I think we're being vetted," I murmured to Marco, who was already photographing the table setting.

"In Italy, they would have already asked about my family, my job, and if I am married," he replied. "The English are more... private?"

"Reserved," I corrected. "They're waiting to see if we commit any cardinal sins before they decide whether to speak to us."

The proprietress poured my tea with a steady hand, placing a silver strainer over my cup. The green liquid arced gracefully into delicate bone china, which Marco watched with clear appreciation.

She gestured to the three-tiered stand. "Scones are still warm. Enjoy, dears."

As she retreated to attend to another table, Marco surveyed the spread before him with intensity. He picked up a scone, weighing it in his palm as if assessing its credentials.

"It is very light," he observed, breaking it in half to reveal a fluffy interior.

Ryan was already assembling his vegan version with methodical precision, too engrossed in documenting the process for his followers to notice Marco's technique. "Just taking a few photos for the 'gram," he muttered, angling his phone to capture the optimal scone-to-natural-light ratio.

Marco reached for the jam – a crucial detail I registered a half-second too late. With the confident flourish of a man who had decorated countless tiramisus, he spread a generous layer of strawberry jam across the cut surface of his scone, creating a glistening red canvas. Then, with an artist's eye, he topped it with a perfect spiral of clotted cream, his knife creating a white peak at the centre.

The reaction was immediate but utterly British in its restraint – a collective intake of breath from the surrounding tables, felt more than heard. The twin-permed ladies by the window froze mid-sip. Teacups hung suspended in the air as if time itself had stopped. The tweed-clad newspaper reader lowered his broadsheet by precisely two inches; his eyebrows ascended by the same measure. Even the cat on the windowsill, methodically cleaning its paws, paused to stare.

The proprietress, returning from the kitchen with a fresh pot of tea, visibly faltered, her professional smile momentarily replaced by an expression one might wear upon discovering a slug in one's lettuce.

Marco, blissfully unaware of the cultural chasm he had just tumbled into, raised the assembled scone to his lips. His face was alight with anticipation, a man about to tick off a significant item on his British experience checklist.

I cleared my throat softly. "Marco," I murmured, but it was too late. He had already taken a substantial bite, eyes closing in evident pleasure.

"Magnifico!" he declared, a crumb escaping to his chin. "This cream – it is like nothing we have in Italy. So thick, so sweet but not too sweet." He gestured with the remaining half of his scone, inadvertently showcasing his jam-first assembly technique to anyone who might have missed it the first time.

The woman nearest to us – one of the permed duo – leaned toward her companion and whispered something that sounded suspiciously like "Cornish spy." Her friend nodded grimly.

Marco caught my expression, his exuberance giving way to uncertainty. He glanced around, registering the room's muted disapproval. His cheeks, already flushed with enthusiasm, darkened further.

"What?" he whispered, leaning across the table. "What did I do wrong? Is it bad manners to express enjoyment?"

I took a deliberate sip of tea, buying time. "It's not that," I said quietly. "It's... the order of assembly."

"The order?" His brow furrowed. "I don't understand."

"You put the jam on first," I explained, keeping my voice low. "Then the cream."

He looked down at his half-eaten scone, then back at me, confusion mounting. "Yes? This is logical. The jam is sticky. It holds the cream in place."

"Logical, perhaps, but we're in Devon. Here, it's cream first, then jam. What you've done is the Cornish method."

Marco's eyes widened with the dawning horror of someone who's just realised they've committed a social sin of catastrophic proportions. "This is... bad?"

"It's practically treason," I said, allowing myself a small smile. "You've inadvertently declared allegiance to Cornwall while sitting in a Devon tea room. It's like wearing a Manchester United shirt to a Liverpool match."

Ryan, finally tuning into the conversation, looked up from his phone. "What's happening? Did Marco cause an international incident?"

"Worse," I replied. "An inter-county one."

Marco set down his scone as if it might detonate. "I had no idea," he whispered, genuine distress in his voice. "In Italy, we have many food rules, but they are the same in all regions."

"Not true," I countered. "What about the carbonara debate? Pancetta versus guanciale?"

His eyes narrowed. "That is different. There is only one correct way – with guanciale. The other is an abomination."

"Well, there you have it," I said, gesturing around the room. "To these good people, jam first is the abomination."

The proprietress approached our table again, her professional demeanour restored but slightly strained around the edges. She eyed Marco's partially eaten scone with the pained tolerance of a primary school teacher confronted with a well-intentioned but fundamentally flawed art project.

"Everything to your liking?" she asked, her tone carefully neutral.

Marco's face had achieved a shade of red previously unknown to the human spectrum. "It is delicious," he managed, then added with genuine contrition, "I am so sorry for my mistake. I did not know about the... correct procedure."

The woman's expression softened slightly. "First time with a cream tea, is it?"

Marco nodded vigorously. "At home, we have nothing like this. It is all new to me."

"He's Italian," I explained, as if this single fact might excuse any number of cultural transgressions. "His first time in Devon."

"Ah, well then," she said, visibly relaxing. "Can't expect you to know all our ways straight off, can we? Though between you and me," she lowered her voice to a conspiratorial whisper, "My late husband was Cornish, and honestly, forty years of marriage and he never did get the knack of it – not once! I must have threatened him with divorce at least five separate times." She grinned, a flash of sweet memories, as if the recollection of his repeated failures gave her as much pleasure now as annoyance then.

Marco glanced around the room, where the other patrons had gradually returned to their conversations, though occasionally a curious eye would drift in our direction. "Do you think they will forgive me?"

I followed his gaze to the twin-permed ladies, who were now engaged in an animated discussion, periodically glancing our way. "Eventually," I said. "Though I'd avoid mentioning Cornwall for the rest of our stay, just to be safe."

Marco nodded solemnly. Then, with renewed determination, he reached for his second scone, ready to attempt redemption. He carefully applied a generous layer of clotted cream to his scone half, then topped it with a modest spoonful of jam, his movements deliberate and almost ceremonial. He held up his creation, seeking my approval. "Is this correct? The Devon way?"

I nodded. "Textbook. You'll be granted honorary citizenship if you keep that up."

The proprietress, who had been keeping a weather eye on our table, approached with a fresh pot of tea.

"Getting the hang of it, I see," she observed, noting Marco's properly assembled scone.

Marco beamed at her. "Yes! I am learning the Devon way."

She laughed, a warm sound that seemed to release the last of the tension from the room. "You'll do," she said, refilling our cups. "Where are you all headed after this, then?"

"Dartmoor," I replied. "We're showing Marco South West England – he's documenting the British experience through fresh eyes."

The man with the newspaper had lowered his shield entirely, revealing a face weathered by decades of Dartmoor winds.

"If you're heading to the moor," he offered, his voice gruff but not unfriendly, "take the road through Widecombe. Best views that way."

"And don't miss Haytor," added one of the permed ladies. "You can climb right up it on a clear day. Though you'll want proper shoes." Her eyes drifted down to Marco's feet, where his butter-soft Italian loafers gleamed with the kind of polish that had never encountered moorland mud. His green Wellies, still drying from yesterday's downpour, would have been the wiser choice for Dartmoor's unforgiving terrain.

"Thank you," Marco said, genuinely touched by the locals' acceptance. "I will photograph everything. Maybe even the famous Dartmoor ponies?"

"Oh, you'll see them right enough," the proprietress assured him. "Bold as brass, they are. Come right up to the car looking for treats."

As we finished our tea, I outlined our route on a small map spread between the teacups. "We'll head north through Moretonhampstead, then onto the high moor. There's a stone circle I want to photograph, and if the weather holds, we might catch sunset at Brentor Church."

Ryan scrolled through his weather app, brow furrowed. "It says 'changeable conditions' for Dartmoor. That could mean anything from mild drizzle to biblical deluge." He looked up at me accusingly. "I told you we should have packed the extreme weather gear."

"We'll be fine," I assured him, though privately I knew that 'changeable conditions' on Dartmoor was meteorological code for 'prepare for all four seasons in a single afternoon.'

When I settled the bill, the proprietress wrapped two extra scones in waxed paper and handed them to Marco. "For the road," she said, giving him a conspiratorial wink.

Marco accepted the package as if receiving a sacred text. "Grazie! My Mamma will not believe this. I must learn to make these at home."

"Good luck finding proper clotted cream in Florence," Ryan said, zipping up his jacket in preparation for departure.

"I will improvise," Marco declared with the confidence of someone who had never failed a culinary challenge. "Perhaps mascarpone with a little... what is the English ingredient that makes everything better?"

"Gin?" suggested Ryan.

Outside, we found the afternoon had brightened, with earlier clouds now revealing patches of blue sky. As we walked to the car together, Marco turned to me, thoughtful.

"This is what I love about England," he said. "You take simple things – cream, jam, scones – and turn them into matters of profound importance. In Italy, we are the same with coffee. One wrong word about cappuccino after noon, and you are dead to your family."

"Cultural identity is often found in the smallest details," I agreed, unlocking the car.

The transition to Dartmoor's austere expanse was abrupt, as if someone had flipped the page from a pastoral watercolour to a charcoal sketch. One moment, we were cocooned in hedge-lined lanes. Next, we'd emerged onto an open vista where granite tors erupted from swathes of heather like the knuckles of a giant buried beneath the earth. The sky expanded, suddenly vast and uncompromising. Clouds seemed determined to outpace our little electric car as we climbed steadily into the heart of the moor.

Marco reacted immediately. He pressed himself against the rear window, camera forgotten in his lap, eyes wide as saucers. "Mamma mia," he breathed, "it is like the end of the world. No people, no houses, just... stone and sky."

"Welcome to Dartmoor," I said, guiding the car around a bend that revealed yet more of the same – an endless ripple of land that seemed to breathe with ancient, inhuman patience. "It's been this way for thousands of years."

"In Italy, we would have built at least a pizzeria," Marco murmured, his voice tinged with equal parts awe and mild distress. "Where are all the people?"

"That's rather the point," I replied. "You come to Dartmoor to escape people."

Ryan had been suspiciously quiet since we'd crossed onto the moor. Suddenly, he perked up, a gleam in his eye that I recognised all too well. It was the look Ryan got when presented with an opportunity too perfect to resist – in this case, a credulous Italian and a landscape steeped in folklore.

"Do you know about the witch?" Ryan asked, his voice dropping half an octave into what he clearly believed was a storyteller's register. He twisted around in his seat to face Marco, who instinctively leaned back.

"What witch?" Marco yelped, his voice climbing several notes in the opposite direction.

I caught Ryan's eye and saw the barely suppressed delight. I should have intervened. Still, I confess I was curious to see where this would go. Besides, every visitor to Dartmoor deserved at least one proper ghost story.

"Look there," Ryan said, pointing through the windscreen to a peculiar tor in the distance – a stack of granite that, with minimal imagination, resembled a human face in profile. "That's Bowerman's Nose. He was a hunter who was turned to stone by the witch Vixana."

Marco followed Ryan's finger, squinting at the distant rock formation. "That is a nose? It looks more like a... how do you say... thumb?"

"Well, it's weathered a bit since the 16th century," Ryan conceded, already reaching for his phone. "Let me just check the details of the story... Ah, here we go." He scrolled rapidly, the blue phone light casting his face in a ghoulish glow. "Bowerman was hunting with his dogs when they chased a hare – actually, no, wait – it was the witch herself, transformed into a hare to trick him."

Marco's eyes widened further. "The witch could transform?"

"Oh yes," Ryan nodded solemnly. "All the best ones can. Anyway, Bowerman and his hounds charged through a gathering of witches, disrupting their ritual. Vixana was so angry, she turned Bowerman to stone." He paused for effect. "His dogs, too. Those smaller rocks around the base? All dogs. Still guarding their master after five hundred years."

I glanced over at Ryan, impressed despite myself. He'd clearly been doing his homework on local legends. Marco was now pressed against the car door, alternating between staring at the tor and casting nervous glances at Ryan.

"This is... a story, yes? Like a fairy tale?" Marco pleaded, his voice taking on a desperate quality.

"Well," Ryan said, in a tone that suggested nothing of the sort was obvious. "People do report strange happenings around the tors. Especially near Vixen Tor, which we're approaching now."

As if on cue, a massive granite outcrop loomed ahead, sharp-edged and forbidding against the sky. Clouds began to gather around its peak, giving it an ominous, almost sentient appearance. I had to admit, if witches were to live anywhere on Dartmoor, Vixen Tor would be prime real estate.

Ryan lowered his voice dramatically, leaning closer to Marco. "Our next photo spot is exactly this Tor. But we need to be careful. They say Vixana still haunts this area. On misty days – like today – she lures travellers off the path. They follow what they think is a hare, or sometimes a beautiful woman, and they're never seen again."

"Madre di Dio," Marco muttered, crossing himself discreetly. He edged closer to the centre of the back seat, away from the windows, and began to whisper something in Italian that had the cadence of a prayer.

"Ryan," I warned, my tone carrying a hint of caution.

But Ryan was on a roll, his storytelling enthusiasm overpowering his better judgment. "There was a case just last year," he continued, now fully committed to his tale, "where a hiker reported seeing a woman in old-fashioned clothes standing on top of Vixen Tor. When he called out to warn her it was dangerous, she turned to him and her face was – "

"Stop!" Marco burst out, his voice high and tight. He had now moved directly behind my seat, seeking some protection against moorland witches. His fingers clutched his phone like a talisman, though the screen showed no signal bars. "I do not want to hear the end of this story."

"Ryan," I said firmly, "you've had your fun."

Ryan had the grace to look slightly sheepish, though not entirely repentant. "I might have embellished a bit," he admitted. "The hiker story was just something I read on a paranormal forum."

"The tors are granite," I explained, slipping into the factual tone I reserved for explaining away Ryan's more elaborate tales. They formed over 280 million years ago when molten rock cooled beneath the Earth's surface. Millions of years of weathering exposed them and created these distinctive shapes. Nothing supernatural about it – just time, pressure, and erosion."

Marco nodded slowly, his breathing returning to normal. "So... just rocks."

"Just rocks," I agreed. "Magnificent, ancient rocks that happen to make excellent subjects for photography." I nodded toward his camera, which had remained untouched since we entered the moor.

He looked down at it, then back at Vixen Tor, his expression shifting from fear to tentative interest. "It is... dramatic. The light on the granite," he said.

"Exactly," I encouraged, opening my door. "Come on. Let's

get some proper shots. I promise the only thing that will steal your soul is my composition."

As we stepped out into the wind, Marco straightened his shoulders, embarrassment replacing fear. "I knew it was just stories," he insisted, though his darting glance at the tor suggested otherwise. "In Italy, we have many tales of witches, too. But our witches prefer cities, with good espresso."

Ryan emerged from the passenger side, looking both amused and slightly contrite. "Sorry if I went overboard," he apologised to Marco. "Though you have to admit, it's a cracking good story."

"Next time," Marco promised, already raising his camera to frame the tor, "I will tell you about La Befana, the Italian witch who delivers gifts to children. Sometimes coal. But much nicer than your English witches. And she doesn't turn anyone to stone."

The gravel track to Nun's Cross Farm stretched the concept of "road" to its breaking point. What began as merely rough became more theoretical with each passing mile. Soon, we navigated a Morse code of potholes. The little electric car had so far borne our journey with stoic resilience, but now emitted a mechanical sigh as we bounced toward the isolated farm building, which appeared on the horizon like a mirage in stone.

"Are we still in England?" Marco asked, clutching the door handle as we navigated a particularly ambitious rut. "Or have we somehow crossed into purgatory?"

"Still Dartmoor," I replied, wincing as something beneath the car made a sound no vehicle should ever make. "Though some might argue there's little difference."

The farm itself seemed dropped on the moor by a careless giant. The granite building crouched against the elements, its slate roof blackened by centuries of rain.

"Cheerful," Ryan muttered, zipping his jacket to his chin.

The moment the name "Nun's Cross Farm" left my lips, Marco and Ryan exchanged a look that made my stomach sink.

"Isn't that..." Marco began.

"Just like Knowlton Church," Ryan whispered. "Another haunted site."

"There!" Marco hissed, grabbing Ryan's arm. "Something moved by that doorway!"

I squinted at the abandoned structure where shadows pooled beneath a sagging lintel. At first, I saw only weathered stone and determined tufts of moorland grass pushing through cracks in the masonry. Then, a flicker of darkness shifted in the deeper black.

"It's her," Marco's fingers whitened around Ryan's sleeve. "The nun. She's followed us all the way from Knowlton."

I exhaled slowly. "Oh boys. Not again."

"We should leave," Marco urged, retreating. "Now. Immediately."

I sighed. The ghost stories had clearly done more damage than I'd anticipated. "Wait here," I said, using the tone one might reserve for nervous toddlers. "I'll investigate."

"Brianna, no!" Marco's voice was an urgent whisper. "In horror films, the curious one always dies first!"

I ignored him and strode toward the outbuilding. Wind rippled the grass, sending dust and leaves spiralling upward. Ivy blanketed part of the wall, its glossy leaves a veil against grey stone.

The "shadow" Marco had spotted was still there – a darker patch partially obscured by the ivy. Not moving, not human-shaped, and certainly not supernatural.

I reached out and parted the ivy. Behind it, a small, weathered wooden box was set into the wall. It was the size of a hardback book, its surface carved with simple, elegant patterns.

"Come over," I called. "It's not a ghost. It's a letterbox."

They exchanged glances, neither wanting to go first. Eventually, curiosity overcame fear; they crept forward, wary of nuns appearing from every rock.

"A letterbox?" Marco's brow furrowed. "Like for mail?"

"Not exactly," I explained. I opened the small wooden door to reveal a compartment. Inside were a logbook, a rubber stamp, and an ink pad – each protected by a waterproof bag. "This one is for letterboxing."

Ryan's fear faded. "Letterboxing? Like Victorian geocaching?"

"Precisely," I said. "It began here on Dartmoor in 1854. A local guide named James Perrott placed a bottle at Cranmere Pool for visitors to leave their calling cards in. Eventually, it evolved into this – hidden boxes containing stamps and logbooks. People find them, stamp their personal notebook, leave a message, and move on to the next one."

Marco peered in, fascinated. "So, a treasure hunt? But with no treasure?"

"The stamps are the treasure," I said, demonstrating by pressing the rubber stamp onto a page of my small notebook. "Each one is unique to its location. Collectors try to find as many as possible."

Marco's eyes lit up. "In Italy, we have nothing like this. We would put recipes in the box, I think."

I handed him the stamp. "Go on, have a go. You've found your first letterbox."

He took the stamp with careful reverence, brows furrowed in concentration. Pressing it onto a blank page in his notebook, he slowly revealed a slightly smudged but recognisable outline – the farm buildings against the moor.

"Magnifico!" he exclaimed, suddenly enthused. "And there are more of these? All over Dartmoor?"

"Hundreds," I confirmed. "Some have been in place for decades. Others are temporary. Serious letterboxers use clues and compass bearings to find them."

Marco, who had been leafing through the logbook with growing interest, looked up. "These messages go back years," he said. "Families, couples, solo hikers – all leaving their mark." He picked up the pen that was attached to the book by a string and carefully wrote his name, the date, and "Ciao from Italy! I love your country, but we have better coffee." in neat script.

After Dartmoor's raw, elemental landscape, the manicured tranquillity of the Grand Western Canal seemed so neat and orderly it felt almost staged. The moor had offered windswept drama and granite permanence. By contrast, the canal gave a gentler vision of England: placid water reflecting weeping willows, towpaths edged with wildflowers, and the occasional duck making perfect concentric ripples. After the spectral panic at Nun's Cross Farm, this pastoral idyll seemed determined to soothe us with a display of almost aggressive quaintness.

"I can't believe this is the same county." Ryan stretched his legs as we emerged from the car. "One minute we're being haunted by non-existent nuns, the next we're in a Constable painting."

Marco was already at the water's edge, camera raised. His initial shots were methodical: the languid curve of the canal, the neat hedgerows on the far bank, a pair of swans gliding with aristocratic hauteur beneath a stone bridge. Then he spotted our destination and lost his professional composure.

"Look! A horse! An actual horse pulling a boat!" His voice carried across the water, startling a moorhen into indignant flight. "This is incredible! It is like a museum, but alive!"

The object of his enthusiasm stood patiently by the small wooden jetty. It was a magnificent shire horse, at least eighteen hands high, with feathered fetlocks and a gleaming chestnut coat. Harnessed to a traditional canal barge painted in glossy green and adorned with elaborate roses and castles, the horse exuded calm dignity. It seemed to have been posed for tourists since the dawn of photography.

The boat itself showed careful work – a long, narrow craft with shiny brass parts, checkered curtains at the small windows, and wooden benches for passengers on each side. A small sign stated it was "The Tivertonian, Est. 1974," making it fairly new among English heritage sites.

Marco approached the horse, his camera clicking rapidly as he circled for the optimal angle.

The horse's handler – a man of no easily guessable age, but with the sort of red, battered complexion you get from spending years locked in noisy argument with the wind and sun and rain – watched Marco's fit of photography with the tranquil forbearance of someone who has witnessed this exact performance more times than he's had hot dinners.

"She's called Duchess," he offered, patting the horse's substantial neck. "Sixteen years old and knows this canal better than I do."

Duchess acknowledged her introduction with a soft snort and the gentle swish of her tail, which Marco immediately captured in a burst of shots.

"Magnifico!" Marco lowered his camera only to raise his phone for a quick social media update. "My Italian followers will not believe this."

As more passengers arrived, we were invited to board. The barge settled lower in the water as we found our places on the wooden benches, the interior smelling pleasantly of varnish, tea, and history.

Marco positioned himself near the front, where he could maintain visual contact with Duchess. As the handler prepared to cast off, Marco suddenly rummaged in his bag and produced the remnants of his lunch – a slightly squashed sandwich with crusts intact.

"For Duchess." He leaned precariously over the side to offer the bread to the horse. "A thank you for pulling us."

The handler, who had been untying the mooring rope, paused. His expression underwent a subtle but profound transformation. A raised eyebrow, a slight tightening around the mouth, and an almost imperceptible inhalation all signalled a five-alarm emergency in British non-verbal communication.

"Ah," he said, his tone neutral. "It seems I've perhaps been remiss in my introduction to Duchess's routine. My fault entirely."

Marco, bread still extended toward the horse, looked confused. "Sorry? You have done nothing wrong!"

"It's nothing, really," the handler continued, in a voice that suggested it was very much something. "Just that Duchess has a rather sensitive stomach, you understand. But I clearly failed to mention it, so the oversight is mine."

Marco looked from the handler to the horse, who was eyeing the bread with undisguised interest. "But she wants it," he said, as Duchess stretched her neck toward the offering.

The handler stepped forward, inserting himself between horse and sandwich.

"I'm sure she appears keen," he said. He still smiled, though it now seemed fixed by an invisible force. "Horses are rather like children in that respect. What they want isn't always what's best for them. Perhaps I might have better explained her regime."

Marco withdrew the bread, looking increasingly perplexed. "I do not understand. Is the bread bad?"

"No no, not bad as such," the handler clarified, in a tone that clarified nothing.

Ryan, who had been watching this exchange with growing amusement, leaned toward me and whispered, "Ten quid says Marco offers his sandwich to the handler next."

I ignored him, watching as Marco's confusion deepened. The cultural chasm between Italian directness and British obliqueness widened by the second.

"But I have fed horses before," Marco insisted, still clutching the sandwich. "In Italy, they eat everything. Bread, apples, sugar cubes..."

The handler's smile remained fixed, but a new note entered his voice – a strained politeness that suggested he was approaching the outer limits of his British reserve.

"Perhaps you would prefer to enjoy your sandwich yourself? I wouldn't want you to miss out on your lunch."

Marco's eyes darted between me and the handler, his brow furrowed in confusion. "I do not understand this man," he whispered urgently. "He speaks many words but tells me nothing, and keeps saying sorry, but for what?"

I decided to intervene before we found ourselves in an international incident over sandwich crusts. "Marco," I said gently, "he's asking you to stop feeding his horse."

"Then why does he not say this?" Marco asked, genuinely perplexed. "One sentence – 'Don't feed the horse' – would be enough."

"That's not how we communicate in England," I explained, as the handler focused on the ropes, pretending not to hear. "Here, being too direct can seem rude. So instead of saying exactly what we mean, we often imply things or suggest them indirectly. Sometimes we even blame ourselves, not because we believe it's our fault, but to avoid making someone else uncomfortable. Or we rely on putting up signs everywhere, hoping to avoid awkward conversations. We do almost anything to steer clear of confrontation."

Marco looked incredulous. "This is confusing to me. It feels like I must guess. How does anyone understand each other?"

"We don't, half the time," Ryan chimed in cheerfully. "That's why we drink so much tea. Gives us something to do while we decode each other's sentences."

The handler, having secured the barge, returned to his position. His expression had reset to professional affability, the sandwich crisis apparently resolved. "All settled, then? Wonderful. We'll be underway momentarily. If anyone has any questions about the canal's history or wildlife, I'm happy to answer. Just not about Duchess's diet." This last was delivered with a smile that, for the first time, reached his eyes.

As the barge slipped away from the jetty, Duchess leaning into her harness with practised ease, Marco shook his head in lingering disbelief. "In Italy, if someone fed something wrong to my horse, I would shout, they would shout back, then we would drink espresso together and become friends."

"In England," I replied, watching the towpath unspool beside us, "we'll all go to our graves never having mentioned the sandwich again, but secretly writing about it in our diaries for decades."

Marco laughed, finally relaxing. "I will never understand the English," he declared, raising his camera to capture Duchess's steady progress along the towpath. "But I think I am beginning to like them anyway."

We nosed the car into Ilfracombe. The town began its slow reveal: first, the curve of the harbour emerged, then the boats with their flaking paint and self-importance. The water glinted so brightly it forced us into an involuntary squint.

"A perfect day for the coast," I announced. "We've actually got sunshine. In North Devon. In England."

Ryan squinted at the sky with suspicion. "Don't get too excited. I checked my weather app, and there's a 60% chance of precipitation by lunch."

I was already heading toward the harbour's edge. "Come on, both of you. There's history to absorb before the inevitable downpour."

Marco slid from the car, instantly shifting from travel-weary passenger to alert photographer. Camera already in hand, lens cap off, finger poised over the shutter.

"This is fantastico," he exclaimed, spinning in a slow circle to take in the vista. "So authentic! Real fishing boats, not just tourist attractions. In Italy, our harbours are all yachts, designer sunglasses and overpriced aperitivos now."

I led them along the curve of the quay. Fishing vessels with names like "Perseverance," "Lady Luck," and "Atlantic Spray" knocked gently against the stone. Salt and diesel hung in the air, mingling with the tang of fresh catch and the saccharine scent of nearby doughnut stands.

"Ilfracombe's been a working harbour since the 12th century," I explained, pausing to let a trio of fishermen pass with crates of gleaming mackerel. "These smaller boats go out daily for their catch, while the larger vessels used to handle coal, lime, and even prisoners bound for the Colonies."

Ryan's attention had already drifted toward a chippy advertising "Devon's Best Fish and Chips" in faded lettering, but Marco was enraptured, photographing every weathered rope and rusting cleat.

We continued our circuit of the harbour, past the RNLI lifeboat station where a gleaming orange rescue vessel stood ready for emergency, and toward the protective seawall. The morning remained stubbornly pleasant, with only the faintest breeze ruffling the water's surface and sending the occasional gull wheeling overhead.

"There's something you should see just ahead," I said, deliberately casual. "A rather distinctive piece of public art. It's called 'Verity,' by Damien Hirst, a well-known contemporary British artist."

Marco's eyes lit up. "Damien Hirst? The one with the shark in formaldehyde? The dots? He is famous even in Italy."

"The very same," I confirmed. "Though this piece is a bit more... anatomical."

Ryan suppressed a snort. "That's one way of putting it."

As we rounded the final curve of the harbour wall, Verity came into view – all twenty metres of her. Sword raised skyward, scales of justice held aloft, pregnant belly exposed to the elements and the judgment of every passing tourist.

Marco stopped dead in his tracks. "Mamma mia," he whispered, camera forgotten at his side. "She is enormous."

He approached slowly, eyes tracing the figure from base to sword tip. I followed at a discreet distance, waiting for the inevitable moment of realisation. It came precisely as Marco circled to view the statue's right side.

The transition was magnificent in its completeness – from artistic appreciation to visceral horror in the span of three seconds.

For Verity's right side, now visible to Marco's unblinking gaze, was an anatomical cross-section. The pregnant woman's internal organs, muscles, cranium, and womb were fully exposed, the developing foetus clearly visible within.

"Dio mio!" Marco staggered backwards, one hand clutching his stomach, the other making rapid, fluttering gestures in the air before him. "What is this? Why? Why is she cut open like this?"

A stream of Italian followed, too rapid for my limited linguistic capabilities, but the tone suggested either fervent prayer or creative profanity.

I stepped forward, slipping into tour guide mode. "It's meant to represent truth and justice – Verity, from the Latin 'veritas.' The exposed anatomy symbolises transparency and the search for objective truth. The scales and sword are traditional symbols of justice. The pregnancy represents fertility and future potential. The whole thing's a meditation on the legal principle of 'truth, the whole truth, and nothing but the truth.'"

Marco's eyes were still fixed on the exposed womb, his expression suspended somewhere between fascination and nausea. "But why must it be so... graphic? In Italy, our public statues have fig leaves, not... internal organs."

"It's characteristic of Hirst's work," I continued, maintaining my calm exterior while privately enjoying his discomfort. "He's rather fond of making us confront mortality, anatomy, and the physical realities we prefer to ignore."

"Very much so," Ryan said with a wry grin, appearing beside us after perusing the ice cream stand's menu. "Remember his diamond-encrusted skull? Or the cow cut in half? His style is certainly... consistent."

Marco swallowed hard, looking distinctly green around the edges. "But this is for everyone to see. Children. Grandmothers. Tourists eating ice cream!"

"That's rather the point," I said. "Art in public spaces forces us to engage with ideas we might otherwise avoid. It's caused quite the controversy since its installation in 2012. Some locals campaigned to have it removed, calling it obscene. Others see it as putting Ilfracombe on the cultural map."

Marco was now backing away from the statue, his camera hanging forgotten around his neck.

Ryan clapped a hand on Marco's shoulder. "I think what our friend needs is some proper sustenance. Nothing settles a stomach quite like food."

As if on cue, Ryan's stomach growled loud enough to send a nearby seagull fluttering into the air.

"Perfect timing," I said, glancing at my watch. "It's nearly lunchtime anyway."

Marco cast one last haunted look at Verity, muttering something that sounded like a promise to light a candle at the next available church, before allowing himself to be steered away toward the harbour restaurants.

"Lunch," Ryan declared, pointing at a small café with weathered blue paintwork. "No more anatomical surprises. Just reliable British food."

Marco's face suggested he found this reassurance only mildly comforting.

The café Ryan selected had clearly embraced its maritime location with the enthusiasm of a first-time sailor discovering knots. Fishing nets draped from the ceiling. Weathered buoys hung at rakish angles from the walls. The tables were solid, scarred wood that had endured decades of elbows and spilt tea. Each was decorated with a small jar of shells and sea glass. The effect hovered between charming local authenticity and a set designer's vision for a low-budget production of "The Tempest."

"Perfect," Ryan declared, steering toward a corner table with an unobstructed view of the harbour. "We can see the boats, but not the statue."

Marco followed like a man recently rescued from a shipwreck.

"I am better now," he pronounced to the room at large. "Some things cannot be unseen, but perhaps they can be... overlaid with new images. Like food."

"That's the spirit," I chimed, taking the seat opposite him. "Nothing cures artistic trauma quite like deep-fried potatoes."

The café's interior hummed with the gentle percussion of coastal dining: the clink of cutlery, murmured conversations about tides and weather, and the thud of the kitchen door as waitstaff emerged with seafood. Salt-flecked windows, perpetually in need of cleaning, framed the harbour like living paintings, fishing boats nodding in the gentle swell.

A waitress materialised at our table, order pad at the ready, her expression suggesting that whatever we might request, she had served stranger things to stranger people.

"What can I get you?" she inquired, pen poised.

Ryan took the lead. "Do you have any vegan options? Specifically, vegan fish and chips?" he queried.

The waitress didn't blink. "We do tofu fried in batter with

chips. We call it 'Not Fish and Chips' on the menu."

How very creative, I thought.

"Perfect! I'll have that, please," Ryan beamed. "And a pot of tea."

"Bean burger for me," I said. "With chips. And a green tea, if you have it."

Marco, still contemplating the menu, finally looked up from the laminated page. He set it down. "Just chips, please," he muttered, his voice slightly hollow. "And water. No ice."

"You sure that's enough?" Ryan asked. "They do a lovely looking pasta with–"

"No. Just chips," Marco repeated firmly. "My stomach needs... simplicity. After the statue."

The waitress nodded, as if sculptural distress was a common dietary consideration, and retreated to the kitchen.

"It will pass," I assured Marco. "The first Hirst is always the most shocking. By the third or fourth, you'll be completely desensitised to anatomical cross-sections."

Our food arrived with impressive speed, suggesting either exceptional kitchen efficiency or the strategic deployment of microwaves. Ryan's plate featured golden-battered rectangles of tofu arranged around a mountain of thick-cut chips, accompanied by mushy peas of an improbable green. My bean burger sat proudly on a brioche bun, garnished with rocket and a slice of tomato so pale it might never have encountered actual sunlight. Marco's portion of chips was generous enough to feed a small family, golden and glistening with just the right amount of oil.

"Now this," Ryan observed, surveying his meal with satisfaction, "is proper British seaside dining."

He reached for the collection of condiments clustered at the table's edge, bypassing the ketchup and vinegar in favour of a squat brown bottle. With the practised motion of a chemist adding a crucial reagent, he upended the bottle over his plate, unleashing a thick, brown cascade that pooled around his Not Fish and spread insidiously toward the chips.

Marco watched this procedure with growing alarm. "What is that?" he asked, leaning forward to inspect the dark substance.

"Brown sauce," Ryan replied cheerfully, now spreading the condiment with his fork to ensure maximum coverage. "It's a British institution. HP Sauce, to be specific. The HP stands for Houses of Parliament, believe it or not."

Marco's expression suggested he most certainly did not believe it. "But it is... so brown. What is in it?" he persisted.

"Tomatoes, molasses, dates, tamarind, vinegar, various spices," Ryan listed, already cutting into his battered tofu. "It's sweet, tangy, and a bit spicy. British answer to ketchup, just better. Goes with everything."

Marco eyed the bottle with the caution one might reserve for an undetonated explosive.

"Don't knock it till you've tried it," Ryan encouraged through a mouthful of Not Fish. "Go on – just a little dab on one chip. It's part of the authentic British experience."

Peer pressure works, even when delivered by someone with a mouthful of vegan fish substitute. Marco hesitantly reached for the bottle, fingertips pinched around its neck. He tipped it carefully, letting a controlled drip of sauce fall onto the farthest edge of his plate. He eyed the pile of chips, picked out the smallest, and nudged it toward the dab of sauce for the experiment. He dipped the chip with the delicacy of someone testing bath water, ensuring only the very tip made contact with the brown substance. Then, with a glance that suggested he was memorising our faces in case these proved to be his final moments, he took a tentative bite. Marco's face twisted through surprise, confusion, horror, then settled on disgust. His eyes watered, and he reached for his water glass.

After a substantial gulp, he gasped, "What is this? Sour? Sweet? Spicy? All together? In one sauce?" He placed a hand over his heart, as if to prevent it from escaping his chest in protest. "This is what you English call sauce? My Mamma would rather go on a no-pasta diet than allow this on our family table!"

Ryan continued eating happily, unfazed by Marco's culinary crisis. "It's an acquired taste," he conceded. "But once you acquire it, nothing else will do on a full English breakfast." He was reaching for the sauce again. "It's practically a national treasure. The Queen had it on her breakfast table. There's a Royal Warrant on the bottle and everything."

I observed the scene with amusement, taking a bite of my bean burger. "British culinary contributions to world cuisine are generally an acquired taste," I remarked. "Much like our sense of humour and our weather."

I leaned forward in the driver's seat, squinting through the windscreen. According to Ryan's latest foodie app, St Columb Major was supposed to be home to Cornwall's finest vegan Cornish pasties. Instead, we found a village that looked as if everyone had left in a hurry: boarded-up shops, empty streets, and an eerie quiet hanging in the air like mist. I glanced at Ryan, who was audibly calculating how many minutes had passed since breakfast.

"Five hours and thirty-two minutes," he announced, squinting at his phone. "I've gone precisely five hours and thirty-two minutes since my last meal. According to my nutrition tracker, I'm officially entering the danger zone of low blood sugar."

"The danger zone being the point where you become unbearable?" I asked, raising an eyebrow.

Ryan ignored me, scrolling through his app. "It should be right there – Cornish Comfort Bakery. Five stars for vegan pasties. Seventeen glowing reviews."

Behind us, Marco pressed his face against the window. "This is very suspicious," he whispered, his Italian accent thickening with each word. "In my country, when all shops close like this and people disappear, it means only one thing – La Cosa Nostra - la mafia!"

"I highly doubt the Cornish mafia is after pasties," I said, though the boarded windows and all those nails were a bit unsettling.

"You do not understand," Marco insisted, gesturing wildly enough to hit the car ceiling. "First, they make everyone stay inside, then they take over the businesses one by one. Protection money, you know? "

"Or," I suggested, "there's a perfectly reasonable explanation that doesn't involve organised crime."

Ryan's stomach growled. "Whatever the reason, my app says I've burned 1,742 calories and only eaten 842."

"Let's at least get out and investigate," I said, unclipping my seatbelt. "There has to be someone about."

As we got out of the car, a distant roar drifted over – not traffic, not machinery, but definitely human. Marco grabbed my arm, a little too dramatically.

"You hear that? They are coming!" His eyes were wide with alarm. "The families are fighting for territory!"

"Marco," I said firmly, "this is Cornwall, not Sicily. The most dangerous thing here is likely to be an angry seagull."

We walked down the deserted high street. The shouting in the distance was getting louder. Ryan trailed behind, one hand on his stomach, the other gripping his phone as if it might conjure a pasty if he stared at it long enough.

"Look," I pointed to a handwritten sign in one window that had been hastily taped to the inside of a board: "CLOSED FOR HURLING DAY – BACK TOMORROW."

"Hurling?" Ryan frowned. "Like... being sick?"

"I think it's some sort of game," I replied, vaguely remembering an article in a cultural magazine. "Traditional Cornish sport, if I'm not mistaken."

As if summoned by our conversation, an older man appeared from a side street, his face flushed with excitement. He wore a faded rugby shirt and carried a walking stick that he waved enthusiastically as he approached.

"You lot aren't from around here, are you?" he asked, grinning broadly. "Come for Hurling Day and got lost?"

"Actually, we came for vegan pasties," Ryan said. "It's been five hours and forty-one minutes since breakfast."

The man let out a bark of laughter. "Ah, you're after Sally's place. She's closed up today, same as everyone. Can't risk the windows on Hurling Day."

Marco stepped forward. "What is this 'hurling'? Is it dangerous? Is it... controlled by certain powerful families?"

I nudged him sharply in the ribs.

"Controlled? Not at all!" The man chuckled. "Hurling the Silver Ball is the most chaotic tradition around. Centuries old."

Marco's face lit up. "Hurling? The Irish sport with the sticks?"

"No, no, Cornish hurling," he said. "Centuries old. Townsmen vs. Countrymen, fighting for the silver ball. The whole parish – seventeen square miles – is the field."

Ryan's expression shifted from hunger to curiosity. Only odd local traditions can distract him from food.

"So that's why it's all boarded up? A ball game?" I asked.

The man chuckled. "It's a bit more than a ball game, love. Hundreds of men running through the village and countryside, no real rules to speak of. Things can get a bit... enthusiastic."

A particularly loud cheer erupted from somewhere beyond the church.

He proceeded to explain, with evident pride, that Cornish hurling was a game played across the entire parish – a territory spanning seventeen square miles. Teams of "Townsmen" and "Countrymen" battled for possession of a silver-coated apple wood ball, trying either to carry it to a stone goal or across the parish boundary to score.

"So it's like rugby without boundaries?" I asked.

"More like medieval warfare," he corrected. "Only real rules: don't throw or hide the ball, no cars. And try not to kill anyone. Though that's more of a guideline than a rule."

Marco looked horrified. "People have died playing this?"

"Not for decades," Bill said reassuringly. "Just a few broken bones and the odd concussion these days."

The distant roar suddenly swelled, and he glanced over his shoulder. "That'll be the game coming this way. They're moving through town. Game can go on for hours. Record is over eight, I think."

"So all the shops are closed for this?" I asked, turning back to Bill.

"Aye, safety precaution. Sally had her bakery window smashed three years ago when the ball went through it. Insurance nightmare, that was."

Ryan looked horrified. "And this is legal?"

"Been happening since before 'legal' was a concept round here, lad. After the game, everyone shares silver beer – that's beer with the ball dipped in it." He caught our expressions and laughed. "Don't worry, they clean it first. Usually."

The clamour grew louder – now I could pick out individual shouts and what sounded like splitting wood.

"What about the pasties?" Ryan asked desperately. "Is there anywhere else?"

The man studied Ryan's woeful expression for a moment, then his face softened. "Tell you what – my wife's made some vegan ones for our daughter who's gone all plant-based. Been experimenting with recipes. We've got plenty extra if you'd like some."

Ryan went from despair to delight in seconds.

"You're an angel sent from vegan heaven," he breathed.

Five minutes later, we were hurrying back to our car, clutching a paper bag containing three generously sized pasties still warm from the oven. Behind us, the shouting had reached a fever pitch, and as we slammed the car doors, I caught sight of a surging mass of people rounding the corner of the high street.

"Drive!" Marco yelped, spotting the crowd. "The families are coming!"

I rolled my eyes but braced for action, admitting a strategic withdrawal was wise. Ryan already cradled the paper bag like a newborn, inhaling deeply through the top.

"Five hours and fifty-three minutes," he said with reverence as we pulled away. "Worth every second of the wait."

In the rearview mirror, I watched as a wave of people filled the street we'd just left, chasing a small, glinting object.

We'd settled ourselves on a tufted patch of grass, just above the broken spine of Cornwall's mining past. Everywhere you glanced, the land was staked with abandoned engine houses: crumbling stone, poking up at the low pewter sky as if to defy it. The sea, a slab of Atlantic grey, blurred into the clouds so there was no finding the horizon at all.

Ryan made a beeline for the flattest bit of ground. He smoothed out the brown paper under his pasty and began dissecting his lunch with a sort of surgical attention. The astonishing view – the cliffs, the engine houses, the endless sea – all of it was relegated to a painted backdrop. "Crust held up well," he said, giving the edge a critical look. "Wheat flour, but vegetable shortening, not lard. Classic Cornwall pasty uses beef suet." As if that settled things.

Marco had barely finished half his pasty before the lure of the camera got him. He circled the outcrop, kneeling, then lying flat on the cold grass for a different angle. When he liked a shot, he'd make a little sound of satisfaction. "These buildings – so dramatic!" he called over, sounding genuinely surprised. "Like the skeletons of a civilisation!"

"That's not far off," I said, steadying my own pasty on my knee while I pointed to the nearest engine house. "These were the powerhouses of industrial Cornwall. From the early eighteenth century, these mines made the region one of the most important metal mining areas in the world."

Marco paused, camera poised. "What did they mine? Gold?"

"Tin and copper, primarily," I told him. "Cornwall produced two-thirds of the world's copper at one point. These engine houses contained massive beam engines – steam-powered pumps to keep the mines from flooding. Some of the mines ran for more than half a mile under the sea."

Ryan, mid-bite, stopped chewing. "Under the sea? That sounds absolutely terrifying."

Marco was back to composing shots, but I could tell from the way he lingered that he was listening.

We were halfway through this impromptu history lesson when a figure appeared along the path: a man in a stormproof jacket, striding at a good clip, with a black and white Dalmatian shadowing him. The dog saw us and perked up, but stayed obedient at heel.

"Afternoon," the man called, raising his hand in greeting. His accent was pure Cornish, the vowels stretched out, slow and golden. "Fine day for pasties and photography."

Ryan raised his pasty. "Is there a bad day for either?"

The man laughed and came to a stop at a polite distance from our picnic. The dog sat as if on cue, eyes bright.

"Wheal Owles," the man said, nodding to the engine house commanding the bluff. "That's where you're looking at. Bad history, that one. Nineteen men and one boy lost when they broke through into an old working. Flooded in minutes."

Marco lowered his camera, face suddenly serious. "The men who worked here – they died?"

"Mining was dangerous work," the man said. "Still is, wherever you find it."

His attention flicked to Marco's pasty, specifically to the thick D-shaped crimp running along one side.

"Ah, I see you've got proper pasties there. Traditional shape and all."

Marco held his up. "Why this rope edge?"

The man's eyes lit up, delighted to be asked. "That's the crimp. Vital part of a Cornish pasty," he said, warming to his subject. "The miners would carry these down for their 'crib' – their lunch, you see. Their hands got covered in arsenic, copper dust, tin. Nasty stuff."

Ryan, who had been getting along nicely, froze. "Arsenic?"

"Aye," said the man. "Terrible stuff. The crimped edge was your handle. You ate the pasty, threw away the crust that was contaminated."

"Ingenious," I said. "Functional design before it was fashionable."

He nodded, and after a quick look round as if checking for eavesdroppers, dropped his voice to a confidential tone.

"There's another reason for leaving the crusts, mind," he said.

Marco leaned in, interested. "What reason?"

"The Tommyknockers," he said, barely above a whisper.

Ryan looked bewildered. "The what?"

"Tommyknockers," the man repeated. "Spirits of the mines. They'd knock on the walls – sometimes warning of a cave-in, sometimes just mischief. Miners left the crusts for them, as an offering. You cross the Tommyknockers, you might never see sunlight again."

Marco's eyes widened. He crossed himself, muttering in Italian.

"Superstition," Ryan said, but I noticed he was looking at the ruined walls with more caution than before.

The man shrugged. "Call it what you like. Miners who forgot to make an offering often met with accidents, that's all I'm saying."

Ryan, keen to move the conversation back to food, asked, "What was in a traditional pasty? Besides the, er, arsenic-covered crust."

"Beef, potato, swede, and onion," said the man. "Every family had their own recipe, though. Some put in carrot, some wouldn't hear of it. Caused arguments, that did."

He patted his thigh for the Dalmatian, gave us a last nod, and strode on. No sooner was he out of earshot than Marco stood up. He propped his half-eaten pasty against the skyline of Wheal Owles, nudged it left and right, then started snapping photos from every angle.

"What are you doing?" I asked, though I already knew.

"Documenting," he said, with a solemnity only Marco could manage, "the most dangerous lunch in all of England! The pasty that feeds both miners and spirits."

Ryan rolled his eyes at me, but I noticed he was picking at his crust, a little less sure than before.

"You don't actually believe in mine spirits, do you?" I said quietly.

"Of course not," he said, a touch too quick. "But maybe I'll leave some crust. Tradition, after all."

I smiled into my green tea from the thermos, watching as the weak Cornish sun briefly pierced the clouds, lighting the ancient stones against the Atlantic.

Rows of stone seating carved directly into the cliff face, dropping precipitously toward the turquoise waters of Porthcurno Bay below. Nature had provided the dramatic backdrop of the Minack theatre; human hands had merely accentuated what was already there. Ryan, who'd been scrolling through TripAdvisor reviews for the entire winding drive from the mining heritage site, finally looked up from his phone and let out an involuntary "Blimey" that seemed to perfectly capture the sentiment of first-time visitors.

"It says here that a woman built this with her gardener in the

1930s," Ryan announced.

"Is this not the most spectacular thing?" Marco called back to us, his Italian accent stretching the word 'spectacular' into something with at least twice the necessary syllables. "It is like ancient Greece, but in England! With the sea! Magnifico!"

We followed a narrow stone path that curved downward, each step revealing more of the theatre's impossible geometry. Carved granite seating spread in a semi-circle, facing a stage that seemed to hover between land and sea. The back of the stage was open to the elements, framing nothing but the endless Atlantic horizon.

"Do you think they ever lose actors over the edge?" Ryan asked, peering down the steep drop with an expression of fascinated horror. "One dramatic exit too many and – whoops – straight into the sea."

"That's precisely the sort of question that makes me travel with you, Ryan," I replied dryly. "Your unique ability to find the morbid angle in any beautiful situation."

A small cluster of people had gathered near the stage area, their voices carrying up to us in fragments. They appeared to be in the middle of some sort of crisis, judging by their animated gestures and the distinctly stressed tone of their conversation. One woman in particular – tall, with a shock of silver hair cropped close to her head – seemed to be the focus of their attention.

As we stepped onto the main seating level, the silver-haired woman turned abruptly from her group, striding toward us with measured, determined steps.

"Welcome to the Minack," she greeted us. "I'm Eleanor. Are you here for the performance this evening?"

"We hadn't planned to be," I admitted, "but now that we're here, it seems like too good an opportunity to miss. What's playing?"

"A Midsummer Night's Dream," she replied. "Though at this precise moment, it's more of A Midsummer Night's Nightmare."

"Problems with the production?" I enquired, noting the tension in her shoulders despite her light tone.

Eleanor sighed. "Our Puck has food poisoning. Bad mussels, apparently. He's currently communing with the porcelain deity rather than the fairy king. She rubbed at her eyes, tired but determined. "You wouldn't happen to know of any decent actor nearby? Someone Oscar-level, with so much spare cash they wouldn't even bother charging us a fee?" She smiled.

Ryan saw his chance. He perked up immediately. "I could help and jump in! I did amateur dramatics at university," he volunteered, straightening his posture in what I recognised as his attempting-to-appear-taller stance.

Eleanor gave him a polite but dismissive once-over. "That's kind, but Puck requires a very particular physical presence. We're doing an experimental production – a mime version. Our director has rather specific visual requirements."

At that moment, Marco bounded back up the steps toward us, gesturing wildly at a seagull that had swooped particularly close to his head.

"Did you see? The bird, he tried to attack me! Like Hitchcock!" Marco's entire body was engaged in the retelling, his hands sketching the seagull's flight path while his face cycled through expressions of surprise, outrage, and dramatic peril.

Eleanor froze, her eyes fixed on Marco with sudden intensity. She tilted her head slightly, like a bird of prey that had just spotted movement in the undergrowth.

"You," she said, pointing directly at Marco. "What's your name?"

Marco paused mid-gesticulation, surprised at being addressed so directly. "Marco. Marco Ricci," he replied, unconsciously striking a pose that wouldn't have looked out of place on a Renaissance painter's canvas.

"Marco," Eleanor repeated, as if testing the name. "Have you ever acted before?"

"Well... no... yes..." Marco stammered, flapping at the air as if he might catch a firmer answer mid-flight. "Not really on stage... but... I am Italian?" He threw that out, obviously trying to be helpful.

Eleanor's face lit up. "Perfect. Absolutely perfect"." As if the mere fact of being Italian ticked every box for a Shakespearean

CV. "Would you consider stepping in as our Puck tonight? As I was explaining to your friends, it's primarily movement-based. No lines to learn, just physical expressiveness and a touch of mischief."

Marco's eyes widened. "Me? Play Shakespeare? But I am not English actor!"

"That's precisely why you're perfect," Eleanor insisted. "Puck isn't meant to be conventionally English. He's other-worldly, mercurial, completely uninhibited. Everything about you – your gestures, your expressions, even the way you move – it's exactly what our director has been trying to coax out of our regular actors for weeks."

Ryan stepped forward, clearing his throat. "Actually, I mentioned that I have acting experience. Classical training, in fact. I played Bottom in my university production."

Eleanor gave him another, more thorough examination, but her expression remained unchanged. "I'm afraid you're too..." she paused, searching for a diplomatic phrase, "...conventionally English-looking for what we need. Our Puck needs to stand out from the mortal characters. To be visibly different."

"I'm too ordinary, you mean," Ryan translated, his shoulders slumping slightly.

Marco, who had been watching this exchange with growing excitement, now bounced on the balls of his feet. "I could do it! I would be honoured to play the little fairy man!"

"Woodland sprite," Ryan corrected automatically, his tone distinctly sulky.

"The rehearsal room is just through there," Eleanor said, pointing to a small stone building nestled against the cliff. "Our costume designer will get you fitted, and our movement director can run through the basic choreography with you. You have three hours to prepare yourself."

As Marco bounded off, following Eleanor's directions with puppyish enthusiasm, Ryan turned to me with an expression of betrayal. "Can you believe that? 'Too conventionally English-looking.' What does that even mean?"

"Eleanor doesn't know you and your dramas," I replied, patting his arm sympathetically. "The first look at you might make her think you are the typical outdoorsy dogwalker. Not exactly sprite material."

Ryan's scowl deepened. "I could be otherworldly."

We killed the hours until the shows started by taking more photos of the beautiful scenery, Ryan maintaining a stony silence, hardly speaking a word to me. Marco was busy rehearsing. As the amphitheatre gradually filled around us, the evening air carried a salt tang from the sea below, and the sky was beginning to soften toward sunset, promising a backdrop that no conventional theatre could hope to match.

"Look at it this way," I offered, breaking the silence. "Marco's going to be prancing around in what I assume will be some sort of ridiculous outfit. You get to sit here and judge his performance with the ruthless criticism of someone who 'could have done it better.'"

A reluctant smile tugged at Ryan's lips. "I would have been brilliant," he muttered, but I could tell his mood was beginning to thaw.

Eleanor materialised beside us just as the theatre lights began to dim. She looked considerably more relaxed than when we'd first met her.

"Your friend is a natural," she whispered, sliding into the empty seat next to me. "Our director is beside himself with excitement. Apparently, Marco has 'reinterpreted the essential Puck-ness of Puck.'"

"That sounds like Marco," I agreed.

Eleanor laughed softly. "I should tell you – I knew Rowena Cade, the woman who built this place. She was like a grandmother to me. She would have adored your friend's enthusiasm."

"You knew her personally?" I asked, genuinely intrigued. "The woman who created all this?"

"Oh yes," Eleanor nodded, her gaze sweeping across the theatre with evident affection. "I grew up nearby. As a child, I would help her mix concrete and carry stones. She was already in her seventies then, still working on the theatre every day. Hands like leather, but she could carve the most delicate designs into wet concrete."

Our conversation was interrupted by the beginning of the performance. The actors playing Theseus and Hippolyta strode onto the stage, their voices carrying remarkably well in the open-air setting.

The production was innovative – minimal sets, relying instead on the natural drama of the location. As the mortal characters became entangled in the forest, lighting subtly shifted to create an impression of enchantment. And then, with a leap that seemed to defy gravity, Marco burst onto the stage as Puck.

He was transformed. Someone had applied glitter to his hair and painted elaborate swirls across his cheekbones. His costume consisted of what appeared to be strategically draped silk in shades of green and brown, with vines woven through. But it was his movement that truly captured attention – fluid and unpredictable, somehow managing to suggest both animal and sprite, mischievous and ancient.

Ryan, who had been maintaining a posture of critical readiness, slowly straightened in his seat. "Oh," he said in awe. "He's actually... good."

Marco's Puck danced between the other characters, his expressions conveying everything that Shakespeare's words normally would. When he mimed applying the love potion to the sleeping lovers' eyes, his face reflected such gleeful mischief that the audience laughed aloud.

By the final scene, even Ryan was leaning forward, completely absorbed. When Marco delivered his final bow – an elaborate, courtly gesture that somehow incorporated both ballet and what looked suspiciously like Italian football victory celebrations – Ryan was on his feet with the rest of the audience, applauding with genuine enthusiasm.

"I couldn't have done that," he admitted as we made our way backstage after the performance. "Not in a million years."

Marco greeted us with sweat-dampened hair still sparkling with glitter, his face alight with the particular ecstasy of performance adrenaline.

"Did you see?" he demanded, grabbing Ryan's shoulders. "I was flying! Not really flying, but in my soul, I was flying!"

"You were brilliant," Ryan conceded, without a trace of his earlier resentment. "Truly otherworldly."

Eleanor joined us, carrying a bottle of champagne and four glasses. "A toast to our emergency Puck," she declared, expertly popping the cork with minimal spray. "Rowena would have loved tonight's performance."

We settled onto a small patio overlooking the now-darkened sea, the sound of waves providing a gentle soundtrack to our conversation. Eleanor filled our glasses and then raised her own.

"To Rowena," she said, "and to spontaneous magic."

After we'd clinked glasses and Marco had recounted his favourite moments from the performance – with full physical re-enactments – I turned to Eleanor. "Tell us more about Rowena. Building this place must have been an extraordinary undertaking."

Eleanor's face softened with memory. "She was the most practical visionary I've ever known. Started building this place in her late thirties, which was considered quite scandalous for a woman in the 1930s. She'd bought the cliff-top house you can see up there, called Minack House, and local amateur theatre groups needed somewhere to perform The Tempest."

"So she just... decided to carve a theatre into a cliff?" Ryan asked incredulously.

"Essentially, yes," Eleanor nodded. "She and her gardener, Billy Rawlings, moved tons of earth and stone by hand. Used concrete mixed in a wheelbarrow. She couldn't afford proper tools, so she carved the intricate Celtic designs you see on the seats using kitchen knives and forks."

Marco, who had been listening intently, looked around with new appreciation. "One woman did all this? With garden tools?"

"And continued working on it well into her eighties," Eleanor confirmed. "During the war, the theatre was commandeered by the military – they installed a gun post right over there." She pointed to what now appeared to be a small box office. "After the war, Rowena simply incorporated it into the theatre design. Waste not, want not, as she always said."

"That's extraordinary," I said, genuinely moved by the story. "To have such vision, and the determination to realise it."

"She used to say that she wasn't building something new, just completing what nature had begun," Eleanor replied, her gaze drifting over the darkened amphitheatre. "The cliff already resembled a theatre; she merely helped it fulfil its purpose."

As we drove away later that evening, Marco was still riding high on his unexpected theatrical debut. This moment he will recall, and probably retell to all his Italian relatives, many times.

We drove along Somerset's back roads until Wells started to appear in the distance. The cathedral spires were the first thing we saw, slowly rising above the rooftops.

"Last stop," I reminded them, a tinge of melancholy in my voice. After two weeks of Ryan's constant hunger and Marco's operatic moods, I'd grown oddly attached to our dynamic. "Marco's bus is at four."

"Four? That's three hours, twenty-two minutes. Time for lunch or only sightseeing?" Ryan asked, glancing at his watch.

"You and your stomach," I sighed, without real irritation. "Yes, time for both. I want Marco to see Vicar's Close – oldest purely residential street, all originals."

"Older than Roman streets?" Marco was sceptical. "In Rome, we have–"

"All original buildings," I emphasised, anticipating his objection. "The street layout is medieval, and every single structure still standing is original, just with modernisations inside. It's a perfect example of medieval urban planning."

"Urban planning? In medieval times?" Marco laughed.

We found a parking space near the cathedral and made our way through Wells' quiet streets. The city had a serene quality that afternoon. It was a pleasant change after Cornwall's windswept drama. Elderly couples ambled along the pavements. Their pace was unhurried, as if they had long ago surrendered their watches to retirement. A group of schoolchildren in matching burgundy uniforms filed past. Their excited chatter softened to whispers as they passed the cathedral's imposing façade.

"This way," I guided them, moving past the cathedral's west front with its hundreds of medieval carvings. "Vicar's Close is just behind the cathedral complex."

We approached through a stone archway. Suddenly, it was there – a perfect medieval street unfolding before us like an architectural mirage. Two rows of identical stone houses faced each other across a narrow cobbled lane. Chimneys and gables created a rhythmic pattern against the sky. The street stretched away from us in a straight line. It seemed to extend far into the distance.

"Now this," I said, pausing for effect, "is what I wanted you to see. The oldest purely residential street in Europe, built in the 14th century for the cathedral choir men."

Marco had stopped in his tracks. "It is so... straight," he finally managed, as if straightness were an exotic architectural feature.

"That's not even the clever bit," I continued, leading them further into the street. "Watch as we walk. The entire lane is built with forced perspective: it is only about 140 meters long, but looks much longer because it starts wide and tapers as it extends, and the last houses at the north end are built smaller in height and width than those at the entrance. The stone setts of the cobbled lane are tighter together toward the end, exaggerating the effect."

"Optical illusion architecture? In the 1300s?" Ryan raised an eyebrow. "That's rather sophisticated for people who still thought bathing was dangerous."

"Medieval architects were cleverer than we think," I said, setting up my tripod. "They used this in cathedrals too – to make spaces seem larger or pull your gaze to the altar."

Marco circled around me, his camera forgotten momentarily as he absorbed the perfect symmetry of the street. Then, as if physically struck by inspiration, he let out a gasp and began speaking rapid Italian.

"Mamma mia! Questo è impossibile! In Italia, niente è dritto, tutto cresce come funghi selvatici!" His hands carved elaborate shapes in the air as he spoke, drawing invisible architectural plans.

"Translation?" Ryan prompted, amused.

Marco switched to English without missing a beat. "This is impossible! In Italy, nothing is straight, everything grows like wild mushrooms! Medieval Italian streets turn and twist like drunk snakes!" He gestured emphatically, nearly knocking my camera in the process. "But this – this is like someone used a ruler! In the Middle Ages!"

I finished setting up my camera, framing the shot to capture the forced perspective. "The uniformity is remarkable, isn't it? Each house had the same layout: a hall and one room downstairs, two bedrooms above, and an attic. They've been modified over the centuries, of course. But the external façades are largely unchanged."

Marco had now set up his tripod in the middle of the street and was taking rapid-fire shots while muttering to himself in Italian.

For the next hour, we moved up and down Vicar's Close, with Marco directing us into various positions while he captured shot after shot. His enthusiasm was infectious, and even Ryan eventually found himself pressed into service as a photographic subject, standing awkwardly in doorways or walking down the centre of the street with exaggerated casualness.

"I never realised medieval urban planning could be so exciting," Ryan muttered as he posed for the twelfth time.

As our time in Wells drew to a close, I took a final look at Vicar's Close – this perfect slice of medieval England that had survived plague, reformation, civil war, and centuries of change.

The Wells bus station was more an optimistic stretch of pavement with a single glass shelter than a station. Yet the British talent for orderly waiting was on full display. About eight people had formed a perfect straight line, no barriers or markings, just a collective social consciousness that needed no external direction.

Ryan checked his phone. "Marco's bus is in Glastonbury, two minutes late. Fifteen minutes to go," he said.

Marco barely registered this information. He was lost in his camera's display screen, scrolling through the hundreds of photos he'd taken of Vicar's Close, muttering appreciative Italian phrases to himself each time a particularly pleasing composition appeared.

"Should we join the queue?" I suggested, eyeing the orderly line of waiting passengers.

But Marco, still absorbed in his photographic review, had wandered away from us toward the shelter. To my horror, he casually positioned himself at the very front of the queue, just beside the bus stop sign, continuing to flick through his photos with cheerful obliviousness to the social catastrophe he had just engineered.

The reaction was immediate, though understated enough that an untrained observer might have missed it. It seemed as if a silent alarm had triggered a series of finely tuned British distress signals: eyebrows raised by precise millimetres, lips compressed, throats cleared with deliberation. Someone near the back of the queue emitted a "tut" so perfectly pitched and brief it deserved musical notation.

"Oh god," Ryan whispered, frozen in place. "He's queue-jumped."

I hurried to Marco and hissed, "You can't stand there."

He looked up, confused. "Why not? The bus stops here, yes?"

"Yes, but there's a queue," I explained, gesturing toward the line of people whose expressions had now shifted from disapproval to that particular brand of satisfaction that comes from witnessing justice served. "In Britain, you always join the end of the queue. Always."

Marco blinked at me, then at the line of people. "But why? The bus comes at the same time for everyone, no? No matter where we wait!"

His voice carried across the bus station with unfortunate clarity. Several people in the queue exchanged glances filled with complex emotions – a mixture of disbelief at such queuing heresy being openly voiced, and a certain anthropological interest in this rare glimpse into the mind of a queue jumper.

"It's not about efficiency," I explained in a lower voice, guiding him toward the end of the line. "It's about fairness and order. In Britain, queue-jumping is practically a criminal offence."

"But this is madness!" Marco protested, though he allowed himself to be led. "In Italy, we just wait in a group, all together. We talk, we laugh – sometimes we push a little, but in a friendly way! When the bus comes, everybody gets on."

A woman near the front of the queue visibly shuddered at this description, clutching her handbag closer to her chest as if to protect it from the mere concept of such chaos.

Ryan joined us at the end of the queue. "The British invented queuing," he said with the gravity of someone imparting sacred knowledge. "It's part of our national identity."

Marco looked unconvinced but made what appeared to be a good-faith effort to join the queue. Unfortunately, instead of standing behind the last person, he positioned himself to their left, inadvertently creating a parallel line and causing immediate confusion among the waiting passengers. Several heads turned, calculating whether this constituted a new, competing queue or merely the actions of a confused foreigner.

"Not like that," Ryan said, sighing as he repositioned Marco by the shoulders. "Behind me. In a straight line. One person after another."

"This is very strange," Marco observed, allowing himself to be arranged into the correct queuing formation.

An elderly couple standing a few positions ahead of us in the queue had been listening to our conversation with undisguised interest. The woman turned slightly, contributing to the discussion while maintaining perfect queuing posture.

"Young man," she addressed Marco with the gentle firmness of a retired schoolteacher, "queuing is the cornerstone of civilisation. Without it, there would be anarchy."

Her husband nodded sagely. "During the war," he added, though which war remained unspecified, "people queued for hours. Never complained."

"I'm starting to understand why the British conquered so

much of the world," Marco whispered to me. "With this kind of patience for standing in straight lines, you could outlast anyone."

A young man who joined the queue behind us – who had been pretending not to listen while absorbing every word – unsuccessfully suppressed a snort of laughter.

"Remember," Ryan instructed Marco, "when the bus arrives, you board in order. No rushing forward."

Marco nodded solemnly, though I caught a mischievous glint in his eye. "I will be the perfect British person. Very orderly, very quiet, very sad in the face."

"We don't look sad," Ryan protested. "We look... composed."

"Like this?" Marco arranged his features into an expression of such exaggerated stoicism that he resembled a palace guard trying not to sneeze.

Despite my best efforts, a laugh escaped me, earning disapproving glances from several queue members.

The bus rounded the corner and lumbered toward us with the unhurried confidence of public transport that knows its passengers have no alternative. Its arrival triggered a subtle shift in the queue – a collective straightening of spines, a rustle of tickets being retrieved from pockets and purses, a mental calculation of optimal seating strategies. Marco, however, seemed to have forgotten about the bus entirely. His face had transformed, the excitement of imminent departure colliding with the realisation that our peculiar trio was about to disband.

"This is it," he said, his voice suddenly thick with emotion. "Our adventure ends."

The bus wheezed to a halt before us, its doors folding open with a pneumatic sigh. The queue began its orderly procession forward – each person maintaining perfect spacing, tickets extended like offerings.

"Get your ticket ready," I murmured. We were three from the front.

Instead of reaching for his ticket, Marco dropped his backpack to the pavement and turned to face us with the dramatic intensity of a tenor preparing for his final aria. What followed was a masterclass in Italian farewell protocol.

First came the embrace – not the brief, shoulder-patting approximation that passes for physical contact among the British, but a full-bodied hug that spoke of genuine affection and imminent continental separation. He lifted me off my feet with unexpected vigour.

"Brianna!" he exclaimed at a volume better suited to addressing someone across a busy piazza. "You have taught me so much! Your eye for beauty, your patience, your endless supply of green tea!"

Before I could respond, he released me and swivelled toward Ryan, who had begun a strategic retreat that was foiled by Marco's superior speed and determination. Ryan found himself captured in an equally enthusiastic embrace, his arms pinned to his sides, his expression cycling rapidly through alarm, resignation, and finally a grudging acceptance.

"Ryan!" Marco continued at the same volume. "My friend! My fellow photographer! The man who can find vegan food in the most unlikely corners of this strange island!"

The queue had now paused entirely, the orderly boarding process suspended as everyone turned to witness this unprecedented emotional display. The bus driver leaned forward in his seat, watching with the interested expression of a man whose route rarely offered such entertainment.

Having completed the hugging phase, Marco progressed to the next stage of his farewell – the double-cheek kiss. I received mine with the practised ease of someone who had travelled enough in Europe to anticipate the left-right sequence.

"You have shown me the true England!" Marco proclaimed, now addressing not just us but apparently the entire bus queue, several of whom were studying their shoes with intense fascination. "The ghosts in the mines! The deep fry of everything! The strange sauce that you put on food that needs no sauce!"

"Brown Sauce," Ryan muttered automatically.

"I will never forget this journey!" Marco continued, undeterred. His hands carved elaborate shapes in the air as he spoke, as if physically sculpting his memories. "The cliffs! The medieval street that is so straight it hurts my Italian soul! The way everyone apologises when you try to poison their horses!"

Marco was clearly not yet finished with his emotional adieus. Tears – actual, glistening tears – had formed in the corners of his eyes. He brushed them away with an expressive sweep of his hand.

"I will send you my mother's recipes," he promised, clasping my hands in his. "Her pesto will change your life."

He scooped up his backpack and joined the queue properly. But as he shuffled forward, he continued his declarations over his shoulder.

"I will write to you both! Real letters, not just emails! With Italian stamps! And you must visit me in Florence – my family will welcome you like their own children!"

Marco reached the front of the queue and handed his ticket to the driver, who accepted it with the bemused expression of someone who had just witnessed an unexpected one-man show. With one foot on the step, Marco turned for a final, theatrical wave.

"Arrivederci, my British friends! Until we meet again!"

He boarded the bus with a flourish, immediately engaging the nearest passenger in animated conversation as he made his way down the aisle. Through the windows, we could see his gestures continuing unabated, likely explaining to his seatmate the entire history of our friendship and travels.

As the bus pulled away, I found myself waving with unexpected enthusiasm. Beside me, Ryan's hand rose in a more contained farewell gesture, but his expression had softened into almost fondness.

"Well," he said as the bus disappeared around a corner, "that was very..."

"Marco," I finished for him.

"Exactly," Ryan nodded. "Completely, utterly Marco."

We stood for a moment in the peculiar vacuum that follows an exuberant departure. The contrast between Marco's emotional whirlwind and the quiet Somerset afternoon was almost comical.

"You know," Ryan observed as we turned toward the car park, "I think I might actually miss him. The way everything – literally everything – was either a tragedy or a miracle."

I nodded, understanding precisely what he meant. "He experienced more in two weeks than some people do in years. Every cream tea was the best cream tea. Every church was the most beautiful church. Every sunset was nature's masterpiece."

We reached our car, and I unlocked it with a beep that seemed unnecessarily loud in the quiet street.

"Oxford next," Ryan said, settling into the passenger's seat and immediately checking his food app. "There's apparently an excellent vegan café near the Bodleian. We could have an early dinner when we arrive."

I settled into the passenger seat with a small sigh of relief. As much as I'd enjoyed Marco's exuberance, the thought of our next companion - a German photography student with a portfolio as precisely arranged as a mathematical proof - promised a welcome change of pace. Ryan caught my expression and nodded knowingly. We were trading operatic farewells for punctual arrivals.

A GERMAN IN SOUTH CENTRAL ENGLAND

The M4 ahead was gridlocked, cars idling in drizzle. My wipers drummed steadily as our two-hour drive from Wells slowed to a crawl. Brake lights shimmered ahead, the sat-nav desperate for alternatives. I tapped the steering wheel, watching the minutes vanish as we inched forward.

Ryan scowled at his phone. "It's recalculating again. We're now arriving at... Four seventeen. Forty-seven minutes late!" He jabbed at the screen. "What if we take the next exit? There's a road that runs parallel."

"That road will be just as congested," I replied, inching forward before braking again. "Everyone is getting the same sat-nav suggestion. It's the digital lemming effect."

Ryan's stomach groaned so loudly it briefly drowned out Sara Cox's banter on Radio 2. He placed a protective hand over his midsection, his face echoing a universal truth: being stuck in traffic makes every hunger pang feel more dramatic.

I indicated and eased into the middle lane, hoping to make up any time at all and perhaps gaining ten seconds. "We'll survive, Ryan. Humans can go three weeks without food."

"That's average," he shot back. "I'm sure my personal threshold is significantly lower – three hours, four at most."

The rain intensified. Fat droplets hammered the windscreen with urgency. I adjusted the wiper speed and peered through the watery veil at an endless procession of red lights on the horizon. This was the quintessential British motorway experience: simultaneously moving and stationary, progressing at a pace that made an unmotivated snail appear dynamic.

"Do you think she'll wait?" Ryan asked suddenly, his voice tinged with genuine concern. "The German photographer. Katrin."

"I did text her about the traffic," I replied. "Hopefully, she'll understand that even the most meticulously planned journey is no match for the M4 on a Friday afternoon."

Ryan nodded, but his expression was unpersuaded. "Germans have a different relationship with time, don't they? More... severe."

"I wouldn't generalise about an entire nation's temporal philosophy," I said, though I sympathised with his anxiety. After

Marco's Italian expressiveness, German efficiency sounded a little intimidating. "But yes, Katrin probably prefers things a bit more orderly."

I was honestly curious about Katrin. Her CV landed on my desk, thick as a phone book, packed with degrees and awards, all before she turned forty. She'd studied Sociology and Anthropology, added Psychology on the side, then switched to documentary photography to track how society shifts. Her articles had a good reputation in German academic circles. And now she was turning her attention to us Brits, with all our odd habits we like to think are perfectly normal. As we got closer to Oxford, I couldn't shake the feeling Katrin would notice everything we usually try to brush under the rug, and write it all down, even the bits we'd rather ignore.

The traffic lurched forward, granting us another thirty metres, then settled back into immobility. Through the rain-streaked window, I saw frustrated travellers – a businessman whose lips were moving to some unseen listener through a hands-free, a woman applying lipstick with surgical precision, and a family with children whose entertainment options had long expired.

"This is uniquely British, you know," I observed, gesturing toward the surrounding vehicles. "There's a resigned acceptance of traffic as inevitability – like drizzle at Wimbledon or a delayed train. No one honks. No one tries to create an extra lane. Just quiet, dignified suffering."

Ryan wasn't listening. His phone had migrated from navigation to a vegan restaurant review site, where he was now scrolling through Oxford dining options.

"There's a place near the Bodleian," Ryan muttered to himself. "The reviews mention a coconut-based cheese alternative that apparently 'transcends the limitations of non-dairy products'." His stomach growled again, as if responding directly to this information.

"Perhaps focus on meeting our new colleague before planning dinner?" I suggested mildly.

"I'm multitasking," Ryan replied, without looking up. "Planning dinner while also tracking our delay, while also researching German cultural expectations." He held up his phone, displaying a webpage titled 'Understanding German Time Culture: A Guide for Chronically Late Britons'. "Did you know that in Germany, arriving five minutes early is considered 'on time', while arriving at the scheduled time is technically late?"

"Great," I said, moving into the faster lane. "Katrin's definitely going to judge us."

"That's not helping." Ryan switched back to the navigation app and groaned. "ETA four thirty-one now. We're haemorrhaging time."

The next forty minutes passed in a similar fashion.

When we finally reached the outskirts of Oxford, Ryan had progressed to a state of hunger-induced philosophical despair. "Do you think time moves differently when you're starving?" he wondered aloud. "Einstein said time was relative, but did he account for blood sugar levels in his calculations?"

I navigated through the familiar streets. The university buildings glowed softly despite the grey skies above. After the purgatory of the M4, the city felt like a medieval sanctuary – albeit one we were now approaching nearly an hour later than planned.

"She's still waiting." Ryan scanned a text message with palpable relief. "Though her message contains precisely zero emojis and ends with a full stop, which I'm interpreting as restrained disapproval."

I pulled into a parking space near the Bodleian with a small sigh of relief. Ryan unbuckled his seatbelt with remarkable speed, his hunger temporarily eclipsed by the more immediate concern of making a good impression on our new companion.

"Remember," I cautioned as we gathered our things, "no lengthy explanations about British traffic philosophy. Just a simple apology for the delay."

"And then food," Ryan added firmly. "Immediate, substantial food."

The Bodleian Library loomed before us, its stonework glowing with history. Even after many visits, I always felt a moment of reverence as I approached it. Today, however, urgency replaced awe. We were fifty-four minutes late, and Katrin Becker was waiting. I spotted her immediately: tall, angular, geometric brown hair, wire-rimmed glasses catching the watery sunlight. She checked her watch as we approached.

"Almost an hour," she greeted us, her English perfect, consonants crisp, vowels measured – an unmistakable German accent. Her gaze flicked between us, cataloguing our bedraggled appearance. "I expected delays from the M4 traffic reports, but my calculations suggested thirty-two minutes maximum."

"I'm terribly sorry," I offered, extending my hand. "The traffic was particularly apocalyptic today. I'm Brianna, and this is Ryan."

Katrin shook my hand firmly, then turned to Ryan. He fumbled to smooth his travel-rumpled shirt with one hand as he extended his other to greet her.

"We've been crawling along the motorway for hours," he explained. His voice carried the haunted quality of someone who had just escaped captivity. "The sat-nav kept adding minutes as if it enjoyed our suffering."

"I arrived one hour and twenty minutes early," Katrin replied. Her tone suggested this was the only sensible approach to appointment-keeping. "To account for any difficulties like train delays or locating the meeting point." She gestured to the iconic building behind her, which has been in the same location since the 14th century and features on most Oxford postcards. Hardly a place to miss easily.

Ryan nodded as if this made perfect sense. "Very wise. Very... thorough."

Katrin adjusted the strap of her camera bag, a technical marvel of compartmentalisation. It made my own equipment storage look like a teenager's bedroom. "While waiting, I compiled research on Oxford's literary connections," she continued. From her bag, she retrieved a sleek leather-bound notebook. "Organised by chronological period, by geographical location within the city, and by thematic significance."

She opened the notebook carefully, angling it toward us so we could see the pages. They were marked with colour-coded tabs, neat margin notes, and precise hand-drawn maps.

"This is..." I began, struggling to find an appropriate response to this monument to thoroughness.

"Extraordinary," Ryan finished, leaning closer with undisguised reverence.

A flicker of something, maybe the faintest hint of pleasure, crossed Katrin's face. "It is simply efficient," she replied. Her fingers lingered affectionately on a complex colour-coded timeline. "I have divided the authors into seven categories, with twenty-three subcategories based on period, style, and thematic preoccupations."

"Seven categories," Ryan repeated, as if memorising an incantation. "With twenty-three subcategories. That's... that's beautiful."

I glanced between them, marvelling at the unlikely connection forming before my eyes. Where Marco had bonded with Ryan over their shared appreciation for food, Katrin was capturing his attention through the seductive power of extreme organisation.

"May I?" Ryan asked, gesturing toward the notebook.

Katrin hesitated for a moment, her fingers hovering over the edge of the notebook before passing it to Ryan. As Ryan carefully turned the pages, Katrin leaned in and pointed to a section. "The blue tabs indicate Tolkien locations," she said, then gestured at other colours. "Green for Lewis. Purple for Carroll."

Oxford has long been a cradle of imagination, its cloisters and cobbled lanes inspiring some of the most famous stories ever written. Tolkien, who lectured on Anglo-Saxon at the University, was responsible for The Hobbit and The Lord of the Rings; his friend C.S. Lewis, professor of English literature, conjured up The Chronicles of Narnia. Both were members of the Inklings, a literary group that gathered in pubs to share drafts and ideas. Decades before that, Lewis Carroll, a mathematician at Christ Church, invented Alice's Adventures in Wonderland for the college dean's young daughter. It was hard to walk through Oxford and not feel as if the city itself was both a living college and some half-imaginary landscape on the literary map.

And Katrin has sorted this out, just like that, while she was waiting.

"It's... It's like looking at the Rosetta Stone of literary Oxford," Ryan murmured, his voice hushed.

Katrin's posture relaxed by approximately two degrees – a seismic shift in her body language. "Most people find my organisational systems excessive," she admitted, adjusting her glasses.

"Most haven't witnessed the glory of categorisation," Ryan replied with unexpected passion. He looked up from the notebook, his eyes wide with sudden inspiration. "Could you – would you consider – helping me organise my phone apps? I have seventy-three of them, with no logical system whatsoever. It's digital chaos."

I suppressed a smile, recognising the peculiar alchemy taking place.

"Seventy-three applications with no organisational principle?" Katrin's voice contained a note of genuine distress. "This is... inefficient."

"Catastrophically inefficient," Ryan agreed eagerly. "I have three separate weather apps, five different mapping systems, and nine – nine! – food-related platforms, not including delivery services."

Katrin inhaled sharply, as if physically pained by this information. "This requires immediate intervention," she declared. Her earlier frostiness melted in the face of this organisational emergency. "We must establish primary categories by function, then develop a nested hierarchical structure."

"Yes," Ryan nodded vigorously. "Nested hierarchies. That's exactly what I need."

Rain resumed its gentle patter on the ancient stone, but neither Ryan nor Katrin noticed; they huddled together over the notebook, absorbed in their shared world where colour-coding and categories mattered deeply.

"Perhaps," I suggested gently, "we could continue this conversation somewhere dry? And possibly with food?" I directed this last part to Ryan. His hunger-induced motorway philosophy had been forgotten in the face of Katrin's organisational prowess.

"Food," he repeated, as if reacquainting himself with the concept. "Yes, food would be excellent. Though..." he glanced at his watch with sudden concern, "I don't want to disrupt the schedule."

"I have researched three café locations nearby." Katrin produced a small map with three coloured dots. Beside it was a chart comparing their merits across several criteria.

"The King's Arms has superior tea selection but substandard ambient noise levels," she explained, pointing to a yellow dot. "The Covered Market café offers eight vegan options but only four power outlets. The University café on Broad Street presents the optimal balance of nutritional options, ambient noise, and proximity to our next photography location."

Ryan was staring at Katrin with undisguised admiration. "You've quantified café ambience," he whispered, awestruck. "With comparative metrics."

"It is simply logical," she replied, though I noticed a hint of colour rising in her cheeks – the first evidence that our Germanic companion might be susceptible to flattery.

"The Broad Street café sounds perfect," I interjected, before Ryan could request a detailed explanation of her ambient noise measurement techniques. "Shall we?"

As we gathered our belongings, I saw Ryan lean toward Katrin and lower his voice conspiratorially. "I have a spreadsheet tracking every meal I've eaten for the past three years," he confided, showing his phone. "With caloric estimates and satisfaction ratings."

"Three years of nutritional data?" Katrin's eyes widened with genuine interest. "This could yield valuable consumption pattern analysis." She leaned closer. "Have you established baseline variables for comparative assessment?"

"I... no," Ryan admitted, looking suddenly enlightened by the possibility. "But I could."

I led the way toward Broad Street, listening to their animated conversation. Behind us, the Bodleian stood solid and unchanging. It had witnessed centuries of academic obsessions come and go. Ahead, I could only imagine what our journey with Katrin would bring. It would undoubtedly be the most meticulously documented travel experience in history.

The university café, just off Broad Street, had a quiet, typical Oxford charm. It was smart but unpretentious. The mismatched chairs and tables had seen years of student arguments and sudden insights. Light came in through tall windows, catching shelves of battered paperbacks and jars of tea. The steady hum of conversation was just right – not so loud you had to shout, not so quiet you felt you had to whisper. It was, in short, precisely the sort of place where one could imagine Lewis and Tolkien huddled over manuscripts, though they would likely have found the vegan brownies and oat milk options somewhat bewildering.

We walked up to the counter together. Ryan went first, studying the menu board as if he were solving a puzzle. Katrin followed, standing straight, her eyes moving quickly over the choices and the staff behind the counter.

"I'll have the green tea, please," I requested, "loose leaf if you have it."

The barista nodded and reached for a glass jar behind her. Ryan started his usual round of vegan questions, a routine I had seen in cafés all over Britain.

"The raspberry flapjack – are you certain there's no honey?" Ryan leaned in. "And the dark chocolate topping – do you know the cocoa percentage? Some lower percentages sneak in milk solids."

The barista wore the patient expression of someone used to Oxford's unique culinary interrogation. She answered each question with admirable detail. Ryan, after much consideration, settled on a cinnamon-apple muffin – its vegan credentials had been established to his satisfaction. He also ordered a soy milk latte, but not before requesting further specifications about the bean's origin and roast profile.

Katrin's order was quick and to the point, with no small talk. "Black coffee," Katrin ordered. "No sugar. In a ceramic cup, not paper." She hesitated. "The Ethiopian roast, if available. If not, the Guatemalan is acceptable."

The barista, to her credit, didn't flinch, merely nodding.

We found a corner table, a small oak affair scarred with the initials of generations of students.

"So," I began, preparing to navigate our first proper conversation as a trio, "shall we discuss our photography plans for—"

"Entschuldigung," came a voice from behind me, hesitant yet hopeful. "Bist du aus Deutschland? Are you from Germany?"

I turned and saw a young woman standing near our table, watching Katrin. She looked about twenty-five, with a hesitant smile and the rumpled look of someone deep in essay season.

"Ja," Katrin replied, switching effortlessly to German. They exchanged several rapid sentences before Katrin turned back. "This is Jana. She is a student here, from Germany. She heard me speaking with my German accent and wished to say hello."

"Would you like to join us?" I asked, gesturing to the empty chair at our table. "We're just getting acquainted ourselves."

Jana paused, holding her coffee cup with both hands. "I don't want to interrupt your meeting…"

"Nonsense," Ryan said, already shifting his chair. "The more the merrier. And I need someone to help me convince Katrin that my app chaos isn't terminal."

Jana laughed, a bright sound that didn't match her nervous look, and took the empty chair. "Thank you. It's just… It's nice to hear German sometimes. Even though I've been here three years."

"You're studying at Oxford?" I asked, taking a sip of my perfectly brewed green tea.

"Comparative literature," she said, nodding. "Final year now." Her face changed. "My last year, regardless."

"You don't wish to continue your studies?" Katrin asked, pen poised above her notebook, apparently cataloguing this new acquaintance with the same methodical approach she applied to everything.

Jana's fingers traced nervous patterns on her coffee cup. "I can't," she said simply. "Brexit. The regulations have changed. International student fees have tripled. The research grants I'd need for postgraduate work are no longer available to EU citizens. Not like before."

"That's awful," Ryan sympathised, pausing mid-bite of his meticulously vetted muffin. "After three years here."

Jana nodded, looking both resigned and a little stunned. "I have to leave in four months. Back to Germany." She said it flatly, as if she were talking about a place that didn't quite feel real.

"But that's home, isn't it?" I asked gently. "Returning must have some appeal."

"Germany doesn't feel like home anymore," Jana confessed. Her voice lowered slightly. "It feels like... a foreign country now. Here are all my friends. My life. I do feel home here. But the UK is sending me away." She tried to smile, but it didn't quite reach her eyes. "I'm caught between places. Neither fully belongs to me now."

Katrin had been writing in her notebook, her pen moving in neat, quick strokes as she listened. When Jana finished, Katrin paused and looked up, her face showing something like sympathy.

"This is a common experience," Katrin observed, not unkindly. "Cultural displacement following prolonged immersion in a different environment. There are documented psychological frameworks for this phenomenon."

Rather than being offended by this clinical assessment, Jana seemed comforted. "Yes, exactly. I'm neither fully German nor British – just somewhere in the uncomfortable middle."

"What do you love most about Oxford?" I asked, trying to move the conversation to something lighter. "What will you miss?"

The question changed everything. Jana's face lit up with real enthusiasm. "Oh, there's so much! The libraries, of course. The way the light hits the Radcliffe Camera at sunset. The secret gardens. But mostly..." She leaned in, lowering her voice. "The traditions. The weird, wonderful, completely bonkers traditions that make no sense but everyone takes incredibly seriously."

"Such as?" Ryan prompted, clearly enchanted by this shift in energy.

"The Time Ceremony at Merton College," Jana replied immediately. Her eyes sparkled. "It's my absolute favourite. Every autumn, when the clocks change from British Summer Time to Greenwich Mean Time, students gather at 2 a.m. in the Fellows' Quad."

"For what purpose?" Katrin asked, pen hovering above paper.

"To maintain the integrity of the space-time continuum, of course," Jana replied with a perfectly straight face. "You see, the theory goes that when the clocks go back and the same hour occurs twice, there's a risk of a temporal paradox. So students drink port – for courage – and walk backwards around the quad for an hour. They recite Latin verses and sing hymns. This backwards movement counteracts the backwards movement of time and prevents reality from unravelling."

Ryan was grinning broadly now. "That is gloriously absurd."

"That's what makes it wonderful," Jana insisted. "It's utterly ridiculous, yet everyone – including brilliant professors of physics and philosophy – participates with complete solemnity. For that one hour, the rational academic world embraces the absurd, and it's... magical."

I watched as Katrin carefully wrote "British Unlogical Academic Rituals" at the top of a fresh page in her notebook, underlining it twice.

"What else?" Ryan encouraged, leaning toward Jana with genuine interest. "What other mad traditions have you embraced?"

As Jana launched into descriptions of May Morning celebrations and the peculiar sport of Tortoise Racing at Corpus Christi College, I observed our group dynamic evolving. Jana's animated storytelling provided a perfect counterpoint to Katrin's methodical documentation. For each tradition Jana described, Katrin added another precisely worded entry to her growing list. She occasionally paused to ask clarifying questions about dates, participants, or historical origins.

I sipped my tea, watching this curious cultural exchange unfold before me. Where Marco had brought Mediterranean warmth and chaotic enthusiasm to our travels, Katrin was introducing Teutonic precision and analytical depth. Different but equally valuable companions for our photographic journey through England.

Jana was now describing an elaborate college dining tradition involving standing on tables and drinking from specially designed horns, while Katrin dutifully recorded this information in her growing catalogue of British peculiarities.

I smiled. Katrin's methodical style, combined with Ryan's cheerful chaos, would make our England trip interesting.

Highclere Castle's tea room distilled centuries of British aristocratic tradition into a single, elegantly arranged space. Afternoon light filtered through tall windows onto crisp white tablecloths, precisely placed bone china, and silver three-tiered stands awaiting their delicate cargo.

"This is," Katrin declared, "exactly as I expected an English castle tea room to appear." She withdrew her camera, adjusted three separate settings with quick, decisive movements, and captured a series of images from slightly different angles.

Ryan, meanwhile, had developed a laser-like focus on the nearest cake stand. "Those scones look properly made," he murmured, more to himself than to us. "Golden tops, good rise. I wonder if they have vegan clotted cream?"

We dropped into our chairs. I rubbed my legs under the table, glad to be off my feet after walking the grounds all morning.

A waitress appeared with menus, though they seemed largely superfluous given the standardised nature of a traditional afternoon tea. Katrin, however, studied hers as if it were a critical historical document.

"I would like," she announced with careful enunciation, "the complete High Tea experience, please."

The waitress offered a polite nod, though it couldn't quite

hide her exasperation. She sighed softly, her lips moving in a barely audible mutter as she headed back toward the kitchen. Katrin furrowed her brows and glanced at me, puzzled. Ryan, always ready to explain British culinary customs, cleared his throat.

"Well, technically," Ryan leaned forward. His eyebrows rose as they always did when food terminology was at stake. "This is Afternoon Tea, not High Tea. People mix them up all the time." His smile took the edge off the correction. Katrin didn't seem to mind – in fact, her expression brightened at the clarification. She lifted her pen from her notebook and pointed to the menu with the tip of it. "But here..." she tapped the heading twice, "...it says 'Traditional English Tea Experience.' That's High Tea, isn't it?"

"Tea as in the beverage, not tea as in the meal called tea. That's actually dinner, except sometimes lunch is called dinner, particularly in Northern England," Ryan explained. He somehow made this labyrinthine explanation sound almost reasonable.

Katrin stared at him.

"Perhaps I should explain," I said, smoothing the napkin across my lap just as our three-tiered stand arrived – a gleaming silver structure placed squarely before us, brimming with delicacies.

On the bottom tier were finger sandwiches with the crusts cut off: cucumber and mint butter, egg and cress, smoked salmon and cream cheese, and vegan versions for Ryan.

The middle tier featured warm scones, accompanied by little pots of jam and clotted cream.

On top were small cakes and pastries: Victoria sponge, lemon squares, chocolate éclairs, and fruit tartlets, all just a couple of bites each.

"What we're having here now," I continued, tilting the stand for Katrin's camera, "is Afternoon Tea."

"Afternoon Tea begins at the bottom tier," Ryan added, already reaching for a cucumber sandwich. "Savoury before sweet, sandwiches before scones, scones before cakes. There's a proper order to everything."

Katrin nodded, making rapid notes. "And High Tea? This is a different meal entirely?"

"Completely different," I confirmed. "High Tea was actually the working-class evening meal, much heartier than Afternoon Tea. It included substantial fare such as meat pies, fish, potatoes, and cheese on toast – essentially a proper dinner eaten at a dining table after returning from work, accompanied by strong tea. By contrast, Afternoon Tea is light and meant for the afternoon."

"So High Tea is..." Katrin paused, pen ready.

"Dinner," I supplied. "Or tea, depending on where in Britain you're from."

"But tea is also this," she gestured at our three-tiered stand, "and also the beverage."

"Exactly," Ryan said cheerfully, examining a vegan sandwich with approval. "Perfect clarity."

Katrin's brow furrowed as she attempted to diagram this linguistic tangle in her notebook. "And dinner can also be lunch?"

"In some regions, yes," I nodded. "Particularly in working-class northern communities, the main meal of the day was traditionally taken at midday and called dinner. The evening meal was tea."

"So lunch can be dinner, dinner can be tea, and tea can be..." Her hands hovered in the air above our elaborate spread, then dropped in surrender.

"This elegant arrangement before us is the real Afternoon Tea," Ryan confirmed, "though it might also be called Low Tea because it was traditionally served on low tables in drawing rooms. High Tea, however, was served at high dining tables."

Katrin regarded Ryan for a beat, then forcefully scratched out her previous notes with a flourish. "This system," she declared, tapping her pen down, "is not efficient."

"Spectacularly inefficient," I said, picking up a cucumber sandwich. "But efficiency was never the point. Afternoon Tea started because a duchess got hungry between meals. In the 1840s, Anna, Duchess of Bedford, wanted something to eat in the late afternoon. The upper classes ate dinner late, sometimes at eight or nine, so there was a long gap after lunch."

Ryan grinned. "I must be related to that duchess," he said, patting his stomach. "If not by blood, then at least in spirit. I get hungry at four every day."

"The duchess created an entirely new meal category because she was hungry between meals?" Katrin clarified, her tone suggesting this ranked among the more bewildering British eccentricities she'd encountered.

"And then it turned into a social event," I said. "The upper classes used it to show off their best china, silver, and their social connections, of course."

Ryan moved on to the scones, spreading vegan cream and jam with care. "The big debate," he said, waving his knife, "is whether you put jam or cream first. Cornwall and Devon argue about it. Our last photographer from Italy nearly started a fight in a tearoom over this."

"There's a debate about the jam and cream order?" Katrin asked, pen poised.

"Fierce debate," Ryan confirmed seriously.

Katrin shook her head, clearly struggling with the concept. "So the same meal has multiple names, depending on class and region, and the components of the meal are assembled in different orders depending on geography?"

"Welcome to Britain," Ryan and I said in unisono, raising our teacups in a small toast.

"It doesn't really matter what you call it," Ryan interjected philosophically, carefully selecting a vegan pastry from the top tier. "High Tea, Afternoon Tea, cream tea, Duchess tea – the important thing is whether it's delicious and whether they've made proper vegan alternatives." He bit into his pastry with evident satisfaction. "And I'm pleased to report that they have."

Katrin made one final note in her book. I caught a glimpse of what she'd written: "British naming conventions – entirely dependent on context, history, region, and class. No logic. Accept and adapt."

It looked like Katrin was learning the first rule of British culture: when things make no sense, just carry on and pour another cup of tea.

A quiet laugh behind me interrupted our conversation about British tea terms. I turned to see our waitress, Mary, her name badge pinned to her shirt. She looked at us with a hint of amusement, holding a fresh pot of tea with steady hands.

"Heard your tea debate," she said, setting the pot down. "I've worked here twenty years, and tourists still ask for 'High Tea' when all they want are fancy cakes." Her Hampshire accent was smooth, like a pebble in a stream.

"Twenty years?" Ryan perked up, momentarily distracted from his meticulous dissection of a vegan éclair. "So you were here when they filmed Downton Abbey?"

Mary's face lit up. "Oh yes, right from the beginning. Cameras, costumes, actors everywhere." She looked around the tea room and checked her watch. "I'm on break. Mind if I sit? I don't often get to talk about those days."

Katrin shifted her chair to make room before we could reply, her usual reserve gone. "You worked here during filming? You met the actors?" For the first time since we'd met her, Katrin sounded almost excited.

Mary sat down with a sigh. "Been on my feet since six. Not sure why I still do this, but here I am." She poured herself tea. "Did I meet them? Love, I served them tea, fixed their costumes when pins came loose, and once had to run halfway across the estate to fetch Dame Maggie Smith's reading glasses."

At the mention of Maggie Smith, Katrin made an unexpected sound – something between a gasp and a squeak. Her pen froze above her notebook.

"Maggie Smith?" she repeated, her voice uncharacteristically hushed. "You met Maggie Smith? In person?"

Ryan and I exchanged surprised glances. We'd grown used to Katrin's measured responses and analytical approach to everything from cathedral architecture to sandwich fillings. This sudden display of fan behaviour was unexpected.

Mary nodded, clearly pleased by the reaction. "Oh yes, many times. Proper legend, she was. Not one for small talk, mind you, but always polite. She had this way of looking at you – right through you, really. It was like she could see every thought in your head and found most of them rather amusing."

"She was a goddess," Katrin declared with startling conviction. "A complete goddess of acting." Her usual precise language gave way to unexpected hyperbole. "I was deeply affected when she died. I watched The Prime of Miss Jean Brodie seventeen times. Seventeen."

Mary's expression softened. "She was something special, no doubt about that. Had her own chair, you know – no one else was allowed to sit in it. And she was the only one permitted to have tea while on set."

"Really?" I prompted, intrigued by this small detail.

"Oh yes. Everyone else – actors, directors, the lot – they were strictly forbidden from eating or drinking around the antiques. Too valuable. Too irreplaceable. But Dame Maggie? She'd be sitting there, script in one hand, cup of Earl Grey in the other, bold as brass. Lady Carnarvon herself would bring it to her sometimes."

"Lady Carnarvon? The actual countess?" Ryan asked, leaning forward with interest.

"The very same. Lovely woman, if a bit... particular." Mary lowered her voice conspiratorially. "She had this system for all the security codes around the estate during filming. Instead of normal numbers, she'd use historical dates. Drove everyone absolutely mad."

"Historical dates?" Katrin's professional precision had returned, her pen once again poised above her notebook.

"Oh yes. You'd ask for the code to get into the storage room, and she'd say something like, 'It's the year of the Crimean War' or 'The succession of George III.' Then, when you'd look confused, she'd just say 'Look it up!' with this little smile." Mary shook her head, laughing. "The production assistants were constantly on their phones, googling British history in a panic."

"That seems needlessly complicated," Katrin observed.

"That's aristocrats for you," Mary said. "They have time for things like that." She went on, "The logistics were a headache. Sometimes the last tourist would leave at closing, and the Downton Abbey trucks would already be waiting in the car park, ready to come in as soon as the gates shut. It felt like a military operation."

Ryan stopped eating, caught up in Mary's stories. "Were there any disasters? Did things ever go wrong on set?"

"Oh, the dogs!" Mary exclaimed, clapping her hands together once. "Lady Carnarvon's dogs were always causing chaos. Labradors and cocker spaniels, the lot of them. Not trained for television, were they? One time, they were filming a very serious scene in the library – all dramatic music and important dialogue. Suddenly, Ellie, her old Labrador, comes bounding in with this antique slipper in her mouth, tail wagging like a metronome gone mad."

"Did they ruin the take?" I asked.

"Ruined plenty of takes. Nearly knocked over a Ming vase worth more than my wages." Mary sipped her tea. "But no one could tell them off. They were the countess's dogs. The director just waited for someone to lure them away with treats."

Katrin had filled nearly a page with notes. "And Dame Maggie – she liked the dogs?"

"She loved them. Carried treats. Said they behaved better than most actors she'd worked with." Mary leaned in closer. "Want to hear something really interesting? Some of the crew refused to work in parts of the castle after dark."

"Why?" Ryan asked, his voice dropping to match Mary's conspiratorial tone.

"Ghosts," Mary whispered dramatically. "The castle's full of them, if you believe in that sort of thing. Footsteps when no one's there. Doors opening on their own. Cold spots in the middle of rooms in summer. One cameraman swore he saw a woman in Victorian dress walk through a wall in the upstairs corridor. He refused to go back up there alone."

"Did Dame Maggie ever experience anything... supernatural?" Katrin asked, her pen now hovering expectantly.

Mary smiled. "If she did, she never mentioned it. Not the type to get flustered by a mere ghost, was she? Though she did say once that she felt 'observed' in the library, even when she was alone. Said it felt like someone was reading over her shoulder."

"Remarkable," Katrin murmured, making another note.

"Quite the fan, aren't you?" Mary said, watching Katrin.

Katrin straightened in her chair. "I appreciate exceptional talent and precision in all forms," she stated, though her flushed cheeks betrayed her. "Dame Maggie Smith represented the highest calibre of theatrical discipline and technical proficiency."

"She made you laugh and cry, did she?" Mary suggested with a knowing smile.

A small, almost imperceptible softening appeared at the corners of Katrin's mouth. "Yes," she admitted quietly. "She did."

I watched the exchange, interested. Under Katrin's methodical surface was a devoted fan, a refreshing contrast to her usual analytical style. Ryan caught my eye across the table. His raised eyebrows and quick grin matched my own surprise at this new side of our German companion.

In that moment, I saw that Katrin's notebook held more than just data. It included things that mattered to her, things that stirred feeling beneath her efficient surface. And Dame Maggie Smith had earned a place among the architectural measurements and historical dates in those carefully documented pages.

Mary's tales of aristocratic eccentricity were abruptly curtailed by the arrival of a harried-looking man in his sixties. He wore the slightly desperate expression of someone perpetually chasing solutions to problems that multiplied faster than they could be resolved. A name badge identifying him as "Robert – Café Manager" was pinned somewhat haphazardly to his waistcoat, tilting at precisely the angle that would have caused Katrin physical discomfort had it been attached to her own person.

"Sorry to interrupt, Mary," he said, running a hand through what remained of his grey hair, "but that tap in the kitchen's gone from dripping to practically weeping."

Mary nodded but stayed seated. "Wrapped a cloth around it?"

"Tried that," Robert sighed. "Soaked in ten minutes. Lady Carnarvon will have kittens if the bill jumps. Maybe Dave from the village can come."

Katrin, who had been quietly taking notes about Maggie Smith, put down her tea and frowned, looking suddenly concerned.

"Dave?" she asked. "A certified master plumber?"

Robert blinked. "Dave Tompkins. Fixed things here thirty years. Retired undertaker. Great with his hands."

I saw Katrin's polite interest shift to real concern. Her pen paused over her notebook, as if she wasn't sure what to write.

"But is he qualified?" she pressed, accent sharp.

"Qualified?" Robert echoed. "Don't know. He fixed the vicarage boiler last winter, replumbed half of Church Lane after the big freeze. No complaints."

Katrin sat up straighter at every answer.

"In Germany," her tone sharpened, "such repairs require a certified Handwerksmeister. There's a years-long apprenticeship – Ausbildung – then master certification."

Robert stared at her, mouth slightly ajar, as if she had suddenly begun speaking in tongues. "Right," he said after a moment, clearly having absorbed none of this. "So I'll just give Dave a ring then, shall I?"

"I'll help," Katrin said, phone out. "I have apps for certified tradespeople."

Mary hid a smile behind her teacup. Robert looked at Katrin as if she'd just landed from another planet.

"That's very... thoughtful," he managed, taking a small step backwards, as if Katrin's organisational efficiency might be contagious. "But Dave's the best, believe me, dear."

Ryan, quietly enjoying this, now chimed in with enthusiasm. "She's right, though, about potential issues," he said, already on his phone, researching 'plumbing advice for listed buildings'. "A dripping tap in a building with original Victorian pipes could indicate pressure irregularities in the system. Modern compression fittings might not suit legacy infrastructure, especially with mixed metals that could accelerate galvanic corrosion."

Robert's expression had transitioned from bemusement to something approaching alarm, as if he'd innocently mentioned a dripping tap and now found himself confronted with the possibility of catastrophic structural failure.

"Dave usually just replaces the washer," he said weakly.

"Temporary at best," Ryan nodded, scrolling through his phone. "If the valve seat's eroded, a new washer is like a plaster on a broken leg."

Katrin nodded, glad for Ryan's support. "Exactly. In Germany, even for a tap, a preservation specialist must approve repairs in historic buildings!"

"Dave brings his own toolbox," Robert offered, as if this somehow addressed all concerns.

I watched, amused. It was a classic clash: the German way of doing things properly and by the book, meeting the British habit of making it up as we go and trusting anyone who's 'been at it for years'. A major repair to the historic listed castle certainly requires approval from the Local Planning Authority. But a leaky tap in the tea room? That's just another job for our Daves.

Mary laughed outright at this conversation. "She's got you there, Robert. We do love our Daves, don't we? Every village has one – the bloke who can fix anything with duct tape, WD-40, and a bit of know-how picked up along the way."

"If it leaks again, we know who to blame," Robert shrugged. "Been working that way for centuries, hasn't it? Castle's still standing."

Katrin looked like she was about to say something, then thought better of it. She wrote something in her notebook. I guessed it was along the lines of 'British repairs: chaotic, informal, somehow still working'.

Robert, perhaps sensing an opportunity to escape before further plumbing theories could be proposed, began backing away toward the kitchen. "Right, well, I'll just go and... ring Dave then. Thanks for the... advice."

As he retreated, I distinctly heard him mutter, "Not trusting Dave... What's the world coming to?"

Mary watched him go with amusement. "Don't take it personally," she told Katrin. "We're funny about our local experts. The Daves who fix plumbing, the Ediths who know everything about everyone's medical symptoms but aren't actually doctors, the retired Mr Peterson who'll argue with your architect about load-bearing walls based on nothing but 'forty years of watching buildings go up.'"

"But how do you know they're right?" Katrin asked, perplexed.

"We don't," I said. "That's part of the British approach to home repairs. We are rather a DIY nation. Born of stubbornness and being broke most of the time. We start projects with a mix of faith, superstition, and the belief that anything can be fixed with makeshift tools and a cup of tea. "

Ryan nodded. "And nowadays, with YouTube. I'm convinced it was invented for British DIY emergencies."

"This is... interesting," Katrin declared, making another note in her book.

"And yet," Mary observed with a smile, "the village has remained standing for hundreds of years, through wars, weather, and generations of Daves applying their undocumented expertise to its maintenance."

Katrin pondered. "This should not work. Yet somehow, it does."

"That's Britain," I said. "Where things work despite our best efforts to the contrary."

Once Mary returned to her work and the tale of Dave the unofficial plumber concluded, we finished the last morsels of our afternoon tea in contemplative silence. The tiered stand, now empty, stood as a silver monument to Anglo-Saxon culinary tradition – somehow essential to the national character. Ryan carefully dabbed the corners of his mouth with his napkin. Katrin made a few final notes in her notebook, undoubtedly categorising our tea experience with her own elaborate system.

"Shall we settle the bill?" I suggested, gathering my belongings. "Let's see the gardens before they close."

Ryan checked his watch. "Two hours, seventeen minutes until last entry for the Egyptian Exhibition. The Earl of Carnarvon sponsored Tutankhamun's dig. Did you know–"

"Perhaps we can save the Egyptological lecture for the actual exhibition," I interjected gently, knowing that once Ryan embarked on a historical tangent, we might never reach the gardens at all.

We walked to the counter and joined the short queue of people getting ready to leave. The tearoom was much busier than when we arrived, filled with the sounds of cups and quiet talk. At the till, a young woman handled the card machine quickly and confidently.

Katrin stepped forward. "I'll pay. It's a research expense – documentation of British tea culture."

Before we could object, she had produced her wallet and a large banknote. "This should cover it," she said, handing it over.

The young woman at the counter stopped, her hand hanging in the air. She looked from the banknote to a sign next to the till that read 'CARD PAYMENTS ONLY' in large letters.

"I'm sorry," she said. "We don't accept cash. Card payments only." She gestured toward the sign with a weary movement.

Katrin stared at the note. "Cash?" she repeated. "You don't take cash?"

"That's right," the cashier confirmed, pointing toward the card reader. "Contactless preferred, but chip and PIN is fine too."

Behind us, the queue had developed the particular energy of British people forced to wait longer than expected – a subtle shifting of weight, the occasional pointed sigh, and meaningful glances exchanged between strangers, united by the experience of a queue delay.

"But this is money," Katrin stated, examining the banknote as if to confirm its authenticity to herself. "Legal tender issued by the Bank of England."

"I understand that," the cashier replied with admirable patience, "but we're cashless since the pandemic. Health and safety."

"In Germany," Katrin began, her accent sharpening. "Cash is king. It's reliable, needs no technology, and keeps your business private." She spoke as if declaring a human right.

The queue behind us had grown by two more people.

"That's fascinating," the cashier responded, in a tone that suggested it was anything but. "Still no cash."

Ryan, who had been watching this exchange with growing excitement, suddenly sprang forward. "I can help!" he announced, phone already in hand. "I have seven different payment apps."

He jumped between Katrin and the cashier, thumb working. "Apple Pay, Google Pay, two banking apps, PayPal, a cryptocurrency wallet – though probably not relevant – and one with an unknown function but definitely money."

The cashier now looked bored, as if this was more than she had signed up for. Behind us, a man in line checked his watch in a way that made sure everyone saw.

"Perhaps," I suggested, gently moving between them and presenting my own card to the terminal, "we could continue this fascinating discussion of payment evolution after we've completed the transaction?"

With a decisive tap, my card connected with the reader, producing the confirmatory beep that seemed to release the collective tension in the queue behind us.

"Britain rushed to cashless recently," I told Katrin as we left the counter. "Before the pandemic, cash was everywhere. Now, few places accept it."

"It's inefficient," Katrin said, tucking her banknote away. "What about people without digital banking, the elderly, the disconnected?"

"Those are real concerns, but most people ignore them in the rush for progress," I said. "Britain has a habit of jumping into new technology without much planning, and a lot of people get left out."

Katrin had already opened her notebook, creating a new entry with a heading: "British Payment Customs – Illogical Transition to Cashless Society."

"I must document this," she murmured, writing with quick,

precise strokes. "In Germany, attempts to reduce cash usage have met with significant cultural resistance – many people feel uncomfortable without it. There is a saying: 'Nur Bares ist Wahres' – only cash is true."

"I think that cashless is brilliant," Ryan interjected, still scrolling through his collection of payment apps. "The future of currency is digital. Did you know there are cafés in London that accept payment in cryptocurrency? I tried to use Bitcoin once for a vegan burger, but the transaction took forty-five minutes to process, and the chip shop's Wi-Fi kept dropping out."

"You know," I observed as we stepped into the sunlight, "you're creating quite the anthropological study of British peculiarities."

Katrin nodded seriously. "It is important to document cultural anomalies systematically. The British approach to daily life contains numerous inefficiencies and contradictions that must be recorded to understand them."

"And yet," Ryan added thoughtfully, "there's something rather wonderful about it all, isn't there? The weird traditions, the Dave-based repair systems, the confusing meal names."

Katrin considered this for a moment, her expression softening almost imperceptibly. "It is chaotic," she conceded. "Disorganised. Frequently illogical." She paused, glancing back at the castle behind us. "But also... unexpectedly charming."

W e slipped into the Cotswolds with our electric car barely making a sound, the landscape shifting from motorway monotone to a patchwork of neat fields. Stone cottages flickered past the windows, each one prompting a small twitch of interest from Katrin, who was already lining up her camera for the next shot. With every bend, another village materialised, each one like an illustration from a children's book.

"The harmony is remarkable," she said, sliding her glasses up. "Consistent architecture, but each building has character. Efficient local materials."

Ryan twisted in the passenger seat to face her. "Efficient? They're not efficient – they're beautiful. That's the whole point."

"Beauty and efficiency aren't opposites. See German engineering," Katrin replied, eyes on the window.

I navigated a particularly sharp bend, the tyres crunching on loose gravel as a row of cottages came into view, their windowsills bright with cascading geraniums. "We'll reach Bibury in about five minutes. It's often dubbed the prettiest village in England – William Morris thought so, at least."

"The textile designer?" Katrin was already noting it down.

"The very same," I confirmed. "He called it 'the most beautiful village in England' in the 1800s, and the tourism industry has been quoting him ever since."

As we rounded the final bend into Bibury, a jarring change stole away any lingering sense of calm. I'd expected the quiet of the river and the usual postcard scene, but the village was packed. At least six tour coaches, engines idling, jammed the narrow street. Tourists swarmed the single lane, some clustering in large, chattering groups, others hustling to the bridge for photos. Selfie sticks waved overhead, guidebooks flipped open to annotated pages, cameras clicked in rapid succession. The air buzzed with a dozen languages, none of them English.

"Oh," Ryan said, disappointed. "It's Piccadilly Circus with better architecture."

I manoeuvred our car as far to the side of the lane as possible, trying not to block the massive coaches whose engines idled noisily, adding a background drone to the multilingual cacophony. "This is... rather more crowded than I expected," I admitted.

Katrin had already opened a fresh page in her notebook. At the top, she wrote: "Overtourism Phenomenon – Bibury Case Study."

"The coach registration plates are primarily from London tour companies," she observed, counting methodically. "Six large coaches, approximately sixty to seventy passengers per vehicle, equals approximately four hundred visitors in a village with a population of..." She looked at me questioningly.

"Less than a hundred permanent residents," I supplied, watching as a tour guide with a small flag attempted to herd a group of visitors toward Arlington Row.

We exited the car and were immediately swallowed by the crowd. Ryan, caught between a determined German family and a group of enthusiastic Japanese photographers, stumbled slightly as he tried to maintain his footing on the uneven cobblestones. Katrin forged ahead with determination, her camera bag clutched protectively to her chest, while I tried to keep both of them in sight.

"We need to reach Arlington Row," I called over the noise. "It's just through this narrow..."

My words were cut short by sudden chaos. A new batch of tourists, freshly unloaded from one of the coaches, surged forward in a determined wave, cameras up and elbows out. Their single-minded focus was on reaching Arlington Row within their limited window – exactly seventeen minutes to take photos before returning to their coach. Ryan, swept into their path, was jostled hard by an enthusiastic man with a camera whose huge lens bumped him aside.

"Ow!" Ryan yelped, stumbling against a low stone wall. "My ankle!"

The photographer barely paused and continued to rush towards Arlington Row. I reached Ryan, who tested his right foot, face tight with pain.

"Are you all right?" I steadied him by the elbow.

"Just twisted," he winced, stepping carefully. "I'll need a minute."

Katrin returned, frowning at the crowd, then focused on Ryan. "We should get out of here." Her notebook was forgotten.

We slipped down a quiet side lane. The noise faded. Ryan limped beside me in silence.

A woman called nearby. "Is your friend hurt?"

I turned to see a woman in her sixties kneeling in a front garden, secateurs in hand, surrounded by a magnificent display of roses. Her silver hair was pulled back in a neat bun, and she wore gardening gloves that had seen many seasons of use. She regarded us with concern, her eyes lingering on Ryan's awkward gait.

"Just twisted his ankle – ran into the crowd," I said.

The woman's expression darkened slightly. "Those coach tours are getting worse every year." She rose to her feet with the fluid movement of someone who had spent a lifetime tending gardens. "I'm Sally. You look like you could use a sit-down and perhaps a cup of tea. Would you care to come in?"

Before I could formulate a polite refusal, Ryan had already stepped forward. "That would be wonderful," he said, his pain apparently forgotten at the prospect of tea. "If you're sure it's no trouble."

Sally smiled. "Nice to have visitors without selfie sticks." She led us toward her shining oak door. "Come in."

I glanced at Katrin; she nodded, pen out. "Time to document local views on tourism," she murmured.

Inside Sally's cottage, the shift was immediate. It felt as though we had crossed into another world. The interior matched every Cotswold ideal – low-ceilinged rooms, exposed beams, uneven flagstones layered with faded Persian rugs, and windows casting diamond-patterned light. She led us to the kitchen, where gentle heat from an Aga cooker mingled with the sight of dozens of teapots – some plain, some ornate – arranged on open shelves.

"Please, sit down," Sally gestured to a solid oak table surrounded by mismatched chairs. "I'll put the kettle on."

While Sally made tea, a large black cat with amber eyes walked in, looked us over, and jumped onto Ryan's lap.

"That's Lucifer," Sally explained over her shoulder. "Don't be fooled by the name – he's an angel. Most of the time."

Ryan, clearly delighted by this development, began gently stroking the cat, who settled into his lap with a rumbling purr that seemed too substantial to originate from such a modestly sized creature.

"Lovely home," I said, absorbing the warmth.

Sally placed a teapot – shaped like a thatched cottage – on the table, along with a matching milk jug and sugar bowl. "It was my parents' before me, and my grandparents' before that," she said, distributing mugs with practised efficiency. "But living here isn't what it used to be."

"Because of tourism?" Katrin prompted, notebook open beside her mug.

Sally nodded, a sigh escaping her lips – equal parts resignation and bitterness. "We are the lucky ones. We live on a rather quiet street. But even we can't open our curtains on some days," she murmured, voice tight with fatigue. "They peer through the windows, faces inches from the glass. It feels like being under siege."

"That's a clear invasion of privacy," Katrin said.

"Last summer, we were having Sunday dinner – my daughter and her family were visiting – and I looked up to find three different people taking photos through the window. They were actually discussing the 'authenticity' of our family meal, as if we were some sort of museum exhibit."

Ryan looked up from petting Lucifer. "That's awful."

"It gets worse," Sally continued, warming to her subject. "They trample through the gardens – my poor roses have been decimated more times than I can count. That particular bed you saw me tending? I've replanted it three times this year alone." She stirred her tea with perhaps more force than necessary. "And the roads – a trip to Cirencester that should take fifteen minutes? It can take more than an hour when the coaches are here, blocking the roads. It feels like a battle just to buy groceries some days."

Katrin was writing furiously, occasionally pausing to ask precise questions. "Has there been an impact on property values? Are there local regulations in place regarding privacy protection? What percentage of local businesses derive their primary income from tourism?"

Sally answered each query with the patient thoroughness of someone who had given these matters considerable thought. "Houses on Arlington Row sell for astronomical sums – not that they come up for sale often. The last one went for over a million pounds, and it's barely the size of this kitchen. As for regulations..." She shook her head. "The council makes sympathetic noises, but nothing changes. And yes, most businesses here now depend on tourism. The traditional shops have all converted to selling souvenirs or cream teas."

As the conversation continued, I realised that gradually the true theme of our cultural exchange began to emerge. Outside, the village continued to pose dutifully for the endless crowds, its picturesque calm just an illusion. But within the room, England's mask slipped; we glimpsed the other side of that flawless coin. England wasn't just the picture on the postcards most tourists see. Many visitors do not notice the real challenges that people here deal with every day.

When we reached Snowshill, the contrast with Bibury was obvious. The buildings and gardens were just as carefully kept, all that familiar Cotswold stone. What set it apart was the peace. No tour groups, no crowds with cameras. The village was quiet, except for the odd car and the steady sound of Katrin taking photos. Ryan's ankle seemed fine again after a short break and a few of Sally's homemade ginger biscuits. He claimed they possessed healing powers that doctors had not yet discovered.

We wandered along the narrow high street. The cottages leaned toward each other across the lane, like elderly neighbours sharing secrets. Katrin captured doorways, window frames, and the occasional architectural quirk with unwavering attention to detail. She paused at a fine example of a mullioned window, adjusting her camera settings with small, deliberate finger movements.

"The geometric consistency is remarkable," Katrin said, not looking away from her viewfinder. "These were constructed before standardised manufacturing, yet the proportions are nearly identical across different buildings."

"Beautiful craftsmanship," I agreed, admiring the way the afternoon light caught the leaded glass. "They built things to last back then."

Ryan, who had been inspecting a display of local honey in a nearby shop window, rejoined us with a bounce in his step that suggested his ankle had indeed fully recovered. "There's a craft shop just ahead," he announced, pointing toward a small storefront with a hanging wooden sign. "Might be worth a look."

The shop spread across the ground floor of what must once have been a weaver's cottage. Its doorway sagged low, forcing Ryan to duck as he entered. Inside, the space brimmed with local crafts: hand-turned wooden bowls gleaming with wax, tightly woven willow baskets, mugs dipped in glazed earth tones, and shelves packed with preserves and chutneys in neat jars. A bell chimed quietly over our heads, summoning the grey-haired man at the counter. He nodded briefly and resumed reading his newspaper.

Katrin wandered among the shelves, studying each item as carefully as she had studied the buildings outside. She picked up a mug, checked the maker's mark, and set it back exactly where it was.

As we prepared to leave, Katrin reached the door first, pulled it open wide, and stepped through without looking back. An elderly woman, who must have been browsing among the shelves earlier, followed several steps behind, moving slowly. Katrin released the door, which began to swing closed. I started to call out a warning, but before I could, the door swung back and thudded softly against the elderly woman's shoulder.

"Oh! I'm sorry!" the woman exclaimed immediately.

Katrin stopped, half in and half out of the shop, looking confused. The elderly woman just smiled at her and continued on her way.

Katrin remained in the doorway, watching the elderly woman walk away, her expression one of disbelief. Then she turned back to me, searching for an explanation.

"Did she just..." Katrin began, then stopped.

"Apologise to you for you letting the door hit her?" I supplied. "Yes, she did."

"But that makes no sense." Katrin furrowed her brow. "I am the one who should apologise. I failed to hold the door, causing it to strike her. The error was clearly mine."

"That's Britain," Ryan chuckled, guiding us both fully onto the pavement to free the doorway. "Land of the backwards apology."

We kept walking through the village, Katrin deep in thought about what had happened. On the village green, two old men sat beneath a big oak tree, trading short remarks about the weather and falling into long silences.

At that moment, we witnessed the second incident. Along the edge of the green strode a middle-aged man in a waxed jacket and Wellington boots. He focused so intently on a sheaf of papers that he failed to notice the cast-iron lamppost ahead. Without looking up, he collided with it – his shoulder taking a glancing blow. Katrin, surprised by what followed, stopped in her tracks.

"Sorry," the man muttered to the lamppost. He adjusted his jacket, nodded at the inanimate object, and continued on his way without breaking stride or showing any sign he found the event unusual.

Katrin watched him go, then looked at us as if she was doubting her English. She took out her notebook, opened to a new page, and wrote at the top: "British Apology Rituals." Then she started a list, writing quickly.

"Is this a common issue, a certain mental problem in Britain? Or is this some cultural code I don't understand?" Katrin asked, genuine concern in her voice, looking up from her notebook.

Ryan burst into laughter, drawing a glance from one of the elderly men on the bench. "It's definitely a cultural code," he assured her.

She looked at both of us, trying to sum it up. "So this is normal? The person who didn't do anything wrong apologises, and so does the person who did?"

"Precisely," I confirmed. "And often, the person less at fault will insist that they are, in fact, more at fault, which the original fault-bearer must then vigorously deny."

"It's like a conversational dance," Ryan said. "Everyone knows the steps, but we all act like it's spontaneous."

Katrin still looked puzzled. "And what about the man and the lamppost?"

"Ah, that's a higher level," I said. "Saying sorry to things you bump into is the black belt of British politeness. It's when 'sorry' is so automatic you say it to everyone and everything, every single time."

Katrin made another note, then looked up, starting to understand. "This explains a lot about British colonial history," she said. "Maybe they built an empire just to have more people to apologise to."

Ryan laughed so loudly that both old men on the bench turned to glare at us, their faces showing clear disapproval. That was about as close as you get to a serious telling-off.

It's a place you can't miss. Broadway Tower rises from the hilltop, a miniature fortress – medieval in look but built much later. Its eccentric shape captures the English fondness for creating things that seem ancient, built for simple pleasure.

The path twisted gently upward, leading us through a field dotted with grazing sheep, who seemed largely indifferent to both the tower and the small parade of tourists crossing their land. As we drew closer, Katrin stopped every few metres to photograph it from different angles, focusing on its hexagonal shape and faux-battlements.

"The architectural influences are chaotic," she said, adjusting her lens. Gothic details appeared alongside Saxon features and a seemingly invented turret system. Though her tone was critical, her camera clicked twice as often as usual at historic sites.

Climbing to the top of the tower meant navigating a narrow spiral staircase that wound through three levels. As we approached the stairs, Ryan, who had been unusually quiet since we left the car, glanced at the steps and finally spoke up as we started our ascent.

"There isn't a lift, is there?" he asked, eyeing the stone steps with the trepidation of someone who viewed unnecessary physical exertion as a personal affront.

"It was built in 1798," I reminded him gently. "So no, there isn't a lift."

"The Swiss built lifts in their castles so more tourists actually make it to the top alive," he muttered, but started climbing anyway, his hand trailing along the ancient stone wall for support.

By the time we reached the tower's summit, the exertion seemed worthwhile. We stepped onto a viewing platform, where a spectacular panorama awaited. In every direction, the Cotswold landscape spread out – fields of green and gold stitched by dry stone walls, their patterns reminiscent of ancient runes. On days like this, the Black Mountains in Wales appeared in the distant haze.

"Thirteen counties visible from this vantage point," announced a voice behind us. "On a clear day, that is."

We turned to see a man in his fifties with a benevolent expression. He looked ready to offer information, whether asked or not. Dressed in a tweed jacket with leather patches, he seemed cast as the quintessential English guide. His neat silver hair and half-moon spectacles gave him an academic air as he surveyed us.

"Welcome to Broadway Tower," he continued, gesturing expansively at our surroundings. "One of England's most delightful architectural follies. I'm volunteering as a guide here – been sharing the tower's story for fifteen years now."

"It's quite remarkable," I offered politely. "The views are spectacular."

"Ah, but do you know why it was built?" the guide asked, his eyes twinkling with the anticipation of someone about to deliver a favourite anecdote. "That's where the real story lies."

Katrin, who had been making notes about the structural elements of the tower, looked up with professional interest. "I assume for military observation or territorial surveying?"

The guide's smile widened. "Not at all, not at all. This tower exists because a bored aristocrat wanted to test a theory about light visibility." He paused dramatically, clearly enjoying Katrin's confused expression. "Lady Coventry, you see – that's the Countess of Coventry – wondered whether a beacon lit on this hill could be seen from her home in Worcester. That's some twenty-two miles away."

"A beacon?" Katrin repeated, her pen frozen above her notebook. "Like a fire?"

"Exactly," the guide said, tapping the railing. "She was curious – that's what ladies did back then, if they had money and little else to fill the day. Wondered about things. One day, Lady Coventry asked if a light from here would be visible from her drawing room. Idle curiosity, really. Just a passing thought. But the Earl, hopelessly smitten with his wife, decided to settle it. They built a bonfire, and the flickering light reached her doorstep. She was delighted. He was likely relieved. As a gesture of affection, the Earl hired James Wyatt, who was a bit of a show-off, to build something permanent – a folly to mark the spot forever."

Katrin's eyebrows had risen steadily throughout this explanation, until they threatened to disappear entirely into her hairline. She blinked, processing the story. "So this entire structure exists," she clarified, "because a bored aristocrat wanted to test the visibility of light across counties?" Her disbelief mingled with a grudging fascination.

"Absolutely!" the guide confirmed with evident delight.

Katrin pressed further, now writing quickly in her notebook. Her eyes remained on the guide as she asked, "And after this experiment was completed? What purpose did the tower serve then?"

"None at all," the guide replied, cheerful as ever. "That's the mark of a true folly – not meant for practical use. Occasionally, the Earl entertained guests here. Imagine bringing your friends all the way up simply to marvel at your wife's curiosity – and your deep pockets!"

The guide, pleased by Katrin's reaction, went on. "The style? Just whatever the Earl fancied. Saxon, Gothic, Moorish – all mixed together. He wanted it to look old and mysterious, but it was brand new. Even the arrow slits are fake. No one ever used them."

Katrin muttered something in German – though I couldn't translate it precisely, I caught the distinct phrase "pathologisches Niveau," which required little imagination to interpret. She then made another note in her book, striking the pen down with more force than usual.

"English eccentricity – pathological levels," she said now in English. Yet her voice carried reluctant admiration.

Ryan, meanwhile, had been listening to the guide's explanation with growing delight. Unlike Katrin's bemused scepticism, his expression was one of pure enchantment with the absurdity of it all.

"That's brilliant," he declared, moving to the edge of the viewing platform to take in the panorama again. "Building an entire tower just to see if light travels in a straight line. That's exactly the sort of thing I'd do if I had aristocratic levels of wealth."

The guide beamed at Ryan, clearly recognising a kindred spirit. "The folly tradition is a uniquely English approach to architecture," he agreed. "Building something purely because it pleases you, with no regard for practicality or purpose. There's something rather wonderful about that, don't you think?"

I watched as Katrin finished her notes.

"Only the English," she concluded, closing her notebook with decisive finality, "would consider 'because I was curious' sufficient justification for a major construction project."

The first thing I noticed was the hand-painted sign – a rabbit so anatomically improbable it could only have been drawn by someone who knew rabbits by rumour alone. The pub, 'The Crooked Hare,' tilted at conflicting angles, as if every section strained to pull away. Inside, squat oak beams – scarred by unwary tall patrons – spanned a ceiling stained by centuries of wood smoke and nicotine. The interior felt snug, even claustrophobic, yet unexpectedly comforting.

We entered during the peaceful lull between lunchtime rush and evening service. At that hour, pubs doze in amber anticipation. A fire crackled in an ancient stone hearth, as though it had warmed drinkers since Tudor times. Mismatched wooden chairs and tables sprawled across the room, each appearing to have been discovered over decades, not as part of a uniform set.

Katrin stepped in behind me and froze. Her shoes made a distinct peeling sound with each step – the unmistakable soundtrack of footwear on an adhesive surface. She looked down in growing horror, lifting one foot experimentally. The carpet clung to her shoe before releasing it with obvious reluctance.

"This floor," Katrin whispered, her tone tight with restrained panic, as if she'd stumbled into a biohazard. "It is... sticky."

Ryan nodded knowingly as he navigated the sticky expanse. "You know it's a real British pub if you hear that sound underfoot. It's practically mandatory."

Katrin leaned in, looking worried. "This can't be up to health code. The bacteria on this carpet..." She glanced around, half-expecting to see something growing. "How is this allowed in a place that serves food?"

"It's tradition," I explained, steering her to a corner table where the carpet seemed marginally less hazardous. "English pub carpets have been sticky since forever. Some historians claim the gluey floors deter bar fights – it's difficult to launch an attack when your shoes are semi-glued down."

Katrin looked unconvinced by this dubious historical theory. "But surely modern hygiene standards would require..."

"It's England," I cut in, gently. "Tradition always wins out over hygiene, especially in the countryside. The stickier the carpet, the more genuine the pub. And wait for it: some of our loos are carpeted, too!"

She shook her head in bewilderment but followed me to the table, where she removed a packet of antibacterial wipes from her bag and discreetly cleaned her hands. "This is not how we would operate a Gaststätte in Germany," she muttered.

While Katrin processed her new surroundings, Ryan had already seized the laminated menu and was examining it with focused attention. His expression shifted from one of concentration to surprise, and finally to undisguised delight.

"They have a vegan nut roast!" Ryan exclaimed, eyes bright, as if he'd found a buried treasure. "An actual proper Sunday roast, but with a nut and mushroom base instead of meat." He clutched the menu to his chest. "How very 90s! This is hilarious, I could weep."

The landlord, a stocky man with a red face typical of someone who belonged behind a bar, greeted us with a nod. He took our orders quickly and efficiently, not writing anything down, his expression brisk but neutral, then quietly disappeared into the kitchen.

Our meals arrived swiftly: nut roast for all. Each plate brimmed with crisp, golden roast potatoes and Yorkshire puddings swollen into airy bowls. Bright vegetables with gravy that pooled on the plate, creating a glossy brown lake as each pea and carrot floated like a tiny archipelago.

Ryan regarded his vegan roast with reverence, photographing it from multiple angles before taking his first bite.

We ate in appreciative silence. The only sounds were the gentle clink of cutlery against plates and the occasional satisfied murmur. When we finished, the landlord came back, hands behind his back, wearing the polite look of someone about to ask the usual question.

"Is everything all right with your meals?" he inquired, his tone suggesting this was a question that required – indeed, permitted – only one possible answer.

Katrin, however, interpreted this as a genuine request for feedback. She set down her knife and fork with precise movements, wiped her mouth delicately with her napkin, and launched into a detailed assessment.

"The vegetables are cooked perfectly," she began, her tone measured. "Not too soft, which is unusual for British cooking in my experience. The gravy is too salty, with about twenty percent more sodium than ideal. The nut roast," she nodded to Ryan's empty plate, "was very well spiced, with a good balance of textures. The portion size is adequate for lunch." She paused and added in the same calm voice, "But the plate is slightly chipped on the left edge."

The landlord's smile faltered. Colour vanished from his cheeks before returning in force. A flush crept from collar to hairline. He opened and shut his mouth twice but produced no sound – like a fish abruptly beached, reconsidering its life choices.

"Everything's lovely, thank you," I interjected, using the classic British tactic of social rescue. "Really delicious, we've enjoyed it immensely."

Relief washed over the landlord's face, though he continued to eye Katrin with the wary expression of someone who has encountered a previously unknown species and is unsure of its dietary requirements or potential for aggression.

"Very good, very good," he muttered, backing away slightly. "Glad to hear it. Very good."

Once the landlord left, Katrin turned to me, puzzlement creasing her brow. "He asked about the meal. I answered honestly, even complimented things. Why does he look so put out?"

Ryan snorted into his beer, hastily converting the sound into an unconvincing cough.

"He didn't really want a real answer," I said. "It's just something people say. When a British person asks, 'Is everything all right?' they're not really wanting to hear any feedback. They're performing a ritual that expects 'Yes, lovely, thank you,' even if your food is barely edible."

Katrin's brow furrowed. "But how does anyone improve if customers never say what they really think?"

"That's not the point," I said. "The idea is to keep things running smoothly, without any fuss or arguments. Most of us in Britain are not very good at complaining. We'll quietly eat a disappointing meal rather than mention it. If we do complain, it's usually in private. Giving direct feedback is seen as quite rude. Unless someone specifically asks for it, maybe in writing on a comment card that no one reads."

"But I said several positive things," Katrin protested. "The vegetables were perfect. The nut roast was well-spiced. In Germany, honest feedback is valued after a meal – it's how establishments improve."

"You also said the gravy was too salty and the plate was chipped," Ryan said. "Here, that's like saying someone's kid is ugly but has good shoes."

Katrin reached for her notebook with a sigh of resignation. She flipped to a page already headed "British Communication

Rules" and added a new entry: "Rule #4: Never say the truth." This time she underlined it three times, then added in smaller letters beneath: "Politeness requires dishonesty."

"It's not exactly dishonesty," I attempted to clarify. "It's more like... social lubrication. The truth, but filtered through a complex system of understatement, implication, and mutually understood codes."

"So if the meal had been truly terrible," Katrin asked, pen poised above her notebook, "what would be the appropriate response to 'Is everything all right?'"

"'Yes, fine, thank you,'" Ryan and I replied in unison.

"And if it had been the most exceptional meal of your entire life?"

"'Yes, lovely, thank you,'" I confirmed. "Though in that case, you might add a slightly more enthusiastic nod."

"British communication is like your sticky pub carpet," Katrin mused. "Inefficient, problematic, yet somehow considered charming by those who are used to it."

I laughed. "That's probably the best description of British communication I've heard," I said. "We really do put politeness first."

While settling the bill – paid by card, to Katrin's continued disapproval – I reflected on how our German companion revealed facets of British culture I'd long taken for granted. Through her observations, our national quirks became more than quaint habits. They seemed to be a complex system of codes and compromises. Illogical, perhaps, but undeniably ours.

After eight centuries, a place like this seems serenely indifferent to intruders. Morning sunlight gilded the honeyed limestone buildings of Chipping Campden, tracing long, delicate shadows along the arc of the High Street. We'd arrived before the world woke, driven by Katrin's conviction that early light sharpens every photograph. For a while, the street belonged to us – and to the invisible presence of the wool merchants who shaped the town.

"This is exceptional Perpendicular Gothic," Katrin said as she aimed her camera at St James Church. The sound of her shutter broke the morning silence with a steady rhythm. "The size of this wool church shows how rich the town was in the 15th century. The height of the tower and the length of the nave create a pleasing, balanced look."

Ryan yawned beside me, still bleary-eyed from our early departure. After yesterday's pub lunch and an evening spent sorting through Katrin's exhaustive categorisation of British communication oddities, we'd retired early to a small B&B outside Stow-on-the-Wold. The landlady had served us tea in chipped mugs, which Katrin had examined with the forensic attention of a health inspector before cautiously sipping.

"Is that building wearing a hat?" Ryan asked, pointing toward an unusual structure perched at the edge of the churchyard.

"The East Banqueting House," I supplied as I consulted my mental catalogue of architectural curiosities. It was built in 1613 by a wealthy merchant for entertaining guests. They would gather there after gorging themselves at his main house.

"So it's a dessert house?" Ryan's face brightened with immediate interest. "An entire building dedicated to pudding? The 17th century suddenly makes much more sense to me."

Katrin was already across the churchyard, tripod balanced on her shoulder. She set it up with her usual care and adjusted for the uneven ground. Once the camera was steady, she began photographing the East Banqueting House – a small, square building with a domed roof – from every angle. Each shot was carefully recorded in her notebook.

"The architectural excess is fascinating," she called over her shoulder. "Completely unnecessary ornamentation with no practical function. Very British."

We continued along the High Street, a gently curving thoroughfare lined with a parade of limestone buildings. Most medieval towns grew organically, often in a chaotic manner. Chipping Campden's main street, though, displayed a harmony of design. This suggested either remarkable cooperation among its original builders or the controlling hand of a single wealthy patron.

"The street curves deliberately," I explained as Ryan admired a particularly elaborate doorway. "It was designed this way in the 14th century. Apparently, it creates a more appealing vista as you walk through the town."

"Medieval urban planning with aesthetic priorities," Katrin said. "Not great for traffic, but it looks good." She sounded brisk as usual, but I could tell the town's golden stone had made an impression.

As we approached the village green – a modest triangle of grass bordered by more immaculate stone buildings – we noticed a small gathering near its centre. Five men, dressed in what looked like white nightshirts, stood in a rough circle. They surrounded a larger figure who demonstrated a peculiar hopping movement.

"Right, lads," the central figure boomed in a rich Gloucestershire accent that rolled across the green. "Remember, it's all in the stance. Feet shoulder-width apart, weight on your back foot until the moment of impact."

We paused at the edge, watching as the man demonstrated what appeared to be a carefully calibrated kick aimed at the shin of an imaginary opponent.

"Excuse me," Katrin called, already striding up to the group with that energetic, unhesitating German manner – a kind of directness you'd never see from a Brit. It was oddly invigorating. "What activity are you engaged in?"

The man turned, revealing a face creased with laugh lines and a pair of startlingly bright blue eyes beneath bushy eyebrows. He swept off a flat cap and executed a small bow that managed to be simultaneously ironic and courtly.

"Shin-kicking practice," he announced with evident pride. "I'm George Hawker, though most folks call me Shins. Been champion of the Cotswold Olimpick Games shin-kicking competition seven years running."

"Shin... kicking?" Ryan repeated, his expression vacillating between horror and fascination.

"Oldest sport in the Cotswolds!" George gestured for us to come closer and proclaimed, "Been doing it since 1612, we have. Part of the Cotswold Olimpick Games – that's Olimpick with a 'k', mind you, very traditional spelling."

Katrin produced her notebook and pen. "Please explain the rules and techniques." She sounded as if she were documenting an important anthropological discovery, not an organised form of lower leg assault.

George beamed with the delight of a man who rarely encountered genuine interest in his peculiar passion. "Well, now, it's quite simple in theory but requires great skill in execution. Two competitors face each other, wearing traditional white smocks." He tugged at his own garment, which I could now see was padded to a considerable thickness around the lower legs. "Smocks must be stuffed with straw – that's the padding, see?"

He bent down, patting his shin. The movement produced a rustling sound, confirming the presence of what sounded like half a haystack within the fabric.

"Then, when the referee gives the signal, you take it in turns to kick each other's shins until one man gives in." He delivered this explanation with the same casual tone one might use to describe the rules of croquet.

"Is protective equipment permitted?" Katrin scribbled in her notebook as she spoke.

"Just the straw in your smock," George replied, looking mildly offended at the suggestion of additional protection.

"And people do this voluntarily?" I wondered aloud.

"Been doing it for over four hundred years!" George confirmed cheerfully. "It's about strength, technique, and most importantly, who can endure the most pain without crying out."

I looked at Ryan, expecting horror, but he was watching George's stance with a worrying amount of interest.

"Could I have a go?" he asked, taking a step forward before I could intervene.

"Ryan," I said, "maybe just watch this time–"

"Excellent!" George clapped his hands together. "Always good to see a newcomer interested in our traditional sports!"

Before I could formulate a more emphatic objection, George was guiding Ryan to a spot on the green, instructing one of his trainees – a stocky young man with a farmer's ruddy complexion – to act as Ryan's opponent.

"We'll just do a friendly demonstration," George assured me. He apparently misread my concern as fear for Ryan's life, not exasperation at his impulsiveness. "One kick each, no competition rules."

While Katrin watched from the perfect spot, her pen hovered above a new notebook page. She titled it "Traditional English Alpha Male Contest Disguised as Sport: Shin-Kicking Rules."

"Is there an official governing body for this activity?" she inquired, somehow maintaining a perfectly straight face.

"The Cotswold Olimpick Games Committee," George confirmed, pride evident in his voice. "We maintain the ancient traditions and ensure the rules are properly followed."

While Katrin documented this information with her customary thoroughness, Ryan was fitted with a borrowed white smock. He stuffed generous handfuls of straw into it.

"Now then," George instructed, stepping back to assess his handiwork, "remember what I showed you. Weight on your back foot, then transfer forward as you strike. Aim for the middle of the shin – that's where it hurts most."

Ryan nodded. He squared off against his opponent. The man watched him with the indulgent look of one who had seen many enthusiastic novices come and go – most of whom limped away.

"Ready?" George called, raising his hand like a starter at a race. "Begin!"

Ryan lunged forward, overly enthusiastic. His kick lacked any of the technical refinement George had just demonstrated. His opponent, clearly experienced, sidestepped the worst of the impact and delivered a precise counter-kick. It connected solidly with Ryan's shin, despite the straw padding.

Ryan let out a strangled gasp, hopping back and grabbing his leg. His face managed both regret and sudden understanding.

"Bloody hell!" he wheezed, hopping toward a nearby bench. "That's – that's not what I expected."

"Didn't get your padding distributed right," George observed sympathetically, helping Ryan to the bench. "You want it concentrated over the shin bone, not spread around the calf."

Ryan collapsed onto the bench, massaging his injured leg with the theatrical misery of a football player seeking a penalty. He looked up at me, his expression somehow combining self-pity with a plea for sympathy. "I could have been a contender," he lamented.

I couldn't help but roll my eyes. "If only someone had warned you that voluntarily being kicked in the shin might result in pain."

"Good spirit, though!" George encouraged, patting Ryan's shoulder. "Most newcomers don't even attempt a proper kick – they just flinch away. You went for it, lad. That's what counts in shin-kicking."

Katrin snapped her notebook shut with a decisive sound. "Online I have found seventeen distinct rules and eight historical variations of this activity," she announced. "It appears to be simultaneously primitive and highly regulated. Fascinating cultural contradiction."

"That's us Brits all over," George agreed cheerfully, though I suspected he wasn't entirely following Katrin's anthropological assessment. "Tradition and good sportsmanship, that's what it's about."

Ryan continued to rub his shin, his initial anguish slowly transforming into a kind of rueful pride. "Do I get some sort of certificate?" he asked hopefully. "Something that says I participated in traditional shin-kicking?"

"Better," George replied with a wink. "You get a proper Cotswold story to tell, and the knowledge that you've joined a tradition older than most countries. Not many tourists can say they've done that, can they?"

Ryan, still wincing, managed to look genuinely pleased. For all his impulsiveness, I had to admit he was always willing to dive into local traditions – sometimes literally.

George started packing up his things. A few onlookers had gathered, probably unsure if they were watching a bit of history or just an odd local sport. George slung a bag of straw over his shoulder and gave us a nod, looking pleased to have introduced another visitor to the joys of shin-kicking.

"Right then," he said cheerfully, extending a weathered hand first to Ryan, then to Katrin, and finally to me. "Lovely meeting you all. See you later!"

He had turned to rejoin his trainees when Katrin's voice stopped him in his tracks.

"At what time, precisely?" she asked, already extracting her notebook from her bag.

George turned back, his bushy eyebrows drawing together in confusion. "Sorry?"

"You said 'see you later,'" Katrin elaborated, pen poised above a fresh page. "I need to know what time would be convenient for you. The Eight Bells pub appears to be the highest-rated establishment in the village according to three separate review platforms. Would seven o'clock be acceptable? Or do you prefer to eat earlier?"

A peculiar silence fell over our small group. George's mouth opened slightly, then closed again, his expression cycling through bewilderment, amusement, and finally a sort of cautious concern, as if he suspected he might be the unwitting target of an elaborate prank.

"I think," I interjected gently, "there's been a small misunderstanding. When George said 'see you later,' he wasn't actually suggesting a specific arrangement to meet again."

Katrin's pen paused mid-air, her brow furrowing. "But he clearly stated his intention to see us later."

"It's just a manner of speaking," I explained. "A common British farewell expression. It doesn't literally mean that he expects to see us again."

"Then why say it if a meeting isn't planned?" Katrin asked, genuinely baffled.

George shrugged. "It's just something we say. Like 'cheers' even if we're not drinking."

"Ah!" Katrin's face cleared momentarily, as if one mystery had been solved, only to cloud again with fresh confusion. "It's like yesterday, yes? When the pub landlord comes over, asks 'Is everything all right with your meals?' but doesn't really want to know the answer?"

"Exactly," I confirmed. "British English is full of phrases that don't mean what they seem on the surface."

Ryan, who had been observing with growing delight, limped over to join us, clearly sensing an opportunity to contribute to Katrin's cultural education.

"Oh, we have dozens of these," he announced proudly, as if British linguistic inconsistency were a national achievement worthy of celebration. "Like when someone asks, 'How's your day been?' they don't actually want a detailed account of your day. They're expecting 'Fine, thanks' regardless of whether your day involved winning the lottery or discovering your house has subsided."

"It's not the words that matter so much," I said, "as the whole ritual of saying them."

"Like 'I'll be there in a minute,'" Ryan continued enthusiastically. "Which means anywhere from thirty seconds to half an hour, depending on who's saying it."

"Or 'Help yourself,'" I added, warming to the theme. "Which doesn't mean take whatever you want, but rather 'take a small, socially acceptable amount while pretending you don't really want it.'"

George, who had been following this conversation with the increasingly bewildered expression of a man who had unwittingly triggered an avalanche, shifted his weight from one foot to the other.

"Or 'Just round the corner,'" Ryan forged on, apparently cataloguing every British linguistic peculiarity he could recall. "Which could mean anything from ten metres to twenty miles away."

Katrin's pen was flying now, each phrase documented with a small notation regarding its actual meaning versus its literal interpretation.

"The worst is 'We must get together sometime,'" I noted. "Which almost invariably means 'We will never voluntarily meet again unless forced by circumstance.'"

George protested, looking genuinely distressed at this characterisation. "Sometimes people really do want to meet again."

I grinned. "And that's the real British challenge – figuring out when someone is only socially sweet-talking or actually means what they say. You need a built-in language decoder, a kind of seventh sense for reading between the lines. But honestly, most of us don't have one either. So we can't really blame visitors for getting lost."

We continued our journey through Cotswold's undulating landscape. Ryan had at last dropped the theatrical wincing, though every so often he'd reach down and massage his battered shin, wearing the look of a man relishing a fresh story – determined to make his injury central to the day. "This shin-kicking made me exceptionally hungry!" he announced, as if it explained everything. Exceptionally hungry? As if his normal appetite ever left room for improvement.

He pressed on. "Can we stop for snacks? My injury's crashed my blood sugar. I can't be held responsible until I eat."

He had barely finished when Katrin made a noise of surprise. "Stop!" She tapped my arm from the backseat. "What is this? It looks nothing like Britain, almost Italian!" She had discovered the Bliss Tweed Mill.

Ryan groaned, not keen on any stop that did not involve food, but I was already pulling over. The Bliss Tweed Mill stood in full view, round and solid, with a tall chimney that looked almost like a church spire. Katrin was reaching for my camera before the car had even stopped.

"This mill was built in 1872," I said. "Famous for its unusual circular design."

Katrin, already setting up her camera, frowned at the building. "Strange design. Not efficient for manufacturing, which usually needs straight lines. Why make a round mill?" Before I could answer, she was off with her tripod, looking for a better angle. Ryan and I followed more slowly. Ryan especially moved as if each step was a test, wondering if he might survive.

Katrin had finished her shots and was just brushing off her hands when we noticed an elderly man watching us from across the lane.

Ryan rushed over at once, hunger overriding any social caution. "Excuse me, we are starving, do you know a place where we can get anything to eat? There seems to be nothing here besides this strange round mill..."

"Tourists, are you?" The old man eyed us, the question mostly rhetorical. "Come to see our famous mill?"

"No," Ryan said, "just looking for food."

"We're photographers," I said, stepping forward with a hand.

"Arthur," he introduced himself. "Worked in that mill for twenty-seven years. Started in 1963, at sixteen years old. Last generation to see it as a real working mill, before they turned it into fancy flats."

Arthur launched into his story without invitation. He told us about the chimney, modelled after a Tuscan bell tower, because John Bliss, the builder, had wanted something people would notice – a showpiece that married beauty and industry.

He then pointed into the valley beyond. "If you're heading for Brockworth, there's a decent shop in Lower Slaughter. You might try there for your snacks." He glanced at Ryan. "Tell Maggie that Arthur sent you. She won't give you a discount, but she may not overcharge you quite as much as she does the other tourists."

With Arthur's ambiguous recommendation, we got back in the car and set out for Lower Slaughter in pursuit of Ryan's much-anticipated snacks.

The village shop in Lower Slaughter was tidy and well-kept. It managed to be both useful for locals and appealing to tourists. The shelves held basics like washing powder, tinned beans, and toilet paper, alongside things for visitors: hand-painted biscuit tins, Cotswold honey with lavender, and tea towels with watercolour sheep.

Ryan made a direct beeline for the crisps section, his gastronomic radar unerringly guiding him toward potential snacks. Katrin followed with unexpected attentiveness, scrutinising ingredient lists with forensic intensity.

"This contains whey powder," she said, blocking his hand as he reached for the packet. "And this one uses milk-derived flavourings." She picked up another packet and angled it toward him, presenting the ingredient list. "This one is free from animal products and uses twenty-seven percent less packaging."

I was a little surprised. Katrin's attention to Ryan's food choices seemed more than just polite. It was almost protective.

While they paid for vegan snacks and drinks, I browsed the guidebook section and half-listened to their conversation with the woman at the till.

"You alright?" the shopkeeper asked Katrin as she began scanning their purchases.

Katrin stopped to reach for her wallet. She looked at me, clearly alarmed.

"Is something wrong?" Katrin asked. "Do I look unwell? Am I bleeding? A spider in my hair?"

The shopkeeper, a middle-aged woman, had the patient look of someone used to tourists from every nation. She kept scanning items with professional efficiency, though her eyebrows rose at Katrin's reaction.

Ryan stepped in, placing a gentle hand on Katrin's arm. "No, there isn't a spider, it's just a greeting," he explained. "Like saying 'hello' or 'good afternoon'. It doesn't actually mean she thinks something's wrong with you."

"But she asked about my well-being," Katrin said, confused.

"The correct response," Ryan continued in the patient tone of a language instructor, "is simply 'Yes, fine, thanks. And you?' It's not a medical inquiry; it's just how people say hello in many parts of Britain."

Katrin stared at him for a long moment, then turned back to the shopkeeper, who was now watching this exchange with the fascinated expression of someone witnessing an unexpected cultural demonstration in her own shop.

"Yes, fine, thank you," Katrin said carefully, as if reciting an unfamiliar phrase in a new language. "And... you? You... alright?"

"All good, ta," replied the shopkeeper, a smile tugging at her mouth. "That'll be twelve pounds fifty, love."

As Katrin paid, I noticed her free hand already reaching for her notebook, continuing the growing glossary of "British Phrases That Do Not Mean What They Say."

Ryan, already halfway through a packet of crisps, nodded

thoughtfully. "Wait until she discovers 'How do you do?' isn't actually a question," he murmured to me as we returned to the car. "That might be the final straw for German-British relations."

Our next destination was nothing but a sharply angled, grassy slope. The dizzying incline seemed tailor-made to snap bones – or perhaps send contestants tumbling after runaway wheels of cheese.

As we crested the final bend in the narrow country lane, Cooper's Hill's festival atmosphere hit us with almost physical force. Hundreds of spectators lined the treacherous hillside. Cheers and laughter carried on the breeze. The scent of crushed grass, spilt ale, and anticipation hung in the air like an intoxicating fog.

"My God," Katrin breathed, her normally composed features rearranging themselves into an expression of horrified fascination. "The angle of descent is approximately seventy degrees at its steepest point. This cannot possibly be safe for human locomotion."

Ryan, who had spent the drive from Lower Slaughter educating Katrin on the finer points of British greeting conventions, leaned forward between the front seats, his eyes widening with delight. "It's not meant to be safe," he explained, with the satisfied air of someone about to witness justified calamity. "That's rather the point."

I manoeuvred our car into one of the few remaining spaces in the makeshift car park. It was essentially a farmer's field, temporarily repurposed for the occasion. We joined the steady stream of spectators making their way toward the hill. The crowd was a curious mixture: locals who had attended the event since childhood; university students, armed equally with cameras and alcohol; and bewildered tourists, who had stumbled upon something far more perilous than their guidebooks implied.

As we claimed a viewing spot midway up the slope, Katrin asked, "So, explain to me again, why perfectly rational adults would voluntarily throw themselves down a near-vertical hill in pursuit of dairy products?"

"It's tradition," I offered, knowing this explanation would be wholly insufficient for Katrin's German sensibilities. "Cheese-rolling has been happening here for at least two hundred years, possibly longer. Some say it has pagan origins – a fertility ritual to encourage a good harvest."

Katrin opened her bag, took out her notebook, and held her pen above a fresh page. At the top, she wrote in her precise handwriting: "Mass Voluntary Injury Event (Cheese-Induced)."

"Fertility ritual," she repeated, writing it down. "Strange that farming and self-injury go together. Maybe it was meant as a sacrifice." She looked around, still making notes.

"Look at the physiological indications of pre-event anxiety," she murmured. She gestured toward the competitors, who were stretching, drinking, or simply staring down the hill. Their expressions ranged from bravado to naked terror. "Pupil dilation, excessive consumption of alcohol as courage-enhancement, ritualistic physical preparations for the activity about to be undertaken."

Ryan had disappeared briefly into the crowd, returning with cups of amber liquid which he offered to us with a flourish. "Local ale," he announced. "Seemed appropriate for the occasion."

I accepted my cup with thanks. Katrin eyed her own cup with suspicion, raised it to her nose, and carefully sniffed its contents before taking a cautious sip. Her eyebrows rose slightly – the Katrin equivalent of enthusiastic approval. She then made a small notation in her book, which I strongly suspected read, "Acceptable fermentation quality."

"The true madness," Ryan continued cheerfully, "is that it's not even about catching the cheese. The cheese gets a one-second head start and can reach speeds of seventy miles per hour. No human could possibly catch it. You're essentially throwing yourself down a cliff face in pursuit of an object that's already won the race before you've taken your first step."

Katrin frowned. "So what are they actually trying to win?"

"To be the first person to reach the bottom," I explained. "The cheese is essentially a symbol – though the winner does get to keep it."

"A nine-pound Double Gloucester," Ryan added, with the reverent tone of someone describing a religious artefact. "Aged for several months. Quite delicious, I'm told, though obviously not vegan-friendly."

A sudden hush fell over the crowd as the master of ceremonies took his position at the top of the hill. He was a local man in his sixties, wearing what appeared to be a cricket umpire's coat. In his hands, he cradled a perfect wheel of cheese, its waxy exterior catching the sunlight like some precious geological specimen. He raised it above his head to appreciative cheers from the spectators.

"The competitors in the first race, please!" he called, his voice carrying surprisingly well across the hillside.

About twenty young men gathered at the summit, forming a ragged line. Some dropped into the kind of starting stances you see in athletics – heads down, fingers splayed on the grass, eyes fixed on the imaginary tape ahead. Others swayed gently, their balance undermined by what looked and smelled like a bold dose of pre-race liquid courage. The gap in their preparations was obvious. A handful wore running shoes, shorts, and performance tops. The rest came straight from the pub, zipped into jeans and laced into trainers that had clearly seen more spilt ale than tarmac.

"They can't possibly be serious," Katrin whispered, her camera now raised, adjusted to capture what she clearly believed would be evidence of collective British insanity.

"I assure you, they are," I replied, just as the master of ceremonies began his countdown. "Women compete too, mind you. But in their own race, separate from the men's."

"Three... two... one..."

The cheese was released, a golden disc hurtling down the slope with blistering speed. A split-second later, competitors flung themselves after it – instantly becoming a cascade of thrashing limbs and piercing yelps. They merged into a writhing mass; any semblance of running was obliterated within metres. Gravity asserted its rule. Bodies pitched, spun, skidded, at times launched skyward before crashing back with bone-jarring impact.

Beside me, Katrin's camera clicked rapidly as she tracked competitors tumbling down the slope. Her face conveyed a mix of professional detachment and genuine horror. "Lateral tibial impact," she murmured, focusing on one unfortunate racer cartwheeled down. "Potential clavicular fracture on subject three. Definite posterior contusions on multiple participants," she added, her pen keeping pace in her notebook.

The first competitor reached the bottom – more through uncontrolled momentum than strategy – and was surrounded by St John Ambulance volunteers. They assessed his condition with the practised efficiency of those who had seen it all before. To my surprise, he stood up, bloodied but triumphant, clutching the now-battered cheese wheel above his head like a war trophy.

"He appears to be enjoying his potential spinal compression," Katrin observed with genuine bewilderment, making another note. "Endorphin response to trauma? Or culturally conditioned pain suppression?"

"Look," Ryan pointed halfway down the slope, where a young man had become entangled in the safety netting, his body contorted into a shape that suggested he might be auditioning for a position as a human pretzel. "That's going to leave a mark."

The St John Ambulance crew is impressively efficient," I noted as they extracted another competitor from a brutal landing. They treat dozens of injuries every year – mostly sprains, bruises, and the occasional concussion. Though there have also been broken bones.

Ryan sipped his ale contemplatively. "You know, it makes perfect sense when you think about it," he declared. "What better way to spend a day off than hurling yourself down a near-vertical slope? All for dairy products you'll probably be too injured to eat!"

"A perfectly sensible British pastime," I agreed with a smile.

"Ale-induced cultural delusion," Katrin muttered, photographing a competitor being stretchered away with what appeared to be a dislocated shoulder.

"Did you know," Ryan announced, "that Cooper's Hill cheese-rolling has been banned officially at least three times? And each time, locals would just show up and do it themselves. No official organiser, no permits, just people determined to hurl themselves down a hill after cheese."

The women's race started – just as chaotic as the first. A mix of pride and embarrassment washed over me; some British traditions always evoke this strange blend of feelings. Objectively, it was ridiculous and dangerous, yet the sheer persistence of it was strangely wonderful. Rejecting health and safety culture, it celebrated a time when risk assessment meant simply glancing down a hill and thinking, "I reckon I could roll down that."

I guided our car back through the narrow lanes snaking between Cotswold villages. At times, the navigation system faltered, faced with roads older than the Romans. Gentle waves of green countryside unfurled, punctuated by dry stone walls. Clusters of grazing sheep regarded our passing with magnificent indifference.

"Castle Combe," I explained as we drove, "has been called 'the most perfect village in England' so many times that it's become a cliché. Unlike most clichés, though, this one happens to be true. The village has remained almost completely unchanged since the 16th century."

"Another tourist village?" Katrin asked, looking up from her notes. "Like Bibury?"

"Much less crowded," I said. "And much better preserved. Castle Combe is in tons of period films because it barely needs set dressing to look authentically medieval."

The village appeared as we rounded a bend: stone cottages set in a wooded valley, their slate roofs catching the afternoon light. I parked at the small lot by the entrance, and we walked down the sloping main street.

Katrin stopped abruptly in the middle of the lane and turned in a slow circle, her expression one of growing bewilderment.

She looked from the perfect cottages, with their hanging baskets of flowers, to the immaculate market cross in the tiny square. Then, her gaze travelled upward, scanning the rooftops with increasingly furrowed brows.

"Where are the satellite dishes?" she asked. Her tone suggested she'd found a glitch in reality. "The solar panels? The television aerials? The electrical wires?" She pointed at the rooflines with an accusatory finger. "Every house in Germany has these things. Every house in every other British village we've visited has these things."

"They're banned," I said. "Castle Combe is a designated conservation area under some of the strictest preservation orders in the country. Modern alterations to exteriors are essentially barred."

"But how do people watch television? Access the internet? Generate renewable energy?" She gestured toward a particularly picturesque cottage with climbing roses framing its doorway. "These are functional dwellings, yes? Not film sets?"

"Real homes," I confirmed. "The modern amenities are all hidden. Satellite dishes are tucked into back gardens where they can't be seen from the street. Internet cables run underground. Solar panels are only permitted if they're completely invisible from public thoroughfares."

Katrin scrawled in her notebook with deliberate force. I caught the heading: "Excessive British Nostalgia – Impractical Devotion to Aesthetics over Utility."

"It's rather impressive, though, isn't it?" Ryan observed, admiring the flawless street view. "Like stepping into a time capsule. No ugly modern intrusions, just pure, preserved history."

As we continued past the market cross, a small group was gathering nearby. A young man in his late twenties stood addressing them with the practised charm of a professional guide. We drifted toward the group just as he was introducing himself.

"Welcome to Castle Combe," he announced with a warm smile that managed to appear genuine despite what must have been its thousandth iteration that week. "I'm Oliver, your guide for today's historical walking tour. We'll be exploring not just the architecture of what many call England's most perfect village, but also the social history that shaped it – from its medieval origins as a thriving wool town to its present-day life as a community that balances preservation with modern living."

Oliver Blackwood embodied a certain type of English charm. He was articulate and knowledgeable, but not pompous. Friendly, but never overbearing. He wore smart-casual attire that blended traditional elements – a tweed waistcoat – with modern style: dark jeans and boots. His wavy dark hair occasionally fell across his forehead, prompting a habitual motion of brushing it back with his hand. The gesture seemed to endear him to the two middle-aged American women at the front of the group, who exchanged appreciative glances each time he did it.

We joined the group of about a dozen tourists and followed Oliver through the village. He stopped at intervals to point out architectural details or share bits of history. He spoke with the confidence of someone who enjoyed his subject, not just repeating memorised facts.

The tour ended at the church lychgate, where Oliver gave his final remarks. As the group began to disperse, he invited us to join him for a drink at the pub, a 12th-century building that had served travellers since before the Magna Carta.

"It's quite traditional inside." Oliver's warm smile brightened the invitation. "Low beams that have been concussing tall visitors for eight centuries, and locally brewed ales that make the potential head injury entirely worthwhile."

Most of our fellow tourists nodded enthusiastically at this proposition. The two American women exchanged glances that suggested they found the guide as appealing as the historical architecture, while an elderly couple who had asked particularly insightful questions throughout the tour were already discussing which local beer they might sample. Ryan, predictably, had perked up at the mention of refreshments.

The Castle Inn matched expectations for a Cotswold pub: low ceilings, heavy oak beams, stone walls, and a large fireplace. Horse brasses and old farm tools hung on the walls. The landlord, used to tour groups, greeted Oliver with a familiar nod.

We sat at two tables near the fireplace, where a small fire warmed the room. We ordered drinks: local ale, cider, and green tea for Katrin and me. The tea arrived with more ceremony than expected. Ryan, after questioning the barman about the chips, ordered a plate for himself.

As the drinks arrived, conversation followed the usual pattern for British strangers. The weather was discussed in detail, its current state noted, and future prospects considered. This led to polite comments about the village, phrased to show appreciation without too much enthusiasm.

"The light here is quite remarkable." The American woman's tone was pleasant, her observation bland enough to be universally acceptable. "The way it catches the stone in the afternoon."

"Yes, quite lovely." The elderly gentleman nodded with measured approval. "Though we've been fortunate with the conditions today. Last Tuesday was rather overcast."

"The forecast suggests it might hold through the weekend," Oliver contributed, demonstrating the British ability to extend weather-based discussions indefinitely if social necessity requires it.

At precisely this moment – amidst the delicate, unspoken negotiation of conversational boundaries – Katrin set down her teacup. She launched herself directly into territory no British person would willingly enter without several years of acquaintance and, possibly, a signed confidentiality agreement.

"The accommodation prices in the Cotswolds are completely unreasonable since COVID," she announced in a clear, carrying tone. "Our B&B charges 175 pounds per night for a room that would cost 70 euros in Germany. The bathroom was small enough that one must sit sideways on the toilet to avoid knee contact with the shower door."

A silence fell over the table. The elderly couple paused with their glasses in mid-air. One of the American women coughed. Oliver kept smiling, though it looked more forced now.

Oblivious to the conversational rift she'd created, Katrin pressed on with her signature thoroughness. "And, of course,

Brexit has complicated everything for European visitors. Passport control took seventeen minutes longer than in my last visit in 2015."

The elderly couple exchanged a look, then finished their drinks and left, mentioning the need to get back before dark. A middle-aged couple who had said little during the tour followed soon after, citing dinner plans.

Undeterred by this exodus, Katrin turned her attention directly to Oliver, who was now staring into his half-empty glass as if contemplating diving into it headfirst.

"Are you married?" she inquired with the direct manner of someone conducting a census. "I noticed you do not wear a ring, but this is not definitive evidence of marital status."

Oliver's smile wavered momentarily, like a signal struggling through fog. "I, ah, no. Not married."

"Interesting," Katrin said, nodding as she made a small note in her book. "And what is the salary for a tour guide in the Cotswolds? Is it enough to purchase property in the area? The housing market here must be extremely competitive given the strict planning regulations and limited stock."

The remaining American women suddenly discovered urgent text messages that required their immediate attention. Within moments, they too had departed, leaving only our small group and Oliver, whose complexion now resembled the soft pink of the roses climbing the pub's exterior.

I reached out and touched Katrin's arm gently, leaning in so my words would be private. I whispered, "Perhaps we could discuss different topics? In Britain, certain subjects are considered private."

Katrin paused mid-sentence, her brow furrowing in confusion. She looked around at the now-empty tables surrounding us, then back to Oliver's strained expression, a dawning comprehension slowly replacing her usual analytical certainty.

"Have I violated another social protocol?" Katrin's voice lowered, but remained perfectly audible to everyone within a five-metre radius.

"Just a bit," Ryan said cheerfully, popping another chip into his mouth. "You've hit the unholy trinity of British conversational taboos in under five minutes. Quite impressive, really."

Oliver, demonstrating the remarkable resilience that must be a job requirement for anyone working in British tourism, managed to reclaim his professional equilibrium. "Not to worry at all," he assured Katrin with forced joviality. "It's just that we Brits tend to be a bit... reserved... about certain topics until we know each other better."

"Or until we're dead," Ryan added helpfully. "Whichever comes first."

We finished our drinks with strained politeness. The conversation was now confined to the safest topics: the age of the pub beams (ancient), the quality of the local ale (excellent), and the historical significance of Castle Combe (considerable). Oliver maintained his professional demeanour admirably. Still, I noticed his eyes occasionally darting toward the exit with the longing of a trapped animal sensing freedom.

As we walked back to the car, the afternoon sun cast long shadows across the immaculate village street. Katrin walked beside me, unusually quiet, her hands clasped tightly. Finally, as we reached the car park, she stopped and turned to me, genuine confusion on her face.

"I have caused social discomfort," she stated, not as a question but as a fact requiring verification.

"It's not your fault," I assured her, unlocking the car. "British social rules are unwritten and often illogical. But generally speaking, there are three subjects we avoid with people we've just met: politics, money, and personal questions."

"But these are precisely the topics that contain actual substantive information," Katrin protested as she slid into the back seat. "Weather patterns and comments about visible architectural features convey no meaningful data that isn't already apparent to all participants."

"That's the point, really," I said, settling back as the car shuddered out of its tight parking space. "Small talk doesn't exist for the actual words – it's a ritual, a sort of verbal handshake, laying down a bit of carpet so one can get acquainted comfortably. In Britain, the idea of talking about money or prying into a stranger's personal life feels like skipping several essential steps in a relationship."

Katrin was already documenting these insights in her notebook.

"Exactly," Ryan confirmed from the passenger seat, where he was already researching our next destination on his phone. "The weather isn't really the topic – it's just the vehicle for the actual communication, which is 'I am a non-threatening person willing to engage in meaningless exchange to make you comfortable.'"

"Highly inefficient," Katrin concluded, closing her notebook with a decisive snap. "But I will adapt to the protocol."

As we pulled away from Castle Combe, its perfect medieval silhouette receding in the rear-view mirror, I couldn't help but smile at Katrin's determined expression. She had approached British social customs with the same methodical thoroughness she applied to everything – analysing, categorising, and preparing to adapt with German efficiency to our peculiar island ways.

The journey to High Wycombe carried an unmistakable air of conclusion – a peculiar blend of satisfied fatigue and faint melancholy. It's the feeling that lingers at the end of any worthwhile adventure. Katrin's immaculate suitcase, already packed that morning, waited in the boot of our electric car. It was a silent reminder that our trio would soon become a duo again. In the weeks since she had joined us, Katrin documented British peculiarities with the thoroughness of a Victorian naturalist cataloguing exotic species. Today would be her final opportunity to complete her extensive taxonomy of our national eccentricities.

"Google Maps says left in two hundred metres," Katrin announced. "Given British roads, I'd say there's a sixty-seven percent chance of error."

Ryan twisted in the passenger seat to face her. "I'll miss your statistical approach to absolutely everything, Katrin. My life will feel distressingly imprecise without you."

The tea room appeared accurately where the navigation system had predicted – a small miracle that Katrin noted in her book with a satisfied nod. The building, a converted Victorian townhouse, had eschewed the shabby-chic aesthetic that plagued many such establishments in favour of genuine period charm. Bay windows overlooked a modest garden where summer roses nodded gently in the breeze, and a hand-painted sign above the door announced "The Duchess's Secret" in an elegant cursive that somehow managed to suggest both exclusivity and welcome.

Inside, it smelled of fresh baking and Ceylon tea. White tablecloths covered the tables, spaced out and tidy. Someone played the piano quietly in the corner.

"Afternoon Tea for three, please," Katrin said as the waitress approached, giving us a proud look – as if to ensure we noted her progress since Highclere Castle.

"Very good," the waitress replied with a small bow of her head. "Would you prefer the window table or perhaps something more private toward the back?"

We selected the window seat, settling ourselves as the waitress departed to prepare our order. Katrin placed her camera bag on an empty chair and surveyed the room with the analytical gaze I had come to recognise as her data-gathering expression.

"Excellent consistency," Katrin observed. "No anachronisms. Genuine Wedgwood china. Very authentic."

Not long after, the three-tiered stand arrived, and I watched Katrin put her new Afternoon Tea skills into practice. She laid her napkin on her lap, picked a finger sandwich from the bottom tier, and took a careful bite without dropping a crumb. She'd clearly done her homework.

It was as we were progressing to the scone tier that I noticed the woman at the neighbouring table. She sat alone. Her posture was impeccable; her appearance meticulously arranged down to the last detail. Her brown hair was styled in a professional bob, somehow appearing both fashionable and appropriate for a woman in her early fifties. She wore a perfectly tailored navy suit that whispered of discreet expense rather than shouting it. A string of pearls caught the light whenever she moved.

What caught my attention was her behaviour. Though she had a full Afternoon Tea before her, she eyed it with conflicted desire. After a quick check in a compact mirror, she reached for a plain scone, assembled it with care, and took a small bite, visibly uneasy and setting it down after two nibbles. Her eyes glanced around the room as if anticipating judgment.

Katrin had noticed my attention wandering and followed my gaze. "The woman appears to be experiencing significant food anxiety," she observed in a voice that, while lowered, was still perfectly audible to anyone within three metres. "Her body language suggests conflict between desire and restriction. Classic disordered eating patterns."

"Let's discuss this later," I said, smiling apologetically at the woman.

To my surprise, the woman returned my smile. "Your friend is quite observant. And correct. I'm losing this tea stand battle."

"It's a challenging opponent," I agreed, warming to her humorous reply. "I'm Brianna, by the way. This is Ryan, and our friend Katrin is visiting from Germany."

"Victoria Pembroke," she replied, inclining her head slightly. "How lovely to meet you all."

Ryan, who had been surreptitiously checking his phone beneath the table, suddenly looked up with renewed interest. "Pembroke? As in the incoming Mayor of High Wycombe?"

Victoria raised an eyebrow, clearly impressed. "You're very well-informed about local politics."

"I just googled you, actually," Ryan admitted with characteristic honesty. "Your photo's on the town council website. Though I must say, you're much more glamorous in person than in your official portrait."

Victoria laughed, a genuine sound that momentarily replaced her careful composure with something more relaxed. "Council photographers specialise in making one look simultaneously constipated and menacing. It's a particular talent."

Katrin opened her notebook. "As Mayor, what are your responsibilities?"

Victoria seemed momentarily taken aback by Katrin's directness, but recovered quickly. "Mostly ceremonial, to be honest. Opening fêtes, attending functions, chairing council meetings. We're rather big on tradition in High Wycombe."

"Speaking of tradition," Ryan interjected, scrolling through his phone, "does High Wycombe still do that thing with the scales? The public weighing ceremony for mayors?"

Victoria's carefully composed expression flickered for just a moment. Her hand moved, almost involuntarily, to smooth her already immaculate jacket. "Yes, indeed," she replied. Her voice maintained its pleasant tone, though I suspected it was with considerable effort. "One of England's more unusual civic traditions. The Mayor is weighed at the beginning and end of their term of office."

"Fascinating," Katrin scribbled in her notebook. "Why is this tradition kept?"

"It dates back to the medieval period," Victoria explained, her fingers now fidgeting slightly with her napkin. "The idea was to ensure that the Mayor wasn't growing fat at taxpayers' expense during their year in office. If you gained weight, the crowd would boo and jeer – a public shaming for abusing your position for personal gain."

"It's public?" Katrin clarified, pen paused.

Victoria nodded, glancing at her watch with a barely disguised flash of anxiety. "Completely public. Right in the town centre, with a crowd of spectators." She attempted a light laugh. "Rather barbaric when you think about it – a public weigh-in with hundreds watching. Mine's scheduled for next Thursday at eleven, actually."

The tension in Victoria's voice was unmistakable now. I noticed her eyes drifting back to the untouched pastries on her stand, while Ryan remained oblivious to her discomfort, already deep into a Google search about the history of public weighings.

"Do they use historical scales?" he asked eagerly. "Like those big beam balance things with weights on one side?"

"Yes," Victoria confirmed, her smile strained. "The same old scales, only used for this event." She glanced at her watch. "It's nerve-wracking, I admit."

Victoria tapped her fingers on the table, then folded her hands and tried to smile. "Listen to me, fretting about a silly weigh-in like a teenager before prom. I'm not really made for being in the spotlight. I'm more rhino than Bambi – not exactly the delicate mayoress people might expect."

Ryan glanced up. "Rhinos are magnificent – endangered, strong, great skin. That's a compliment."

"I've tried seventeen diets since my nomination and lasted about half an hour on each," Victoria admitted. "My willpower is like a toddler – easily distracted and temperamental."

Katrin's brow furrowed as she listened, her pen paused above her notebook. Victoria, encouraged by our attention, kept going with her self-mocking stories.

"I've tried everything – that peculiar diet where you only eat foods of a single colour each day, the one where you consume nothing but soup for a fortnight, even that bizarre Hollywood regimen involving baby food." She rolled her eyes expressively. "I'm absolutely useless at looking even half as elegant as a Mayor ought to. My personal trainer has threatened to resign twice, claiming I'm that particular client who gains muscle mass only in her biscuit arm."

"Biscuit arm?" I inquired, unable to resist.

"The arm used for opening biscuit tins," Victoria said mock seriously. "My best muscle."

Ryan laughed. I glanced at Katrin, noting how she had gone from confusion to genuine worry. Katrin watched Victoria's hands intently, as if trying to reconcile the confident woman in front of us with the way she talked about herself.

Victoria leaned in. "Truth is, I'm addicted to midnight chocolate. The corner shop must think I'm running a confectionery ring. The weigh-in will reveal all – I'm more representative for Cadbury's than model Mayor."

At that, Katrin closed her notebook with a snap, making Victoria stop mid-sentence. Katrin sat up straighter.

"This is unacceptable," she declared with quiet intensity.

Victoria blinked, clearly uncertain whether she had somehow caused offence. "I'm sorry?"

"Your negative self-assessment is both inaccurate and psychologically harmful," Katrin continued, her German accent becoming more pronounced as it tended to do when she was particularly emotionally involved. "You appear to be a healthy weight with normal body composition. These extreme measures you describe are unnecessary and potentially dangerous."

The conversation stopped. Victoria looked at Katrin, half confused and half amused.

"I recommend a balanced approach," Katrin forged ahead, completely missing the social abyss opening beneath her feet. "Vitamin D supplementation has been shown to support metabolic function, particularly in the British climate where sunlight exposure is insufficient for natural synthesis. I can suggest an excellent German fitness application with scientifically validated protocols for maintaining optimal health without extreme dietary restriction."

Victoria stared at her, momentarily speechless, as Katrin unlocked her phone and began scrolling through it with efficient thumb movements.

"Additionally," Katrin continued, "there are effective psychological techniques for improving body image that do not involve self-denigration. The constant negative commentary you direct toward yourself creates neural pathways that reinforce–"

"I think," Victoria interrupted gently, her social training finally overcoming her surprise, "that perhaps I've given you the wrong impression. I apologise for misleading you; I was just making a bit of a joke, you know. Having a good laugh about myself."

Katrin looked up, bewildered. "But you called yourself a rhinoceros, your willpower a child's, and described yourself as 'absolutely useless' with a chocolate problem. Those aren't jokes."

An awkward silence descended upon our table, thick enough to slice and serve with clotted cream. Victoria and Katrin stared at each other across a cultural gap wider than the English Channel, mutual incomprehension rendering them temporarily mute. Ryan caught my eye, his expression silently communicating that the situation required my intervention before Katrin potentially offered to create a personalised nutrition spreadsheet for the future Mayor of High Wycombe.

"I think," I said smoothly, "that we're witnessing one of those fascinating cultural differences that make international friendships so enriching." I turned to Katrin with a gentle smile. "In Britain, self-deprecation – joking or speaking humorously about one's own flaws – is a form of social etiquette. The more accomplished the person, the more they're expected to downplay their achievements and exaggerate their flaws. It's not meant to be taken literally."

Katrin's expression shifted from confusion to dawning comprehension. "This is another example of British statements that mean the opposite of their literal content," she clarified, reopening her notebook. "Like when someone says 'I'm fine' but actually means they are experiencing significant emotional distress."

"Exactly," I confirmed. "The more Victoria disparages herself, the more it signals to other British people that she's confident enough to joke about her insecurities. It's a complex social code."

Katrin, pen poised, said, "So when a Brit claims to be 'absolutely useless,' it actually signals modesty rather than a lack of self-confidence?"

Victoria, who had been following this exchange with growing amusement, nodded. "Precisely. If I were truly concerned about my appearance, I'd probably say something like 'I've been trying to eat a bit healthier lately' while looking perfectly calm."

"The greater the claimed inadequacy, the less it is actually believed," Katrin murmured, making a note.

Ryan chuckled. "In Britain, clarity is considered somehow vulgar. We prefer to navigate through layers of irony, understatement, and self-mockery. It keeps things interesting."

"And confusing," Katrin added, writing with renewed vigour. She had started a fresh page with the heading "British Self-Negation Protocols".

Victoria watched this documentation with evident fascination. "I never realised how strange our communication style must seem to outsiders," she admitted. "It's rather like speaking a second language that uses all the same words as the first, but with entirely different meanings."

"The vocabularies are identical, but the semantic frameworks are incompatible," Katrin agreed, appearing relieved to have identified the source of the misunderstanding. She turned to Victoria with newfound clarity. "So you do not actually believe you resemble a rhinoceros?"

"Good heavens, no," Victoria laughed. "Though I maintain that rhinos are magnificent creatures."

"And your relationship with chocolate is within normal parameters?"

"Well," Victoria said with a wink, "I wouldn't go that far."

I glanced at my watch, surprised we'd spent nearly two hours dissecting the finer points of British social conventions. The tea had grown cold in our cups. The remaining pastries sat neglected. Afternoon light had shifted to that golden quality that signals the day's slow surrender. "I'm afraid we need to be making tracks," I announced, reluctantly interrupting Victoria and Katrin's surprisingly animated discussion about cultural communication differences. "We're due in Brighton to meet our next photography student."

Victoria's expression shifted from animated to polite disappointment. "What a shame. I've quite enjoyed this unexpected cultural exchange." She extended a perfectly manicured hand toward Katrin. "Thank you for the vitamin D recommendation. Perhaps it will help me face the scales with more confidence."

Victoria gathered her belongings and bid us farewell, promising to look up Katrin's recommended fitness app. I watched with quiet amusement as our German companion began the methodical process of preparing for departure.

"Your organisation puts Marie Kondo to shame," Ryan remarked with a grin. He watched as Katrin placed her notebook, pens, and camera lenses into their correct compartments inside her bag.

"I am unfamiliar with this Kondo person," Katrin replied, not looking up, "but efficiency in packing is not a competitive activity."

I smiled, already missing the way Katrin took Ryan's comments at face value. Her lists of British oddities had shifted from scientific record to a fond, if still puzzled, catalogue of our national quirks.

Ryan approached the counter to settle our bill, extracting his phone with characteristic enthusiasm. "I don't suppose you accept BitSprout?" he asked the waitress, his expression hopeful. "It's a vegan cryptocurrency. Completely plant-based blockchain. Each transaction plants a virtual tree that becomes a real tree when enough people water it digitally."

The waitress stared at him with blank indifference. "We accept only cash," she replied flatly after a moment, gesturing toward a handwritten sign that stated the card reader is out of order.

Ryan turned to us with a helpless shrug. "I think I've got about forty-seven pence in actual coinage," he admitted.

Katrin's expression brightened considerably. She reached into her handbag and extracted the same large-denomination note she had attempted to use at Highclere Castle. "I can pay with this," she declared triumphantly, presenting the note with a flourish that suggested she was finally able to deploy a long-thwarted weapon.

The owner accepted it with a nod, making change from an ancient cash register that produced mechanical clanking sounds reminiscent of Victorian engineering. Katrin received her coins with a pleased expression, as if her worldview had been momentarily validated.

We stepped outside into the late afternoon sunshine. The air carried that peculiar English blend – exhaust fumes, municipal planting, and the indefinable scent that presages early evening. The High Street stretched before us. Its medieval layout remained utterly unconvinced by centuries of modern traffic management.

Katrin straightened her jacket and looked at us, earnest and a little sad. It was time to say goodbye.

"Thank you for guiding me through British cultural practices," she said, extending her hand with the formality of a diplomat. "Your insights will help as I continue exploring."

I accepted her handshake. "It's been our pleasure," I replied, meaning it sincerely. "You've made us see our own country through fresh eyes."

Katrin turned to Ryan, offering a small, precise nod that acknowledged their shared journey without requiring physical contact. "Your explanations of British humour patterns have been most illuminating, if occasionally confusing. I now understand seventeen percent more of your jokes than when we first met," she stated.

Ryan clutched his chest in mock offence. "Only seventeen percent? I've been operating at peak wit just for you!" he protested.

"That was a joke," Katrin deadpanned. "My attempt at British humour. I learned."

Ryan and I exchanged glances, both a little startled and then unexpectedly touched. That had to be the first time Katrin deployed her freshly minted sense of British irony – a subtle triumph in our cultural exchange.

"Safe travels," I said, shouldering my camera bag. "Do stay in touch."

"WhatsApp messages are acceptable," she nodded. "Though I prefer email for detailed communications. Less prone to misinterpretation."

Ryan and I turned toward our car, the moment of departure having arrived with its inevitable awkwardness. We had taken perhaps five steps when Katrin's voice called after us, her usual measured tone slightly elevated.

"Wait."

We turned to find her exactly where we'd left her, her expression uncharacteristically uncertain. She took three precise steps forward. Then, in a movement so unexpected it stunned us, she opened her arms and briefly embraced me, then Ryan.

"Thank you for the wonderful days," she said, voice muffled against my shoulder. As she pulled back, her cheeks flushed pink in a fleeting moment of embarrassment.

"Have I now breached another unspoken British protocol by displaying public affection?" she asked somewhat hesitantly. "But honestly, right now I don't care. I just want you to know how much I enjoyed myself, and that I'll miss you both."

For a moment, none of us spoke. The days of shared experiences seemed to hang in the air between us, a silent acknowledgement of connections formed through mutual bewilderment and growing understanding.

Then, as if needing to reclaim her composure, Katrin straightened and gestured toward the town centre with a brisk, professional movement. "But why must every old city have such an illogical one-way street system? It defies all sense of order! The route to my accommodation requires seven unnecessary turns. A direct path exists, but it's forbidden by arbitrary directional restrictions."

Ryan burst into laughter, the tension of farewell broken by this quintessentially Katrin observation. "And here I thought we'd corrupted you with our British chaos."

"Never," she replied warmly, the hint of a smile playing at the corners of her mouth. "Though I have made a separate notebook for 'Inexplicable British Practices That Function Despite Their Irrationality.' It is quite thick already."

With a final wave, she marched toward the town centre, notebook in hand. We watched her go, both of us smiling, amused and fond of her steadfast precision.

"Brighton then?" Ryan prompted, turning toward our car.

"Brighton," I agreed. I glanced back at Katrin. She now paused to photograph an illogical traffic sign. "I think I'm going to miss her."

A FRENCH IN SOUTH EAST ENGLAND

I am always amazed by how Brighton manages to be simultaneously regal and rakish, elegant and eccentric. The Grand Hotel, with its cream-coloured Victorian façade facing the Channel, stood like an imposing dowager. It showed the city's dignified side. As we pulled our car into the valet area, I caught Ryan eyeing the building with his usual mix of admiration and mild anxiety, the kind expensive places provoked in him.

"Bit posh, isn't it?" he murmured, tugging self-consciously at his rumpled shirt. "I feel like I should have ironed... well, anything."

"Our new student insisted," I said, retrieving my camera bag from the boot. "Apparently, staying anywhere less than four stars constitutes a human rights violation in her book."

The lobby enveloped us in a cocoon of understated luxury. Muted lighting, plush upholstery, and the gentle tinkling of a piano created an atmosphere where time moved more languidly. The air carried the faint scent of lilies and expensive perfume. It was a marked contrast to the musty, tea-and-dog aroma that had characterised many of our Cotswold accommodations.

We settled into a pair of elegantly curved armchairs. My practical hiking boots looked decidedly out of place against the pristine cream carpet. Ryan immediately began scrolling through his phone, while I consulted my watch with growing frequency.

"Thirty minutes late," I remarked as the hotel's ornate clock struck the half-hour. "Katrin would have had an aneurysm by now."

"Katrin would have arrived forty-five minutes early and reorganised the reception desk filing system while waiting," Ryan replied without looking up from his screen. "I miss her already. Her horrified expression when confronted with British inefficiency was becoming the highlight of my day."

I smiled, glancing down for a moment as a twinge of fondness for our departed German companion crossed my face.

"Fleur Rousseau," Ryan read from his phone, "award-winning fashion photographer from Lyon, specialising in avant-garde portraiture... Oh, look, she did that famous Vogue shoot with the models posed as quantum physics concepts. Quite brilliant, actually."

"And quite late," I added, though without any real irritation. Where Katrin's orderliness could feel relentless, Fleur's disregard for schedules was rebellious – almost invigorating after so much precision.

It was at precisely that moment that Fleur Rousseau made her entrance. And an entrance it undoubtedly was, rather than a mere arrival.

She descended the grand staircase with the deliberate grace of someone who knew she was being observed and had no intention of disappointing her audience. Her dark bobbed hair caught the light with each step, swinging with precision. It seemed cut by mathematical calculations rather than by mere scissors. She wore a perfectly tailored black jumpsuit that was both avant-garde and classic, accessorised with a single, dramatic scarlet scarf. It fluttered behind her like a personal wind machine effect.

I looked down at what I was wearing: practical trousers still showing signs of our Cotswold trip, a wrinkled linen shirt for comfort, and old hiking boots. The difference between us couldn't have been more obvious.

"Ah, there you are," Fleur called, spotting us. "Brianna and Ryan, yes? Enchantée." She extended both hands in a greeting that felt more suited to a film premiere than a business meeting.

"We were just–" I began, but Fleur had already launched into speech, her English impeccable but emphatically French in its musicality.

"This hotel," she announced, gesturing expansively, "is adequate, though the pillows lack proper structure. But the bathroom – mon Dieu!" Her hands flew upward in a gesture of magnificent despair. "What is this British peculiarity? The taps?"

Ryan nodded enthusiastically. "The separate hot and cold?"

"Precisely!" Fleur seized upon his understanding with evident relief. "It is barbaric! Either I freeze my hands like a fisherman in the North Sea, or I scald them as if preparing lobster. There is no civilised middle temperature." She demonstrated with her elegant hands, moving them rapidly between imaginary taps, her expression shifting from exaggerated shock to theatrical pain.

"I suppose mixer taps would be more practical," I agreed, biting back a smile at her passionate denouncement of British plumbing.

Ryan was already tapping at his phone. "The separate tap system dates back to Victorian plumbing regulations. Something about preventing contamination between potable and non-potable water supplies."

Fleur waved away this historical context with an elegant flick of her wrist. "History is no excuse for suffering. The Victorians also thought arsenic made excellent wallpaper. We have evolved past this, non?"

Before either of us could respond, Fleur pivoted to her next grievance, her body language transforming to communicate a fresh outrage. "And the sockets – where are the sockets in the British bathroom? How does one achieve the perfect coiffure when forced to style one's hair in the bedroom, away from the mirror, like some kind of primitive camping experience?"

She patted her immaculate hairstyle, which showed no evidence of the hardships she described. "This," she declared, gesturing to her head, "was created under conditions of extreme adversity. In France, our bathrooms are temples of self-care, with proper lighting and electrical access. Here, it's as if beauty is considered suspicious – something to be hidden away, perhaps performed in a dark cupboard while apologising."

I caught Ryan's eye over Fleur's shoulder and saw him struggling to maintain a serious expression. "Britain does have rather strict rules about electrical outlets in bathrooms," he said, looking up from his phone. "Safety concerns about water and electricity mixing. Though I see your point about the inconvenience."

"Safety!" Fleur repeated, as if the concept were an obscure philosophical position she found intellectually interesting but practically irrelevant. "The French have managed to blow-dry their hair for decades without mass electrocution. It is a risk we accept for beauty."

As Fleur kept up her dramatic complaints about British bathrooms, I had to hide a smile. The difference between her and Katrin was clear. Katrin studied our quirks with careful notes, while Fleur reacted with big gestures and stories. Both were confused, but in their own ways.

The contrast couldn't have been more perfect. We had farewelled our German friend, only to immediately encounter her temperamental opposite. Both were Europeans. Both were brilliantly talented in their fields. And both were utterly bewildered by the strange island nation they found themselves in. It was going to be an interesting few days.

The Brighton seafront promenade spread before us like an architectural timeline. Victorian grandeur gave way to Regency elegance. Art Deco boldness followed, with occasional modernist intrusions. All faced the eternal grey-blue of the English Channel with varying confidence. Fleur walked slightly ahead. Her perfect silhouette drew appreciative glances from passing locals. Ryan trailed behind us, his attention split between his phone's navigation app and the compact drone case slung over his shoulder.

"The light here is different," Fleur observed, pausing to frame an imaginary shot with her elegant hands. "It has a clarity, yes? A certain British crispness that we don't have in Lyon. Though of course, the French light has superior warmth and character."

I smiled at her instinct to affirm French superiority, even while recognising Brighton's unique light. The low afternoon sun cast long shadows and gilded the seafront in a soft golden glow.

"Look," Ryan called suddenly, pointing toward the eastern end of the promenade. "Something's happening over there."

At first, I thought he simply wanted to divert us from his ongoing struggle with the drone's online manual. But when I looked over, I spotted an odd crowd near the Palace Pier.

"How strange," I murmured as we drew closer. "This looks like the Burning the Clocks parade, but that's a winter solstice event in December."

We approached the growing assembly. Adults and children carried handmade paper lanterns in shapes of clocks, stars, moons, and suns. Each glowed from within, lit by LED lights instead of candles. This safety concession didn't lessen their ethereal beauty.

"What is this bizarre paper parade?" Fleur asked, brow arched in obvious curiosity.

Before I could answer, a woman in her thirties with cropped hair and an official-looking clipboard approached us with a welcoming smile. "Hello there! Here to watch the Summer Solstice Clocks?"

"I thought Burning the Clocks was a winter event." I met her gaze, still puzzled.

"It is," she confirmed. "This is a special summer edition we've organised to raise funds for the Royal Alexandra Children's Hospital. Same concept as December – handmade paper lanterns, community procession, symbolic burning, but with fewer layers of clothing and much less hypothermia." She grinned. "We're calling it 'Lighting the Clocks' instead of burning them, just to differentiate."

Ryan had already unzipped his drone case, his expression that of a child on Christmas morning. "Would it be all right if I captured some aerial footage? I've got all the proper certifications," he added hastily, producing a laminated card from his wallet with the speed of someone frequently asked to prove their credentials.

"That would be lovely," the organiser replied. "Just keep it below fifty metres and away from the actual burning area later on. Health and safety would get a nervous breakdown otherwise."

While Ryan prepared the drone, I noticed Fleur standing

apart, watching the crowd with unexpected intensity.

"This commitment to charity," she said, her voice softer than I'd yet heard it, "it is so... British. In France, we have many festivals, but they are for tradition and pleasure, not so often for others." She gestured at a family group working together on an elaborate lantern shaped like an astronomical clock. "And they make these by hand? For no personal gain?"

"It's part of the charm," I explained, watching Ryan's drone rise into the air. It hovered like an anxious parent before gaining confidence and ascending to capture the spectacle. "The lanterns represent the passing of time. In winter, it's about letting go of the year and looking forward to the light returning. For this summer version, I suppose it celebrates the height of light – and maybe hopes for an actual British summer."

"Hope dies last," Ryan called over his shoulder, his face lit by the drone's control screen. "Though hoping for reliable British sunshine may be wishful thinking – almost as bold as trusting the Channel Tunnel to run on time during a bank holiday."

The procession began to form – a snaking line of glowing paper sculptures moved like a luminous river through the dusk. Musicians played acoustic guitars, hand drums, and recorders. Their gentle soundtrack somehow avoided the usual discordance.

"The whole thing ends on the beach," I explained as we walked with the procession. "Traditionally, they burn the lanterns as a symbol of letting go."

"Isn't that rather wasteful?" Fleur said, her eyes lingering on the handmade lanterns, the usual judgment missing from her tone. "All this work, just to destroy it?"

"That's the point." I offered a gentle smile. "Impermanence makes it meaningful. Like a sand mandala or cherry blossoms – beauty that exists briefly, then returns to the elements."

Ryan's drone hovered above us, capturing the trail of light winding toward the beach. He followed behind, focused on both his controls and the path. Occasionally, he stumbled over uneven paving stones, never taking his eyes from the screen.

As we approached the beach, the procession slowed, participants gathering in a wide circle around a metal fire pit that had been set up just above the tide line. The organiser we'd spoken to earlier stood on a small platform, using a megaphone to direct the assembled crowd.

"Welcome to our first-ever Summer Solstice Clocks event," she announced. "Thank you all for coming and for your generous donations. Together, we've raised over eight thousand pounds for the children's hospital!"

A cheer rose from the crowd, and Fleur looked genuinely impressed. "Eight thousand? Just from this?"

"British people are remarkably generous when it comes to children's charities," I explained. "It's one of our better national traits."

As the organiser continued her speech, a small girl, perhaps six or seven, approached Fleur, clutching a tiny paper lantern shaped like a simple clock face. With the solemn dignity of a child on an important mission, she extended it toward the French photographer.

"For you," she said simply. "Mummy made extra."

Fleur froze, clearly unprepared for this interaction. For a moment, I thought she might refuse – maintaining her role as the sophisticated observer rather than participant. But something in the child's earnest expression seemed to reach her. With surprising gentleness, she accepted the lantern, bending slightly to meet the girl's eye level.

"Merci beaucoup, petite," she said softly. "It is very beautiful."

The child beamed and rejoined her mother. Fleur examined the modest paper creation with an expression I couldn't quite decipher – something between bewilderment and unexpected emotion.

When the signal came for lantern bearers to move forward, Fleur surprised me by quietly stepping away from our group. She cradled her gifted lantern and slipped into the line of participants making their way to the fire pit. Though her striking appearance set her apart from the other families, Fleur blended in smoothly as she walked with them, her steps steady and her focus wholly on the processional ritual.

As darkness settled fully over Brighton beach, people placed the lanterns one by one into the fire pit. Their paper structures caught quickly. The lanterns transformed from solid objects to curling flames, then to ash and memory. Fleur held her small clock lantern for a moment before releasing it into the fire. She watched it burn with an intensity that suggested she was seeing beyond the transformation. Perhaps, she was understanding, in some small way, the peculiar British magic of creating beauty specifically to release it.

We decided to take a nightcap in The Railway Arms. The pub blared its theme with a foghorn. Surfaces overflowed with relics of Britain's railway heritage. Signal lanterns dangled from beams. Framed 1950s timetables lined the wood-panelled walls. Tables, crafted from carriage doors, gleamed with brass in the dim light. Even the bar arched like a platform, with spirits stacked on a rack mimicking a Victorian departure board. It was a haven for true train obsessives and a masterclass in immersive design.

"Mon Dieu," Fleur murmured, her eyes pausing on a glass-encased station master's hat before shifting to a collection of vintage railway company logos rendered in stained glass behind the bar. She shook her head slightly, lips pursed in amused disbelief. "The British and their... how do you say... fixations?"

"Obsessions," I supplied helpfully. "And yes, we do tend to take our themes rather seriously."

Ryan had already moved across the room and positioned himself beneath a framed map of the pre-Beeching British railway network. His expression shifted to one of nostalgic reverence as he reached up and traced a vanished branch line with his finger. "It's magnificent," he declared. "Look at all these connections that don't exist anymore. The country was actually properly connected back then."

Fleur blinked, her eyebrows tucked into a neat question mark. "Pre-Beeching? Was that some kind of vicious storm?"

Ryan let out a low chuckle. "You could call it that. Back in the 1960s, there was this Dr Richard Beeching, right? His solution to making the UK railways pay was to cut great swathes of them away. He axed a load of rural lines, just like that. They even called it the Beeching Axe. People didn't love it, as you can imagine. Cities still got their trains, but out in the countryside? Forget it. Trains are a rare species now. Sometimes they put on buses, but they're about as regular as blue moons. If you live properly rural, you basically need a car to get anywhere. Not great for the planet, come to think of it..."

Fleur nodded, lips pursed. "Ah. In France, we never went quite so far with closing the lines. Not all or nothing, like you Brits. When you do something, you really do it, don't you?"

The evening crowd presented a curious mix. Some tourists wandered in, eyes scanning the decor with obvious fascination. Others, tired commuters, slouched at tables, seeking liquid consolation after daily rail-based tribulations. Among the latter, one man drew my attention for the way his immaculate posture contrasted with his otherwise exhausted demeanour.

He sat alone at a small table with a half-empty pint. Sometimes he glanced at his smartphone, scrolling through messages. At other times, he opened his leather notebook and wrote a few quick notes, tapping his pen against the page in thought. Tiredness showed in the lines on his face, but he still sat up straight, as if he knew slouching would only make the day feel worse. His tailored suit had a few creases and signs of wear. It was proof that his day had lasted longer than the designer had expected.

As we approached the bar to order drinks, the man glanced up. His gaze met mine with the quick, impersonal acknowledgement city people use to avoid conversation in crowded spaces. My obviously outdoorsy appearance made him look again, this time with a flicker of interest.

"Not from around here, I take it?" he offered as Ryan attempted to decipher the railway-themed cocktail menu ("The Delayed Departure" appeared to be a gin and tonic with "signal failure bitters").

"Just visiting," I confirmed. "I'm Brianna, this is Ryan, and our friend Fleur is from France."

"Richard Whitman," he replied with a nod that managed to be both economical and perfectly polite. "Though most people around here know me as 'that poor bastard on the 7:15 to Victoria.'"

This introduction, delivered with the dry precision of someone stating a meteorological fact, immediately endeared him to me. I recognised in his tone the particularly British blend of stoicism and irony that serves as our national emotional coping mechanism.

"Would you mind if we joined you?" I asked. "We're documenting different aspects of British life, and you've just identified yourself as a commuter, which is definitely on our list."

"By all means," Richard replied, gesturing to the empty chairs at his table. "Though I should warn you that commuter stories are like holiday photos – fascinating to those who lived through them, mind-numbing to everyone else."

Once we had our drinks – local ale for me, something vegan-friendly for Ryan, and red wine for Fleur, who accepted it with the look of someone making the best of limited choices – we joined Richard at his table.

"So, you commute to London?" Ryan prompted.

Richard took a measured sip of his beer before answering. "Three hours round trip, five days a week. Up at 5:30 AM to catch the 7:15 from Brighton to Victoria. Home by 8 PM if the trains are running properly, which is approximately as reliable as British summer weather."

He delivered this information without complaint or drama. He simply stated the parameters of his daily existence. His phone displayed a real-time train tracking app, which he checked out of habit. He had learned that, however distressing, information is preferable to uncertainty.

"Tuesday was actually quite good," he continued, checking his notebook. "Only seventeen minutes late. Monday was the usual chaos – signal failure at Haywards Heath, stuck for forty minutes just close enough to London to see the skyline but not actually arrive."

Fleur, who had been listening with increasing dismay, set down her wine glass with a sudden motion that drew our notice. "Three hours? Every day? C'est fou! This is madness!" she exclaimed. "You spend fifteen hours each week just... travelling?"

"Fifteen hours on a good week," Richard corrected with a small, mirthless smile. "More typically, seventeen to eighteen, accounting for delays. Today was particularly exciting – a 'passenger incident' at Gatwick meant we all got to enjoy an impromptu tour of the rarely-used Redhill loop line."

"But why?" Fleur persisted, her French directness cutting through the layers of British understatement. "Why not live closer to your work?"

Richard's face showed this was a question he'd mulled over many long journeys, staring at the rain-streaked countryside. "The maths is simple but harsh," he said. "A comparable job in Brighton pays about forty percent less. A similar home in London costs roughly eighty percent more." He spread his hands in resignation. "The choice is simple: long commute or no mortgage."

"It's become a defining feature of English life," I added, noting Fleur's continued bewilderment. "As property prices in London have skyrocketed, people have been forced further and further out, creating these 'commuter belt' towns. Brighton's actually a good example – plenty of Londoners here."

Ryan nodded. "The South East of England has essentially become one giant suburb of London, connected by increasingly expensive and unreliable train services."

Richard's expression brightened slightly, the way enthusiasts do when their specialist subject arises. "The Brighton Main Line is particularly interesting from an infrastructure perspective," he began, straightening almost imperceptibly. "Originally built in the 1840s, it suffers from Victorian engineering constraints that make it uniquely vulnerable to signal failures, particularly in the Balcombe Tunnel section."

He paused, perhaps noticing from our expressions that he'd veered into territory only fellow enthusiasts appreciate. "Sorry," he said with a smile. "One develops peculiar interests after spending enough time on trains. I can tell you the precise minute each station kiosk opens. I know which vending machines are most likely to malfunction and the best carriage for both seat availability and proximity to Victoria's exits."

"That's actually quite impressive," I said, genuinely meaning it. There was something oddly touching about his mastery of this challenging aspect of daily life.

"Survival skills," Richard replied with a modest shrug. "After seven years of the same commute, you either develop strategies or lose your mind entirely. I've opted for the former, though some days it's a close call."

Fleur watched the exchange with fascination. She placed her hands lightly on her wine glass and traced its rim with her fingers. Tilting her head, she asked, "And your family? They are... accepting of this arrangement?"

A shadow crossed Richard's face briefly before his composed expression returned. "My wife has adapted. The children less so. My daughter has a chart where she marks the days I'm home in time for bedtime stories. Some months, there aren't many marks."

The matter-of-fact way he delivered this poignant detail was perhaps more affecting than any dramatic declaration could have been. Even Fleur seemed momentarily lost for words.

"It's rather like a modern version of those Victorian fathers who went off to manage distant parts of the Empire," Ryan suggested, attempting to lighten the mood. "Except instead of sending postcards from exotic Bombay, you're texting from Hassocks Junction to say you'll be late again."

Richard laughed, a genuine sound that momentarily erased the fatigue from his features. "That's surprisingly accurate. Though at least the Victorian colonial administrators didn't have to deal with replacement bus services."

As our conversation continued, I watched Fleur's expression change. It shifted from incredulity to something like respect. The French are familiar with bureaucratic absurdities. They understand system failures. But Richard's response had a uniquely British touch: detailed documentation, dry humour, and stoic endurance. Suffering transformed into something almost like art.

"In France," she said finally, swirling the remains of her wine thoughtfully, "we would have riots in the streets if the trains were consistently this bad."

"Oh, we complain endlessly," Richard assured her. "There are fierce tweets. Sometimes, someone writes to their MP. In extreme cases, people fold their newspapers in a particularly aggressive manner." He smiled. "It's our way."

The South Downs coastal road curved before us like a pale ribbon against the green backdrop. It seemed designed only to showcase the capricious nature of English weather. One moment, the landscape was bathed in cautious sunshine. The next, it plunged into the grey embrace of sudden cloud cover. All the while, the persistent wind ensured that no hairstyle, map, or conversation remained undisturbed for long. Our electric car purred along, content. It was the only participant in our journey completely unbothered by the atmospheric drama unfolding beyond its windows.

"The forecast says 'occasional light showers.'" Ryan squints at his weather app, lips quirking in a sceptical grin. "Tenner says we'll be swimming before sundown. This looks like flood territory to me."

I caught Fleur's expression in the rear-view mirror. Her eyes were wide with horror, her mouth set in a look of disbelief. She gazed out at the sky, now growing moodier by the minute. She stroked her perfectly coiffed bob, already mourning its imminent destruction.

"We are actually going to walk in this?" Fleur protested, her accent growing more pronounced with each darkening cloud. "This is not weather for promenading. This is weather for staying inside with blankets and Netflix."

"It's perfect walking weather," I insisted cheerfully, pulling into the small car park that marked the start of our coastal path. "Not too hot, not too cold – just right for appreciating the landscape without overheating."

Fleur's response was a sound that somehow managed to combine a scoff, a sigh, and a prayer into a single eloquent exhalation.

As soon as we stepped out, the wind greeted us with enthusiasm. It met Fleur's styled hair like a long-lost friend it was eager to rearrange. She clutched her silk scarf as it threatened to make its return flight to France independently.

"Mon Dieu!" she exclaimed, extracting a compact umbrella from her handbag with the determined air of a knight unsheathing a sword. "This is not wind – this is harassment!"

We began our walk along the cliff path. The Channel spread out below in grey-blue splendour, white-capped waves crashing with percussive regularity. The rain had politely held off, but now began to make tentative advances – not quite a proper downpour, but rather the particularly English phenomenon of precipitation that somehow approaches from all directions at once.

Fleur's umbrella immediately registered its protest by turning inside out with an audible snap.

"C'est pas possible!" she wailed, wrestling with the rebellious accessory as the wind transformed it into a useless metal flower. "This country actively tries to make people miserable! The weather is malicious – actually malicious!"

As she battled with her inverted protection, a middle-aged man jogged past us, his bare legs exposed to the elements in running shorts that might have been appropriate on the Côte d'Azur in August but seemed wildly optimistic on the English coast. His T-shirt proclaimed "Brighton Half Marathon 2022", and he nodded a cheerful "Afternoon!" as he passed, apparently experiencing an entirely different meteorological reality than the one Fleur was enduring.

"Sixteen degrees!" Fleur called out after him, though the wind carried her words in the opposite direction. "It is sixteen degrees Celsius! Where are your trousers?"

"That's considered tropical here, I'm afraid," Ryan said, tugging his jacket higher. "The minute it's fifteen degrees, you'll see shorts and legs everywhere. Over twenty? Watch us whinge about the insufferable heat wave and pray for rain."

We continued along the path, passing a parked car positioned to face the sea view. Inside, an elderly couple sat with contentment etched into their faces, a thermos open between them, steam rising from small cups as they methodically worked their way through what appeared to be egg and cress sandwiches. They were watching the rain-streaked sea with the same peaceful appreciation one might direct at a fine painting in a gallery – as if the grey drizzle were simply another brushstroke in a masterpiece they had come specifically to admire.

"Are they... picnicking? In a car? In the rain?" Fleur exclaimed, her voice rising to compete with the wind.

"It's called 'making the best of it,'" I remarked. "It's a sacred British rite – a car picnic with a rain-blurred sea."

Fleur's complaints grew as the path became muddier. Her French leather boots – clearly picked for looks, not practicality – gathered a rich patina of English countryside with each step.

"My hair is ruined," she lamented, trying to smooth wind-tousled strands now framing her face in a messy halo. "My clothes are damp. My boots – mon Dieu, my boots are destroyed! Why do this? Where's the pleasure in this activity?"

As if in direct response to her question, a cheerful procession of dog walkers appeared around the bend ahead. Their anoraks – in various shades of sensible green, navy, and that peculiar shade that outdoor clothing manufacturers insist on calling "berry" – rustled with waterproof efficiency. Their dogs bounded alongside, utterly delighted by the adverse conditions, which provided additional mud to roll in and puddles to investigate.

"Lovely day, isn't it?" called the leader of this weatherproof parade as they passed us, their face glowing with the particular sheen that comes from genuine enjoyment of fresh air, regardless of its moisture content.

Fleur stared after them in mute incomprehension. Eyebrows knit. Her lips parted. A strand of hair plastered across her forehead like a question mark, perfectly illustrating her bafflement.

"The British relationship with weather is complex," Ryan explained. "It's part stoicism, part denial, and part national identity. We don't have extreme weather like other countries, so we've developed an extreme relationship with moderate weather instead."

I caught Ryan's eye over Fleur's increasingly bedraggled form. His slight shrug conveyed volumes – an acknowledgement of the peculiar British pride in enduring discomfort, and the unspoken understanding that explaining this to non-Brits was essentially impossible.

"Perhaps we should head back to the car," I suggested gently, as Fleur attempted to salvage what remained of her dignity by fashioning her sodden scarf into a makeshift headscarf. "The lighthouse isn't too far by road, and the visitor centre will have hot tea."

"Tea," Fleur muttered. "No. No tea. But hot coffee. In a dry place. With walls and a roof. This is a good British idea." She cast a final, accusatory glance at the sky. "Your weather is a form of psychological warfare. No wonder you invaded half the world – you were looking for somewhere dry to sit down."

Our next destination appeared through the mist. It looked almost like a Victorian engraving come to life. Belle Tout lighthouse stood as a tower – poised, elegant, seemingly ready to topple right off the edge of the cliff.

Rain streaked the windscreen as we approached, bathing the world in a shimmering silver glow. The wipers cleared the drizzle, offering moments of sharp visibility before the mist reclaimed the glass.

"Belle Tout." I pointed toward the lighthouse as we pulled into the small car park just below it. "Our next stop."

Fleur's head snapped up from her contemplation of her ruined boots. "Belle Tout?" she repeated, her accent caressing the words with newfound affection. "This is a French name?"

"Sort of," Ryan replied, scrolling through his phone. "Belle is French, meaning beautiful. Tout might come from Old English 'tot,' meaning lookout. So, it's a Franco-English hybrid, 'beautiful lookout.'"

This linguistic connection lifted Fleur's mood at once. She pressed her forehead to the rain-speckled window, peering out with renewed interest at the scene outside. Her previous complaints were forgotten as she focused on the lighthouse, its walls gleaming despite the absence of sunshine.

"It is quite beautiful," she admitted, reaching for her camera bag. "Even in this English... moistness."

We dashed from the car to the lighthouse, where a small crowd gathered around a middle-aged man. His navy jumper displayed the lighthouse trust's embroidered logo, and he spoke with the fervour of someone who had found his calling.

"...one of the most remarkable engineering achievements in British coastal conservation," he was saying as we joined the group. "Belle Tout lighthouse was literally moved, in its entirety, seventeen metres inland in 1999."

"Moved?" Fleur repeated, curiosity overtaking her earlier irritation. "The entire structure?"

The guide, whose name badge read 'Ian,' turned to us with a welcoming smile. "Indeed! The whole lighthouse, all 850 tons of it, had to be relocated due to coastal erosion. The cliffs here recede by about thirty to forty centimetres each year. By the late 1990s, Belle Tout was perilously close to the edge."

Fleur's eyes widened with genuine interest.

"Rather than lose this landmark, a bold engineering solution was devised," Ian continued, clearly delighted by Fleur's enthusiasm. "The entire lighthouse was separated from its foundations and set on a massive concrete platform. Using hydraulic jacks and greased rails, they pushed the whole structure inch by inch to its new spot, farther from the edge."

"How long did this process take?" Fleur asked, leaning in with keen interest.

"The actual move took just four days," Ian replied. "Preparation took months. They had to detach the lighthouse from its original foundations – an incredibly delicate process. One wrong calculation, and centuries of history could have been reduced to rubble."

He led us to a display showing photographs of the move: the structure balanced on its concrete platform, the system of jacks and rails, and the painstaking progress as the lighthouse inched to safety.

"The hydraulic jacks could only move the structure about fifty centimetres at a time," Ian explained. "After each movement, the crew had to reset and reposition them. It was like watching an 850-ton chess piece slowly advance across a board."

"Genius!" Fleur declared as she took the photograph of the display. "In France, we would have simply built a new one and complained about the old one falling into the sea. This is... stubbornness, yes, but admirable stubbornness."

Ian beamed at this assessment. "The lighthouse has quite a cinematic history as well," he added, sensing a receptive audience. "It's appeared in several films and television programmes. Perhaps most famously in the James Bond film 'The Living Daylights.'"

This revelation elevated Belle Tout to an entirely new status in Fleur's estimation. She began photographing the lighthouse from various angles, completely oblivious to the persistent drizzle that continued to reshape her once-perfect bob into something more closely resembling a windswept Brontë heroine.

"The light quality is extraordinary," she said, crouching to capture the lighthouse against the dramatic cloud formations. "This grey light – it creates a mood that we never achieve in the South of France. So atmospheric, so... English."

I watched this transformation with quiet amusement. What struck me was how much more naturally beautiful she looked. Her controlled appearance had surrendered to the elements. The wind brought colour to her cheeks, and her hair moved wildly. She seemed almost British – a dishevelled elegance from valuing experience over appearance, substance over style.

"She's been Britainised," Ryan murmured beside me, evidently reaching the same conclusion. "Give her a few more hours and she'll be apologising to inanimate objects when she bumps into them."

"I heard that!" Fleur called without looking away from her viewfinder. "I will never apologise to furniture. This is where I draw the line."

The rain intensified, shifting from drizzle to a steady deluge. Ryan muttered, "I'll check the route to our next stop," and ducked into the car. Fleur, however, remained surprisingly unbothered by the downpour. She dropped and stretched out on her stomach in the sodden grass, angling her camera for a dramatic lighthouse shot.

I decided to also take advantage of the shifting light for moody shots. As the weather grew harsher, the photographic opportunities became even more striking. This is a British phenomenon, often overlooked, but a secret delight for landscape photographers.

By the time we persuaded Fleur to return to the car, she was soaked through but triumphant, clutching her camera with the satisfied expression of someone who had captured something precious.

"I have decided," she announced as we settled back into the car, "that English weather is terrible for humans but excellent for photography. It is a fair trade, perhaps."

The White Cliffs of Dover looked just as impressive as we'd hoped, though our visit was brief. Rain seemed to follow us everywhere in southern England. We finally got a break at Leeds Castle, but the name puzzled Ryan. "Why is it called Leeds Castle when we're in Kent?" he asked, clearly frustrated. "It's nowhere near Leeds. It's like calling Buckingham Palace 'Manchester Residence' or the London Eye 'The Liverpool Wheel.'"

I told Ryan the castle was named after its original builder, a Saxon lord called Led or Ledian, who built a wooden structure on the site in 857 AD, not the city in Yorkshire. Still, Ryan felt it was unfair. He kept grumbling about "misleading names" as we stopped next to one of Kent's most unique buildings: a traditional Oast House. It looked like something straight out of a

Victorian painting of the English countryside.

The building stood in front of us, with its brick base and white, cone-shaped roofs that looked like witches' hats on a farmhouse. These kilns were once common in Kent and Sussex, specifically designed for drying hops and transforming them into an essential component of beer.

"C'est charmant," Fleur murmured, her camera already tracking the geometrical perfection of the conical roofs against the cloud-scattered sky. "Like something from a fairytale, non?"

Right after she spoke, someone stepped out from the lower door of the Oast House. He looked weathered and strong, with a flat cap pulled low over eyes that had clearly spent years watching hop plants. He watched us with the cautious curiosity of someone who often sees visitors but never quite gets used to tourists.

"Afternoon," he called, his voice carrying the distinctive cadence of deep Kent – a rural accent that somehow managed to stretch single syllables into multiple ones. "Come to see the hops, have you?"

"If that's possible," I replied, approaching with my camera deliberately visible. "We're photographers documenting traditional British crafts and architecture."

"Photographers, eh?" His face crinkled, possibly a smile or just rearranged wrinkles. "Herbert Ashworth," he said, extending a hand stained by a life in the soil. "Most call me Hoppy, for what I grow."

"I'm Brianna, and these are my colleagues Ryan and Fleur from France," I said, accepting his handshake and noting the calloused strength still evident despite his apparent age.

"France, is it?" Hoppy looked at Fleur with new interest. "You folks know a thing or two about growing things for booze, I'll give you that. It's a different crop, but the idea is the same: right soil, right climate, and knowledge passed down through generations."

This unexpected connection seemed to please Fleur, who nodded with surprising enthusiasm. "Exactly so! Terroir – the relationship between plant and place. It is the foundation of all authentic agriculture."

Hoppy's expression brightened further at this, as if he'd discovered a kindred spirit where he least expected one. "Come on in, then. I'll show you what's left of proper hop farming before it's all replaced by machines and chemicals."

The interior of the Oast House was partly converted into a small museum, but it remained a working facility rather than a polished tourist attraction. When we entered the brick-walled room, we saw it was dominated by massive wooden drying floors. Above those rose the distinctive conical towers we had admired from outside.

"Been drying hops here since 1842," Hoppy informed us, running a proprietary hand along one of the wooden beams. "Five generations of Ashworths have worked this land. I'm the last, mind you. My son's an accountant in Maidstone. Says there's no future in hops these days."

There was no mistaking the sadness in his voice, a quiet sense of loss for something important that was fading away.

"Hop growing's an art and a science," he continued, warming to his subject. "You need the right soil – slightly acidic, well-drained. Kent's perfect for it – that's why they call it the Garden of England. Hops are perennials – same plants come back year after year if you treat 'em right. They grow on strings – eighteen feet high, they can reach in a good season."

While Hoppy listed the hop varieties – "Goldings, Fuggles, Bramling Cross for traditional ales; Northern Brewer and Target for bitter beers" – Ryan walked over to the drying equipment, checking out the mesh floors and the old heating system.

"So the hops would be spread on these floors?" he asked, interrupting Hoppy's monologue about flowering cycles.

"That's right," Hoppy confirmed, clearly pleased by the interest. "Layer about eight inches thick. Heat rises from below – used to be wood fires, then charcoal. Now it's mostly oil burners. It takes about eight to ten hours to dry a batch properly. Used to be a full-time job just watching the temperature. Too hot and you'd scorch 'em, too cool and they'd rot. Proper skill, hop drying was."

"Just like wine," Fleur interjected, surprising me with her continued engagement. "The process matters as much as the raw material. In Bordeaux, my uncle would say the cellar master was as important as the vineyard."

"Exactly so!" Hoppy agreed. "It's the knowledge that makes the difference, the things you can't write down or program into a computer. You know when hops are ready by how they feel and smell. I can tell more with my fingers than any machine ever could." He rubbed his fingers together, remembering the feeling. "There aren't many traditional hop gardens left in Kent now," he added, his voice turning sad again. Where there used to be thousands of acres, now there are only hundreds. Most of the business has moved to big mechanical farms in Herefordshire. "They say it's more efficient. I say it has less character."

Leading us into a small side room, he pointed upwards. Bundles of dried hops hung from the ceiling, filling the air with a unique fragrance – part herbal, part floral, with hints of citrus and spice drifting through the space.

"Here," he said, reaching up to pluck a few cone-shaped flowers from one of the bundles. "Rub these between your palms, then smell."

Ryan and I followed his instructions, but it was Fleur's reaction that proved most interesting. She crushed the delicate green cones between her elegant fingers, then brought them to her nose with the practised motion of a professional scent evaluator.

"Extraordinary," she murmured, her eyes closed. "It is like... pine, grapefruit, and something earthy underneath. Much more complex than I expected."

"Try tasting just a bit," Hoppy suggested. "Just a small nibble, mind – they're powerful bitter."

Fleur obliged, touching her tongue cautiously to the crushed hop. Her expression transformed immediately into one of surprised disgust, followed by reluctant fascination.

"Mon Dieu! So bitter!" she exclaimed. "But also... interesting. Like very intense herbs and something almost – how do you say – resinous? This goes into beer?"

"That bitterness is what gives beer its character," Hoppy explained with evident satisfaction at her reaction. "Balances the sweetness from the malt. Without hops, beer would be just sugary grain water."

He regarded Fleur with newfound respect, clearly appreciating her willingness to engage directly with his craft. "You've got a good nose," he told her. "Could have made a hop farmer out of you in another life."

Fleur laughed. "Perhaps in that life, you would have been a wine maker," she replied. "We are not so different, I think – the hop farmer and the vintner. Both of us are translating the earth into something that gives life more meaning."

Hoppy nodded, pleased by this assessment.

As we prepared to leave, Hoppy presented each of us with a small bundle of dried hops tied with twine – "For luck," he explained. "Traditional house-warming gift, keeps the nightmares away."

Fleur tucked her bundle carefully into her bag, treating it with great reverence. "I will hang this in my Lyon apartment," she declared. "A reminder that in England, there are a few things of charming tradition."

Coming from Fleur, this was high praise indeed.

We were all curious to visit the town that shares its name with something much more famous. Sandwich sits between Deal and Ramsgate on the Kent coast. It has a unique charm you only find in English market towns that have managed to avoid chain stores and lookalike high streets. The medieval buildings tilt at odd angles, their timber frames showing off centuries of history. Narrow lanes wind along paths set by hooves long before cars ever arrived.

"Feels almost illegal not eating sandwiches in Sandwich," Ryan said as we parked in a Tudor-era square. "Like skipping the hamburger in Hamburg."

"I believe this calls for lunch," I agreed, noticing a small café squeezed between a bookshop and an antiques dealer. Its hand-painted sign, "The Daily Bread," showed a sandwich that looked both tasty and oddly shaped.

The café interior embodied the particular British genius for creating spaces that are both cosy and a bit cramped. Tables were close enough for inadvertent eavesdropping, but not so close as to require social interaction. The walls displayed framed black-and-white photographs of old Sandwich. The air carried the scents of baked goods and freshly brewed tea.

We settled at a small table near the window. Ryan, visibly intrigued by the town's name matching the humble food, immediately pulled out his phone, his eyes already searching for facts.

"Did you know," he began, scrolling with purpose, "that the sandwich was named after John Montagu, the 4th Earl of Sandwich? Apparently, in 1762, he asked for meat to be served between slices of bread so he could eat with one hand while continuing to play cards. He was a notorious gambler who didn't want to leave the gaming table, even for meals."

"How very British," Fleur observed, studying the menu with a cautious expression. "Creating a portable meal just to avoid interrupting gambling."

"That's not entirely fair," Ryan countered, still reading. "Sandwich was also First Lord of the Admiralty and a patron of Captain Cook. The Sandwich Islands – now Hawaii – were named after him. The gambling story might be made-up anyway – some historians think he was actually just working at his desk and needed something he could eat without utensils or interruption."

Fleur appeared unconvinced by this historical rehabilitation. She tossed her hair and made a dismissive sound. "Pfft! This sandwich. This... how can I say... emergency food? Now it is your national cuisine!" Her voice shifted into its usual rhythm when she talked about her favourite topic: how British culture falls short compared to France. "I watch you British people all week," she went on, her hands starting to wave. "These sandwiches in plastic! You eat standing up! Or, mon Dieu, even while walking!"

Her voice climbed, drawing sidelong looks from nearby tables where guests quietly chewed the very food now under critique.

"In France," she declared, her hands gesturing more and more, "lunch is sacred. Sacred! A minimum of two hours with family or colleagues. Freshly cooked food. Proper courses. Conversation. Wine! It is a cornerstone of civilisation!"

A middle-aged couple at the next table exchanged glances, their identical tuna and cucumber sandwiches suspended mid-journey to their mouths.

"But here," Fleur continued, oblivious to the attention she was attracting, "I see office people. Educated! Adults! In the rain, they stand! Eating triangles with mystery inside from some factory! Made yesterday! C'est barbare!"

Her right hand sliced the air for emphasis, causing a passing waitress to execute a nimble sidestep to avoid collision.

"The pre-packaged sandwich industry in the UK is worth over eight billion pounds annually," Ryan contributed helpfully, still scrolling through his phone. "That's approximately five million sandwiches consumed every day."

This statistical reinforcement only fuelled Fleur's passionate critique. "You see?" she exclaimed, now addressing the café at large rather than just our table. "An entire nation systematically undernourishing itself! No wonder the British are so... so... reserved. How can one express emotion on a diet of cold, triangular bread with insufficient filling?"

The atmosphere in the café shifted as nearly every patron turned to Fleur, faces reflecting embarrassment, fascination, or outright amusement. In the corner, an elderly gentleman let his newspaper fold closed, his eyes sparkling with the relish of an unexpected performance interrupting his daily ritual.

"The sandwich itself is not the problem," Fleur clarified. Her hands now conducted an invisible orchestra of culinary disapproval. "In France, we have the croque monsieur, the pan bagnat – these are sandwiches of dignity and substance. For me, it is the British way, this casual to not care about the eating experience, which I find very troubling, you know."

I sipped my tea in silence. I had learned that Fleur's gastronomic ramblings were best allowed to run their natural course, like a summer storm that would eventually exhaust itself. Meanwhile, Ryan remained happily oblivious to the social ripples Fleur was creating; he had found the vegan options on the menu.

"They have a roasted red pepper, hummus, and rocket sandwich on sourdough," he announced. "And it's made in-house daily. No plastic packaging involved."

This minor concession to Fleur's principles seemed to momentarily derail her momentum. She blinked at Ryan, then at the menu he was proffering.

"Locally baked bread?" she asked, her tone suggesting she was negotiating a hostage release.

"Apparently sourced from the bakery two doors down," Ryan confirmed. "And they use Kentish vegetables wherever possible."

Fleur considered this information with a serious look, as if calculating moral equations. "And we will eat at this table?" she pressed. "Sitting down, like civilised people? Not standing in the street or walking while eating?"

"We can even use plates and cutlery if you'd like," I offered. "The full sedentary dining experience."

She sighed deeply, as if making a significant concession. "Very well. I will try this Sandwich sandwich. But I maintain that lunch should be a proper meal, not this... functional refuelling."

The waitress approached with commendable composure, considering she had just witnessed Fleur's impassioned critique of the very establishment where she worked.

"Ready to order?" she asked, pencil poised above her notepad.

"Three of your locally-made sandwiches, please," I replied. "And perhaps a pot of green tea for the table?"

"Lovely," the waitress nodded. "And would you like those to take away or–"

"Sit in!" Fleur said quickly. "Here, at the table. With plates."

"Right you are," the waitress agreed, her expression betraying only the faintest glimmer of amusement. "Plates it is."

As she departed, the elderly gentleman who had been watching us from the corner folded his newspaper and approached our table. He paused beside Fleur, his eyes twinkling with good humour.

"Begging your pardon," he said, his voice friendly and gentle, "but I couldn't help overhearing your thoughts on our British eating habits."

Fleur briefly stiffened, concern flickering across her face, perhaps anticipating a sharp rebuttal to her outspoken critique of local habits.

"Just wanted to say," he continued with a smile, "that in forty years of coming to this café, that's the most sensible thing I've heard anyone say. My late wife was French, from Normandy, and she never stopped complaining about how we eat standing up. 'Like horses at a trough,' she used to say."

He offered a small, respectful nod. "Enjoy your seated lunch. Some of us old dogs can learn new tricks, you know."

Maybe one could explain British eccentricity by being confined to a rainy island for centuries. Over time, the weather became less an obstacle and more a theatrical backdrop for peculiar traditions. The Maldon Mud Race was certainly a prime example.

We arrived at Promenade Park in Maldon in the early afternoon. The persistent drizzle settled into a steady, predictable rhythm – like a metronome. It did not increase or decrease but simply existed, a constant reminder of our geographical reality. The mudflats of the Blackwater Estuary stretched before us, exposed by low tide. They glistened with rain and anticipation, transformed from mere geology into an arena for one of the world's most absurd sporting events.

"Perfect conditions," declared a passing local, nodding appreciatively at the rain-slicked mud as if evaluating a fine wine. "Not too wet, not too dry. You want that perfect consistency – like chocolate mousse, but less appetising."

I nodded along and gave the usual polite response. In Britain, talking about the weather always means agreeing, no matter what you really think. And, for sure, I didn't think this mud was anything to call 'perfect'. But each to their own.

We moved through the busy crowd, following Ryan as he led the way and checked to make sure we were close behind. Bright flags showed the path of the muddy course, running across the riverbed from one side to the other. Ryan looked over the event program he had just picked up and told us that competitors have to run, wade, and push through thick mud and water to cross the riverbed, then head back the same way to reach the finish line.

The spectators formed a cheerful, waterproof ring around the course – a sea of wellies, raincoats, and practical hats. Many clasped thermoses of steaming drinks. Children darted between adults, undeterred by the weather. A local brass band played on, determined to ignore their sheet music slowly dissolving in the rain.

Fleur lingered at the periphery, her umbrella hovered above her perfect bob like a protective force field, somehow radiating disapproval. Over the noise, she asked, "Remind me why we're here again?" Her voice barely rose above the hubbub.

"It's for your photo series on British traditions," I reminded her. "The Maldon Mud Race has been happening since the 1970s. It's become quite famous."

"Famous," she repeated, watching with undisguised horror as competitors in various states of costume performed warm-up stretches nearby. Some were already splattered with mud, having tested the conditions with preliminary forays. "This is what passes for fame in Essex? Running through mud in fancy dresses?"

Before I could defend the noble tradition of mud racing, Ryan returned briskly from the registration tent, pamphlet in hand and a notably excited grin on his face.

"Absolutely brilliant," he declared. "They dash across the mud. The course is 400 yards, and most of it is knee-deep sludge. Costumes are strongly encouraged!"

Fleur's gaze shifted from the muddy competitors to Ryan, her expression transitioning from horror to something altogether more calculating. A small, mischievous smile played at the corners of her mouth.

"But you, Ryan," she said, her voice dropping to a silky purr that I hadn't heard her use before, "you must participate, non? It would make such wonderful photographs." She placed a light hand on his arm, her eyes wide. "You would be magnificent in the mud. So... authentic."

I watched this performance with quiet amusement. Fleur, who had spent the past days declaring British customs barbaric, unhygienic, and generally beneath contempt, was now gazing at Ryan as if mud racing were an Olympic sport requiring exceptional skill and courage.

Ryan, predictably, puffed up under this unexpected praise. "Well, I've been thinking about it," he admitted, though I knew for a fact he had mentioned no such intention. "It would be an authentic cultural experience. And great content for my Instagram."

"Exactement!" Fleur exclaimed, her hand still resting on his arm. "Your followers would adore you. And I would personally take photographs – the French perspective on this very British tradition."

A flamboyant voice interrupted this manipulation in progress. "First-timer, are we? I can always tell – that mixture of enthusiasm and abject terror is quite distinctive."

We turned to face a man seemingly engineered to embody "theatrical." He wore a purple velvet waistcoat over a ruffled shirt. His salt-and-pepper hair swept into a gravity-defying quiff despite the persistent drizzle. A name badge on his waistcoat read: "Derek 'Dizzy' Thornton – Race Costume Coordinator."

"I'm Derek," he announced unnecessarily, extending a hand adorned with several chunky rings. "Twenty-three years of mud race experience, though these days I prefer to keep my feet dry and my spirits high by dressing others for their muddy debuts."

Ryan shook the offered hand with a slightly dazed expression. "I'm Ryan. These are my colleagues, Brianna and Fleur. I'm thinking of participating."

"Marvellous!" Derek exclaimed, clapping his hands together with theatrical delight. "A virgin mudder! We need to get you dressed properly, my dear. No one does their first race in ordinary clothes. It's just not done."

He pointed to a vintage VW camper van parked nearby, its sides covered in swirling patterns and the words "Dizzy's Costume Emporium" in bold letters. "My mobile wardrobe is ready. Twenty years of mud race costumes, all sorted by theme, size, and how likely they are to cause a public scandal."

As we followed Derek to his van, he talked of the race's origins.

"Started in the 1970s on a pub dare," he explained, unlocking the van's back doors with a flourish. "One bloke bet another he couldn't race across the mudflats to the pub opposite. The classic British origin: alcohol, reckless bets, and cheerful disregard for personal safety."

Inside, Derek's van was a surprise: a carefully organised costume shop on wheels. Racks of wild outfits lined both sides. Boxes labelled "Hats," "Wings," and "Things That Should Not Bend But Might" were stacked at the back. A full-length mirror hung on one door, slightly warped to make everyone look slimmer. "Good for morale," Derek said with a wink.

Ryan moved quickly among the racks, reaching for hangers and flipping through costumes. He stopped and held up a cape and mask combination – an alarming lime green and purple. He turned to us and asked, "What about this superhero outfit? Or maybe something Viking, with a helmet?"

Derek regarded Ryan with the critical eye of an artist assessing a blank canvas. He circled him once, making small "hmm" sounds, occasionally reaching out to turn Ryan's shoulders or measure his height against an invisible standard. Finally, he nodded decisively.

"I know exactly what you need," he declared, reaching deep into the rack of costumes. With theatrical timing, he slowly withdrew a frilly maid's outfit. The black and white ensemble featured an exaggerated short skirt with petticoats, a lace-trimmed apron, and a bonnet that could only be described as aggressively ridiculous.

"This is perfect for you, love," Derek said with complete conviction. "Trust me, I've been dressing racers for twenty years. The contrast of the pristine white apron against the brown mud? Photographic gold!"

Ryan's face fell as Fleur and I burst into laughter. His expression cycled rapidly through shock, dismay, and the dawning realisation that he had somehow talked himself into a situation that would inevitably involve him wearing petticoats in public.

"But... I was thinking something more heroic," he protested weakly. "Something with a bit more... dignity?"

Derek waved off the concern. "Dignity and mud racing don't go together, darling. Besides, the maid outfit won the 'Most Photographed Costume' award three years in a row. You'll be an absolute sensation."

Fleur's eyes gleamed with delight. "It is perfect," she agreed, her accent thickening with amusement. "Very... how you say... photogenic."

Trapped by his own enthusiasm and Fleur's approval, Ryan accepted his fate with the resigned expression of a man who realised too late he had been expertly manoeuvred. Derek held out the costume, guided Ryan's arms into the sleeves, and straightened the bonnet at a jaunty angle while Ryan stood, mouth slightly open in mild shock.

"The boots can stay," Derek decided, eyeing Ryan's footwear critically. "The mud will claim them as its own regardless."

A horn blast interrupted our laughter and signalled the start of the race. Competitors headed to the starting line, a mix of superheroes, animals, historical figures, and one rather uncomfortable-looking maid. The crowd cheered as an official raised a starting pistol.

"Bonne chance!" Fleur called, blowing Ryan an exaggerated kiss that seemed to both embarrass and encourage him.

The pistol fired, and the race began, though calling it a "race" was a bit optimistic. The competitors lurched forward into the mud, moving like a strange slow-motion ballet as their feet were sucked into the thick surface, released with pops, and trapped again moments later.

Ryan's initial strategy of careful, high-stepped walking lasted approximately fifteen seconds before his first slip sent him sprawling forward, his white apron immediately transforming to a splattered brown. He recovered, but lurched sideways into another competitor dressed as what might have been a chicken.

"C'est magnifique," Fleur declared, her camera clicking rapidly as she captured Ryan's ungainly progress. "The British at play – like children, but with less dignity."

Ryan's trip across the mudflats got more dramatic as he went. Halfway to the cheese platform, he took a spectacular fall, landing face-first in the mud with his arms outstretched, like a diver whose pool had turned into chocolate pudding. The crowd cheered, and even Fleur gasped before bursting into laughter.

"I did not think it possible," she admitted between giggles, "but I am beginning to understand the appeal of your bizarre British traditions."

Ryan's trip across the mudflats got more dramatic as he went. Halfway to the opposite bank, he took a spectacular fall, landing face-first in the mud with his arms outstretched, like a diver whose pool had turned into chocolate pudding. The crowd cheered, and even Fleur gasped before bursting into laughter.

"I did not think it possible," she admitted between giggles, "but I am beginning to understand the appeal of your bizarre British traditions."

Ryan eventually reached the far bank, sporting a triumphant expression that suggested he had accomplished something genuinely significant, rather than simply touching a wooden post while dressed as a domestic servant. His return journey featured two more falls, a near-collision with a mud-covered bride, and a final dramatic slide on his knees toward the finish post.

As he crossed the finishing line, ending his mud-soaked odyssey in approximately 378th place, the cheers from the crowd suggested he had achieved something far more impressive than merely surviving his own poor decision-making. Mud-covered, bedraggled, but grinning widely beneath a layer of Essex estuary silt, Ryan had somehow transformed from reluctant participant to mud race enthusiast in the space of twenty minutes.

"That," he declared as he squelched toward us, his maid's outfit now a uniform brown, "was actually brilliant fun. Absolutely disgusting, but brilliant." He proudly displayed his finisher's certificate with its QR code. "And I get a professional photo of this whole disaster to download! I'm framing it for the office."

"A memento of questionable taste," I observed dryly, capturing his triumphant pose with my camera. "But certainly earned by a survivor."

The next morning, rain still streaked the windows. The sky looked like wet concrete. Fleur really hadn't been lucky with the English weather. Usually, our climate is better than people say. Since Fleur arrived, though, it seemed determined to prove every stereotype right.

For his heroic effort at the mud race the previous day, I had promised Ryan a proper reward: an authentic start to the morning. The fogged-up window announced "Maggie's Breakfast Bar." Below, bold red letters, "Home of the Real Full English," jarred against the washed-out dawn. This seemed the right refuge to recover from mud-weary exhaustion.

Ryan grinned as he pushed open the door. "I'm absolutely starving. Nothing like a bit of proper British breakfast to start the day."

The blast of warm air greeted us with the comforting mix of frying bacon, sizzling sausages, and brewing tea. Mushrooms lent an earthy aroma, while the distinctive smell of baked beans – so odd to Europeans at breakfast – cut through the air. Condensation fogged the windows, forming a steamy barrier between the oily interior and the gloomy day outside. For a split second, I honestly couldn't say which side was preferable.

It was clear Maggie's interior was built for endurance, not charm. Worn leather booths lined the walls, burgundy seats cracked and patched with duct tape, bearing the scars of years of diners sliding in and out. Framed, yellowed newspaper clippings celebrated the café's fleeting glory – including being named "Essex's Best Breakfast" in 1997. A faded photograph depicted, I guessed, Maggie herself, shaking hands with someone resembling a minor royal at an old local event.

At the far end, an open kitchen offered a view of the breakfast theatre. Cooks in stained aprons flipped sausages with the casual precision of those well-practised. Eggs were cracked one-handed into heated pans. Bacon was arranged with architectural care.

We slid into a booth, the leather creaking beneath us. Fleur scrutinised the table's surface with the keen gaze of a health inspector, discreetly running her finger along its edge and frowning at her invisible findings.

"It's clean," I assured her. "Just well-used."

Before Fleur could articulate her concerns, a waitress materialised beside our table. "Morning," she announced, extracting a notepad from her apron pocket. "Full English is two eggs any style, bacon, sausage, black pudding, beans, tomato, mushrooms, and toast. Tea included." She delivered this information not as a sales pitch but as a statement of immutable fact.

Ryan's face illuminated with anticipation. "Brilliant! I'll have the full works, please, but with the vegan options – so the plant sausages, vegan bacon, extra mushrooms instead of black pudding, and could I possibly get avocado on the toast?"

The waitress scribbled briskly. "Vegan Full English. Right." She pivoted to Fleur, her voice braced and ready. "And you, love?"

Fleur glanced around at the nearest tables, her gaze landing on a man in a high-visibility jacket – likely a manual labourer – eating his massive breakfast. As she watched him spear a slab of sausage, her eyes widened, and she pressed her hand to her chest, torn between fascination and alarm at the amount of food.

"This," she said, gesturing toward the neighbouring table's breakfast with the careful gesture of an art critic addressing a controversial installation, "is impossible to eat in the morning! Impossible! In France, we have le petit déjeuner – it is small, civilised." She straightened in her seat, taking on the dignified air of a cultural ambassador. "I will have le petit café and a croissant, s'il vous plaît."

The waitress remained neutral. "We've got tea," she said, tapping her pencil on the notepad.

Fleur pressed, carefully enunciating. "But I would prefer coffee."

"We've got that too," the waitress replied, matter-of-factly. "But tea comes with the breakfast."

Fleur eyed a nearby mug skeptically. "Ah, merci. But... where is the coffee? The small one, with taste? This tea is just tinted water with milk."

"Instant or filter?" the waitress asked, unflappable.

"Filter please. Parfait," Fleur said, though her tone suggested the coffee situation was anything but perfect.

I ordered avocado toast with some mushrooms and beans – a modest compromise between Fleur's continental minimalism and Ryan's full embrace of British excess – and requested a pot of green tea.

Fleur once again glanced at nearby tables, closely watching diners devour their Full English breakfasts. She leaned in, concern sharpening her voice. "Look at this," she whispered. "So much grease. How does anyone function after such a meal? In France, we'd need a nap straight away."

"That's the best way to start a day," Ryan insisted. "It's sustaining. Gets you through until lunch. Perfect for the British climate – you need those calories to generate heat."

Our drinks arrived: my pot of green tea, Ryan's mug of builder's tea strong enough to stand a spoon in, and Fleur's coffee, delivered in a mug – decidedly not the dainty cup she had expected. Fleur wrapped her hands around the mug hesitantly and studied it, her wariness clear.

Taking a careful sip, Fleur's lips twisted in disappointment. "Dishwater," she pronounced, setting the mug down. "This is not coffee. It's just a faint ghost of coffee."

The food arrived before Fleur could elaborate further on her beverage critique. Ryan's vegan Full English was impressively arranged, my avocado toast was modest but appetising.

Fleur looked down at her croissant, frowning as she prodded the dense pastry with her fork. It sat on its plate with the solidity of something meant to survive a nuclear apocalypse. The delicate, flaky creation she expected was nowhere to be found.

She gingerly poked the croissant with her finger as if testing for signs of life. "This," she announced, raising her voice for the nearby tables, "has no resemblance to a real croissant! It looks, smells, and feels like a lump of clay." She lifted it between thumb and forefinger, showing it to the room. Its golden-brown exterior failed to impress her. "A real croissant has layers – feuilletage – created by folding butter into the dough repeatedly. This is just bread shaped like a croissant."

I caught the eye of an elderly woman at a nearby table, who had paused to watch Fleur's performance with clear amusement. I offered her a small, apologetic smile and leaned closer, whispering, "From France..." She responded with a knowing nod, her expression a mixture of sympathy and entertainment.

"Poor girl." The woman's voice dropped. "Must be difficult for her to adjust, French cuisine is really not our forte." She shot a glance at Fleur's bread-croissant, then tried a smile. "But perhaps our Mince Pies will win her over? There's nothing on the other side of the Channel to compare with those little sweet treats."

O ur car glided along the narrow road curving around Bosham harbour. At low tide, small boats rested on exposed mud, waiting patiently for the returning waters. Above a cluster of cottages, the medieval church tower stood sentinel. The weathered stone and painted facades reflected with remarkable clarity in the still waters of the inlet. The village seemed to exist both in reality and in its mirror image.

"This is rather magnificent." I parked in the small area designated for visitors. "Bosham is one of the few places depicted in the Bayeux Tapestry. King Canute's daughter is supposedly buried in the church, and legend has it that this is where he commanded the tide to turn back."

"Unsuccessful, I'm guessing." Ryan pointed toward the exposed mudflats, where several boats were listing at improbable angles.

Fleur, who'd spent most of the drive scrolling through castle photos on her phone, lowered the device and turned her attention outside. The village's atmosphere, and perhaps its history, finally caught her interest. She looked around appreciatively.

"It is very... English," she conceded, which I decided to take as a praise rather than an insult. "The light on the water, the reflection of the buildings – c'est charmant."

We walked along the waterfront, where ancient cottages stood with their feet in the harbour at high tide. This peculiarity had persisted for centuries, despite the obvious impracticalities of waterlogged doorsteps and flooded roads. Ryan captured the scene with his usual enthusiasm, directing us to "move slightly left" or "look more contemplative" as he framed his shots with us as extras.

It was as we approached the ancient church that a modest breeze swept across the shoreline. I tucked a strand of hair behind my ear and continued walking, but beside me, Fleur stopped abruptly and lifted her hand dramatically to her temple, as if she'd been struck by something considerably more substantial than moving air.

"Mon Dieu!" she exclaimed, her voice rising above the gentle lapping of water against the shore. "This malicious English wind is giving me a migraine!"

Ryan and I exchanged glances, each raising our eyebrows.

The light breeze, gentle enough to leave a nearby puddle undisturbed, had seemingly left Fleur in distress. She stood with her eyes half-closed, fingers pressed to her forehead, striking a pose of dramatic suffering.

"It is like needles," she insisted, clutching her scarf tighter. "Sharp, cold needles stabbing straight into my brain."

"There's probably a pharmacy in the village," I suggested, keeping my tone neutral despite the overwhelming evidence that the English climate was, for once, behaving with remarkable restraint. "We could get you some paracetamol."

In the UK, paracetamol is the answer for almost everything. Whether you have a callous, cystitis, or even a broken leg, it always seems to be the solution. At the NHS hospital A&E, the routine is familiar: wait for hours, sit on a hard chair, and listen to the sounds behind the curtains. Eventually, a tired nurse appears – determined and in a hurry. Before you can explain your problem, she hands you two pills. No introductions, no extra questions, and no diagnosis. Paracetamol is expected to fix it all.

"Oui, yes," Fleur agreed. "Something for this terrible pain. The English weather is so... aggressive."

The 'aggressive' weather continued its mild assault as we retraced our steps through the village. We eventually located a pharmacy tucked between a tea shop and a boutique selling nautically themed homeware that no sailor would ever purchase. The pharmacy announced itself with the distinctive green cross – a symbol understood across Europe. It was a rare moment of continental harmony.

"I'll wait out here," Ryan announced, settling onto a conveniently placed bench with his phone. "Need to check if my mud race photos have gone viral yet."

Inside, the pharmacy was brightly lit and clinical. Shelves were filled with remedies for all kinds of problems, but that was just the beginning. It felt more like a warehouse, packed with books, candles, fake tan, baby food, pet beds, and even the classic British kettle. You could find almost anything there. I wondered if they even stocked something so mundane as paracetamol. I turned to suggest that we ask the pharmacist for it, but I found that Fleur was no longer at my side. She had wandered several steps away, pausing before a display of cosmetics. Despite her earlier claim of incapacitating pain, she now examined various foundations and serums with intense concentration, her migraine seemingly forgotten in the face of retail temptation.

Leaving Fleur to cosmetics, I found paracetamol. Waiting at the counter, I watched Fleur move from skincare to makeup with focused attention.

By the time I had purchased the painkillers, Fleur had accumulated an impressive collection of items. She was engaged in a deep conversation with a shop assistant about various mascara formulations. Her earlier distress had vanished, replaced by the animated enthusiasm of someone in their natural element.

Fifteen minutes later, Fleur emerged triumphantly from the checkout with a shopping bag that rustled with promise and potential. Her expression was one of satisfaction rather than pain – the hunter returning successfully from the expedition.

"You seem to be feeling better." I held the paracetamol box, still unopened, in my hand.

Fleur blinked, momentarily confused, then her hand flew back to her temple in belated remembrance of her condition. "Ah, the headache! It is... slightly improved. The shop was a good distraction from the pain."

She turned around and gave the chemist a last, long look.

"In France," she continued, "pharmacies are for medicine, not this... beauty temple with sandwiches!" She gestured toward a small refrigerated section near the entrance where pre-packaged sandwiches sat in neat rows. "Why would anyone want to purchase food in the same place they buy medication for foot fungus?"

I held up the small box of paracetamol I'd purchased. "Well, fortunately for your migraine, I managed to locate some actual medicine amidst the beauty products and sandwiches."

But she was right. British pharmacies really are quite different from their continental counterparts. Initially, apothecaries, chemists, and druggists each had distinct roles. That changed in 1704, when all of them began selling other products to make extra money. They offered things like tobacco, alcohol, cosmetics, and food. These days, it's not so different, minus the alcohol and tobacco.

Fleur accepted the pill box with a gracious nod. We stepped outside. When the gentle breeze touched her perfectly styled hair, she placed her hand back to her temple, but with less drama than before.

As we walked up to Ryan, who was busy taking pictures of a seagull, Fleur adjusted her scarf. "The English air is still terrible," she said, but not as firmly as before. "But maybe I can handle it with the right medicine." She patted her bag of beauty products and smiled. "Who knew you could turn a pharmacy into a shopping mall? That's so British."

The late-afternoon sun stretched shadows across the worn flagstones and lit up the weathered stonework of the Hospital of St. Cross with a soft, golden glow. Founded in the 1130s, St Cross is England's oldest almshouse still in use. Its stone buildings form a quiet quadrangle that feels far removed from the busy world we'd left behind in the car park.

"It's not actually a hospital in the modern sense," I explained as we approached the entrance. "In medieval times, 'hospital' meant a place of hospitality for pilgrims, the poor, and the elderly. St Cross has provided accommodation and care for elderly gentlemen – the 'Brothers' – since the 12th century."

We walked under a stone archway and stepped into the inner courtyard. The chapel's Norman architecture was simple but beautiful. The buildings radiated a calmness born of nine centuries of charity.

"It feels as if time moves more slowly here," Fleur observed, her voice unusually subdued. Even her critical French sensibilities appeared momentarily humbled by the weight of history and the simple dignity of the buildings.

As we walked through the cloister, its stones smoothed by centuries of footsteps, the quiet was suddenly broken by a loud growl from Ryan's stomach. The sound echoed in the stone corridor, making an elderly gentleman in a long black cloak glance over at us with a small, amused smile.

Ryan's expression shifted from embarrassment to sudden excitement. His gaze was fixed on something across the courtyard. "Look!" he exclaimed, pointing toward a small gathering near a wooden door. "They're giving out bread and ale! It's the Wayfarer's Dole!"

His stomach rumbled again in anticipation.

"The what?" Fleur asked, raising a perfectly shaped eyebrow.

Ryan was already fumbling for his phone. His fingers danced across the screen to activate his camera. "The Wayfarer's Dole," he repeated, using the particular cadence he reserved for explaining British traditions. "It's one of the oldest continuous charitable traditions in England. Since the 12th century, any traveller who knocks on the door of St Cross can receive a small portion of bread and ale. It's completely free, no questions asked."

He began recording a reel for his Insta account, narrating with the intensity of a documentary presenter. "This tradition has continued uninterrupted for over 850 years. It survived the Reformation, both World Wars, and the invention of the package holiday. It's the ultimate example of medieval hospitality surviving into the modern age."

Fleur regarded the small queue with a mixture of curiosity and scepticism. "People still want this free bread? After nearly a millennium?"

"It's not about the food itself," I explained, watching as an elderly attendant in traditional dress greeted each visitor with a quiet dignity. "It's about participating in a living tradition that connects us directly to medieval pilgrims who stood in exactly the same spot, receiving exactly the same offering."

Ryan had already joined the queue, his camera ready to document every moment of his impending historical experience.

The attendant, a gentleman whose face and black cloak

made him look like a figure from a historical illustration, greeted us with a small bow. He handed out simple offerings from a wooden tray: a small piece of bread and a tiny cup of ale.

When Ryan's turn arrived, he accepted his portion with exaggerated reverence. He held the bread as if it were a precious artefact. "Thank you," he said, his voice hushed in genuine appreciation.

The attendant's eyes crinkled with particular warmth. "You are most welcome, traveller," he replied, the formal phrase worn smooth with centuries of repetition.

Fleur approached next, her initial scepticism apparently overcome by curiosity. She accepted her portion with surprising grace, examining the simple bread with the eye of someone from a country where bread-making is almost a religion.

"C'est charmant, this tradition," she conceded, turning the small piece in her elegant fingers. "Though a proper French baguette would improve it considerably."

The attendant received this critique with the imperturbable calm of a man who had heard far worse over his years of service.

I accepted my own portion with a quiet "thank you," then moved aside to capture photos of Ryan's enthusiastic consumption. He stood beneath an ancient archway. The light fell across his face. He aimed for a 'thoughtful medieval pilgrim' look, but achieved something closer to 'hungry tourist in fortunate lighting conditions.'

As we left St Cross in the fading sunlight, the gentle tolling of bells shifted our attention to our final destination for the day. Winchester Cathedral awaited us, its massive presence dominating the city centre just a short drive away.

Inside the cathedral, we stepped into a cool, echoing space. It was so large it seemed to have its own atmosphere. Stone pillars rose high above us, leading the eye upward. We walked through the nave. Our footsteps echoed on stone worn smooth by countless visitors.

"Jane Austen is buried here," I mentioned as we approached the north aisle. "She died in Winchester in 1817."

Ryan immediately redirected his attention from the stained glass he'd been photographing. "Jane Austen? Really? I've read all her books – twice."

We stood before the simple stone slab that marked Austen's final resting place. The inscription made no mention of her novels. Her family had chosen to commemorate her virtues, not her literary achievements, which had not yet earned recognition at the time.

"It's rather moving," Ryan said quietly, photographing the grave with restraint. "It makes you realise how someone who created worlds that live on in readers' imaginations can have such a modest resting place. It puts greatness into perspective."

"The English approach to greatness," Fleur observed. The cathedral's hushed atmosphere seemed to soften her voice. "Understated, yet fond."

Soon, as the cathedral staff began the gentle process of encouraging visitors toward the exit – a peculiarly British form of eviction involving meaningful glances and progressively closer hovering – we found ourselves again in the early evening light. The day was drawing to a close, the sun casting long shadows across the ancient city.

Walking back to our car, Ryan summed up our day: "From a coastal chemist to a medieval almshouse to Jane Austen's grave, we've covered quite a bit of English history in a single day."

"And consumed historically authentic bread and ale," I added.

"And survived English wind that causes instant migraines," Fleur concluded with a hint of a smile, acknowledging her earlier dramatics with rare self-awareness.

If you think you'll notice exactly when you enter the New Forest, you're wrong. There's no sign. No clear border. Just a subtle shift – the landscape loosens from trimmed fields to ancient woodland and heathland, untamed since William the Conqueror's time. Our car seemed to shrink as we drove narrow lanes beneath arching trees. Occasionally, sunlight spilt through clearings, revealing purple heather and yellow gorse.

"Map says ponies soon." Ryan peered at his phone. "About five thousand here, roaming freely across the forest."

Fleur leaned in. "Five thousand horses? Wandering? That's allowed?"

"Ponies, not horses," I corrected, slowing near a meadow. "It's protected – one of Europe's oldest land-use systems."

Almost on cue, a small group of ponies appeared at the meadow's edge – shaggy, sturdy creatures with intelligent eyes and an air of complete ownership. Among them, a woman knelt beside one pony, her silhouette outlined by the open landscape as she concentrated on its front hoof.

I pulled the car onto the grass verge and switched off the engine, keeping my eyes on the woman as she worked. Curiosity about her skill drew me. "That looks like someone who knows what they're doing. Shall we introduce ourselves?"

The woman glanced up at our approach but, without pausing, continued manipulating the pony's hoof with experienced movements.

"Morning." I offered a tentative smile. "Sorry to intrude. We're photographers documenting British traditions. I'm Brianna; these are Ryan and Fleur."

"Sarah Blackthorn," she replied without looking up. "Doc Blackthorn to most folk round here." She released the pony's hoof and straightened up, revealing herself to be a woman in her mid-sixties with silver-streaked dark hair tied back in a practical ponytail. "This little one's picked up a stone bruise. Nothing serious, but better attended to sooner rather than later."

She eyed us, focusing briefly on Fleur's city look. "Photographers? Here for pretty pony pictures?"

There was something in her tone – not quite hostile, but certainly protective. She seemed to be evaluating us against some unspoken standard.

"We want to understand the forest's traditions," I said. "How people, animals, and land connect."

Something in my answer seemed to unlock a flicker of trust. "So, you're not one of those tourists who insist on feeding the ponies crisps and biscuits, patting their noses, and generally treating them like oversized Labradors?" She gave a small, approving nod and turned back to the pony, her hand running with clear affection along its warm neck. "Well, you've come to the right place for tradition. My family's been exercising commoning rights here for over three hundred years."

"Commoning rights?" Fleur stepped forward, curious. "That's a legal thing?"

Doc Blackthorn's expression softened slightly at Fleur's genuine curiosity. "It's ancient law. Predates most of your modern legal codes. Commoners – that's people like me who own or rent property with attached rights – can graze animals on the open forest. Been that way since before the Norman Conquest."

She gestured for us to follow as she began walking through the meadow. The recently treated pony trailed behind her like an attentive dog. Other ponies raised their heads as we passed. They regarded us with mild curiosity before returning to their grazing.

"Each pony belongs to someone," Doc Blackthorn continued, "but they live semi-wild, make their own decisions about where to go and what to eat."

"How do you know which pony belongs to which commoner?" Ryan raised his phone to capture images of the animals against the backdrop of ancient oaks.

"It's the mark that matters." The Doc walked over to another pony, a dun-coloured mare with a unique pattern clipped into its coat. "See this? Each commoner has their own mark, a specific way of clipping the coat. This one is the Crosthwaite mark, a four-year-old mare from a family in Lyndhurst."

Fleur moved closer. "And the ponies, they are not... how do you say... disturbed by humans approaching them?"

"They're used to people, but they're not tame. Some even bite," Doc Blackthorn warned. "They aren't pets. These are working animals with a job: managing the vegetation and keeping the ecosystem healthy."

"Magnifique," Fleur whispered. "In France, such animals would be behind fences, controlled."

"Different traditions," Doc Blackthorn acknowledged. "Here, it's the land that shapes the practice, not the other way around."

Ryan, who had been alternating between taking photographs and checking information on his phone, looked up with sudden enthusiasm. "What about The Drift? I've just been reading about it – the annual roundup of ponies. When does that happen?"

For the first time, Doc Blackthorn looked truly animated, eyes bright with pride. "The Drift is our busiest time. Happens throughout August and September, different areas on different days. We gather all the ponies, check their health, mark the new foals, and take out any that need treatment." Her hands flew as she mimed gathering and sorting, her voice quickening. "It's not a tourist spectacle, mind you. It's serious work – dangerous, heart-thumping work if you don't know what you're doing. To round up the ponies, you have to be an excellent rider – fast, bold, a bit wild yourself. People call us New Forest Cowboys, or in my case, Cowgirl."

As we continued walking together, the landscape opened up. Heathland stretched ahead, dotted with grazing ponies. Doc Blackthorn paused occasionally to point out different vegetation types, explaining how the ponies' selective grazing maintained the delicate ecological balance.

"And in autumn," she continued, "we have Pannage – another ancient tradition. We release pigs into the forest to eat the acorns."

"Acorns?" Fleur echoed, surprised.

"Toxic to ponies," Doc Blackthorn explained. "Can cause fatal colic. But pigs love them, digest them with no problem. So every autumn when the acorns fall, commoners with pig rights release their pigs to hoover them up."

When we returned to where our cars were parked, Doc

Blackthorn reached down to pat the pony she'd treated earlier. She looked at us, her hand lingering on the pony's neck. "These ponies are the real commoners of the New Forest," she said, a hint of pride in her voice. "We humans are just their caretakers."

I always loved Brockenhurst. It feels like an island of civilisation in a sea of wilderness. Yet, unlike most islands, the boundary between the village and the forest is remarkably permeable. We parked in the small high street car park and stepped onto the pavement. Signs of equine visitors greeted us immediately. Fresh droppings were arranged like an obstacle course on the tarmac. Hoof prints scored a patch of soft ground near a drain. Locals glanced not only for traffic, but also for large, four-legged obstacles that might be grazing around the next corner.

"So this is a typical English village, yes?" Fleur adjusted her silk scarf in the gentle breeze. "Very quaint, very..." She broke off as her eyebrows shot up. A shaggy pony had just rounded the corner and was now checking out a hanging basket outside the village bakery.

"Mon Dieu!" Her voice rose enough to attract glances from passing locals. "There is a horse. In the street. Eating the flowers!"

The pony, clearly unmoved by the hanging basket's wilted blooms, plodded slowly down the high street. It stopped periodically to nose through stray market debris. A young woman exited the bakery clutching a crumpled paper bag, sidestepping the animal with the ease of someone avoiding a well-known obstruction.

"But... but the animal is just... wandering about!" Fleur waved her hands at the pony, clearly amazed. "No one is controlling it! No rope. No fence!"

"Yes, that's Brockenhurst." I smiled, enjoying her reaction. "It's the only village in England where the forest quite literally comes to town."

We continued down the high street. Fleur swivelled her

head, scanning shopfronts and pavement for equine surprises. She wasn't disappointed. At the post office, another pony lowered its head to drink from a puddle left by the morning's rain. It stood precisely aligned between a red post box and a parked bicycle.

Fleur's camera was immediately in her hands. Her professional instincts overrode astonishment. "C'est magnifique!" She dropped to one knee to capture the juxtaposition of the wild animal against the quintessentially British backdrop. "In France, this would cause such panic! The police would arrive, barriers would be erected, children would be ushered inside!"

A postman emerged from the building, mailbag slung over his shoulder. He navigated around the drinking pony with nothing more than a casual "Morning, Bessie" directed at the animal. Whether the pony was actually named Bessie or this was simply the postman's generic greeting for all equine encounters remained unclear.

Suddenly, our attention snapped to a burst of noise farther down the street. A shaggy, ash-grey donkey, ears twitching, stretched its inquisitive head through the open doorway of a tiny gift shop. It seemed intent on examining the colourful wares inside.

"Absolutely not, Herbert." A voice came from inside the shop. "We discussed this yesterday. Bookmarks are not on your diet."

We approached to find the shopkeeper. She was a woman in her fifties with reading glasses on a chain. She stood with hands on hips, addressing the donkey as if negotiating with a slightly difficult customer.

"Is this... normal?" Fleur's eyes were wide as she whispered.

"Completely," I confirmed. "The animals have been part of village life for centuries."

The shopkeeper noticed our interest and offered a cheerful nod. "Herbert's our regular Tuesday visitor," she explained, reaching out to scratch the donkey's ears with familiar affection. "Thinks the shop is his personal browsing library. Don't you, you old nuisance?"

Herbert's long ears twitched in what might have been agreement.

As we continued our village exploration, Ryan took on the role of forest wildlife interpreter. He pointed out warning signs along the road and explained the unique traffic considerations of the area.

"New Forest animals always have right of way." Ryan indicated a road sign depicting a pony's silhouette. "The speed limit drops to 40 miles per hour on forest roads. This is specifically to protect them. Even then, sadly, there are accidents every year."

"But surely there are fences along the roads?" Fleur's brow furrowed with practical French concern.

"Nope." Ryan replied. "The whole point of the commoning system is that the animals roam freely. Drivers just have to be careful. There's even a special hotline to report injured animals. They call it the Verderers' Office."

Further on, a small herd of ponies had gathered on a village green. They cropped the grass with methodical efficiency under the watchful eye of a large oak tree. Several were younger animals, their coats still carrying the reddish hue of foals.

Fleur stood transfixed by the scene, her camera clicking rapidly.

A group of schoolchildren passed us, their uniforms suggesting they were returning from a sports activity. None of them gave a second glance at a pony investigating a bicycle rack outside the village shop. The animal was methodically trying to extract a canvas shopping bag from one of the baskets.

As we completed our circuit and made our way back to the car park, I noticed how Fleur's initial shock had transformed. She now felt something closer to delight. Her camera had barely left her hands. Her expression conveyed appreciation instead of disbelief.

"It is strange," she admitted as we returned to our car, "but also rather wonderful. This village lets wilderness and civilisation exist in harmony. No barriers, no clear boundaries. Just... coexistence."

Evening approached with the unhurried pace of a British summer day. It seemed reluctant to surrender its light, despite the advancing hour. Our car navigated increasingly narrow lanes. The road seemed determined to return to its original state as a forest path. Branches occasionally scraped against the windows like curious fingers. The satnav, in that particularly calm female voice that remains unruffled even when directing you straight into a lake, announced that we were "arriving at our destination." That statement proved immediately and demonstrably false as we rounded a bend. Our path was entirely blocked by what appeared to be a delegation of extraordinarily hairy, horned beasts. They looked as if they'd wandered straight out of a Highland calendar.

Ryan leaned forward, pressing his forehead against the windscreen as he peered out at the animals and asked, "Are those... cows?"

"Highland cattle," I corrected, bringing our vehicle to a gentle stop several metres from the nearest shaggy behemoth. "Scottish breed. Very hardy. Very... large."

The cattle – five in total – stood across the lane, a perfectly efficient roadblock. Their magnificent horns stretched outward like lethal coat hangers. The horns gleamed in the evening light. Long, russet fur covered their eyes.

"We are not in Scotland, are we?" Fleur's voice from the back seat had risen at least an octave. "We have taken a wrong turn, perhaps?"

"Still firmly in Hampshire," I assured her, assessing our options. The lane was far too narrow for turning. Verges on either side sloped into ditches. Attempting those would mean a thoroughly unpleasant extraction.

Ryan kept his phone in one hand, glancing down as he scrolled. "They're New Forest commoners' cattle," he said. He began searching, likely for 'how to persuade Highland cattle to move using only hand gestures and positive thinking.' "Same principle as the ponies. Free to roam."

One of the cattle – the largest, naturally – turned its massive head toward our car with deliberate slowness. Its movement suggested careful consideration rather than alarm. Despite the fringe of fur obscuring its eyes, its gaze seemed fixed directly on us. The animal regarded us with calm assessment. It was a creature that knew exactly how much its horns could damage our modest vehicle.

A small, strangled sound escaped Fleur as she gripped Ryan's arm, her manicured fingers digging into his sleeve. She leaned forward, her wide-eyed gaze fixed on the cattle. "It is looking at us. Why is it looking at us like that?" she whispered.

"Just curious," Ryan replied, though his reassuring tone was somewhat undermined by the slight tremor in his voice. "They're very docile animals, really. Farmers love them because they're so... gentle."

The word 'gentle' hung in the air, as convincing as a politician's promise. The lead cattle beast took a ponderous step toward us. Its hoof landed with surprising delicacy for something that appeared to weigh roughly the same as a small building.

"I'll try the car horn." I gave it a gentle tap.

The resulting sound seemed only to interest the cattle further. The lead animal tilted its head slightly, as if critiquing our musical offering and finding it wanting.

"Perhaps we should reverse and find another route?" Fleur suggested, her voice tight with controlled panic.

"This is the only road to the cottage," I replied. I tried a more authoritative beep of the horn. This had precisely zero effect on our audience, who continued their implacable bovine contemplation of our vehicle.

I opened my window a fraction and attempted a commanding "Shoo!" Even as I uttered it, I recognised the sound was hopelessly inadequate. It would hardly persuade several tonnes of horned livestock to alter their chosen resting place.

One of the smaller cattle closed its eyes and appeared to doze off while still perfectly blocking our path.

The sound of hoofbeats approaching from behind caused us all to turn. Through the rear window, I spotted a familiar figure on horseback – Doc Blackthorn. She was mounted on a sturdy bay horse and approached at a brisk trot.

She pulled alongside my window, looking down at us with an expression that balanced amusement and professional concern. "Thought you might encounter our Highland welcoming committee," she said.

"They won't move," I explained unnecessarily, gesturing toward our implacable roadblock.

Doc Blackthorn nodded, as if this was entirely expected. "Stubborn beasts, Highlands. But they respond to the right approach." She urged her horse forward and positioned herself between our car and the cattle. With practice, she began issuing a series of low whistles and calm verbal commands.

"Come on then, Fergus," she addressed the largest animal. "You know better than to block the lane. Tourists need to get through, don't they? That's right, shift yourself now."

To my amazement, the enormous beast – apparently named Fergus – regarded her for a moment. Then it let out a deep, rumbling sound, as if from near the earth's core. Reluctantly, Fergus shifted his substantial bulk to one side. The others followed suit, creating just enough space for a vehicle to pass. The margins would require extremely careful navigation.

"Drive through slowly," Doc Blackthorn instructed. "They won't charge or anything dramatic, but best not to startle them with sudden movements."

I inched the car forward, hyperaware of the proximity of sharp horns to our paintwork. Fleur had closed her eyes entirely, murmuring what sounded suspiciously like a prayer in rapid French.

"Regardez," Ryan suggested gently, "they're moving aside for us. Just like London traffic, but furrier."

Fleur opened one eye cautiously, then immediately closed it again as a particularly impressive set of horns passed within centimetres of her window.

Finally, we emerged on the other side of the bovine gauntlet. Ahead lay a scene of quintessential English charm – almost as if staged for a tourism brochure. A thatched cottage stood in a clearing. Its roof resembled a groomed mushroom cap. Windows glowed with welcoming light. Heathland stretched to the horizon, a patchwork of purple and green. A curl of smoke rose from a whimsically crooked chimney.

"Your accommodation," Doc Blackthorn announced, her horse walking alongside our crawling vehicle. "Keeper's Cottage. Built in the 1700s, though the thatch is newer, obviously. Old forest keeper's dwelling originally."

I parked by a small garden gate, its archway festooned with climbing roses.

"It's beautiful," I said, genuinely appreciative of the scene.

We exited the car and stretched after the long wait. Fleur emerged last, watching the distant cattle grazing at the lane's edge.

"They will not... visit during the night?" she asked. Her voice strove for casual inquiry, but landed closer to existential dread.

"Highly unlikely," Ryan assured her as he retrieved our bags. "If they do, think of them as very large, very hairy teddy bears. With weapons on their heads."

Fleur's expression suggested this description had not achieved the reassurance he'd intended.

The ferry to the Isle of Wight cut steadily through the Solent, treating the journey like a familiar bus route. Seagulls performed aerobatics around us, either welcoming us or auditioning for an avian ballet. The mainland faded behind. Ahead, the island's chalk cliffs stood pale and watchful. To me, the island has always felt like England in miniature – familiar elements, condensed and removed from time's flow.

"Isle of Wight," Ryan intoned beside me at the rail, his tone precise, as if reciting from a Wikipedia entry memorised on our drive. "Separated from mainland Britain after the last ice age. Became the UK's holiday destination of choice during Victorian times when Queen Victoria built Osborne House here."

Our car wove from the ferry terminal at Fishbourne, winding through gentle hills and preserved villages. The satnav guided us toward Freshwater Bay, its voice stumbling over the local place names.

"Re-cal-cu-lat-ing," the device intoned, each syllable sharp, almost a warning. The mechanical voice sounded disappointed. Was it just me, or did navigation devices really do this – turn colder when ignored? I always sensed mine lost its warmth the moment I chose another route.

We eventually found ourselves on a narrow lane bordered by hedgerows. Wild roses tangled with brambles there, a collaboration of beauty and mild threat. The lane ended at a cottage that announced its uniqueness from fifty metres away. It was a structure that seemed to reject architectural conformity as a personal philosophy.

"I think we've found it," I said, somewhat unnecessarily.

The cottage was traditional stone, but every surface showed self-expression: a rainbow-painted gate, driftwood and stone sculptures, wind chimes in varied tones, and faded prayer flags fluttering on a line.

As we approached, the front door opened. A figure matched the cottage's eclectic style: mid-seventies, tall, willowy, with silver braids past their shoulders. Flowing robes suggested either cosmic inspiration or a bold fabric purchase. Necklaces – crystals, wood, and metal – caught the light.

"Welcome, fellow travellers!" the man called out, raising a hand adorned with several chunky rings. "I'm Peter, though some days I'm Phoenix. For now, it feels like a Peter day, so we'll go with that. You must be the photographers I've been expecting."

We introduced ourselves as we approached, and Peter greeted each of us with a gentle handshake that lingered just long enough to suggest a genuine connection without tipping into awkwardness.

"Come in, come in," Peter ushered us through the door. "The kettle's just boiled, and I've made some scones this morning. Can't have visitors to the island without a proper cream tea, can we?"

Inside, the cottage overflowed with artefacts from a lived life: framed festival wristbands, old photos, record albums, and a vintage Rolleiflex surrounded by prints – each memento hinting at a vibrant past.

"Sit wherever you can find space," Peter invited, gesturing toward a collection of mismatched furniture that somehow cohered into a welcoming arrangement. "Just move any books or records – they're used to being shuffled about."

Ryan immediately gravitated toward a wall covered with festival posters. "Is this an original Isle of Wight 1970 poster?" he asked, pointing to a faded print that showed a lineup of names that read like a roll call of rock royalty.

"Original indeed," Peter confirmed, moving toward the kitchen area. "I was there, of course. Couldn't afford a ticket, so I climbed over the fence. Nearly broke my ankle, but worth it to see Hendrix. That was just weeks before he died, you know."

We settled onto chairs and a sofa covered with throws. Patterns told of global travels: Moroccan weaves, Indian block prints, South American geometrics. Chaotic, but comfortable – a patchwork of international cosiness.

Peter returned with a tray of tea things, setting it on a coffee table that appeared to be constructed from an old ship's hatch cover. "I'll just get the scones from the kitchen. Made them with spelt flour – easier on the cosmic digestion."

When our host returned from the kitchen, there was an immediate and notable change. The flowing robes Peter had worn had been replaced by a long, elegant skirt and a soft, draped top. More delicate jewellery adorned their figure – small earrings glinted in the afternoon light. The intricate silver braids had been partly swept up with a decorative clip. Ryan paused in mid-pour to exchange a look with Fleur, as if to confirm that the person returning to us was unmistakably the same host.

Noticing our surprise, they explained, "While I was in the kitchen, I felt Phoenix coming forward," their voice now softer and lighter. "Sometimes the change from Peter to Phoenix happens quickly. I just let it happen when it does. At my age, trying to resist the cosmic current is simply exhausting."

Phoenix distributed the scones. "Now, you wanted to know about the island's spiritual history?"

Fleur, who had been uncharacteristically quiet since our arrival, was watching Phoenix with undisguised fascination. Her usual critical French perspective had been replaced by genuine curiosity.

"This fluidity between Peter and Phoenix," she finally said, absent-mindedly accepting a scone, "is it... accepted here?"

Phoenix smiled, a web of lines crinkling around warm eyes. "Oh, the islanders have known me for over fifty years, dear. They've seen all my transformations. When I first arrived, fresh from the festival in 1970, they thought I was just another hippy who'd wash away with the next tide. But I put down roots, became part of the community. Now I'm as much a local fixture as the lighthouse."

"Look at the photos! Phoenix reads tarot at the village fête," Ryan had obviously informed himself while drifting through a gallery of tightly packed mementoes on Phoenix's shelves. "And it looks as if you also taught music at the primary school? I bet everyone knows Phoenix-slash-Peter."

"Every British village needs its eccentric," Phoenix said with a wink. "It's almost part of the rules. There's always one pub, one church, one post office, and at least one person who stands a little apart from the usual. We add a bit of colour, dear. Like human hanging baskets."

"In my village in France," Fleur admitted, "such... flexibility would not be so easily accepted."

"Oh, there was talk here too, once upon a time," Phoenix acknowledged. "But British village life operates on a simple principle. If you're useful and kind, eventually your peculiarities become simply... you. I deliver vegetables to elderly neighbours. I organise the solstice celebrations and remember everyone's birthdays. My gender fluidity is just another aspect of my person, like my silver hair or my terrible singing voice."

Ryan, returning from a brief inspection of a shelf lined with vinyl records, said to me, "He has an original pressing of Electric Ladyland, can you believe it?"

"They," Phoenix corrected gently. "Or she, today. The pronouns shift with the presentation, dear."

Ryan's face flushed with embarrassment. "I'm so sorry – they have an amazing record collection."

"No harm done," Phoenix assured him with a smile. "The cosmic self transcends such earthly labels anyway."

Fleur watched this exchange, her face thoughtful. When she finally spoke, it was with respectful curiosity. "They have created something quite special here," she said, gesturing to the cottage and its assembled treasures. "A life lived authentically, without... how do you say... compromise."

As the afternoon went on, our conversation wandered from topic to topic, much like the sound of Phoenix's wind chimes. Each shift was unexpected, but together they made for a pleasant atmosphere. We had finished the cream tea, and now we were in that relaxed stage of English socialising. We held our tea cups more than we drank from them, and our talk turned to deeper subjects.

"What fascinates me about Britain," Phoenix said, bracelets tinkling, "is these elaborate social codes everyone understands but no one ever explains. Like a secret language of–"

"In France, we are more direct," Fleur interjected, leaning forward. "We do not have this British... how do you say... tiptoeing. We say what we mean, immediately and with passion!"

Phoenix blinked, a flicker of uncertainty crossing their face, and tried again. "That directness can be refreshing. As I was saying, British social codes require–"

Fleur cut in. "It's exhausting! When you say 'that's interesting,' is it good or bad? When you say 'we must have lunch,' do you mean it or just words?"

I saw Phoenix's smile tighten. They pressed their lips together, trying to stay calm. Their fingers tapped nervously on the teacup, showing their growing frustration and impatience.

Ryan, missing the tension, said, "There's a study on British indirect speech. 'Would you mind passing the salt?' isn't truly about willingness, it's just a–"

"Exactly!" Fleur exclaimed. "Why not simply say 'Pass the salt'? In Paris, we do not waste time with these elaborate–" Words escaped her.

Phoenix jumped in, voice suddenly earnest. "May I finish my

thought?"

A hush settled over us, broken only by the distant, tingling wind chimes outside. An uneasy pause hung in the air as Fleur blinked, her brow furrowing in confusion.

"I'm sorry?" she said, the phrase an actual question, not a reflexive British apology.

Phoenix set down their teacup. "I wonder if we might try taking turns? It's likely my fault – I speak slowly. Your enthusiasm is marvellous, truly."

Fleur's confusion deepened. She looked between us. "Taking turns? In France, conversation is back-and-forth. We show interest by responding with our thoughts! If you wait to answer, it seems cold – almost as if you weren't really listening." Her hands drew an overlapping pattern.

Understanding dawned on me. I placed my cup carefully on its saucer and assumed the role I had played so often during our travels: cultural translator.

"I think we're experiencing a rather perfect example of cross-cultural communication differences," I suggested. "In England, we essentially queue for our turns to speak, just as we queue for buses or theatre tickets. Interrupting someone is seen as pushing into the conversation queue – a social faux pas equivalent to cutting in line at the post office."

Fleur looked surprised, a flush rising in her cheeks as embarrassment flickered across her face.

"Whereas French conversation," I continued, "is more like... jazz improvisation. Everyone playing together, overlapping, creating something collaborative and immediate."

Phoenix's face had softened with this explanation, the earlier tension easing from around their eyes. "Is that really how it works in France? Interruption is a form of engagement rather than rudeness?"

Fleur nodded emphatically. "When I jump in, it is because your words have sparked a connection in my mind – this is a compliment, not a dismissal."

"How fascinating," Phoenix mused, their irritation now completely replaced by intellectual curiosity. "So what we perceive as rudeness is actually an expression of engaged enthusiasm. Cultural misunderstandings are so illuminating, aren't they? Like little windows into our unconscious assumptions."

"I am sorry if I seemed... how do you say... impolite," Fleur offered, her usual confident demeanour softened by genuine contrition. "I was not being rude, just French."

This simple explanation – "not being rude, just French" – struck me as so perfectly apt that I couldn't suppress a smile. It was a phrase that could explain so many of our cross-cultural adventures over the past weeks.

The tension thoroughly dissolved, and I sensed relief radiating from all of us. Fleur, now visibly self-conscious, made determined efforts to restrain her French conversational habits – her lips pressed tightly together when interrupting thoughts flashed in her eyes.

Phoenix started pausing more often, giving Fleur a chance to join in. The conversation turned into a pleasant mix, not completely British or French, but something in between. It felt bilingual, not in language, but in the way we interacted.

Evening descended gently. Late afternoon draped the garden in gold, followed by the hushed lavender of dusk. Soon, indigo darkness enveloped the cottage garden like velvet. After our tea-fuelled cultural exchange, our host – having shifted from Phoenix to Peter again – drifted through the garden. He fished fairy lights from wicker baskets, strung them through the trees, and arranged cushions and blankets in a circle around a small fire pit. Nearby, a record player crackled to life with the opening bars of "A Whiter Shade of Pale."

"The garden becomes something else entirely at night." Peter struck a match with theatrical precision to light the first of several hurricane lamps. "The veil between now and then grows thinner after sunset. Makes it easier to revisit 1970."

We settled onto the cushions. The fire pit, a metal basin filled with smooth beach stones, flickered. Small flames twisted between the stones, rising from a hidden fuel source as I reached for warmth.

"Bioethanol," Peter said, noticing my curious gaze. "Much cleaner than wood. We must respect the elements while we commune with them."

Ryan sat with the eager anticipation of a child at story time. His back was straight and his expression focused. Fleur, more reserved but equally interested, wrapped herself in an offered blanket despite the mild evening. Her bob and attentive eyes emerged from a cocoon of softness.

"The 1970 Isle of Wight Festival," Peter began, shifting to a lower, storyteller's register, "was not just a concert. It was a moment when the world turned its eyes to our little island. For one weekend, this quiet corner of England became the epicentre of... everything."

The fairy lights cast patterns across his face. Deep lines, shaped by years of island weather, became clear in the glow. His silver braids caught the light. It looked as if metallic threads ran through his hair.

"Imagine it," he continued, leaning forward slightly. His hands began to paint pictures in the air. "Over six hundred thousand people descended on an island with a population of just a hundred thousand. Every ferry was packed to the gunwales. People slept on beaches, in fields, and on doorsteps. The locals were terrified. They thought it was an invasion."

His eyes reflected the dancing flames, twin points of animated light. "And the performers! Jimi Hendrix, The Doors, The Who, Leonard Cohen, Joni Mitchell, Joan Baez, Miles Davis... gods walking among us mere mortals."

Ryan broke in with characteristic enthusiasm. "I've read that Hendrix's performance was one of his last. Was it as legendary as people say?"

Peter's expression transformed. His features rearranged into something approaching religious ecstasy. "Hendrix," he whispered. The name itself seemed to carry mystical weight. "He came on at three in the morning. Most of us had been awake for days. We existed in that liminal space between exhaustion and transcendence."

After a pause, he stood up and walked over to a worn leather case leaning against a garden chair. He took out an acoustic guitar, a vintage instrument marked by years of use.

"He played a white Stratocaster," Peter said, cradling the acoustic as if it were a far more precious electric model. "The sound... it was like he was channelling something not entirely of this world. When he launched into 'Voodoo Child,' it felt as if the entire island had been picked up and set vibrating to his frequency."

His fingers moved across the strings, producing a simplified but recognisable approximation of the famous riff.

"And The Who!" Peter exclaimed, his volume rising with excitement. "They came on as the sun was setting. Townshend was in full windmill mode. Daltrey swung his microphone like he was trying to lasso the audience."

The guitar shifted to the distinctive opening chords of "Pinball Wizard." Peter's right hand attacked the strings with surprising vigour for someone in their seventies.

"But it wasn't just the rock gods." Peter's voice grew softer. He held the guitar against his chest. "Leonard Cohen came on after Hendrix. Can you imagine following Jimi Hendrix? The crowd was still buzzing from all that electric energy. Cohen walked out, a quiet poet in a suit, and just... stilled everyone."

As Peter spoke, the garden transformed around us. The fairy lights brightened into stage illuminations. The small fire magnified in memory until it held the energy of hundreds of thousands of festival-goers – one pulsing collective moment, shaping a generation.

Peter leaned forward, his face turning serious. "Miles Davis was extraordinary. Most of the crowd didn't know what to make of him. This wasn't the melodic jazz they expected. This was Miles during his Bitches Brew phase – experimental and challenging. Half the audience was confused. Those of us who understood knew we were seeing genius in real time."

"And The Doors without Morrison?" Ryan prompted, his research evidently thorough.

Peter's eyes lit up at the question. "You've done your homework! Jim Morrison was still in the band, but he didn't come to the Isle of Wight. He was in Paris, where he would die the next year. Robby Krieger sang most of the songs. They were good, professional, and tight. But without Morrison's unique presence, something was missing. The door was slightly ajar rather than fully open, if you'll forgive the obvious metaphor."

Fleur listened with uncharacteristic silence before speaking. "You speak of these moments as if they happened yesterday, not more than fifty years ago. The details and the feelings – you have preserved them so perfectly."

Peter smiled. The expression made his lined face seem youthful. Silver hair and weathered skin were forgotten. "Time is a strange thing, my dear. It's less a straight line than a spiral. Some moments stay eternally present. I close my eyes and feel the mud, the incense, cigarettes, humanity, the roar when Hendrix hit the first note."

He set the guitar aside gently and leaned toward the fire. "You know, they tried to recreate the festival in 2004 and again in 2007. Proper organisation, decent toilets, reasonable ticket prices. All the things we didn't have in 1970." He chuckled softly. "They were fine events, I'm sure. But they weren't... cosmic. They weren't moments when the universe seemed to gather around a field in Freshwater."

He looked at our faces, lit by firelight and fairy lights, and smiled warmly. "Thank you for listening. Not everyone wants to hear an old hippy's festival stories these days. Most people prefer their music history pre-packaged and simplified, with all the usual clichés about sex, drugs, and rock and roll. They forget that we were there for the music, for the community, and for the chance to create something new."

"We wouldn't have missed it for the world," I assured him, and meant it. Sitting in Peter's garden, as his words painted pictures in the darkness, we had experienced something far more valuable than a Wikipedia entry or documentary film. In that moment, we touched history through the memories of someone who had lived it.

The Poole ferry terminal looked exactly as you'd expect for a place built for efficiency: grey concrete everywhere, a few thin trees in planters, and some tired-looking flowerbeds. Seagulls wandered about, watching leftover chips and sandwiches with the focus of security guards.

"I cannot believe this is where we part ways." Fleur's voice carried across the waiting area. "After mud races and forest ponies and Scottish cows in English lanes – this soulless concrete box!"

She gestured dramatically toward the terminal, her scarf fluttering like a banner. Despite days of rural adventure, Fleur's French polish remained flawless. Her caramel vegan leather luggage contrasted starkly with our battered camera bags and Ryan's mud-stained backpack.

"How do you do it?" I asked, gesturing toward her pristine appearance. "We've tramped through forests, been rained on, encountered free-range livestock, and you still look like you've stepped out of a fashion magazine. It defies the laws of physics."

Fleur smiled with the serene confidence of someone guarding ancient secrets. "It is simple discipline. And excellent skincare. And perhaps a small travel steamer for emergencies."

The ferry announcement crackled over the loudspeaker. The words were almost impossible to understand, thanks to the muffled audio and the echo in the terminal. Still, Fleur nodded as if she'd heard a clear, personal message.

"It is time," she announced. "My chariot to France awaits."

She turned to me, her expression softening into something genuinely warm. "Brianna, I must thank you properly. In the French way."

Before I could respond, she stepped forward, placed her hands gently on my shoulders to steady me, and leaned in to place a kiss on one cheek, then the other, then returned to the first cheek – the traditional three "bise" of formal French farewell.

Ryan had been watching this French ritual with the rapt attention of someone memorising directions to hidden treasure.

As Fleur turned to him, his expression was bright with anticipation.

She turned to Ryan. "And now, Ryan, we must also say goodbye properly."

Ryan stepped forward with such enthusiasm that Fleur had to quickly put a hand out to steady herself against his sudden approach. He tilted his head awkwardly, clearly aiming for her right cheek as he leaned toward her.

"Left cheek first." Fleur repositioned him patiently. "Then right. Then left again."

Having successfully navigated the first three kisses, Ryan – clearly intoxicated by this continental ritual with a beautiful French woman – leaned in again. His head bobbed left and right in rapid succession as he enthusiastically attempted kisses four and five. People nearby watched with amused expressions.

"Ryan," I intervened, pulling him gently back by his collar, "I think three is the traditional number. We're trying to maintain some British dignity here."

"Sorry," Ryan mumbled to the onlookers, his face flushed. "Just practising international relations."

Fleur appeared more amused than offended.

The final boarding call thundered through the terminal, and Fleur marshalled her elegant luggage with the poise of a general organising a stylish campaign.

"Now I must leave you to your English weather and your polite conversational queuing," she said, her tone softening the teasing words. "It has been... educational. Merci. For everything."

She strode toward the boarding gate but turned back, her scarf billowing like a wind-caught sail. "Remember – left cheek first! And pour the milk only after the tea is brewed, never before!"

As she disappeared into the boarding tunnel, Fleur turned one last time, calling "Au revoir!"

"She's something else, isn't she?" Ryan murmured. He was still staring at the now-empty doorway through which Fleur had vanished. Absently, he rubbed his cheek where her farewell kisses had landed, as if checking whether some essence of French sophistication might have been transferred through the contact.

"Indeed, she is," I agreed, gently steering him back toward the car park. "Come on, we have a long drive to Norfolk ahead, and our American student arrives tomorrow."

Ryan fell into step beside me, still glancing occasionally over his shoulder as if expecting Fleur to reappear for an encore farewell. "Americans," he mused. "They'll seem so... loud after Fleur."

"They're just different," I reminded him. "Just as Fleur was different from Katrin and Marco. That's rather the point of what we're doing – experiencing different perspectives."

As we reached our car, I noticed Ryan standing by the window, watching his reflection. He cocked his head and mimed the three-kiss farewell sequence. His lips made small "mwah" sounds as he moved left, then right, then left again.

"Perhaps save that for our next trip to France," I suggested dryly. "I'm not sure Norfolk is quite ready for continental greeting rituals. Baby steps, Ryan. Baby steps."

He grinned, unembarrassed at being caught.

As we pulled away, I glanced in the mirror as the ferry eased into open water. Somewhere on board, Fleur was surely critiquing the coffee or fellow passengers' fashion – a one-woman mission to bring French standards to maritime travellers.

"She'll be back," Ryan said with surprising certainty, following my gaze to the departing ferry. "People like Fleur don't just disappear from your life. They make dramatic exits only to ensure equally dramatic returns."

I smiled at this assessment, suspecting he might be right. Some people enter your life as brief visitors. Others become permanent residents. Fleur, I suspected, belonged to a third category entirely – the recurring guest who arrives like a force of nature, rearranges your perspective entirely, then departs with the promise of future disruption.

AN AMERICAN IN EAST ENGLAND

The satnav guided us through the Norfolk countryside, seemingly unaware of the realities of English rural roads. "Continue for three miles," it instructed, as the lane narrowed. It was barely wide enough for a cyclist, let alone our car.

Ryan peered dubiously at the hedgerows that seemed to be gradually closing in on either side. "Are you absolutely certain this is the right way?" he asked. "I'm not convinced this is even a public thoroughfare anymore. It has the distinct appearance of someone's extended driveway."

"The glamping site said to follow the satnav to the letter," I replied, ducking instinctively as a low-hanging branch swept past my window. "Apparently they're delightfully secluded." Which in tourism parlance typically means 'impossible to find without specialised equipment and possibly a search party'.

After one final, particularly optimistic instruction to "turn right onto the main road", which manifested as a barely visible opening in a hawthorn hedge, we emerged into a clearing that bore all the hallmarks of a place that was trying very hard to be rustic without sacrificing Instagram appeal. A hand-painted sign read "The Barrel House Retreat" in a font that tried to look spontaneous but must have taken considerable time to create.

"This is it," I announced, parking next to a small reception cabin made of reclaimed timber. "Let's see where our American student is."

We had barely stepped out of the car when a booming voice carried across the clearing.

"Hey there! Y'all made it! Welcome to the Hobbit houses!"

The source of the enthusiastic greeting was clear. Chuck Davidson strode toward us, confident and broad-shouldered, his Braves cap perched atop a beaming face, radiating American optimism to enjoy every moment abroad, no matter the circumstances.

Chuck would be our companion in East England: a forty-something American photojournalist mostly known for NASCAR and college football. His application mentioned a sabbatical to "broaden his horizons" beyond sports and an interest in British landscapes under Brianna's guidance.

"You must be Joe-anna and Ryan!" Chuck boomed, enveloping my hand in a grip that suggested he was accustomed to handling heavy equipment rather than human appendages. "Man, am I glad to see you guys! This place is something else, isn't it? Like staying inside a beer keg!"

He gestured behind him to a row of large wooden barrels, each the size of a garden shed, along the clearing's edge. Round doors and porthole windows made them look like maritime equipment washed ashore and repurposed by castaways.

"It's Brianna, actually," I corrected gently. "With an 'a' sound at the end, not 'anna'."

"Joe-ah-na," Chuck repeated, striving for accuracy as his accent transformed my name into something barely recognisable. "Got it! Sorry about that. Come on over and check out my barrel. It's wild!"

As we approached, it was clear the accommodations weren't designed for Chuck. The round door was chest-height, forcing him to duck dramatically. Inside, the curved walls were charming but tight – his shoulders nearly touched both sides.

"Home sweet home!" Chuck declared, turning awkwardly and bumping a shelf, nearly toppling a display of mugs, which he steadied with practised reflexes.

Ryan, entirely immune to the spatial challenges, was examining the interior with the delighted curiosity of a child discovering a particularly elaborate playhouse. "This is brilliant! Look at how they've utilised every centimetre of space. The bed folds into the wall, the table becomes a desk, and is that a bucket shower concealed behind that panel? Ingenious!"

Chuck's accommodation was a masterclass in spatial efficiency. For our American companion, though, it was more challenge than delight. Every surface was crowded with equipment – massive lenses, specialised tripods, and three camera bodies. He seemed ready to document anything, from a distant bird to a subatomic particle.

"I had to leave half my gear at home," Chuck admitted, gesturing to an enormous case that took up most of the limited floor space. "This is just the essential stuff. You should see my

NASCAR setup. I've got a lens that can capture a bumblebee on a driver's helmet from across the track."

He reached for his phone, which was connected to a charger the size of a generator. He said, "I've mapped out our route. We have three days to cover all of East England." He scrolled through an itinerary that could challenge a race driver. "We hit the big spots today: Norwich Cathedral, the Broads, maybe dash up to the coast if the light's good. Tomorrow we can – "

"That's... ambitious," I interjected, hoping to add a note of realism to the proceedings. "Landscape photography isn't really about covering ground quickly. It's about patience, waiting for the right light, the right moment. Sometimes you need to sit in one spot for hours to get the perfect shot."

Chuck looked at me, first confused, then almost horrified, before finally settling on polite disbelief.

"Hours? In one spot?" He checked his watch – an enormous digital affair with multiple dials and GPS. "But there's so much to see! I have a spreadsheet with 64 essential East Anglian photography locations. That's twenty-one each day, factoring in travel time and brief stops – for charges, both vehicle and human."

Ryan, who had been investigating the barrel's ingenious folding toilet system, emerged from behind a curved panel. "Brianna's right," he agreed easily. "Some of our best work comes from really immersing ourselves in a single location. Getting to know it intimately."

Chuck's expression suggested rapid recalculations in his spreadsheet. He seemed to be trying to quantify "intimacy with location" in minutes rather than hours. He glanced at his equipment, wondering if he'd brought the wrong tools.

"But that's how I work back home," he said, nodding at an enormous lens that could probably see through time as well as space. "NASCAR is all about capturing split-second moments. You set up, wait for cars, get your shot, then move to the next position."

"Different subject, different approach," I suggested. "Trust me, the English countryside isn't going anywhere fast. It's been here for millennia – it can spare you an extra hour."

Chuck nodded slowly, though his hand still hovered over his phone as if reluctant to release his grip on the meticulously planned itinerary.

I smiled at Chuck. "Now, shall we get your gear into our car? I suspect you'll be more comfortable with a bit more space around you."

Chuck's relief was palpable. "Yes, ma'am. This barrel is cute and all, but I feel like a bull in a china shop. Or maybe a bull in a barrel shop? Is that a saying over here?" he quipped, searching for the right phrase.

"It is now," Ryan replied cheerfully, already reaching for one of the smaller camera bags. "Let's get you liberated from your wooden prison."

Back in my small car, Chuck's photo gear took up every bit of space, the back seat packed tightly around him. He kept checking the itinerary, growing more anxious with every glance at his watch and sigh, almost as if time moved more slowly in England than in America.

"We're making good time," I assured him, catching his eye in the rear-view mirror.

Chuck opened his mouth to respond, but as we entered the outskirts of a small town, he abruptly turned his head toward the window, distracted by something outside.

"Whoa, whoa, what is that?" Chuck said, pressing his face to the window with wide-eyed curiosity. "A shop called 'Boots' that doesn't sell shoes? What's that about?"

I followed his gaze to the familiar blue and white Boots the Chemist storefront, my eyes scanning its large sign as I drove past. It's a fixture of British high streets so commonplace that I barely registered its existence, let alone the peculiarity of its name.

"It's a pharmacy," I replied, glancing back. "A chemist, we call it. Boots is just the name of the founder, Jesse Boot. It's been around since the 1800s."

"But it doesn't sell boots," Chuck insisted, peering out. "Pretty misleading if you ask me."

"It's just a name," Ryan said.

Chuck didn't stop there. As we drove slowly down the street, he pointed out more unusual British shop names, sounding more excited with each new find.

"Wait, that one says 'Curry's', but it's full of TVs! Not a spice in sight!"

"Electronics retailer," Ryan explained. "Also named after a family, not the food."

"And 'Fat Face'? That sounds like a boxing club or maybe a wrestling place. But it's clothes?" Chuck's voice got louder, as if he was trying to solve a puzzle that didn't quite fit. "And 'Office' sells shoes, not office supplies? Are you all doing this just to confuse people?"

I shared an amused look with Ryan, raising my eyebrows as I glanced in the rear-view mirror to catch Chuck's reaction. Through Chuck's confused American perspective, I began to notice these shop names anew. They had always just been part of my everyday life; I never thought they were odd until Chuck pointed them out.

"I've never really thought about it," I admitted, slowing to allow an elderly woman with a tartan shopping trolley to cross the road. "They're just... shops."

"But the names should tell you what's inside! That's the point!" Chuck protested.

Ryan turned in his seat, eyes lighting up at the chance to share trivia: "Oh, that's nothing compared to our pub names," he began, his voice growing animated. "We've got The Drunken Duck, The Jolly Taxpayer, The Bucket of Blood..."

"The Bucket of Blood?" Chuck echoed, his expression hovering between horror and disbelief. "Please tell me that's a vampire-themed bar."

"Perfectly ordinary pub in Cornwall," Ryan assured him. "Named after a local legend involving a well and a murder. Quite picturesque, actually. Then there's The Frog and Nightgown, The Dewdrop Inn – get it? 'Do drop in'? – and my personal favourite, The Hung, Drawn and Quartered."

Chuck's face had transitioned through a fascinating range of expressions, finally settling on something approaching existential despair. "Is this some kind of elaborate British practical joke? Did you all get together some hundred years ago and decide to name everything in the most confusing way possible?" he demanded.

"I suppose it is rather strange," I conceded, navigating around a delivery van parked with the kind of optimism that suggests the driver believes hazard lights work as legal immunity. "But every country has its quirks. Surely American shop names have their own peculiarities?"

"We have Foot Locker for shoes, Burger King for burgers, Home Depot for home stuff," Chuck countered. "Names say what's inside. That's it!"

"How literal," Ryan said dryly.

I shrugged and smiled as I drove along the river. "That's just culture," I said. "The strangest things become normal when you grow up with them. Sometimes you need someone from outside to notice what's odd."

"Well, consider me your official American perspective-provider," Chuck declared. "Next topic: why do you guys put vinegar on perfectly good fried potatoes? And why call them 'chips' when they're clearly fries?"

"I think we've created a monster," Ryan whispered, just loudly enough for me to hear. "A monster with extremely valid questions about our national peculiarities."

"Don't worry," I whispered back. "Wait until he encounters his first British plug socket with a switch to turn it on and off. That should keep him occupied for hours."

As we neared the turn for St Benet's Abbey, I looked in the rear-view mirror. Chuck was staring out the window, clearly making a mental list of every strange British name he saw. This was a culture that sold pharmaceuticals under the name of footwear and thought "The Slaughtered Lamb" was a perfectly reasonable name for a place to enjoy a quiet drink.

St Benet's Abbey stood before us, a picture lifted directly from a history book. Its weathered stone walls, quietly rooted in the marshes, seemed to have watched centuries slip by with little fuss. This place was once a powerful Benedictine monastery that controlled the local waterways; now, it exists as a striking ruin. The silhouette – remaining walls and a lone windmill built into the old gatehouse – was as much a part of Norfolk as the reeds that waved around it.

The car stopped. Chuck's door flew open. He unfolded from the passenger seat, surprisingly agile despite having been wedged among camera cases. In a flash, he gripped his camera and aimed its huge lens at the ruins.

"Incredible," Chuck said, already clicking away. "How old is this place?"

"Founded around 956," Ryan said, checking his phone. "Most ruins are from the 12th to 14th centuries. The windmill's an 18th-century addition."

Chuck's response was lost in a flurry of camera adjustments and rapid repositioning. He moved from one vantage point to another with the focused intensity of someone who suspects the ruins might suddenly decide to relocate if not thoroughly documented within the next thirty seconds.

"You might want to pace yourself," I suggested, retrieving my own, considerably more modest camera from the boot. "The ceremony won't start for another twenty minutes."

I observed other visitors gathering – a mixture of locals and tourists. Many made their way toward the river flowing past the abbey, a modest ribbon of water connected to the broader network of the Norfolk Broads.

"The ceremony begins on the river," I said. "Abbots and bishops used to arrive by boat – waterways were the main routes."

Chuck hurried back from his circuit of the abbey's perimeter. Without looking up from adjusting the settings on his second camera, now fitted with a long lens, he called out, "So, what exactly are we waiting for out here?"

Before I could answer, the crowd grew noticeably excited. Everyone turned to look at a bend in the river. A unique boat came into view. Unlike the usual modern boats on the water, this was a mahogany sailing boat with a high stern and smooth, classic lines. Its most eye-catching feature was a large, ochre sail, faded by the sun and full in the gentle afternoon wind.

"Is that a wherry?" Chuck asked, camera ready.

Ryan nodded, voice shifting into his familiar tour-guide narration. "Indeed. A Norfolk wherry – traditional sailing barge of the Broads, used for centuries as the main cargo vessel until the railways. This one's a pleasure wherry, though, not a trading wherry. See the more elegant cabin? That's the clue."

The wherry moved closer, gliding smoothly. Sunlight caught its sail, making the brown cloth look almost glowing. At the front, a man stood in elaborate church robes; his mitre perched high as he held a staff. Gold thread in his vestments sparkled in the afternoon sun.

"Is this real, or are they filming a movie?" Chuck whispered, now shooting video.

"Nope, 100% real," I assured him quietly. "That's the Bishop of Norwich arriving for the annual ceremony."

The wherry docked with practised precision. A small reception party moved forward to greet the bishop. Chuck, momentarily forgetting his self-assigned role as documentarian, lowered his camera and simply stared.

"Why's a bishop arriving at a ruined abbey by boat?" Chuck asked, drawing glances.

Ryan whispered, "Centuries-old tradition. The Bishop of Norwich is also the Abbot of St Benet's – the only bishop in England with both titles. The Abbey was never officially dissolved during Henry VIII's Dissolution of the Monasteries in the 1530s."

"Really?" Chuck said, interested. "They missed one?"

"Not quite," Ryan said. "Henry VIII gave the abbey's lands directly to the Bishop of Norwich instead of seizing them. The bishop is still technically abbot. The ceremony reaffirms that connection."

The wherry docked with practised precision. A reception party stepped forward to greet the bishop. For a brief moment, Chuck forgot his self-assigned role as documentarian. He lowered his camera and simply stared.

The ceremony proceeded at a measured pace, reflecting a tradition refined over centuries. The bishop, pastoral staff in hand, walked along a path lined with local schoolchildren and parishioners toward the remains of the abbey church. There, beneath the open sky where a vaulted ceiling had once stood, he took his place at a simple wooden lectern to deliver an address.

"This is something else," Chuck murmured. "A living tradition, not just for tourists. They'd do it even if we weren't here."

I agreed quietly. "Some traditions continue because they're meaningful to the people who maintain them, not because they're Instagrammable."

When the ceremony ended and the afternoon light faded, the crowd dispersed. Some stayed to talk with the bishop; others headed to the car park.

"The light's perfect for exploring the ruins now," I said, nodding to the sunlit stone. "Let's spend an hour capturing the abbey and the surrounding marshland before heading back."

Chuck looked up from his camera screen with a worried expression. He checked his watch and glanced at the sun, clearly feeling rushed.

"We're burning daylight!" he exclaimed, already beginning to pack his equipment. "We need to see the Broads before sunset. It's the whole reason people come to Norfolk!"

"But we're already at a spectacular location with perfect light," I countered, gesturing toward the ruins where the lengthening shadows were creating dramatic patterns across the ancient stonework.

"But my itinerary says sunset at the Broads," Chuck insisted. "It's what the travel blogs recommend."

"The Broads will still be here tomorrow," I pointed out, though I could already see from his determined expression that the battle was lost before it had properly begun.

Chuck's tone was matter-of-fact. "Tomorrow's light is never exactly like today's," he persisted, already halfway through packing. "And tomorrow: north Norfolk coast. It's all on the spreadsheet."

Soon, we found ourselves at a small boatyard a few miles from the abbey. There, a collection of modest motor cruisers was available for hourly rental, and the elderly proprietor regarded Chuck's enthusiasm with patient tolerance. He probably had encountered many excited tourists over the decades.

"Just a small one for the evening," I told the proprietor, as Chuck surveyed the boats. "We want to explore before sunset."

The proprietor nodded, gesturing toward a neat, blue-and-white craft with an open seating area. "The Marsh Harrier will serve you well. She's steady, reliable, and the electric motor won't disturb the wildlife. Three hours enough for you?"

After a quick safety talk, a short demo of the controls, and a hand-drawn map of routes, we set off from the wooden jetty into the Norfolk Broads. Chuck took his place at the front with his cameras ready. Ryan handled navigation, spreading the map across his knees as he gave me directions.

The water stretched before us in a channel about forty feet wide. On either side, dense reeds bordered the water, swaying gently in the early evening breeze. Occasionally, gaps in the reedy perimeter revealed broader expanses of water. Where the channel widened into open areas, small lakes or lagoons appeared, mirroring the gradually reddening sky.

"This is like the UK's Disneyland," Chuck remarked. His tone was bright and lightly teasing as he looked around. "Man-made canals for tourists, yeah? Pretty impressive, you guys dug all this up just for vacations."

I shook my head, reducing our speed as we approached a narrower section. "They're not man-made. These are natural waterways that have been here for centuries. It's a unique wetland ecosystem."

Chuck looked unconvinced, gesturing toward the geometric regularity of some of the channels. "Come on, these are way too perfect to be natural. They're dug in straight lines in some places!"

Ryan, who had been alternating between consulting the map and his ever-present phone, looked up. "Actually, you're both wrong. The Broads are man-made, but not for tourism. They're flooded medieval peat excavations."

We both stared at Ryan, surprised.

"Peat pits?" Chuck repeated.

"Exactly," Ryan said, grinning with the satisfaction of revealing a surprise. "In the 12th to 14th centuries, people dug for peat. When sea levels rose, the pits flooded. No one really knew until the 1950s, when archaeologists proved it. Everyone just assumed they were natural."

Chuck paused, taking this in with a slow nod. "So all these lakes are basically ancient open-cast mines? Flooded by accident? That's actually kind of awesome. It's like landscape recycling!"

Ryan beamed, clearly pleased by this reaction. "Exactly. What seems untouched now is shaped by centuries-old industry. The flooding turned these old pits into some of Britain's best wetlands."

Slowly, we moved through the waterways as the setting sun filled the sky with deep oranges and pinks. The colours reflected in the calm water, making it look like there were two sunsets. Several old windmills dotted the banks, their shapes standing out against the colourful sky.

"Those must have been for grinding grain, right?" Chuck asked, photographing one particularly well-preserved example. "Old-school flour production?"

"Not quite," Ryan replied. "They're drainage mills, actually. Used for pumping water to manage the marshy landscape for agriculture. The Broads are below sea level in many places, so they needed constant drainage to keep the farmland usable."

I guided our boat into a wider part of the water, giving us a clear view of the sunset. The reds and oranges grew deeper, and purple streaks appeared at the top of the sky. The water was so still that it reflected everything perfectly, making it feel like we were floating between two skies.

Without being asked, I cut the motor, allowing the boat to drift silently. The sudden absence of mechanical noise revealed the subtle soundscape of the Broads at dusk – distant waterfowl calls, the gentle rustle of reeds, and the occasional splash of a fish breaking the surface.

No one spoke. Even Chuck paused, his camera raised but idle for now, as he took in the scene.

When Chuck finally began taking photographs, his approach was noticeably different from the rapid-fire technique he had used earlier. Each shot was carefully composed, his movements slow and deliberate as he worked with the changing light rather than racing against it.

He gestured toward the spectacular sky and its perfect reflection. "No spreadsheet in the world could have scheduled this. Sometimes you just have to be in the right place and... wait for the world to do its thing."

"Exactly," I agreed. "I suppose that is the difference between landscape photography and sports photography."

As the last sunlight faded and the sky turned deep blue and purple, Chuck checked his watch. This time, he looked satisfied, not worried about time slipping away.

"Not bad for day one," he admitted, carefully stowing one of his cameras. "One ceremony, one boat ride, and about four hundred photos I didn't plan for but wouldn't trade for anything."

"And we've barely started Norfolk," Ryan said, folding the map. "Tomorrow will be even better."

Chuck looked at us, his schedule in hand, but now with an easy grin. "Maybe we don't need to hit all sixty-four locations after all."

I smiled, guiding our boat in a gentle turn to begin our journey back to the boatyard. "Now you're thinking like a proper photographer, not just a tourist with an expensive camera and a tick-off list."

A crystalline early morning light rendered the red and white stripes of the lighthouse in Happisburgh in such vivid definition that they appeared almost artificial against the pale blue sky. We had left our accommodation at what Chuck had termed "an ungodly hour for vacation." I had insisted it was essential for capturing the lighthouse in optimal morning light. Now, as we stood in its considerable shadow, the early rising seemed entirely justified, even to our American companion.

"This lighthouse looks good enough to eat," Chuck called out. "Like a candy-cane! That's a proper lighthouse!"

"Guiding ships since 1791," I said. "One of the oldest in East

Anglia. It used to be much farther from the cliff, but the sea's claimed a lot over the years."

Chuck raised his camera. "Where do you want me? Should I try a wide shot from over there?"

"Let's talk leading lines," I said, guiding him to where the path led to the lighthouse. "We want to draw the viewer's eye to our subject – see how this path does that?"

Chuck peered through the viewfinder. "In sports, the action leads you. Here, it's static."

"That's why composition's so important," I replied, indicating the angle. "Without movement, framing creates interest."

With visible restraint, Chuck adjusted his position as directed. He took several rapid shots in quick succession – the photographic equivalent of nervous fidgeting.

Ryan, who had wandered off during this exchange, returned with the particular spring in his step that invariably signalled the acquisition of new trivia. "Did you know," he announced without preamble, "that the lighthouse keeper's cottage used to house three families? They worked in shifts, maintaining the light 24 hours a day. The children would sleep through the day so their crying wouldn't disturb the keeper who'd been up all night!"

"Families lived there? With kids?" Chuck asked, lowering his camera.

"Indeed," Ryan confirmed, warming to his subject. "The cottage has been renovated for holiday rentals now, but it's still remarkably small. Oh, and until 1929, they used an oil lamp with a series of concentric wicks to create the beam. Had to be wound up every hour, like an enormous clock. Can you imagine doing that through the night during a winter gale?"

Chuck shook his head slowly, then returned his attention to his viewfinder with newfound deliberation. This time, he didn't immediately press the shutter. Instead, he adjusted his position slightly, waited as a small cloud cast a momentary shadow across the scene, then took a single, considered shot.

He reviewed his screen, smiling. "There's something about being deliberate. Feels more intentional, like I created something."

"Exactly," I said, satisfied. "Let's try a new spot."

After leaving the lighthouse behind and making our way along the cliff, I noticed a small group gathered on a windswept bench by the cliff path. Their muddy boots, worn waterproofs, and backpacks full of specimen jars, notebooks, and old field guides made it clear they were researchers, not tourists. Steam rose from their shared thermoses of tea, and foil-wrapped sandwiches caught the sunlight as they chatted in the cool morning air.

"Looks like a research team," I observed, naturally curious. "Shall we see what they're studying?"

Chuck nodded, his camera already lifting to document this new potential subject. Following my lead, we approached the group, and I offered a friendly greeting as we drew near.

"Good morning," I began. "We're working on a photography project about East Anglia. Are you conducting research here?"

A woman with a clipboard nodded and extended a hand. "Dr Eliza Harrison, geomorphology. Yes, we're monitoring the cliff erosion and archaeological exposures. This lot are my students and colleagues." She gestured toward the group, who offered various nods and raised tea cups in greeting.

"Archaeological exposures?" Chuck echoed. "Like Roman ruins?"

One of the younger researchers – a man whose enthusiasm suggested a relatively recent PhD – leaned forward eagerly. "Far older, actually. This beach is the site of the oldest human footprints found outside Africa. Over 800,000 years old."

Chuck's camera lowered slowly, his expression transitioning from polite interest to genuine astonishment. "Eight hundred thousand? As in, nearly a million years old? Human footprints?"

"Homo antecessor, technically," Dr Harrison corrected. "Our ancient ancestors. They were exposed by a storm in 2013. The tide washed away layers of silt that had preserved them. We had less than two weeks to document them before they were eroded away completely."

The younger researcher nodded with enthusiasm. "It was absolutely frantic. We were literally racing against the tides. We took photographs, made casts, and recorded measurements, all before the sea took them back."

"And did you save them?" Ryan asked, having joined our small gathering. "The actual footprints, I mean."

Dr Harrison shook her head. "Only in documentation. That's the hard truth of coastal archaeology: the same forces that reveal these treasures also destroy them. The actual footprints disappeared within two weeks of being found. But we saved them through photogrammetry and laser scanning."

"Families," Chuck said quietly, almost to himself. "Actual families walked here. Before there was an England. Before there was... anything really!"

"Exactly," Dr Harrison agreed. "A family group, adults and children, walked along what was once the bank of an estuary. We could see which way they were going. We saw the marks of their toes and could even guess their heights from their stride lengths. It was just an ordinary moment in their lives, saved by chance for nearly a million years."

After our dive into palaeontology, we, or really Ryan, started to feel hungry. We made our way down to the beach along a narrow path that zigzagged down the cliff. Chuck was much more nervous than excited about the descent. He muttered about "health and safety standards" that would have made such a path illegal in at least thirty-eight American states.

Now, on a relatively flat section of sand, Ryan unpacked what looked like provisions for a minor expeditionary force.

"I've got three types of sandwiches," Ryan declared, extracting carefully wrapped packages from his seemingly bottomless rucksack. "And some pies!"

"Ryan," I said, laying out my neutral density filters in preparation for the afternoon light, "there are only three of us, and you've brought enough food to sustain a small village through a moderately harsh winter."

He pressed on, now producing a Tupperware container. "Homemade vegan sausage rolls," he offered. "The B&B owner insisted I take them. Apparently, her grandmother's recipe veganised. And – oh! – some local apple juice."

Chuck, who had been examining the cliff face with the critical eye of someone assessing structural integrity, perked up at the mention of food. "Did you say sausage rolls? I've been wanting to try those ever since I saw them on the Great British Baking Show."

While Ryan gave Chuck enough food to last a sea voyage, I spotted someone sitting alone on a bench at the top of the cliff, outlined against the sky.

"I'm going to explore a bit," I called, gathering my camera. "The light on those cliffs is rather extraordinary."

I ascended the path, grateful the morning's exertions had left Chuck temporarily immobile with food and fatigue. This spared me his commentary on European path maintenance. Nearing the top, I saw the woman more clearly – she sat a few paces from the path, silver-haired, impeccably dressed in a tweed skirt suit from a generation that preferred proper attire to technical fabrics for coastal walks. Her hands were clasped in her lap, knuckles white with tension despite her composed demeanour.

I approached with the cautious respect one affords strangers who appear lost in thought. "Good afternoon," I greeted. "It's a lovely view from here."

She turned, her face arranging itself into a polite social mask. "Indeed it is," she replied, her accent refined. "Though rather changeable, as views go."

Something in her tone suggested this was more than casual observation. "I'm Brianna." I extended a hand. "I'm a photographer working on a project about different aspects of British life and culture. We're showing an American colleague around. That's him down there, being fed by my other colleague."

This produced a small but genuine smile. "Margaret Cliffton," she responded. "Though it's Madge to my friends." She gestured to the space beside her on the bench. "Please, do sit if you'd like. The bench still has an excellent view, though considerably less garden around it than when I installed it."

As I sat, the significance of her words registered. "This was your garden?"

Margaret nodded, looking toward the cliff edge. "Until last year, yes. This bench was surrounded by lavender. There was a stone path from the cottage, about fifteen meters from today's cliff edge."

"I'm so sorry," I murmured, genuine sympathy welling as I realised the full meaning of her vigil.

"Twenty-seven years I lived there with my late husband," she continued. Her voice remained even, only her hands betrayed her with a slight tremor. "It was our dream – a little cottage with a sea view." She let out a short, bitter laugh. "We definitely got the sea view. More of it every year."

I observed her profile as she spoke – the straight back, the carefully applied lipstick, and the pearl earrings. They spoke of a generation that did not easily surrender its dignity.

"The erosion has sped up a lot in recent years," she said, her tone turning more matter-of-fact, as if to protect herself. "Climate scientists say it's because of rising sea levels and stronger storms. The cliffs here are mostly sand and clay, so they're very soft. They've always worn away, but it's happening almost twice as fast now as it did ten years ago."

She pointed toward the water's edge. "Do you see that dark patch of sand down there? That's what remains of my vegetable garden. I grew the most magnificent runner beans. Prize-winners at the village show three years running." Her voice caught slightly on that last word, the only crack in her composure.

"My London friends used to envy my coastal retreat," she added after a moment, a mordant smile on her lips. "But they forgot the price it often comes with in England. The sea gives, and the sea takes away. Recently, it's been much more interested in the taking part. They had to tear down my house because the cliff beneath it was crumbling apart. I'm not the only one – over 30 houses have been lost to the sea in the last 20 years."

The sound of heavy footsteps on the path announced Chuck's arrival, his face flushed from the climb and his camera already in hand. "Joe-ah-na! Ryan said you'd found something interesting up here. The light on those cliffs is amazing right now," he called.

I performed the introductions, watching as Margaret automatically extended her hand. She did this with the formality of someone for whom social niceties remained important, regardless of circumstances.

"You lost your home to the ocean?" Chuck asked. His American directness both bracing and a little unsettling. "Man, that's terrible. But you'll rebuild inland, right? I mean, insurance must cover that kind of natural disaster."

Margaret's expression shifted subtly – not with irritation at his directness, but with a rather tired resignation that she was once again explaining realities that seemed at odds with common sense.

"There is no insurance for coastal erosion in England, Mr Davidson," she explained. "It's considered inevitable, not accidental. And there's no rebuilding – the land itself is gone. One simply... moves on." Her hands twisted in her lap. "Though that's rather easier said than done when you're seventy-three and the property market is what it is."

"But that's crazy!" Chuck exclaimed, his volume causing Margaret to wince slightly. "The government must do something, right? Build sea walls or whatever?"

"Cost-benefit analysis," Margaret said, her voice making it clear she'd heard those words too often. "My cottage and the others lost in the last five years aren't worth the millions it would take to protect this part of the coast. The money goes to places with more people or important buildings."

She gestured toward the village in the distance. "Happisburgh itself will eventually go the same way. The church, the pub, the post office – all of it. Perhaps not in my lifetime, but certainly within this century if current projections hold. We're witnessing the slow drowning of coastal England, Mr Davidson. One garden, one cottage, one village at a time."

Chuck fell silent, his expression suggesting he was recalibrating his understanding of a problem that couldn't be solved with American optimism or technological intervention.

From the beach below, Ryan's voice carried up to us. "I've got some kind of local fruit cake! Is anyone actually hungry?"

Neither Chuck nor I responded, both of us silenced by the gravity of Margaret's story. Margaret managed a small smile. "Your friend seems determined to feed an army. It's a very

British response to uncertainty – provision of tea and sandwiches in the face of calamity."

"Where are you living now?" I asked gently.

"A campervan, if you can believe it," she replied, a flicker of something like pride crossing her features. "It's parked in my niece's garden in Norwich. I call it my 'mobile estate.' One adapts, you know. The English have always been rather good at that – adapting. Though I do miss my runner beans."

Margaret rose from the bench with the careful movements of someone managing unseen pain. "I should be going. I try to avoid being here when the soft afternoon light starts. Makes me just more melancholic, thinking of better times, my husband and I enjoying our tea in our comfy conservatory." She straightened her jacket with precise movements. "It was lovely to meet you all. Do enjoy your photography project."

As Margaret left along the cliff path, her posture stayed upright. The sea had taken her home but not, I noted with admiration, her composure.

Chuck watched her go, then turned to me with an expression of genuine bewilderment. "How does she do that? Just... carry on?" he asked.

"It's rather what we do here," I replied simply. "Have a cup of tea and carry on."

After our sobering encounter with Margaret, Chuck grew unusually quiet on the way back. His usual American confidence – thinking every problem has a quick fix or a safety net – had just met the harsh reality of England's eroding coastline. We were halfway to the main road when he suddenly brightened, clutching his phone. "We absolutely have to visit the North Norfolk Railway," Chuck exclaimed. "They filmed parts of 'Dad's Army' there, the greatest British sitcom ever. I even have the complete DVD collection – limited edition, with bonus features."

'Dad's Army' is stitched into the fabric of British TV history. First aired in 1968, it followed the bumbling antics of the Home Guard during World War II. These were mostly too-old, too-young, or otherwise unfit-for-service men left to "defend" Britain if the Nazis invaded. The humour was character-driven – not slapstick – gently poking fun at British class quirks, patriotism, and the unique ability to muddle through chaos with tea and politeness. The show was huge. At its peak, 18 million watched, which is staggering. It became a national institution – so much so that its catchphrases entered daily language. 'Don't Panic! Don't Panic'! You could say it at the pub, the office, or at home, and everyone knows what you mean. Repeats have rarely been off television since.

Ryan, juggling his digital map and mentally counting his remaining picnic supplies, perked up, looking from his phone to Chuck. "Excellent suggestion! Weybourne Station was used as 'Walmington-on-Sea' in several episodes. It's a heritage railway now – steam trains, original signal boxes, the full historical experience."

"You don't mind?" Chuck pressed, turning to me with an expression that suggested he was prepared to plead his case with considerable vigour if necessary. "I know it wasn't on the original schedule, but after that cliff erosion stuff... I could use something a little more, you know, stable."

I found myself smiling at the unconscious pun. "Of course not. Heritage railways are quite photogenic, actually."

Forty minutes later, we reached Weybourne Station. The place looked straight out of a 1940s railway poster: a charming country station with spotless red brick and cream-and-red canopies. The most eye-catching feature was a shiny black steam locomotive, breathing silvery steam as it prepared to leave. Vintage luggage trolleys, brass-handled weighing scales, and old enamel advertising signs, reminders of products from the past, were scattered along the platform.

Chuck bolted from the car with barely contained excitement. "This is AMAZING!" he exclaimed, camera already in hand. "It's like walking onto a movie set, except it's all REAL!"

"That's what heritage railways try to do," I explained as we made our way toward the ticket office. "They preserve not just the trains themselves, but the entire experience of railway travel from a particular era."

Chuck was barely listening, his attention consumed by the steam engine. He circled it with reverent steps, photographing every valve, wheel, and rivet from multiple angles. "The detail is incredible," he breathed, crouching to capture the massive driving wheels. "You don't get craftsmanship like this anymore."

While Chuck continued to take photos of the locomotive, I noticed a group of older men in spotless uniforms talking near the signal box. Their navy blue jackets with shiny brass buttons, sharply peaked caps, and mirror-polished boots stood out. One tall man with impressive white moustaches looked over at Chuck's enthusiastic picture-taking and seemed pleased.

"Morning," he called out, approaching us with a pocket watch in hand. "Admiring our Britannia class, are you? She's a beauty, isn't she? Built in 1951 at Crewe Works. Still runs like a dream, with the right care."

Chuck straightened up, his face alight with genuine admiration. "She's absolutely gorgeous, sir. I've never seen anything like her up close. The detailing is incredible," he marvelled.

"Arthur Simmons," the gentleman introduced himself, extending a hand that bore the ingrained oil stains of someone who worked regularly with machinery. "Volunteer driver and occasional station master, depending on who's called in sick with their backs playing up."

I introduced our small group, explaining the photography project we were working on. Arthur nodded with interest, his gaze lingering on Chuck's professional camera equipment.

"Americans are often our most enthusiastic visitors," he observed with a smile. "You folks seem to appreciate these old trains even more than we do sometimes."

"Is it true this is where they filmed 'Dad's Army'?" Chuck inquired.

Arthur's face lit up. "Indeed it is! Weybourne stood in for Walmington-on-Sea in several episodes. The Home Guard used to patrol along this very platform." He gestured toward the station building. "Captain Mainwaring and Sergeant Wilson stood right there during the episode where they were guarding a captured German pilot."

"I've watched every episode," Chuck announced, as if presenting his credentials. "At least three times!"

"Are all of you volunteers?" I asked, noting the various uniformed figures now busy with pre-departure checks around the platform.

"Every last one," Arthur replied proudly. "From the ticket office to the engine footplate, it's all run by volunteers. Most of us are retired now – engineers, mechanics, teachers – brought together by our love of steam. We take care of everything ourselves: the engines, the carriages, the stations, the track. More than three hundred volunteers help keep this little piece of history alive."

Ryan, who had been examining the locomotive with quiet appreciation, turned at this. "How do you source parts for repairs? I imagine they're not exactly available at the local hardware shop," he asked.

This question appeared to delight Arthur, who immediately launched into a detailed explanation that involved terms like "boiler certification," "triple expansion valves," and "Stephenson valve gear" – all of which Ryan received with enthusiastic nods of understanding while Chuck and I exchanged looks of benign incomprehension.

As the two men got lost in technical talk, I took the chance to snap some candid photos of the other volunteers at work. There was something touching about these men in their sixties and seventies. They carefully polished brass fittings or checked signal mechanisms with the focus of people who saw precision and correctness as a matter of personal honour, not just a job. Each one carried the quiet pride of someone who had found purpose in preserving not only machines, but also knowledge, skills, and a way of working that has mostly disappeared from today's world.

Chuck, who had been photographing the station's vintage signage, rejoined our group. "Those signal levers in that box up there – do they actually work? Or are they just for show?"

Arthur looked mildly offended at the suggestion. "Of course they work! Every signal, every point change on this line is controlled mechanically, just as it was eighty years ago. Nothing computerised here."

"Could I... maybe see how it works?" Chuck ventured, his tone suggesting he was requesting an audience with royalty rather than access to a railway signal box.

Arthur thought for a moment and checked his pocket watch. "Well, we've got fifteen minutes before the next train leaves. I guess a quick demonstration would be fine." He beckoned us to the raised signal box, a small wooden building with windows on every side, giving a clear view of the whole station and the tracks in both directions.

Inside, the signal box was a marvel of Victorian engineering. There was a row of large levers painted in different colours, brass instruments for communication, and a big diagram of the track layout on the wall. Chuck looked delighted as Arthur explained what each lever did and the strict rules for using them.

Soon we were back on the platform, and Chuck was unusually quiet, looking thoughtful. "You know what strikes me?" he finally remarked as we watched the steam engine get ready to leave. "In America, all of this would be automated behind the scenes, with actors in costume for the tourists. But here, it's the real deal – actual people doing real work to keep something from the past alive and running."

He pointed to Arthur and his colleagues, who were busy with the final checks before departure. "These guys aren't playing at running a railway – they're actually running one, using skills that would otherwise be lost. That's... I don't know... kind of beautiful, in a way."

I nodded. "That's British heritage preservation at its best. It's not about putting history behind glass, but about keeping it alive through hands-on experience and sharing knowledge."

As the guard's whistle blew and the steam engine released a magnificent cloud of white vapour before beginning its stately departure, Chuck captured the moment with a single, carefully composed shot rather than his usual rapid-fire approach. Progress, indeed.

For the evening, our plan was to visit a show at Cromer Pier, a British landmark jutting into the North Sea and back into a bygone era of entertainment. As we walked to the Pavilion Theatre at the pier's end, wooden planks echoed with decades of holiday footsteps. Bathed in amber light, the theatre's white façade and ornate features glowed. Chuck, absorbed in his phone since we left the railway, looked up and grinned. Nearing the entrance, he said, "Traditional end-of-pier variety show," as if unearthing a rare gem. He added, "My research shows it's one of the last authentic British seaside entertainments. These shows are relics of the golden age of coastal holidays."

Ryan immediately adopted his tour guide demeanour. "The tradition dates back to the Victorian era," he began as we joined the queue for tickets. "Seaside entertainment was the popular culture of its day – before cinema, television, or the internet. Families would save all year for their week at the coast, and the evening show was the highlight of their holiday."

He pointed to the theatre entrance. "Places like this helped launch some of Britain's biggest entertainers. Comedians would spend years perfecting their acts here before moving on to TV. Variety shows are great because they offer a little of everything – comedy, singing, maybe a magician or dancers – so there's something for everyone, no matter their age or background," he said.

Chuck nodded, already photographing painted trim, vintage lights, and the theatre's slightly weather-beaten grandeur. "We had vaudeville in America," he said. "Similar idea, but it faded with movies and TV. You've kept it alive here."

"Most pier theatres have been converted to amusement arcades or demolished entirely," I clarified. "This is the world's last remaining full-season traditional 'end-of-the-pier' variety show."

Inside the Pavilion Theatre, it felt like stepping into a well-preserved time capsule. Rows of faded red velvet seats faced a stage framed by detailed plasterwork. Brass lights with frosted glass shades cast a warm glow throughout the room. The ceiling showed that even practical buildings once had touches of beauty and skill. The carpet, patterned with swirls and stylised flowers in burgundy and gold, was worn thin in the aisles from years of holiday visitors, marking the paths people had taken over time.

"It smells like my grandmother's living room," Chuck whispered as we took our seats – a middle row that offered a good view of both stage and audience. "Kind of musty but in a nice way. Like old books and furniture polish."

The theatre slowly filled with a mix of holidaymakers and locals. Families with children holding ice creams sat nearby. Older couples seemed like regulars, and groups of younger people, some looking amused rather than simply entertained, also found seats. When the lights dimmed and the red velvet curtain rose to reveal a small but lively house band, it felt like we were part of something set apart from today's usual entertainment.

The show might have taken place any time in the last seventy years. A compère in a polished suit presented acts with crisp banter and subtle innuendo. There were singers, an accomplished dance troupe blending tap with contemporary moves, a comedian adept at family humour, and an exceptionally skilled ventriloquist.

As the show concluded with the entire company performing a medley of patriotic songs that prompted much of the audience to join in, I observed Chuck's expression of genuine delight. There was something touching about his wholehearted embrace.

The applause was warm and sustained as the performers took their final bows. As the house lights came up, Chuck turned to us.

"That was AWESOME!" he exclaimed, his volume causing several nearby audience members to glance our way. "So authentic, so skilful! I've never seen anything like it!"

"Rather good," Ryan nodded. "That ventriloquist stood out."

As we made our way toward the exit, weaving through the crowd, Chuck noticed several of the performers greeting audience members in the lobby area. His face lit up. Without hesitation, he pointed and quickened his pace. "Let's go tell them how amazing they were!" he said, already angling himself towards the ventriloquist.

Before we could respond, he went straight to the ventriloquist, who was chatting with a small group. We followed, arriving just in time to witness Chuck's unique style of appreciation.

"You were ABSOLUTELY AMAZING!" he exclaimed, his voice projecting as if addressing someone across a considerable distance rather than standing two feet away. "The BEST ventriloquist I have EVER seen! And I've seen them in Vegas! You're BETTER than the Vegas guys! That bit with the singing puppet – GENIUS! ABSOLUTELY GENIUS!"

The ventriloquist, a man in his fifties whose stage confidence seemed to fade during this exchange, replied with tight smiles and quiet thanks. His body language showed he was looking for a way out of Chuck's enthusiastic praise. Other performers nearby noticed the scene. Their faces showed everything from amusement to mild concern at Chuck's loud and intense compliments.

I stepped forward and put a hand on Chuck's arm. "Let's give them a bit of a break after that performance," I said, steering him gently toward the door.

Once outside on the pier, the sea air cooled our faces, and the sound of waves provided ambient cover for our conversation. I turned to Chuck.

"Chuck," I said, still smiling at the ventriloquist's expression, "we need to talk about how the British handle compliments."

Chuck looked genuinely confused. "Did I say something wrong? I was just telling them how great they were."

"You meant well," I said. "But here, enthusiasm is a bit more restrained. Too much can make people uncomfortable."

"But they were really good!" Chuck protested. "Why wouldn't they want to hear that?"

"They do like praise," I agreed. "But in Britain, 'I enjoyed that' or even 'That was rather good' is high praise. We tend to understate."

Chuck's brow furrowed as he processed this information. "So you're saying that in Britain, 'that was rather good' actually means 'that was amazing'?"

"Exactly," I said. "Americans are more direct with praise. Here, it's more subtle. What sounds mild to you can be strong praise here, and your usual enthusiasm can feel a bit much."

Chuck stopped for a moment, clearly trying to process. "So it's not about feeling less enthusiasm," he clarified, "it's about expressing it differently."

"Right," I said. "It's not that people here are less appreciative. It's just a different way of showing it. A different dialect of enthusiasm, really."

Chuck nodded slowly, then grinned. "A different dialect of enthusiasm," he repeated. "I like that. I've been speaking American Enthusiasm in a country that uses British Enthusiasm. No wonder I've been getting strange looks."

Chuck was quiet for a few paces, shoes thudding on the boards. "Alright. Tomorrow I'll try it your way. I'll begin with 'very good.' If I'm impressed, I'll move to 'quite good.' Should I be astonished, I'll dare a 'really rather good.' And if I'm truly blown away..." He paused dramatically.

I looked at him expectantly.

"...I'll whisper, very softly, 'Not bad at all.'"

The next morning, we met in the gravel car park of The Barrel House Retreat. Chuck's luggage was scattered around him in small clusters. He gave an exaggerated goodbye to his wooden cabin. The early light caught his face, showing a mix of relief and exhaustion, like someone who had survived a rough night's sleep and was already planning to turn it into a good story.

"Goodbye, barrel prison," Chuck called out to the wooden structure. "You were very cute – and I mean that in the most British, understated way possible – but a man of my proportions was not meant to sleep curled like a pretzel in a wooden tub."

Ryan grinned as he stacked his bags in the boot like a large spatial puzzle. "I rather liked my barrel. It had a certain charm."

"That's because you're the size of an actual hobbit," Chuck

countered good-naturedly. "I kept waking up with my feet pressed against one wall and my head against the other. And that shower..." He shuddered as though recalling wartime privations. "A bucket system is not a shower. I don't care how eco-friendly it is."

Our car navigated the narrow Norfolk lanes. Chuck sat in the back seat, his knees nearly touching his chin. Even with the front passenger seat pushed as far forward as Ryan could tolerate, he was cramped. The countryside rolled past, shifting almost imperceptibly from Norfolk's flatness to Suffolk's more rolling land. The change was subtle, yet it marked a wholly different geological history.

"So this B&B," Chuck began, hope brightening his tone, "it has real beds? And actual bathrooms? With running water that doesn't require manual bucketing?"

"All the modern conveniences," I assured him, catching his eye in the rear-view mirror. "It's a converted Victorian rectory – proper plumbing, comfortable beds, and an excellent breakfast, according to the reviews."

"Thank the Lord," Chuck breathed, letting his head tilt back against the headrest in visible relief. "I need a proper shower."

The journey to our Suffolk accommodation continued. Chuck peppered us with questions about British B&Bs. Would we be expected to make conversation with the owners at breakfast (possibly)? Would there be other guests (likely)? Would the bathrooms be shared (no, en suite)? His enthusiasm for what most British travellers considered ordinary was genuine and touching.

When we arrived, the B&B proved to be everything promised and more. It was a handsome Victorian building with bay windows and neatly trimmed hedges. The house sat back from the road in a garden that suggested someone spent considerable time with secateurs and a watering can.

The owner, a woman somewhere in her early seventies, looked exactly like someone who'd spent decades making beds and frying eggs for paying guests. She greeted us with a polite warmth.

"You'll be in the Constable Room," she informed Chuck after completing the check-in formalities, "up the stairs and second door on the right. Bathroom's en suite. Breakfast is served from seven-thirty to nine. Any questions, I'm usually in the kitchen or the garden."

Chuck accepted his key – an actual metal key on a heavy brass fob rather than an electronic card. As we climbed the stairs together, he gripped the handrail tightly, deliberately slowing his pace to better absorb the well-preserved Victorian features: the carved bannister, the patterned carpet runner held in place with polished brass rods, and the framed botanical prints lining the walls. His eyes widened appreciatively at each detail.

"This is more like it," he whispered as we reached the landing. "Actual history, not glamping folly."

We dispersed to our rooms, agreeing to meet downstairs in an hour to plan our afternoon excursion. My room, the Gainsborough, was a model of English B&B comfort. It had a brass bedstead and floral curtains that matched the bedspread precisely. The bathroom had modern fixtures. The water pressure, though, was as unpredictable as you'd expect from retrofitted historical plumbing.

After unpacking my things and responding to several emails in my room, I went down, but I realised that our agreed-upon meeting time had passed with no sign of Chuck arriving. Ryan was already waiting in the small sitting room downstairs. He was leafing through a local guidebook with the absorbed interest of someone mining for obscure facts to deploy later.

"No Chuck?" I asked, checking my watch.

"Not yet," Ryan said, looking up from the guidebook. "Perhaps he's fallen asleep. Those barrels didn't provide optimal rest conditions for him."

Another fifteen minutes passed before my concern for Chuck prompted me to check on our American companion. I climbed the stairs and approached the Constable Room, pausing to listen for signs of life before gently knocking on the door.

"Chuck? Are you alright in there?"

The door opened immediately. Chuck stood there in a dressing gown, looking as if he had been engaged in unexpected physical exertion. His face was flushed and his hair uncombed. He clutched his phone, its screen displaying a YouTube video titled "UK Shower Systems Explained for Americans."

"I can't make the water come out," he said without preamble, frustration and embarrassment warring on his face. "I've been in there for like, forty-five minutes, turning every knob and pushing every button I can find."

The particular tone of bewilderment in his voice – the confusion of a competent adult confronted with a task that should be simple but has somehow become insurmountable – caught Ryan's attention. He quickly came up the stairs to join us.

"Shower troubles?" Ryan teased, barely able to contain his delight at this development.

Chuck nodded. "I feel like I'm taking a test I didn't study for," he said as he stepped back to let us both enter his room. "The dial thing on the shower wall doesn't seem connected to anything. Then there's this pull cord in the bathroom – it turns on a light, but no water. I've tried everything short of performing a rain dance."

"Ah," Ryan said, with the satisfied air of someone about to deploy specialist knowledge. "The Great British Shower Mystery. A classic cultural barrier."

We followed Ryan into Chuck's bathroom. The bathroom appeared in the state one might expect after forty-five minutes of increasingly desperate experimentation – towels disturbed, complimentary toiletries rearranged, and the shower curtain askew.

"The problem," Ryan explained, assuming the tone of a particularly patient museum guide, "is that British electrical safety regulations don't allow standard power switches in bathrooms due to the risk of water contact. Hence, the dual-switch system."

Chuck stared at him blankly. "The what now?"

"There should be a second switch," I clarified, walking from the bathroom into Chuck's bedroom to look for it. "Ah, here we are."

I pointed to a switch on the wall outside the bathroom door, positioned at approximately head height and labelled "Shower" in small, faded lettering.

"You see," Ryan continued, warming to his subject, "the power for the electric shower must be controlled from outside the bathroom. You turn this on first, then use the dial inside for water and to adjust temperature and flow."

Chuck's face transformed with dawning comprehension. "Are you kidding me? There's a second switch OUTSIDE the bathroom? Why would anyone design it that way?"

"Safety," Ryan and I replied in unison.

Ryan demonstrated the process – flicking the outside switch to the "on" position, then entering the bathroom to adjust the dial on the shower unit. After a moment's hesitation, water began flowing from the showerhead, prompting a whoop of triumph from Chuck that was probably audible throughout the B&B.

"Double Switch!" he exclaimed, his face alight with the particular joy of someone who has finally solved a maddening puzzle. "I'm going to make a TikTok about this for other Americans. You guys have no idea how weird this is to us."

Ryan and I left Chuck to enjoy his long-awaited shower. Soon, we heard the water running and Chuck singing loudly and off-key to 'Rule, Britannia!' It sounded like he was trying his best to be very British in a very British shower.

"Fancy a cup of tea while we wait?" Ryan suggested as we descended the stairs. "I have a feeling there's a wealth of cultural confusion yet to come."

The pebbled beach in Aldeburgh stretched before us, a natural defence against the sea. Behind us, pastel-coloured houses lined the promenade in neat rows. The late morning light glinted off the North Sea, creating a silver pathway toward our destination – the controversial Scallop sculpture that had divided local opinion since its installation in 2003.

"There it is!" Chuck exclaimed, quickening his pace across the unsteady pebbles. He adjusted to the rocky terrain with each step, his eyes fixed on the distant sculpture. "Man, that's bigger than I thought it would be!"

The sculpture stood on the shingle, four metres tall, made of two interlocking steel scallop shells with the words 'I hear those voices that will not be drowned' cut into them. In photos, it looked just interesting, but seeing it in person was actually impressive.

"It's caused quite the local controversy," Ryan explained. "Some residents campaigned to have it removed – they felt it spoiled the natural landscape. Others defended it as an important artistic landmark."

Chuck circled the sculpture, his camera raised to capture the structure from every conceivable angle. "The way it catches the light is incredible," he observed, crouching to photograph the sculpture silhouetted against the sky. "And those cut-out letters – that's some serious artistic thinking right there."

"The artist, Maggi Hambling, intended it as a tribute to Benjamin Britten, who lived in Aldeburgh," I said, joining Chuck as he examined the text cut into the steel. "The line is from his opera Peter Grimes – about a local fisherman who becomes an outcast."

"Fitting for something that's caused so much debate," Chuck said. "Art that makes people argue is usually doing something right."

As we explored the sculpture, I noticed an elderly couple approaching from the promenade. They moved with the comfort of people who had walked this beach countless times. The man carried a small sketchbook, the woman a flask, presumably of tea. They paused at a respectful distance from Chuck's photographic orbit, the man settling on a piece of driftwood to sketch.

After several minutes of companionable silence – broken only by the sound of waves, the scratch of pencil on paper, and Chuck's occasional murmurs of artistic appreciation – the elderly man looked up from his sketchbook with a mildly apologetic expression.

"I don't suppose any of you might have a rubber I could borrow?" he inquired with the particular diffidence of someone who dislikes imposing but finds himself with no alternative. "I seem to have forgotten mine, and I've made rather a mess of this line."

Chuck, who had been adjusting his camera settings, froze as his hand hung motionless over his lens cap. His brow knitted in sudden confusion, followed by wide-eyed disbelief as he slowly turned to look at the elderly gentleman.

"A... what?" he stammered, voice suddenly high.

The elderly man, clearly confused by this reaction, repeated his request with careful enunciation. "A rubber. For my sketch. I've made an error with this perspective."

"He means an eraser," I said quickly, noting the elderly couple's growing confusion. "In Britain, an eraser is called a rubber."

"An eraser?" Chuck sighed with relief. "Oh! An ERASER! Let me check my bag."

As Chuck rummaged through his equipment, the elderly man turned to his wife with a look of bewilderment. "What on earth did he think I meant?"

Before I could step in, Chuck located a small eraser in his bag and walked over, handing it to the elderly man with a smile that was awkward at best. "Here's your... rubber. Sorry about that. In America, that word means something, uh, completely different."

The man accepted the eraser with a nod of thanks, still clearly puzzled by the exchange. His wife, however, showed a dawning comprehension.

"Oh!" she exclaimed, a slight blush colouring her cheeks. "I believe I understand the confusion. How amusing these language differences can be."

Attempting to move past the awkwardness, Chuck lifted his camera again and gestured enthusiastically toward the sculpture. "It's really something, isn't it? Kind of homely, but still interesting."

This comment led to another moment of confused silence. The elderly couple exchanged glances, both looking surprised as they tried to make sense of what Chuck had said.

"I think it's rather striking," the woman replied. "But homely?"

"No offence meant," Chuck said quickly. "It's got character. Not pretty, but compelling."

Ryan, who had been observing this exchange with quiet enjoyment, stepped forward. "Another language difference," he explained to the couple. "In America, 'homely' means 'plain' or 'unattractive', whereas here it means 'cosy' or 'comfortable'."

"Good lord," the man remarked, lowering his sketchbook. "We really are two nations divided by a common language, aren't we?"

That comment set off a series of language mix-ups, each one highlighting just how different British and American words can be.

"I was wondering why Brianna gave me her very special look when I told her I ruined my pants during last night's photo shoot."

The elderly woman's eyebrows rose slightly. "Your... pants?"

"After a while, I figured he meant trousers," I clarified quickly.

"Ah," the woman nodded.

"It's like when my suspenders broke during a car race last year," Chuck continued, warming to the subject of clothing vocabulary. "Had to hold my pants up with one hand while shooting with the other."

The elderly couple's expressions suggested they were now visualising scenarios that combined undergarments and photography in concerning ways.

"Braces," Ryan translated. "He means braces for trousers, not what we would call suspenders."

"Which are garter belts here," I added, "typically worn by women to hold up stockings."

Chuck's face registered growing alarm. "Wait, so when I told that guy in the store in Norfolk I needed new suspenders..."

"You basically asked for lingerie," Ryan said, grinning. "And it's called a shop here in the UK."

The conversation became increasingly tangled as Chuck struggled with the language differences.

"I was mad at myself for forgetting my tripod this morning," he said, triggering more confusion.

"Angry," I translated. "In Britain, 'mad' primarily means 'insane', not 'angry'."

"And I left my cellphone in the car trunk," Chuck added, determined to list every language mix-up.

"The what?" the elderly man asked.

"The boot," Ryan said. "I think you mean boot, Chuck, trunk in your language. And it's a mobile phone. A trunk is something else entirely here in Britain."

By this point, the elderly couple watched this verbal tennis match with bemused fascination, their eyes wide and lips pursed as they tried to keep up.

"I needed to get some money from my fanny pack, but–" Chuck began, causing the elderly woman to make a small, involuntary sound of surprise.

"Bum bag!" Ryan interjected hastily. "'Fanny' has a rather different anatomical reference here."

"Female anatomical reference," I specified, seeing Chuck's confusion.

"Oh my God," Chuck whispered. "What else am I saying wrong? Is 'watch' something dirty here? Or 'camera'? Is 'what's up' actually an insult?"

The elderly gentleman, whose initial wariness had transformed into evident enjoyment of this cultural exchange, chuckled warmly. "Language is a fascinating thing, isn't it? Same words, entirely different meanings."

As we said goodbye to the couple and Chuck got his borrowed 'rubber' back, I noticed him typing quickly on his phone.

"Creating an Anglo-American dictionary," he said without looking up. "For my own survival. Next entry: 'Rubber – UK: eraser, US: contraceptive.'"

"Perhaps we should work on that over lunch and take it easy the rest of the day, having an early evening," I suggested, guiding him back toward the promenade. "Before you oversleep and someone needs to knock you up in the morning." Of course, I knew this had a completely different meaning in the US, and I grinned while waiting for the predictable reaction.

"What does that mean here?" he asked with genuine alarm.

"To wake you by knocking on your door," Ryan said cheerfully. "Rather different from its American implications."

Chuck's groan was audible all the way to the fish and chip shop.

One of the best things about living in England is seeing those beautiful and idyllic countryside scenes like Flatford Mill, where the view closely matches John Constable's "The Hay Wain". The mill, cottage, and stream have remained largely unchanged since the 1800s, reflecting England's enduring commitment to its pastoral heritage. In the afternoon, sunlight came through the old trees and made shadows on the water, just like in Constable's famous painting.

"This is literally BLOWING MY MIND!" Chuck shouted, startling a flock of birds into the air. "Dude, it's straight out of the painting! I mean – come on, how does that even happen?"

"Preservation," Ryan intoned, barely glancing up from his phone. "The National Trust bought most of this in 1943 to safeguard exactly these Constable landscapes. They keep things almost obsessively accurate."

Chuck dashed forward, camera primed. "Okay, look at that shot! The river pulls your eyes into the cottage, then, boom – trees frame the whole thing. Constable totally knew what he was doing."

We followed at a more measured pace, allowing Chuck his moment of artistic communion.

"Look at that reflected light on the water!" he called, crouching at the stream's edge. "That's the exact same light effect Constable captured. Exact same!"

Nearby, a small cluster of art lovers exchanged wary glances at Chuck's running monologue. A woman with a thick tome on Romantic painting looked visibly pained as Chuck declared Willy Lott's Cottage to be "super cute."

"Maybe we should see the gallery," I suggested, gently steering Chuck away. "They have Constable reproductions and info about his techniques."

Inside the gallery, high-quality reproductions of Constable's works and informative panels about his life lined the walls.

Chuck moved from image to image, his interest piqued as he temporarily forgot his camera.

"The dude was revolutionary," he remarked, studying a reproduction of "The Hay Wain" beside a photograph of the scene we'd just admired. "Painting ordinary places instead of grand scenes. That was pretty radical for back then, right?"

"Exactly," Ryan said, reading. "He made rural scenes into high art at a time when everyone else painted mythical themes."

As we examined a particularly fine reproduction of "Dedham Vale," Ryan made a casual observation: "Of course, the originals themselves are almost always in the hands of the upper class."

Chuck looked up with sudden interest. "Upper class? You mean rich people, right?"

Ryan and I exchanged a glance, the kind you share when an awkward but familiar topic comes up: the British class system. Even if we try to deny it, it remains very much a part of life in the UK.

"Not quite," I said. "Here, class and wealth aren't always the same."

Chuck's brow furrowed with genuine confusion. "But in America, that's basically what class means. If you've got enough money, you're upper class. That's the whole point of the American Dream – anyone can move up in class if they make enough money."

"The British class system is...more complex," Ryan said.

"Impenetrable, some might say," I added.

Chuck looked between us. "So if it's not about money, what is it?"

We headed outside to continue our conversation by the river, settling on a bench with a view of the mill pond. A family of ducks floated by.

"In Britain," I began, "class isn't just about money. It's a complicated mix of family background, education, accent, cultural tastes, and sometimes wealth. 'Upper class' usually refers to the aristocracy and landed gentry – people who inherit titles, own old estates, and went to certain schools. Even if you suddenly become rich, that doesn't always mean you'll be considered upper class. It's just as much about social history and having the right connections as it is about money."

Chuck's eyes widened. "Wait, you mean real Lords and Ladies – like, actual Downton Abbey stuff?"

"Exactly," Ryan agreed. "To be honest, some 'upper class' people can hardly afford to heat their big, drafty houses, but they're still considered upper class."

"Meanwhile," I continued, "if someone grows up in public housing, speaks with a strong regional accent, and becomes a millionaire, British society might still see them as middle class at best. Many people believe you can't become upper class just by getting rich – you generally need the right family history, lifestyle, and social circle to cross that boundary."

Chuck was now typing notes into his phone with the concentrated focus of an anthropologist. "So you're saying Jeff Bezos wouldn't be upper class here just because he's rich?"

"Not unless he had generations of the right family background, education, and social circles," Ryan confirmed. "Though he could pay himself into the right peer groups to get an invitation to Ascot."

Chuck frowned. "But that sounds...sort of random. Weird, even."

"It is," Ryan agreed. "The markers are subtle. Accent, habits, and manner show background."

Chuck shook his head slowly. "In America, if you've got the cash, you can buy your way into pretty much any circle. Sure, old money might look down on new money, but money is still the ticket."

"The British system is changing," I acknowledged. "It's less rigid than it was fifty years ago. But it hasn't disappeared. You still see it in politics, in media, in business. The top positions are disproportionately held by people from particular educational backgrounds and the right families."

Chuck slipped his phone into his pocket. "Sounds exhausting, honestly. Watching how you talk and act all the time."

"Most people don't think about it consciously," I explained. "It's just how they were raised. But yes, for those attempting to navigate between classes, it can be rather like performing in a play where everyone else knows the script but you're improvising."

We continued our walk along the river, passing the spot where the hay wain – the horse-drawn cart – would have stood in Constable's famous painting. Chuck paused to take several photographs, but I noticed his usual running commentary had been replaced by thoughtful silence.

"So when that lady at the tea shop yesterday said I was 'very American,'" he finally said, "she wasn't just talking about my accent, was she?"

"Probably not," I admitted. "Though she almost certainly meant it affectionately."

"Your directness, your enthusiasm, your volume," Ryan elaborated. "All very American traits that the British tend to notice immediately."

Chuck considered it, then grinned. "Cultural signals. I'm waving the Stars and Stripes, you guys are waving – whatever your group or class is. Most of the time, you don't even realise, right?"

"Precisely," I agreed. "And just as you can't help sounding American, most Britons can't help signalling their class background."

Chuck gazed at the unchanged landscape. "Constable was painting more than just a pretty view, wasn't he? He painted a whole social world, the working class."

"Indeed," Ryan confirmed. "And the fact that we're still dissecting British class structures while standing in exactly the spot he painted two centuries ago suggests some things change rather more slowly than others."

Southwold's high street was lined with independent shops, their windows filled with local crafts, antiques, and practical maritime gear that felt genuinely useful, not just for tourists. The streets twisted in old, medieval patterns, giving priority to ancient footpaths instead of cars. As evening came, golden light washed over the bright cottages, the kind of scene that would have made Constable eager to start painting.

"Whoa, what is that?" He was pointing toward the skyline where, rising incongruously from between a cluster of cottages, stood the distinctive white tower of a lighthouse.

"That's Southwold Lighthouse," Ryan replied. "Built in 1890, still fully operational, guides ships along the Suffolk coast."

"But it's in the middle of town," Chuck said. "Aren't lighthouses usually out in wild places where keepers go mad from isolation?"

"Not this one," I said, smiling at his surprise. "They built it here because it was the highest spot and safe from coastal erosion. They chose practicality over dramatic looks."

Chuck was already heading for the lighthouse, camera in hand. I heard him mumble something about "breaking all the rules of lighthouse placement." We walked after him, taking our time and soaking in the calm of the evening. Southwold had that special English seaside feel, as if it belonged to several eras at once. Victorian buildings stood next to mid-century ones, all glowing in the same light the painter Turner once tried to capture on his canvas.

When we caught up to Chuck, he had been going down to the beach to have an even better view of the lighthouse.

"Amazing," he said, framing a shot of the lighthouse behind the colourful huts. "Do people actually live next to it? Do foghorns wake them up?"

"Indeed, they do live here," Ryan confirmed. "Though the foghorn was decommissioned in 2012 – much to the relief of the neighbours, I imagine. The light itself still operates, of course. Thirty-one miles of visibility."

"I think we've earned a proper pub visit," I suggested as Chuck finally lowered his camera, apparently satisfied that he had enough documentation to impress his friends back home with the 'gardenshed in the shape of a lighthouse'. "The Lord Nelson is just around the corner – one of Suffolk's finest traditional pubs."

The Lord Nelson matched American visions of a traditional English pub: low-beamed ceilings, uneven flagstone floors, and walls with maritime relics. Firelight flickered in the fireplace, and conversation filled the air.

We secured a table in a corner. Chuck volunteered to get the first round of drinks. I watched with mild apprehension as he approached the bar. I was aware that American expectations of beverage service were about to collide with British pub reality.

"Three beers, please," I heard him request from the barman. "And make sure they're nice and cold."

The barman's right eyebrow lifted just a little, which for him was probably as good as a big eye-roll. "What sort of beer did you have in mind?" he asked, his Suffolk accent making the question sound almost musical.

"Um, whatever's popular. And with lots of ice, please," Chuck said, compounding his cultural error.

Ryan shot up from our table, sensing the need to preempt any further breaches of pub etiquette from Chuck.

"We'll have two pints of Adnams Southwold Bitter and three lime and sodas," Ryan interjected smoothly, joining Chuck at the bar. Then, turning to our American friend, he added in a lowered voice, "British ale is served at cellar temperature – about 12 degrees Celsius. Not warm, exactly, but certainly not cold. And never, ever with ice."

Chuck's eyes widened. "But beer is supposed to be cold," he protested, but quietly enough for only us to hear. "That's a universal constant."

"In America, perhaps," I replied. "Here, it's considered essential to taste the full flavour profile of the ale, which cold temperatures would suppress."

The barman placed two pints of amber liquid on the bar, their surfaces crowned with a perfect half-inch of foam. "And lime and soda," he added, setting down noticeably smaller glasses filled with clear liquid, ice, and a wedge of lime.

"Wait, that's it?" Chuck asked, staring at the modest soft drink. "Is that like... a starter size? Do we get free refills?"

The barman's expression suggested he was mentally calculating whether the entertainment value of this conversation outweighed its impact on his evening efficiency. "That's a standard single serving," he explained. "We don't do refills. You pay per drink."

"But it's just soda," Chuck insisted, still confused.

"It is a British pub," Ryan murmured, patting Chuck's shoulder sympathetically while gathering our drinks. "Where soft drinks are treated with the same portion control as alcohol."

We returned to our table. Chuck, still looking slightly unhappy about British drinking customs, took a cautious sip of his ale. His expression shifted through several micro-reactions before settling on polite neutrality.

"It's... interesting," he offered diplomatically. "Kind of... bready? Is it supposed to taste like liquid bread?"

"That's not far off, historically speaking," Ryan replied. "Ale was a staple food back then, often a safer alternative to water in medieval times. The fermentation process killed harmful bacteria."

When Chuck, this time entirely alone, ordered the second round and insisted on paying, he pulled out his phone and began tapping at the calculator app, his thumbs moving with slow deliberation.

"Let's see, twenty percent of that would be..." he muttered, before I gently placed my hand over his screen.

"Another cultural difference," I explained. "Tipping in pubs isn't calculated as a percentage. It's usually just rounding up to the nearest pound, or at most, adding a pound or two if the service was particularly good."

Chuck stared at me as if I'd just announced that gravity was optional in Suffolk. "But... how do the staff make a living?"

"They're paid a proper wage," Ryan explained. "Unlike in the US, servers here don't rely on tips for the majority of their income."

"Or you can say 'and one for yourself' when ordering," I added. "This simply means the barman can add the price of a drink to your bill – a small gesture to show your appreciation. It's a traditional form of tipping, unique to British pubs and welcomed, but not required."

Stepping into the Southwold night, we watched the lighthouse beam sweep across the dark sky – a guiding signal for generations.

"So, to recap today's cultural lessons," Chuck said as we

walked back toward our car, "British people put lighthouses in the middle of towns, drink beer at room temperature, don't believe in free refills, and don't tip properly. Oh, and your class system requires a PhD to understand." Despite his words, his tone carried genuine affection rather than criticism.

"Yet somehow we muddle through," I replied with a smile. "Though I notice you still couldn't quite bring yourself to enjoy the ale."

"Baby steps," Chuck admitted. "I can handle the dual-switch shower system and even the weird rubber-eraser thing, but warm beer might be my cultural bridge too far."

"There's always tomorrow," Ryan observed cheerfully. "Wait until you try Marmite."

Chuck's expression of preemptive alarm was visible even in the gathering darkness. "Do I want to know what that is?"

"Absolutely not," I assured him. "The surprise is half the experience."

If you ask someone to envision a typical academic England, Cambridge would probably come to mind. The town delivered exactly as expected, with academic stereotypes preserved so perfectly they bordered on self-parody. Narrow streets were lined with centuries-old college buildings, cars were outnumbered by bicycles. Students – confident yet dishevelled – moved between ancient institutions. Behind the colleges, the River Cam flowed lazily, while punts, steered by experienced tour guides or hopeful tourists attempting pole navigation, glided past.

Chuck's enthusiasm had been building since our arrival. He seemed almost overwhelmed, as if overcome by spiritual ecstasy. He swivelled his head quickly, trying to take in every architectural detail and passing academic. He looked up at every ancient chimney that I feared for his neck.

"This is unreal," he kept repeating in progressively hushed tones, as if volume reduction might somehow convey increased reverence. "It's like Hogwarts, but with real students. And older. And without the magic. Though maybe with the magic too

– who knows what goes on in those buildings?"

We made our way along King's Parade, the iconic street that forms Cambridge's scholarly spine. We passed the magnificent façade of King's College Chapel, whose Gothic pinnacles reached skyward with medieval ambition. A light drizzle had begun to fall. It was that particularly English precipitation that isn't quite committed enough to be proper rain but is certainly more than mist. We sought shelter in one of the many souvenir shops lining the parade.

The shop was crowded with tourists seeking similar refuge from the weather. The air grew damp and wool-scented as rain-spotted jackets steamed in the heated interior. Glass cabinets displayed college crests on everything from silver cufflinks to chocolate bars. Shelves groaned under mugs, tea towels, and teddy bears dressed in miniature academic regalia.

The bears in their little costumes caught Chuck's eye. He picked up one, a soft toy dressed in a tiny black gown with a red hood, and studied it closely.

"Excuse me," he called to the shopkeeper, a woman of indeterminate middle age. "Do you sell the real versions of these? The actual graduation gowns?"

The shopkeeper looked up from her till. "The academic dress? No, I'm afraid we don't. These are just souvenirs – miniature versions for the teddy bears."

Chuck didn't hide his disappointment. "But I need one to show my buddies back home!" he said loudly enough that a few people looked over. "They'd go wild if I showed up to our poker night in a real Cambridge gown."

"You'd need to be a graduate of the university to wear one legitimately," the shopkeeper explained patiently. "They're not sold to the public. Students and academics hire them from official outfitters for special occasions."

Ryan, who had been examining a display of bookmarks featuring college crests, leaned in to offer clarification. "It's like claiming military decorations you haven't earned."

Chuck's expression suggested he was recalibrating his souvenir priorities in light of this information. He looked at the bear, then back at the shopkeeper, and finally replaced the bear on its shelf with gentle respect, as if acknowledging its superior academic credentials.

But he didn't stay disappointed for long. He spotted a rack of baseball hats with the Cambridge crest and the words "CAMBRIDGE UNIVERSITY" in big letters, plus "established in 1209" underneath. He grabbed a burgundy one, his excitement back. "These are cool too. Real Cambridge! Not as impressive as a gown, but I'll look super British back home," he said.

He most certainly would not. But I let him have his British moment.

After we paid, we stepped back onto King's Parade. The drizzle had stopped. We walked past Corpus Christi College toward one of Cambridge's more recent additions – the Corpus Clock.

Chuck stopped so suddenly in front of the clock that I almost bumped into him. With his mouth open in surprise, he stared at the huge golden disc shining on the college corner. Above the clock sat a giant mechanical insect – part grasshopper, part locust – its appearance a little frightening. Sharp metal jaws snapped together in steady bites, as if each one ate up another second.

"What... is... THAT?" Chuck breathed, his camera already in hand, previous souvenir satisfaction entirely forgotten.

"The Corpus Clock," Ryan supplied, adopting his tour guide demeanour. "Unveiled by Stephen Hawking in 2008. That creature on top is called a 'chronophage' – literally 'time-eater' in Greek."

Chuck circled the clock, capturing the insect from every angle with his camera.

"This is seriously cool," he declared, crouching to photograph the chronophage from below. "The way it seems to be eating the seconds – that's incredible design work. And it's actually keeping time?"

"Sort of," Ryan said, checking his phone for details. "It's made to run unevenly. Sometimes it speeds up, sometimes it slows down, and sometimes it even stops, just like how time can feel to us. The blue lights behind it flash to show the seconds."

"The chronophage blinks every minute," I added, watching

as the creature's metal eyelids briefly closed on cue. "The designer, John Taylor, wanted to remind viewers that time is ultimately devouring all of us."

"Cheerful," Chuck remarked, though his enthusiasm remained undimmed. "But totally British – taking something as ordinary as a clock and making it into a philosophical statement about mortality."

"Actually, there is an element of humour involved," Ryan noted. "The clock is deliberately designed to be slightly inaccurate – a quiet joke at the expense of Cambridge's reputation for precision and accuracy."

"So it's both profound AND a prank?" Chuck looked even more impressed. "That's some next-level British wit right there."

We left the ordinary outskirts behind and suddenly found ourselves at the base of a steep hill. At the top stood one of England's most impressive cathedrals. Twisting streets surrounded it, seemingly avoiding right angles on purpose. Lincoln's medieval character was impossible to miss. We parked at the bottom of Steep Hill and set off on foot, wandering through a maze that had tested visitors long before the Norman Conquest.

We walked through narrow passageways between old buildings, feeling almost surrounded by history. Some upper floors stuck out so far, they looked as if the buildings were taking over the street. Ryan and I were used to these tight spaces. Chuck, however, faced a unique form of architectural claustrophobia.

"These streets weren't designed for someone of your... American proportions," I observed, watching as he twisted sideways to pass a particularly narrow section where two pedestrians could barely walk abreast.

"Were people seriously smaller back then?" Chuck asked, rubbing his shoulder. "Or did everyone just spend their lives walking sideways like crabs? This feels like a street designed for gnoms, not actual humans."

"Medieval people were indeed somewhat shorter on average," Ryan said, sidestepping a low shop sign. "But the streets are narrow because space inside the city walls was limited and cars didn't exist."

Chuck nodded, then immediately winced as his head nearly connected with a low beam above a shop doorway. "It's not just the streets," he continued, now hunching as a precaution. "Everything here seems miniaturised. Your roads! What you call a dual carriageway would be barely a single lane back home. The rooms in that B&B last night? My bathroom at home is bigger than the entire bedroom."

He pointed to a café to prove his point. People sat at tables so small they would seem undersized at a children's tea party in the US. "And don't get me started on food packaging. Those bags of chips, or crisps, look like samples to Americans. The frozen peas I saw in that supermarket yesterday? The package was so tiny it could have been for a doll's house."

"I suspect our NHS might collapse entirely under the strain if we adopted your supersized approach to food," I remarked dryly.

We stopped talking as we left the narrow streets and stepped into the wide cathedral square. The change was striking. We went from tight medieval lanes to the towering presence of one of England's greatest Gothic cathedrals. The weathered limestone front stood tall. Even though I'd visited before, I felt a bit awed.

Chuck stopped abruptly, his neck craned back at what appeared to be a physically uncomfortable angle as he attempted to take in the full height of the central tower. For once, his typical torrent of commentary had dried up completely, replaced by an expression of genuine awe.

"Lincoln Cathedral was once the tallest building in the world," Ryan said quietly. He allowed the structure to make its own impressive statement before adding historical context. "From 1311 to 1549, its central spire reached higher than the Great Pyramid of Giza, which had held the record for nearly four thousand years."

"The spire collapsed during a storm," I added. "What you see today is actually considerably shorter than the original structure."

Chuck released a long, low whistle of appreciation. "Well, I guess there's one thing you Brits actually do make big," he said finally, a grin spreading across his face. "And I gotta say, you nailed it. This place is spectacular."

The cathedral's interior was even more impressive. Its vaulted ceiling soared above us with the particular defiance of gravity seen in the finest Gothic architecture. Columns rose like petrified forests, their capitals blossoming into stone foliage. Light filtered through stained glass, casting coloured patterns on ancient stonework and creating an atmosphere both solemn and theatrical.

As we wandered through the nave, Chuck paused beside a commemorative plaque that detailed the cathedral's dimensions. He studied it with growing confusion. Then he turned to us with an expression that suggested he'd encountered yet another British peculiarity requiring explanation.

"Okay, I need to ask about this," he began, pointing to the measurements listed on the plaque. "The height is given in both metres and feet. The floor area is in square metres only. Then there's something about the weight of the tower in tons – but are those metric tonnes or imperial tons? How do you guys keep all this straight?"

Ryan and I exchanged smiles. Once again, we found ourselves confronted with one of those British quirks we'd long ago given up trying to explain.

"It is rather confusing," Ryan admitted. "Even though the UK officially moved to the metric system decades ago, we still use a mix of metric and imperial units, sometimes even together in the same context, like on that plaque."

"But that's my point," Chuck persisted. "You buy vegetables in kilograms, but weigh yourselves in stones. Short distances are in metres, long ones in miles. You fill your car with petrol in litres, but calculate fuel efficiency in miles per gallon. It's measurement schizophrenia!"

I found myself nodding in reluctant agreement. "I've never really thought about it, to be honest. It's just... how we do things."

"But it makes no logical sense," Chuck insisted, warming to his subject. "It's like you couldn't commit to either system, so you just randomly selected whichever unit you liked the sound of for each different thing you measure."

"Though we all agreed that Celsius makes more sense than Fahrenheit," Ryan added. "Water freezing at zero and boiling at one hundred is clearly more logical than... whatever Fahrenheit is based on."

"Except," I interjected, "for when there's a particularly hot summer day, and all the newspapers inexplicably revert to Fahrenheit to report the temperature because 95 degrees sounds more dramatically sweltering than 35."

Chuck shook his head in bewilderment. "And you guys make fun of Americans for not adopting the metric system? At least we're consistent in our wrongness!"

"Consistency has never been Britain's strong suit," I acknowledged. "We prefer the messier but more characterful approach of gradually accumulating contradictory systems, then pretending the resulting chaos is entirely intentional and possibly even sophisticated."

Later, as we concluded our exploration of Lincoln's old town and searched for a place for refreshments, Chuck reflected on the experience. "You know," he observed, "I think I understand Britain a little better now. You're not actually trying to be difficult with all these contradictions. It's just that you never throw anything away, even outdated measuring systems. You just keep adding new things on top of the old ones, like geological layers."

"A surprisingly insightful observation," I conceded. "Though I suspect most Britons would be horrified to discover they're being quite so comprehensible to an American."

The Magna Carta pub sat in an old building at the top of Steep Hill. After our trip to the cathedral, its low-beamed interior felt like a welcome break. The medieval look gave way to the cosy feel of a classic English pub. Chuck, still excited from our visit, dropped onto a wooden bench, which groaned under his weight.

"Man, I need to document this," he said, reaching for his camera bag. "This place is like Medieval Times but without the cheesy jousting tournament."

"It's actually Georgian," Ryan corrected, examining a framed newspaper clipping about the pub's history. "Though parts of the cellar date back to the thirteenth century. The name references Lincoln's connection to the Magna Carta. One of the four surviving original copies is housed in the castle."

While Chuck set up his camera on the table, I noticed a man at a nearby table observing him closely, as if he recognised a fellow professional. The man, who appeared to be in his mid-forties with simply cut grey hair, sat with deliberate care, keeping his back straight. The way he moved reminded me of my uncle, who had to move cautiously before his back surgery.

After watching us for a moment, the man stood up, picked up his half-empty pint, and carefully approached our table, holding his glass steadily as though trying to avoid any sudden jerks.

"Canon 1DX Mark III, if I'm not mistaken," he said by way of greeting, nodding toward Chuck's camera. "Beautiful piece of equipment. The autofocus tracking is unmatched for sports work."

Chuck's face lit up with the particular delight of finding a fellow enthusiast in unexpected territory. "You know your gear! Yeah, it's a beast for tracking fast action. You shoot professionally?"

"I did," the man said, reaching out his hand slowly. "Peter Steele. Most people call me Steady, a nickname from my days as a sports photographer. It's a bit ironic now, because of my back."

Introductions completed, Peter joined our table at Chuck's enthusiastic insistence. There was something immediately compelling about him. He had a quiet dignity combined with flashes of dry humour that emerged as he and Chuck began comparing notes on the particular challenges of sports photography.

"Premier League for fifteen years," Peter explained in response to Chuck's question about his professional background. "I covered everything from Cup Finals to Champions League nights. Started with film cameras. Remember manually focusing while tracking a midfielder's run? Nightmare. Digital was a revelation."

"NASCAR and college football, mainly," Chuck replied, his usual excitement softened with respect. "I've also covered two Super Bowls and a World Series. The real challenge is always the same, right? Anticipating the moment before it happens."

I watched their conversation with interest. Chuck, who normally speaks quickly, slowed down without noticing. He clearly respected Peter's expertise and seemed to connect with him.

"So what happened?" Chuck asked, gesturing vaguely toward Peter's rigid posture. "You mentioned a back situation?"

Peter took a measured sip of his beer before responding. "Three years ago at a Crystal Palace match. I positioned myself pitchside for the second half. I always preferred ground-level shooting for the drama. One of their players attempted an overhead kick, missed completely, and came crashing into the photographers' area. Two hundred pounds of professional athlete landed directly on my back."

Chuck winced sympathetically. "That's brutal. But you recovered, right? I mean, with proper treatment and physical therapy..."

"That's the ongoing question," Peter replied with a wry smile that didn't quite reach his eyes. "Severe disc damage at L4 and L5. Surgery's the only real solution, but I'm still on the NHS waiting list. Been there for thirty-one months now."

Chuck's expression transformed from sympathy to disbelief. "Thirty-one months? As in, almost three years? Without surgery?"

"That's the National Health Service after the pandemic," Peter said, sounding calm. "Elective surgeries were delayed first, and now the backlog is huge. I'm not sick enough to be a priority, but not healthy enough to work properly. I'm stuck in the middle, like thousands of others."

"But it's free, right?" Chuck asked, sounding both curious and a little envious, as many Americans do when discussing universal healthcare. "You don't have to pay anything for the surgery when it happens?"

"Free at the point of use," Peter confirmed. "Paid for through our taxes, of course. But yes – when I finally get the operation, I won't receive a bill. The ambulance that took me from the stadium to the hospital, the initial MRI, the pain management programme – all covered."

Chuck shook his head slowly, processing this information. "Man, in the States, an injury like yours would bankrupt most people. Even with insurance, the out-of-pocket costs would be insane. My cousin broke his leg skiing – had good insurance through his job – still ended up fifteen thousand dollars in debt."

"The NHS isn't perfect," I contributed. "But it removes the financial anxiety from medical emergencies. When my mother needed cancer treatment, our concern was her health, not whether we could afford her care."

Ryan nodded in agreement. "My grandfather's heart surgery would have cost well over a hundred thousand pounds in America. Here, his biggest complaint was the hospital food."

"Don't get me wrong," Peter said, shifting in his seat and wincing a little. "I'm really grateful for the system. The nurses and doctors are brilliant. When it works, it's great. But the waiting is the downside, and it's only getting worse."

"How do you manage in the meantime?" Chuck asked, genuine concern replacing his initial shock. "Are you still able to work?"

"I've adapted," Peter replied with the particular stoicism that seems encoded in British DNA. "I can't handle the physical side of sideline work anymore. Carrying heavy lenses, moving fast, and unexpected hits are too much now. So I switched to portrait photography. It's easier on my body. Not as exciting, but it pays the bills while I wait."

After that, the conversation moved easily. Chuck asked Peter about changing careers, and Peter was curious about how sports photography works in America.

By the time we got a second round of drinks, it was obvious they had really connected. Even though they came from different backgrounds, Chuck and Peter shared the bond of people who spend their careers capturing moments that most others only see for a second.

Eventually, as our conversation turned to Chuck's remaining time in Britain, Peter remarked, "It sounds like you've got quite the tour planned. Though I notice you're missing out on proper football stadiums. All these cathedrals and quaint villages, but not a single visit to the real churches of England – our football grounds."

Chuck's expression brightened further. "Man, I would love that! But wouldn't we need tickets? Aren't those things sold out months in advance?"

"Not for a tour with me," Peter replied with a small smile. "I still have press contacts at several clubs. Can't get you into matches at this stage, but behind-the-scenes access? That I might manage."

Chuck was looking at Peter as if he'd just offered him the Holy Grail itself.

"Seriously? You could get me into actual Premier League stadiums? The locker rooms? The pitch?" His voice had regained its characteristic volume, drawing glances from nearby tables.

Peter nodded, the movement careful and measured like all his physical gestures. "Old Trafford is out – Manchester's too far. But I could arrange something at Leicester City's ground. It's on your way north, and my former assistant is now their team photographer."

Breakfast at our Lincoln B&B felt like a classic British morning. Guests quietly asked for more toast, passed marmalade jars with care, and silently judged anyone who dared order a full English after 9:30. Chuck, though, missed all these subtle cues. He spoke loudly and excitedly, sharing his new plans with Peter for everyone to hear.

"So Steady's picking me up in an hour." He flicked crumbs from his toast onto the pristine tablecloth. "We're hitting Leicester City's ground today. Maybe Villa Park tomorrow. He says the history in these places is incredible – like your cathedrals but with more crowd chanting."

Ryan, who had been methodically arranging his tofu scramble into a precise mound, looked up with mild alarm. "Today? But we're meant to be heading to York this afternoon. We have accommodation booked."

"That's the thing," Chuck countered. "I was thinking I could split off. Peter says he can show me the soccer Britain – not just the photo version."

I looked at Ryan with surprise. Our carefully crafted itinerary was being casually shuffled over breakfast, but I felt more amused than irritated.

"But how will you manage the logistics?" I asked. "Peter mentioned his back prevents him from driving long distances."

Chuck's expression brightened. "I'm going to drive his car! I've got my international driving permit and everything. Peter says his Volvo has an automatic transmission, so I just need to remember to stay on the left."

The thought of Chuck – who had already bumped into several medieval doorframes due to his poor sense of space – now attempting to drive on narrow British roads from the unfamiliar left side made me genuinely nervous.

"Have you ever driven on the left before?" I ventured, keeping my tone as neutral as possible.

"No, but how hard can it be?" Chuck replied with characteristic American optimism. "Peter's going to navigate, and we'll stick to the major roads. Plus, I've been watching you drive for days now – I've got the basic idea."

Ryan, unable to contain himself, set down his teacup with deliberate precision. "The 'basic idea' of British driving involves more than simply changing lanes, Chuck. There are roundabouts to contend with. Right-of-way conventions that differ substantially from American practice. Road signage that requires instantaneous metric conversion while navigating unfamiliar territory."

"And our motorway service stations are profoundly disappointing compared to American rest stops," I chimed in.

Chuck was unfazed, his excitement unstoppable. "Everything will be alright! Peter says the first hour will be terrifying, and then I'll adjust. He can't drive with his back, and this way he gets to show me his world while I provide the transportation. Win-win!"

A short while later, Peter arrived, marking the next step in Chuck's departure. Through the dining room window, I spotted a practical Volvo estate car parked outside. It looked like the classic British photojournalist's vehicle, its once-clean exterior now showing the wear of many trips carrying camera gear through all sorts of British weather.

The rather strenuous task of transferring Chuck's substantial luggage from our car to Peter's took the next half hour. Peter's physical limitations and Chuck's inability to pack efficiently complicated the process. What had arrived in England as two reasonably sized suitcases had somehow multiplied into an assortment of bags, boxes, and bundles containing everything from souvenir tea towels to what appeared to be a substantial chunk of Lincoln Cathedral gift shop inventory.

"Did you really need three identical models of the cathedral?" I teased, helping Chuck manoeuvre a particularly unwieldy package into Peter's boot.

"They're not identical," Chuck protested. "One's for my mom, one's for my office, and one's for my man cave."

Peter observed this transfer of American consumerism with quiet amusement, offering occasional guidance on the optimal arrangement of luggage to maintain visibility through the rear window.

"I see you've prepared for American driving," I remarked to Peter, nodding toward a Post-it note stuck to the dashboard that read "KEEP LEFT" in block capitals, followed by "NO, THE OTHER LEFT!!!" underlined three times.

When the luggage was finally arranged, the farewell began. Chuck launched into his American enthusiasm – a mix of gratitude, hugs, and promises of future contact that felt both heartfelt and temporary.

"You guys are absolutely INCREDIBLE!" he boomed, sweeping Ryan into a massive bear hug that nearly cracked ribs and left no doubt about his appreciation. "Seriously, you're the GREATEST guides in the whole universe! I mean it – I've picked up a ton about Britain, photography, even how to survive a British shower! This trip? LIFE-CHANGING!"

Ryan, extracted from this enthusiastic embrace, straightened his jumper, clearly uncomfortable with such exuberance. "It's been our pleasure," he said, stepping back to a more comfortable distance. "Do drive carefully. And remember, when approaching a roundabout—"

"Give way to the right, follow the directional signs, signal appropriately," Chuck recited, clearly having received this instruction multiple times already. "I've got it. I've been studying YouTube videos all morning."

Chuck's goodbye to me was just as effusive. Prepared this time, I managed to hold onto my dignity during the extended hug. "Thank you for EVERYTHING, Brianna. I'll NEVER photograph the same way again. You are the BEST EVER photographer!"

"It was good to have you here," I replied sincerely. "And do stay in touch. I'd like to see how your approach to photography continues to develop."

"Oh, I'll definitely WhatsApp you guys!" Chuck promised, already backing toward Peter's car, too excited about what comes next to fully complete what's happening now. "And I'll send all my photos! Maybe come back next year? Wales? Scotland? I've heard the Highlands are AMAZING!"

Peter, who had been observing this farewell display with the quiet patience of someone accustomed to waiting, finally intervened. "We should get going if we want to reach Leicester before lunch," he suggested gently. "I've arranged for us to meet the club photographer at one."

"Right! Soccer!" Chuck exclaimed, as if suddenly remembering the primary purpose of this new arrangement. "We're off to see a proper soccer stadium!" He caught himself, glancing at Peter. "Oh no, it is football, is it? That's what you called it, right? Proper football?"

"Indeed," Peter confirmed with a small smile. "And perhaps save that particular soccer phrasing until we're safely away from any actual supporters. The soccer/football distinction can be rather… passionately debated."

With final waves and promises of digital communication that would almost certainly reduce in frequency with each passing mile, Chuck folded himself into the driver's seat of Peter's Volvo. Through the windscreen, Ryan and I could see Peter providing what appeared to be a detailed orientation to the vehicle's controls, while Chuck's expression shifted between concentration and mild alarm.

The car pulled away with a slight jerk, followed by a more confident acceleration. Chuck's hand emerged from the driver's window in a final enthusiastic wave – a gesture that promptly caused the car to drift alarmingly toward the centre line before a visible correction brought it back to the appropriate lane position.

Ryan and I stood together, watching until the Volvo disappeared around a corner, both noticing that Chuck's understanding of British road positioning remained a work in progress.

"Do you think they'll make it to Leicester?" Ryan asked, genuinely concerned as we watched the car turn the corner.

"Peter seems like a good influence," I replied. "And Chuck is adaptable. I suspect they'll manage admirably." I turned back toward the B&B entrance. "Besides, they clearly formed a great connection. Sometimes the most valuable experiences come from the least expected detours."

Ryan nodded thoughtfully. "They did hit it off, didn't they?"

"This is exactly what we hoped for with this project: a real cultural exchange that goes deeper than just being tourists," I added.

A little later, Ryan and I loaded our considerably more modest luggage into our car. He broke the momentary silence. "Shall we already head to York? We've got three free days before we need to meet our Swedish student. We could use the unexpected free days to explore the area, but without any cultural clashes."

"Good idea," I agreed as I got into the driver's seat. "Speaking of culture clash, I'm actually looking forward to seeing what the Swedish student brings. The application mentioned Scandinavian minimalism - could be an interesting perspective."

As Lincoln Cathedral receded in our rear-view mirror, I found myself genuinely curious about our next cultural undertaking. Each student had brought their own perspective, their own preconceptions about Britain, and their own capacity for surprise as expectations met reality. Chuck had been a whirlwind of enthusiasm and adaptation. Now, with our Swedish student, I anticipated an entirely different set of challenges and rewards.

A SWEDE IN NORTH ENGLAND

Before sunrise, the timber-framed buildings of The Shambles seemed to lean in, their upper stories nearly touching overhead. The narrow passage brimmed with morning mist, swirling under the dim glow of street lamps. Dew slickened the cobblestones as we walked along York's most famous street. Through centuries, this place had witnessed everything: commerce, banter, and now, a steady flow of tourists, all eager to capture a hint of Harry Potter magic.

"Mind the step here." I caught Ryan's arm as he stared at his phone with such intensity he nearly missed a sudden drop in the uneven pavement. I glanced ahead. "What time did Lars say he'd meet us?"

"Five-thirty precisely,"

I checked my watch – 5:24 am.

"I wonder if we should have specified which end of the street to meet at," Ryan muttered as he closed the York old town map app on his phone. He peered down one of the narrow alleyways branching off from The Shambles, then sidestepped to get a better angle and craned his neck, scanning the darkness for any moving shapes. "These Snickelways are impossibly confusing in the dark."

The Snickelways of York, those curiously named, cramped passages wedged between buildings, formed a labyrinth, especially in the faint light of early morning. We reached a juncture where three of these paths converged. Suddenly, footsteps resonated behind us, even, purposeful, as if someone was striding out of the mist.

Ryan jumped back, nearly dropping his phone as he spun on his heel to face the sound. "Good Lord!" he exclaimed.

A figure appeared at the entrance to one of the Snickelways. He was tall and broad-shouldered, with long blonde hair tied back in a neat bun. For a moment, his outline looked like a Viking who had wandered into modern York from another time. The street lamp behind him cast a glow that made him seem even more like a Norse god visiting England.

"Brianna and Ryan, I presume?" The voice was low, careful, softer than his Viking-like silhouette had promised.

"Lars!" I called, stepping forward and extending my hand,

which disappeared completely in his much larger one. "Lovely to meet you. Though I must admit, you gave us quite a start."

He blinked once, a little embarrassed. "I'm sorry," he said quietly, thumbs brushing the strap of his camera bag. "I arrived 20 minutes early to scout spots. I didn't mean to startle you."

Up close, Lars Andersson appeared even more imposing. He towered at least six foot four, with shoulders sculpted by years of trekking through forests and scaling rugged trails. He wore understated, high-performance clothing, chosen purely for utility. His Swedish camera bag hung at his side like it belonged there. It looked hefty, but Lars carried it as effortlessly as someone carrying a clutch on a night out.

"Twenty minutes early?" Ryan said, recovering his composure. He now regarded Lars with fascination. "That's... a very early morning."

Lars offered a small smile. "I figured the street would fill up fast. By eight-thirty, everyone and their camera, especially Potter fans, will be wandering through." When he said "Harry Potter," there was just the faintest twitch at the corner of his mouth, a subtle sign of disapproval.

"Ah, yes, the Diagon Alley connection," I put in. "Though The Shambles actually predates the books by several centuries."

"The timber frames mostly date from later rebuilds," Lars said, brushing a lock of hair behind his ear. "Originally, the street was full of butcher shops. 'Shamel' meant bench, where meat was displayed." He glanced at Ryan and me, his cheeks colouring slightly as if he had just realised he was giving a mini lecture.

"Well, you've certainly come prepared," Ryan said, pulling out his phone again. "Usually, I'm the one who shares all the interesting facts with our guests." He scrolled through his screen. "I was just looking at your portfolio earlier. Your work is quite striking, with its minimalist approach and use of negative space." He kept scrolling. "It's very Swedish in style. It actually reminds me of IKEA furniture: stark, functional, and oddly satisfying."

I suppressed a wince at the cliché comparison, but Lars appeared entirely unbothered by it. He let out a quiet laugh. "I've heard worse," he said, then looked away for a moment, fiddling with a zipper. "Though I consider Hasselblad cameras a more appropriate Swedish design reference than flat-pack furniture."

"I loved your coastal series," I chipped in. "The emptiness feels intentional, contemplative."

He nodded, a hint of a grin tugging at his lips. "Thank you. I think emptiness can be as powerful as fullness."

Above us, the sky shifted from black to deep navy as dawn crept in. The carved beams overhead caught the first pale light, each curve and bump glowing with age.

"We should start," Lars murmured, kneeling to unpack his tripod. "Light changes quickly. I'd like to get the street while it's still deserted."

"Of course," I said. "Any shots you have in mind?"

"Indeed," he replied, carefully fitting a lens. "First, I want to capture the lines of the overhanging buildings, almost like a tunnel. Then, I'll focus on the way the lamp light mixes with the dawn." His voice was steady and sure. He clearly knew what he wanted and had come well prepared.

"All black and white?" Ryan asked.

"For this scene, yes. Colour might take attention away from the shapes." Lars looked at the empty street, as if he could already picture the photo in his mind.

While Lars set up his tripod, I took a moment to enjoy the street as it brightened. The Shambles had a special English quality, feeling both ancient and alive. It wasn't a museum piece behind glass, but a living place that changed with each century while keeping its character.

Once Lars had captured the old streets with enough shots to fill an architectural publication, I turned to him. "What's our plan after The Shambles?" I asked.

He straightened, blinking against the dawn. "I've mapped a route through the Yorkshire Dales. I want to photograph drystone walls – the geometric patterns in the hills."

"That sounds like a full day," Ryan said, checking his phone. "But the Dales are a good drive from here. Should we consider breakfast first? There's a café just off Stonegate that opens at six – supposed to be quite good."

Lars straightened from his camera and faced Ryan, regarding him with what might have been mild surprise. "Breakfast is in my daypack. Rye bread, smoked fish, filtered water." He patted a small bag slung across his back. "I hate missing good light."

Ryan's expression fell slightly, his fingers hovering above his phone where I could just make out the word "pastries" in his search results.

"Perhaps a compromise," I suggested. "We can take some travel cups of tea from the café for the journey? The Dales are quite magnificent in morning light, but Yorkshire without tea would be rather sacrilegious."

Lars considered this, then nodded once, decisively. "Tea in reusable cups is acceptable," he said, tugging at his straps. "But quickly. And no plastic!"

When the first sunlight touched the cobblestones, turning the old stones golden, I smiled at the difference between our last American student and our current Swedish one. Chuck had been loud and enthusiastic, while Lars was quiet and reserved. Still, both shared a real passion for photography, just in very different ways.

"Right then," I said, watching as the medieval street gradually transformed in the growing light. "Shall we begin our Dales adventure?"

Morning light caught the dew on the grass, turning the hillsides bright and lush. Lars walked ahead of us on the narrow trail, moving with quiet purpose. His long legs carried him forward at a steady pace, camera swinging from his neck. Every so often, he would pause, lean in, then step back, waiting for just the right moment. The Yorkshire Dales spread out before us, a green patchwork stitched together by centuries-old drystone walls that traced geometric patterns across the rolling land.

Several paces behind Lars, Ryan trudged along. He dragged

his feet in the muddy path and occasionally glanced up. His weary look said it all. His pace slowed – clearly, he was unprepared for the sheer amount of walking involved in countryside photography.

"Brianna," he called, perfectly channelling that British art of making a complaint sound like polite small talk. "Remind me, why are we slogging along the scenic route? Google Maps says there's an actual road just over there."

"That's hardly the point of coming to the Dales," I said, stopping to let him catch up. "Lars wants the light on those walls from this angle, not from a car window."

Ryan squinted at his phone. "There's no tea shop for miles – though half a mile ahead is a farm with an 'honesty-box cake stand.' Let's hope the sheep haven't raided it." He brightened, then frowned as he read the reviews. "Ah. Apparently, they have."

Ahead of us, Lars had stopped at a dramatic overlook. He stood perfectly still – camera raised, but not yet triggered. He waited. He sought a precise combination of light, cloud, and composition only he could perceive. His patience was almost unnerving.

"Is there perhaps a shortcut to your perfect composition?" Ryan continued his disguised lamenting.

Lars pressed one eye to the viewfinder. He kept his hands steady on his camera, ignoring Ryan's comment. Lars shuffled his feet slightly on the uneven ground to adjust his position, intent on achieving his perfect composition.

"There is no shortcut to a good shot," he finally said, without turning around. "Just as there is no shortcut across these hills. The path exists for a reason."

I suppressed a smile at the unintentional philosophy. Ryan looked less amused, his expression suggesting he was mentally cataloguing every comfortable chair he'd ever taken for granted.

We continued our trek as the landscape shifted, descending into a broad, shadowed valley. Against a steep hillside, a cluster of weathered stone cottages came into view. From one end of the settlement, a thin column of grey smoke twisted into the clear morning air. It was substantial, more than a simple chimney fire.

"Look at that smoke," Ryan mused. "Early Guy Fawkes celebration?"

As we approached, we saw a gathering of people around what appeared to be a well-constructed bonfire in a field near the village. Several figures noticed us and waved in greeting.

"Good morning," called a man in wellies and a weathered waxed jacket that spoke of decades of faithful service. "Come for the fête, have you?"

"We're just passing through," I explained as we approached. "Photographing the Dales."

"Well, you've timed it right," the man replied, gesturing toward the gathering. "Annual village fête. We moved it up this year because of the early harvest. Climate change and all that. The seasons don't follow calendars anymore."

Ryan's face lit up as he eyed the trestle tables. "A fête? Brilliant! For a second, I thought it was an early Guy Fawkes party."

The man, who introduced himself simply as Jim, chuckled and offered us earthenware mugs of hot cider that steamed invitingly in the morning air. "For Guy Fawkes, it is too early, now in summer. Every fifth of November, we celebrate the foiling of the Gunpowder Plot – when Guy Fawkes tried to blow up Parliament back in 1605."

Lars, snapping a picture, interrupted. "Wait – you celebrate someone who tried to blow up Parliament?"

His tone held no judgment, just the precise curiosity of someone attempting to understand an unfamiliar cultural practice.

Jim seemed momentarily taken aback by the directness of the question. He offered a bemused smile. "Well, when you put it like that, it does sound a bit odd. But traditions have a way of outlasting their origins, don't they? These days it's more about community gathering, fireworks, and giving the children a bit of excitement as the nights draw in."

We spent a pleasant hour at the fête, sampling homemade preserves and cakes. Lars captured the gathering with black-and-white photos. Somehow, even this cheerful village event became a melancholy study of rural England in his images.

When we finally left, Ryan was much revived by several slices of Victoria sponge. By then, the sun had climbed high enough to show that midday was near.

"I know a rather good pub near Kettlewell," I suggested as we rejoined the main hiking path. "It's about an hour's walk, but the food is excellent and authentically Yorkshire."

Lars's face brightened just enough for me to see it. He nodded. "The light will be too harsh for landscape photography until late afternoon. A meal break would help."

The Dry Stone Inn came into view just as Ryan's complaints about his sore feet became almost poetic. The old building, dating back to the 17th century, was made from the same weathered stone as the walls around us. It was a welcome retreat from the growing heat.

We settled at a corner table, where Ryan immediately began studying the menu with hungry intensity.

"Yorkshire pudding! They have a vegan version of it!" he exclaimed, looking up with genuine delight. "I'm absolutely having that. Lars, you must try it – it's a proper local speciality."

Lars studied the menu with a slight furrow between his brows. "Pudding is typically a sweet dish, is it not? For dessert?"

"Ah, the endless confusion of British terminology," I said, smiling at his bewilderment. "Here, 'pudding' can mean any dessert. Carrot Cake, Apple Pie, Custard – you name it. Or sometimes, like with Yorkshire pudding, it's not a dessert at all but savoury."

When our food arrived, Lars examined his – non-vegan – Yorkshire pudding, a risen, bowl-shaped savoury bread made from batter, with a careful assessment.

"This is made from flour, eggs, and milk," he stated after taking a precise bite. "Yet it is called pudding. And served with meat and gravy." He considered this information as if reconciling contradictory data.

"Very little about English culinary terminology makes sense," I agreed. "We have black pudding, which contains no milk or eggs but plenty of blood. Spotted dick, which is neither spotted nor... well, you get the idea. And then there's toad-in-the-hole, which contains absolutely no amphibians."

Lars' expression remained neutral, but his eyes betrayed a flicker of amusement. He chuckled. "Swedish food names describe precisely what the dish contains. Köttbullar – meat balls. Ärtsoppa – pea soup."

As we ate, I watched Lars. He carefully separated each part of his meal. Meat went on one side, vegetables on the other. He quartered his Yorkshire pudding and placed it apart. He ate each part in turn, never mixing them. I noticed he left the meat untouched. His eating style matched his photography: everything neat, nothing out of place, no messy combinations.

Ryan caught my eye across the table and mouthed something that looked a lot like "Swedish IKEA instructions," nodding toward Lars' neatly arranged plate. I held back a smile and started thinking about our afternoon hike into the higher parts of the Dales, where the views would give Lars even more to photograph and Ryan's legs even more to complain about.

The next morning, it was all about sore muscles. At least on Ryan's side.

"I'm afraid my legs just won't let me do any more hiking today," Ryan said as we headed to the car. "They've gone on strike, complete with picket lines and strongly worded pamphlets about working conditions." Lars stood by the passenger door, unfazed by Ryan's dramatic complaints, showing the steady patience of a Nordic pine in a gentle breeze.

Ryan cast me a pleading glance as he lowered himself into the back seat with the careful movements of a much older man.

I slipped into the driver's seat, adjusting the mirror to catch Ryan's expression of exaggerated suffering. "The Lake District isn't far. Besides, Beatrix Potter's house is hardly a strenuous expedition."

"Potter? Beatrix Potter is on the itinerary?" Lars turned, surprisingly quickly.

"Indeed," I confirmed, starting the car. "Hill Top Farm in Near Sawrey. It's preserved exactly as it was when she lived there, complete with her original furnishings and possessions. I thought it might offer an interesting contrast to the landscape photography – something more intimate and historical."

Lars nodded once. He returned to gazing out of the window, but something in his posture had subtly shifted.

As we drove along the winding country roads from the Yorkshire Dales to the Lake District, the landscape slowly changed. The open, stone-walled hills of the Dales gave way to more dramatic scenery, proper mountains by British standards. Their slopes were thick with trees and dropped into deep, glacial lakes. The water mirrored the morning sky perfectly. Lars stayed quiet for most of the drive, only asking now and then to stop for photos.

"The Lake District inspired some of Britain's finest poetry," I remarked as we rounded a bend that revealed the silver expanse of Windermere stretching before us. "Wordsworth, Coleridge, De Quincey – they all drew creative energy from these lakes."

Lars kept his eyes on the passing landscape. "The forests back home... they can also make you find your creativity." He paused. "Not much poetry like your Wordsworth. More contemplating while sitting on moss-covered rocks until you forget your own name." A barely perceptible smile touched the corner of his mouth. "It's nice though."

Ryan, who had been suspiciously quiet for the past twenty minutes, suddenly leaned forward between the front seats. "Did you know Beatrix Potter was actually a pioneering mycologist before she became a children's author? Her scientific drawings of fungi were remarkably accurate. She was rejected by the scientific establishment because she was a woman, so she turned to children's books instead."

Lars stayed quiet, but I saw a brief spark of interest flash in his eyes.

Hill Top Farm looked just like it did in photos: a sturdy, slate-roofed stone house set in a garden made to match Potter's illustrations. Pink roses climbed the walls. Vegetables and herbs grew in tidy beds edged with low hedges. It felt less like a real home and more like a storybook come to life, which, in many ways, it was.

As we approached the entrance, I braced myself for Lars's typical methodical assessment of the photographic potential. Instead, he paused at the garden gate, his expression hesitant and eyes lingering on the path beyond.

"There will be many tourists," he observed. Lars's dislike of large crowds was something I understood well – after all, I felt much the same.

"It's actually pretty quiet today," I reassured him, glancing at the nearly empty car park. "It's mid-week, so our timing was good."

Inside, the National Trust had carefully preserved Potter's home. Her small writing desk sat by the window, looking out over the garden that inspired so many of her illustrations. Glass cases held first editions of her books. Familiar items from the stories, like a blue jacket and a small wicker basket, were set just where she had left them. It felt as if Peter Rabbit might hop through at any moment.

In the room with these displays, I witnessed a remarkable transformation in Lars. As he approached the glass case holding a first edition of "The Tale of Peter Rabbit," his introverted expression softened with wonder. He stood perfectly still. His fingers hovered above the glass, not quite touching, but tracing the book's outline with unusual gentleness.

"My mother read these to me," he said quietly. "Every night before sleep. She did different voices for each character." A ghost of a smile appeared and vanished so quickly I might have imagined it. "Her rabbit voice was particularly convincing."

The moment felt so intimate and raw that I instinctively took a step back. Ryan quickly developed a fascination for a display across the room.

Lars remained before the case for several minutes. When he finally stepped away, his gaze lingered on the book, and a gentle softness remained in his posture, a rare openness around his eyes.

The rest of our time in the Lake District passed without more glimpses into Lars's thoughts. He photographed the landscapes in his usual minimalist style, creating stark black-and-white images that captured the region's heart and excluded anything he deemed unnecessary.

"Our final stop today is rather unusual," I announced as we departed the Lake District proper, heading toward the coastal town of Egremont. "Something uniquely British that you won't find in any standard tourist guide."

"Is it a cream tea?" Ryan asked hopefully from the back seat. "My legs might consider ending their industrial action for a proper scone."

"Not quite," I replied. "We're going to the World Gurning Championships."

Lars frowned slightly. "Gurning? This word is unfamiliar."

"Essentially, it's competitive face-pulling," I explained. "Contestants put their heads through a horse collar called a 'braffin' and contort their faces into the most grotesque expressions possible. It's been held annually at the Egremont Crab Fair since 1267."

Lars's frown deepened into something approaching genuine concern. "This is... a competition? For making ugly faces?"

"One of Britain's oldest and most prestigious," I confirmed, suppressing a smile at his bewilderment. "The winner is the person who can produce the most hideous face."

Approaching Egremont, the streets were filled with spectators heading toward the town centre. Temporary stands surrounded a central stage, where a large horse collar waited for the competitors.

"Absolutely brilliant!" Ryan exclaimed, his earlier fatigue apparently forgotten as he surveyed the scene with undisguised delight. "Look at that chap warming up over there – he's practising his technique behind that car mirror!"

Lars stood perfectly still amid the flowing crowd, arms crossed tightly. His face registered a look of perplexed fascination. He watched the first competitor approach the stage, insert his head through the horse collar, and contort his features into an expression of spectacular ugliness. Several children in the front row squealed in delight, hiding behind their parents.

"This is a... competition?" Lars repeated, his voice strained with genuine incomprehension. "And people train for this?"

"Some take it quite seriously," I confirmed. "The champion a few years back could pull his lower lip completely over his nose. There are techniques handed down through generations. Some families are known for their gurning prowess."

"But... why?" Lars asked, his question containing more existential weight than the simple word typically carried.

"Why not?" I countered. "It's harmless fun that brings the community together. No different from your wife-carrying championships, really."

"That is a test of strength, endurance, and teamwork – and it is Finnish, not Swedish," Lars replied with absolute seriousness. "This is..." He paused, apparently unable to find an appropriate word in either English or Swedish to describe the spectacle before us.

Ryan, meanwhile, had been watching the proceedings with increasing enthusiasm. As the current competitor finished his performance to raucous applause, he turned to us with a gleam in his eye that I recognised all too well.

"I'm going to have a go," he announced, already moving toward the queue of aspiring gurners forming at the side of the stage.

"Ryan, are you quite sure?" I called after him. "You do realise people will be taking photographs?"

"Posterity demands documentation of this moment!" he replied over his shoulder, already joining the line of competitors.

Lars watched, bewildered. "He'll make himself ugly? For fun? And let people photograph him?"

"The English have always excelled at not taking themselves too seriously," I explained. "There's a certain freedom in being willing to look ridiculous for the sake of tradition and communal laughter."

"We have fun in Sweden too," Lars replied, still watching the stage with wary fascination. "Usually midsummer. And it involves singing about small frogs while hopping in circles. But our faces remain dignified."

I laughed.

As Ryan's turn approached, he began performing elaborate facial warm-up exercises that seemed to involve every muscle from his scalp to his chin. Lars watched this preparation with interest and a growing amusement.

"Perhaps there is something... liberating about this practice," he finally conceded, raising his camera to document Ryan's approaching performance. "Though I maintain it is deeply strange."

"That," I replied with a smile, "is a perfect summary of many British traditions. Deeply strange, possibly liberating, and absolutely worth experiencing at least once."

When Ryan finally took the stage, he put his head through the horse collar with a dramatic flourish. His face twisted into a truly bizarre expression: lower lip sticking out, eyes crossed in different directions, and his nose somehow seeming to disappear. The crowd gasped in appreciation. Lars caught the moment with a perfectly timed photo.

"We are a long way from Swedish minimalism photography," I laughed as Ryan continued his performance to enthusiastic applause.

"Yes," Lars agreed with a smile, lowering his camera. "But perhaps there is something honest in capturing people at their most uninhibited. Even when it involves..." he gestured vaguely at Ryan's contorted face, "whatever this is." He paused, watching as Ryan took an exaggerated bow to scattered applause. "Though I will not be attempting this activity myself. Some cultural experiences are best observed from a distance."

"A wise policy," I agreed. "Particularly when horse collars are involved."

For a moment, I wondered if we'd gone the wrong way, seeing how much Whitby's quiet fishing harbour had changed. Black-clad figures moved through the narrow streets like an elegant funeral procession missing its corpse. Victorian dresses with impossibly cinched waists brushed against leather trousers lined with chains. Velvet frock coats and lace parasols mingled with platform boots, adding improbable height to their wearers. Everywhere, faces were powdered pale, adorned with dramatic eyeliner and deep crimson lips.

Lars stood motionless by our car, looking as if he was calculating the quickest escape back to Sweden.

"Has there been a mass bereavement?" he asked seriously. "Some national tragedy requiring public mourning?"

Ryan, who had been consulting his phone with growing excitement, looked up with a delighted grin. "Not a tragedy, Lars – a celebration! We've stumbled into the famous Whitby Goth Weekend. Twice a year, thousands of Gothic enthusiasts descend on the town. It's one of Britain's most significant alternative cultural events."

Lars's frown deepened.

"It began in 1997 as a small gathering of pen pals from the goth music scene," Ryan continued, his enthusiasm undimmed by Lars's evident disapproval. "Now it's a major festival with bands, markets, and events. Fascinating cultural phenomenon, really."

Lars shook his head. "In Sweden, we get excited too. Then we go for a walk in the woods or paddle on a lake. This is..." He nodded toward a group walking by, one of them dressed like a Victorian undertaker with a top hat and a cane. "...weird."

"It's actually rather perfect that we're here for this," I observed. "Whitby's Gothic associations run deep – Bram Stoker set key scenes from 'Dracula' here after being inspired by the ruins of the Abbey and the atmospheric churchyard."

Lars remained unconvinced, but before he could say anything else, a small group of festival-goers in elaborate outfits came over to us. The woman leading them wore a black corseted dress and a tall hairpiece, as if she had just walked out of a Victorian mourning portrait. She greeted us with a surprisingly warm smile.

"You look like you could use a guide," she remarked, her contemporary London accent contrasting charmingly with her historical appearance. "First time at Goth Weekend?"

Ryan immediately stepped forward with enthusiastic confirmation, while Lars retreated almost imperceptibly behind his camera, as if hoping it might render him invisible to approaching Victorians.

"We're photographers," I explained. "Here documenting British cultural traditions. This wasn't on our planned itinerary, but it seems too good an opportunity to miss."

The woman, who introduced herself as Helena, brightened further at this. "Oh, you absolutely must participate properly! No one captures the essence of Goth Weekend from the outside. You need to experience it." She gestured expansively toward the crowded street. "We're heading to Pandemonium, the costume shop around the corner. They'll sort you out."

Lars's expression suggested he would rather swim the North Sea in January than don Gothic attire, but I caught his eye, raising my eyebrows in silent encouragement before he could refuse.

"Think of the photographic perspective," I murmured. "Documenting from within rather than as outside observers. Very anthropological."

He didn't say a word, but I could see the reluctant recognition of a valid point. "But I will not wear makeup," he stated firmly after a while. "Or anything with unnecessary buckles."

Pandemonium proved aptly named. The small shop was so crammed with Gothic paraphernalia that you had to take sideways steps and duck to avoid suspended vampire bats. On every surface, velvet capes, striped tights, corsets, and top hats crowded together, while accessories flaunted improbable numbers of skulls, crosses, and ravens.

Ryan disappeared immediately into this theatrical wonderland with the glee of a child released in a sweet shop. We heard occasional exclamations of delight as he discovered particularly dramatic items hidden among the packed racks.

"Perhaps something simple for you," Helena suggested, assessing my practical attire with a professional eye. She extracted a black lace-trimmed dress from an overstuffed rail. "Classic Victoriana, but not too restrictive. You could still manage your camera equipment."

The dress was surprisingly tasteful, with a high neck and delicate lace at the collar and cuffs. I accepted it gratefully. It would let me join in without going overboard into the more dramatic side of Gothic fashion.

Meanwhile, Lars stood by the door with his arms folded and one foot pointed toward the exit, clearly ready to leave. Helena bravely approached him, despite his serious look. She held up what seemed to be the simplest thing in the shop: a neatly tailored black frock coat that could have fit right into a Jane Austen play.

"Just this," she offered. "No frills, no accessories. You could be a very minimalist Victorian gentleman."

Lars inspected the coat at arm's length, his fingers testing the weave, his gaze not without a certain respect for the fabric's weight and finish. "In Sweden, we have a saying about dressing for the weather, not the century," he remarked, but his stance was altogether less dismissive than those words suggested. "A standard windproof raincoat would be more practical."

"But far less authentic," Helena countered.

After a negotiation that felt as serious as international peace talks, Lars eventually agreed to wear the coat, but pointed out it was as far as he would go with dressing up. Still, he cut a rather Darcy-ish silhouette: reluctant elegance and stiff dignity. Catching his reflection in the rain-streaked window, he allowed himself a quick, reluctant smile, then composed his face again, clearly hoping neither of us had noticed. I'm sure he enjoyed looking so unexpectedly dashing. Not that he'd ever say so out loud.

Ryan finally emerged from the depths of the shop. He wore a sweeping black cape lined with red satin, a brocade waistcoat with silver skulls, apparent Victorian riding boots, and convincing vampire fangs that only slightly impeded his speech.

"What do you think?" he asked, executing a dramatic twirl that sent the cape billowing outward. "Too restrained?"

Lars let out a strangled sound, somewhere between a snort and a laugh. "In Sweden, someone dressed like that would be swiftly referred to psychiatric services," he said, though a hint of amusement crept into his voice.

"Perfect, then!" Ryan replied cheerfully, adjusting his fangs with his little finger. "Though I did consider the leather trousers with chains."

"A mercy you resisted," I remarked, emerging from the

changing room in my considerably more subdued Victorian dress. Its high neck and long sleeves gave it a certain authentic severity, while lace details added just enough Gothic flair to avoid looking like I was simply dressed for a funeral.

"Ryan looked at Lars. "You look positively gothic," he observed happily, "A proper Swedish Count Dracula."

"I look like someone who has lost a bet," Lars replied. Yet I saw him stand a little taller and try to look nonchalant, flashing a smile that would have charmed any Victorian lady. For the first time, I realised how very attractive he actually was. Then again, I always had a soft spot for Mr Darcy, which never helped in the real world, where men tended to be more Bart Simpson than brooding hero.

As we got ready to head back outside with the other festival-goers, I thought about how good the British are at reinventing themselves for fun. The same country that has serious bankers and practical village councils also loves to dive into fantasy now and then, whether it's Morris dancers with bells or adults dressing up as Victorian vampires in Whitby. I admired how people here are willing to put aside their usual selves and join in a bit of shared make-believe.

Night came quickly over Whitby. The abbey ruins on the cliff stood out sharply against the sky. Street lamps created small pools of light, but the shadows only grew deeper. It was exactly the sort of night you'd want for a ghost tour. Our guide, Morticia, was in full Victorian mourning gear. Her black veil and jet jewellery glinted as she walked.

"Welcome, unfortunate souls," she intoned. "Tonight we shall ascend the one hundred and ninety-nine steps to St. Mary's churchyard, where the dead rest uneasily, and inspiration struck a certain Irish author with a tale of the undead."

Ryan nodded enthusiastically, causing his plastic fangs to slip slightly. He adjusted them before whispering, "This is absolutely brilliant. I've always wanted to do a proper ghost tour in Whitby."

Lars, stoic in his borrowed frock coat, scanned the group. He muttered, "In Sweden, we do not need costumes to appreciate history."

"Says the man from a place where people celebrate Christmas with a singing girl wearing candles on her head," I replied, watching Lars blink in surprise before composing himself.

"Saint Lucia is a traditional celebration of light during dark winter months," he protested, defending his stance. But I did see him smile.

Morticia ended the cultural debate and gathered us together. Soon, we stood at the bottom of the famous 199 steps. The streetlamps' glow faded, and the old stone stairs climbed steeply from the town up to the church. The climb was hard, and each step took us farther from the busy harbour and deeper into Whitby's mysteries.

"Think about it," Morticia called as we climbed. "In medieval Whitby, people carried coffins up these steps. They stopped on benches not just to rest, but to make sure bodies stayed in the coffins."

This sparked a nervous laugh from the group, whose makeup became more obvious: several 'Goth Weekend' types, not all prepared for a climb. One woman, cinched in a corset, took shallow breaths, visibly struggling. A man in platform boots, wary and unsteady, faced each step as a small ordeal. Lars remained mostly aloof, observing with slight amusement.

"In 1890," Morticia continued, pausing at a wider landing to allow stragglers to catch up, "an Irish theatre manager named Bram Stoker visited Whitby. During his stay, he found himself captivated by the atmosphere of this ancient port. The town had abbey ruins, red-roofed cottages, and tales of shipwrecks. He spent hours in the public library, reading accounts of a Russian vessel called the Dmitry. That ship ran aground on Whitby's shore during a terrible storm."

We kept climbing. The effort made us a little breathless, which added to the spooky feeling. Above us, the Church of St. Mary looked more and more imposing against the night sky. Its old gravestones showed up as even darker shapes in the shadows.

"Stoker turned the Russian ship into the Demeter," Morticia explained. "On that vessel came his immortal creation – Count Dracula, who, as a black dog, bounded up these very steps to the churchyard."

The graveyard unrolled before us, old stones tilting at strange angles, as if the earth shifted beneath them. Pale moonlight filtered through clouds, turning the markers into strange sculptures. Behind them, the abbey ruins looked almost skeletal against the sky.

"Here," Morticia announced, guiding us to a particular gravestone, "lies the mortal remains of Mr Swales – a name that might be familiar to readers of Stoker's novel. The author borrowed not only Whitby's atmospheric setting but also the names from these very gravestones for his characters."

I was expecting Lars to keep up his polite disinterest, but he surprised me. He went over to the headstone, crouched down, and traced the worn letters with his finger.

"The link between a real place and a story," he said quietly, and for a second, he actually looked impressed.

Morticia looked pleased to get a serious comment for once. "Yes. Stoker was smart to use real parts of Whitby's history and character in his story. That made it believable, and that's why people still read it today."

After we finished exploring the graveyard, Morticia gathered us up and we headed back down the steps. The group moved more slowly now, some members walking in thoughtful silence, glancing back over their shoulders at the moonlit stones. In the cool night air, our earlier chatter faded and was replaced by a sense of awe. We followed a path along the West Cliff to the Whale Bone Arch, where two giant jawbones made an arch about twenty feet high and framed a view of the harbour.

"Whitby is known for Dracula," Morticia said at the arch, "but its wealth came from whaling in the 18th and 19th centuries."

As we paused under the arch, taking in the view, something unusual happened. Lars, who had mostly hung back during the tour, suddenly stepped forward and got everyone's attention.

"The whale arch," Lars said, with rare excitement. "A signal of success."

Morticia blinked at the interjection but quickly recovered, her tone warm. "Exactly right. Whaling was an incredibly dangerous profession that offered the possibility of great wealth for those who managed a successful catch. When a fleet returned to port, anxious onlookers would watch for a telltale sign of good news: successful crews would tie a whale's jawbone atop the ship's mast, signalling that they had killed the animal rather than the other way around."

Lars walked up to the arch and studied it closely. He circled it slowly, stopping now and then to take careful photos from different angles, treating the bone with the seriousness of an important historical document, his lips pursed as he focused.

"This is not the original arch," he said at last, sounding disappointed. Maybe his Viking roots gave him a knack for spotting whale bones, a part of his Scandinavian heritage.

"You have a good eye," Morticia confirmed. "The original bones, erected in 1853, deteriorated over time and were replaced in 1963. Those replacements also eventually succumbed to the elements, and what you see now is actually the third incarnation, donated by Alaska in 2003."

"Nordic whaling shared roots with Yorkshire," Lars said, studying the arch. "My great-grandfather was a Swedish whaler. I'm glad both countries stopped this brutal hunt."

Ryan stepped closer to examine the arch himself. "Isn't that interesting how England and Sweden are connected somehow?" he remarked.

"The sea connects more than it divides," Lars said. "Unlike land borders, the ocean is a highway between cultures."

It was a surprisingly philosophical way to end our gothic evening, especially coming from our hesitant Swedish Mr Darcy.

We arrived in Staithes on a morning when the air was unusually clear. Every detail of the village stood out. Rooftops and window frames looked sharper than usual. The cottages, painted in faded reds, blues, and ochres, crowded the steep hillsides. As we walked down the winding road into what locals called 'The Bottom' – the narrow space between the cliffs – the village revealed itself little by little. The tide was out, exposing a small beach where fishing cobles sat at odd angles, waiting for the water to return.

"Three hours here," Lars announced. "The light's perfect for architecture."

After our late-night ghost tour in Whitby, Lars was back to his usual self. His brief moment of Darcy-ish nonchalance had been carefully packed away, along with his borrowed frock coat. Refocused and now dressed again in practical layers of muted technical fabrics, Lars looked over the village below, tracing the steep paths and rooftops with his eyes as he planned his shooting angles.

The side paths into the village quickly narrowed, becoming cobbled alleys just wide enough for two people to pass without brushing shoulders. Cottages pressed in from both sides, some upper floors reaching over the path to create short, shaded tunnels. Over time, the village had clearly grown by building wherever there was space, never worrying about straight lines or uniform width.

"Mind the step here," I cautioned as we navigated a particularly steep section where the cobbles gave way to worn stone stairs polished by generations of feet. "And the drainpipe just above."

We continued along the alleyways until we came out into a wider section – just wide enough for three people to stand side by side. At that moment, a tall, thin teenager in a rumpled jacket appeared from a side alley. About seventeen, he carried the usual blend of awkwardness and confidence you see at that age. Though he stood as if trying to look experienced, he still seemed to be growing into his own height.

"You lot look proper lost," he observed, his accent carrying the distinctive Yorkshire vowels that seemed to stretch certain words while compressing others into near unintelligibility. "Tourist types always get confused in these alleys."

"We're not actually lost," Ryan replied cheerfully. "Though we are indeed tourists. Or rather, photographers documenting traditional British coastal communities."

The young man's face lit up. "Photographers? For social? I've got an Instagram going – mostly sunset content and, like, atmospheric harbour vibes. Trying to build my personal brand before I go location-independent."

Even Lars, surprised by Tom's surprisingly well-articulated social marketing speech, looked up from his camera and raised an eyebrow, intrigued.

"I'm supposed to be stacking shelves at me auntie's mate's shop," the boy said, glancing over his shoulder as if he might get caught at any moment. "But there are only so many tins of beans a person can alphabetise before it gets to you, right?"

I laughed. "That's an old-sounding line. I'm Brianna – these are Ryan and Lars. We're doing a photography project on the Yorkshire coast."

"Tom," he replied with a quick nod. "Look, I could show you around if you want, for a tenner. I know all the proper spots – the secret viewpoints. I've been planning my digital escape route, so I've made a list of all the prime places."

Before we could answer, Tom spun on his heel and darted off, motioning emphatically for us to follow. He slipped sideways into an alleyway so narrow it seemed only a shadow cut between buildings, pausing briefly to ensure we trailed after him.

"This here's the Dog Loup," he said proudly as we squeezed into the passage. "Narrowest street in Britain, this is. Only twenty inches wide at its tightest point. Had to rescue a German tourist last summer who got stuck wearing one of them massive backpacks. Proper wedged in, he was."

Lars eyed the narrow passage, then in a single fluid motion dug into his camera bag, pulled out a measuring tape, and ran it along the tightest stretch of wall.

"Eighteen and three-quarter inches," he announced. "That's a real challenge for tall Nordic men like me."

Tom leaned forward, hands on his knees, watching with fascination. "You're a real odd one, aren't you? I like that though. Being different is good. That's why I can't stay here forever like everyone else." He pointed toward the village. "Everyone here's stuck in the same rhythm as their grandparents. The sea comes in, the sea goes out, boats leave, boats return. It's been the same for centuries."

After squeezing through the Dog Loup, we emerged into a small courtyard where cottages shared a communal clothesline. Tom led us up steep steps – so steep they seemed to head straight into someone's kitchen window. The path then turned sharply, and a narrow viewing platform overlooking the harbour appeared before us.

"I'm saving up for my remote work setup," he went on, leaning against the weathered railing like he owned the spot. "I've already got an ultra-slim laptop, refurbished but still with good specs. I'm planning to go to Thailand first. They have co-working spaces on the beach where you can code with your toes in the sand. Then maybe Bali or somewhere in South America. Places with sick Wi-Fi but low living costs, you know?"

His strong Yorkshire accent made his talk of digital nomad life sound even more out of place.

"I just need to get out of these narrow streets," Tom said, staring at the horizon where the North Sea met the sky in a straight line. "Everyone here has looked at the same view for generations. I want different views. Lots of them. Views you have to cross oceans to find."

Ryan, who had been listening to this monologue with thoughtful attention, finally spoke. "Did you know that Captain James Cook lived in Staithes as a young man?" He pointed toward a building near the harbour. "It was here he first felt the call of the sea that would eventually take him around the world."

Tom just shrugged his shoulders, as if to say it hardly needed mentioning. "Course I know of Cook. Everyone does, round here in Staithes."

"But did you also know," Ryan continued, "that before he became the great explorer who charted New Zealand and discovered Australia, he worked in a grocer's shop as a shop assistant – not unlike yourself. You might say you're a modern Cook with the same hunger for freedom, just with better technology at your disposal."

This comparison appeared to please Tom enormously. He straightened slightly, his gangly frame momentarily assuming a more purposeful posture. "Digital Captain Cook," he murmured, testing the phrase. "I like that. Explorer of virtual seas and that."

As Tom took us deeper into the village, showing us hidden viewpoints and sharing local stories, I noticed how little had changed here over time. The fishing boats, hillside cottages, and narrow lanes all showed how the place was shaped by what people needed and what was possible. Yet, when Tom looked out toward the sea, I could sense the same restlessness that drove Cook to set sail. People here, it seemed, have always itched to see more, to explore further. From Cook's time to Tom's, the urge to look beyond the horizon has stayed the same.

"There's this quote I found online," Tom remarked as we climbed back toward the car park, his impromptu tour concluded, his tenner gratefully received. "'Adventure may hurt you, but monotony will kill you.' That's what I've got as my phone background. Proper motivational, isn't it?"

We said goodbye, and Tom went back to stacking shelves. I wondered if he would actually leave, or if he would end up like others before him, always looking out to sea and only dreaming of escape. Still, his youthful energy was a nice contrast to the old stones of the village.

Our next stop greeted us with a clear view from the cliff top. The path led down past rows of red-roofed cottages to a narrow beach and the open North Sea. Unlike Staithes, which feels tucked away in its valley, Robin Hood's Bay is laid out in full view. Its streets and houses are easily visible at once. Still, there is more to the village than meets the eye. Beneath the rooftops are cellars and hidden passages that once made this place a centre for smuggling along the North Yorkshire coast.

"This place is ideal for capturing how closely everything was built in England," Lars said as we stopped to look over the village before heading down. As we started our descent, the main road quickly turned into a steep cobblestone path, with iron handrails set up in some spots. Lars glanced at the slope and shook his head. "But I have to wonder why anyone would choose to build on such a steep hill."

"Often there was no other choice," Ryan said, breathless. "Fishing, smuggling, and dodging taxes mattered more than gradients."

The village street twisted downward in a succession of switchbacks. Occasionally, we passed beneath arches formed by upper stories built across the path. Narrow alleyways – known locally as 'ginnels' – branched off unpredictably, creating a labyrinth. Even the most determined cartographer would find themselves challenged.

We stopped to photograph a cluster of battered, sun-bleached fishing buoys. Their subdued hues flared against the deep blue of a painted door. Just then, a wiry, middle-aged man slipped from a shadowy ginnel. At his heels trotted a fluffy dog, its breed probably a mix of all the dogs that had ever seen the Yorkshire coast.

"Admiring the view?" the man inquired. "First time in Bay?"

"Indeed. We're photographing traditional coastal communities," I replied.

The man nodded as if this explained everything satisfactorily. "You'll be wanting the smuggling history, then. Everyone does." There was no resentment in his tone, merely the resigned acknowledgement of someone who has witnessed countless visitors discovering the same 'secret' information about his home.

"We are," Ryan said, eager.

This unconcealed excitement seemed to please our impromptu guide. He gestured toward the tightly packed cottages surrounding us. "What you're looking at is the most efficient smuggling operation the Revenue men ever failed to properly disrupt. At its height in the 1700s, it's said that every single resident of the Bay was involved. From the fishermen who made the French rendezvous to the grandmothers who hid brandy under their petticoats, everyone played their part."

He pointed up at the rooftops. No two buildings were the same height or faced the same way, so the pattern looked random at first. The real genius, he said, was in how they were built. Instead of standing apart like most village houses, these were all connected. Back doors led into neighbours' kitchens, trapdoors were hidden between floors, and most importantly, cellars formed a network running from the beach up to the cliff top.

Lars looked up, interested. "A distributed network for moving contraband? That's clever."

"Exactly that," our guide said with a smile. "There was no need for risky moonlit dashes or visible cart tracks for customs men to spot. When a smuggling boat arrived, goods went straight into the cellars at the bottom of the cliff. From there, they moved from cellar to cellar, secretly passing from house to house all the way up to the top, never seen outside."

The fluffy dog, apparently deciding the conversation had gone on long enough, gave a single meaningful look toward its owner before glancing up the path.

"Meg's reminding me we've a schedule to keep." He glanced fondly at his canine companion. "If you're interested in the smuggling history, most cottages have been renovated now. But the Old Coastguard Station at the bottom has a proper exhibition. It shows the tunnel system with models and that."

Our group split up for a while. Lars wandered off to photograph the narrow spaces between buildings, odd window placements, and the occasional visible trapdoor.

From a distance, we watched Lars squeeze sideways through every possible passage between cottages, camera slung at his side. Ryan murmured, 'I suspect he's rather relishing the smuggler's side of the British character.'

Later that afternoon, we regrouped as the combination of steep streets and sea air left us all in need of refreshment. We made our way to The Smugglers, a whitewashed pub near the bottom of the village whose beer garden offered uninterrupted views across the bay.

"I need to retrieve our jackets from the car," I announced, noting the sea breeze that had begun to strengthen as the afternoon shifted toward evening. "The temperature's dropping."

"I'll come with you," Ryan said. "My pedometer says I'm only halfway to my step goal, the walk back up should help me catch up."

Lars nodded. "I'll get us a good table outside and order drinks. The usual for everyone?"

We confirmed our drink selections and left Lars to his table-finding mission while we tackled the considerable climb back to the car park at the top of the cliff.

It took us longer than anticipated. The steep gradient slowed our climb, and Ryan's insistence on photographing several unusual door knockers and what he claimed was a particularly photogenic seagull extended our round trip to nearly forty-five minutes. By the time we returned to the pub, the evening had settled into that golden hour beloved by photographers, casting the entire village in warm amber light.

Lars was waiting at a table in the beer garden, camera on the table and looking more confused than usual. There were no drinks in sight.

"Any trouble finding our drinks?" I asked as I sat down.

Lars frowned. "I've been waiting for service. No one's come. Service here is remarkably slow."

Ryan grinned with sudden understanding. "Lars, in British pubs, you order and pay at the bar. No table service."

Lars blinked. "But there are tables. Why sit if not to be served?"

"That's just how it works. Get a table, decide, then go to the bar, order, pay, and carry the drinks back to the table yourself."

"This is completely insane," Lars declared. "And dangerous. One person carrying several containers of liquid through crowded spaces? Without the right trays or tools?"

I had to admit, I often felt the same way. Not only can carrying everything be a hassle. When I travel alone, I always wonder how to keep a table. Do I leave my bag and jacket to show the spot is taken, even though someone might walk off with them? Or do I try to juggle my camera bag, jacket, and drink, only to come back and find the table gone? That's just how it goes in British pubs. It feels so normal to me now that I've accidentally offended Italian and French waiters by trying to carry my own espresso outside.

Lars stood up, although still protesting, and went inside to sort things out. We watched through the window as he listened to the barman, who seemed to be explaining the different ales.

A few minutes later, Lars returned to the beer garden. He concentrated as he balanced three glasses, two in one hand and one in the other, while awkwardly using his elbow to push the door open.

Unfortunately, the door had a spring that made it close by itself. As Lars tried to step into the garden, the door swung toward his back. What happened next was like watching a small disaster unfold in slow motion. Lars moved forward to avoid the door, the glasses shook, and most of the beer spilt all over his trousers.

I heard what sounded to me like a string of Swedish swear words, though the sharp, clear way Lars let them out made them seem more like someone reading out a set of strict rules than actually cursing.

We couldn't help but laugh at the sight of Lars.

"Heads up, mate," Ryan said, giving him a reassuring clap on the back. "Happened to all of us. It's part of the British pub experience!"

Silver light crept over the horizon, turning the long stretch of concrete into a pale ribbon slicing into the North Sea. The pier arched so precisely it seemed drawn by hand, ending at a slender lighthouse that looked almost fragile under the cloudy sky. Roker Pier. This was our spot for sunrise photos.

Lars had been unusually quiet since his wet experience with British pub rituals the night before, a soggy episode he'd rather forget. But as soon as the pier came into view, a change sparked in him. He stood taller, almost as if the shape of it gave him energy. "This," he said, a new spark in his voice, "is proper architecture."

"Knew you'd like it," I replied, pulling up so the full sweep of pier and lighthouse was visible from the car window. "Early twentieth century. Built between 1885 and 1903. More than 600 metres long. At the time, quite an engineering project."

Ryan contributed a dramatic yawn. He'd been in a sort of travel coma since we'd left the B&B, cradling his tea in his re-usable, plastic-free cup, a present from Lars who insisted Ryan needs to work on his ecological footprint. "Bit early," he grumbled, "for architectural appreciation. The sun hasn't punched in yet."

Lars grabbed his camera bag and was already halfway out the door. "Weather is perfect," he said. I expected him to pull out his camera, but instead, he handed the bag to Ryan. "Can you hold this for a minute? I need my morning run before I start taking photos." He took off down the cliff and jogged onto the pier.

The wind over the cliffs ignored my jacket entirely. It had a direct line to my bones. Lars powered below us, while Ryan trailed at a pace set not by speed but by how much tea he could sip without spilling. I couldn't believe the energy Lars has, no matter how early the morning or how windy the weather.

It was then I noticed her: a woman sitting alone on a bench along the pier's promenade. Blonde hair, hastily tied back. Mid-thirties, I guessed, though the fatigue in her posture made her seem older for a moment, until her features brightened as we approached.

"Morning," I offered, angling my greeting to sound casual, as though we all regularly saluted strangers at sunrise. "Beautiful start, isn't it?"

She turned, offering the kind of smile that makes you realise how tired she must've felt before. "Gorgeous," she agreed. "Though honestly, I'd take any weather, so long as I'm not stuck inside. Out here, rain or shine – it's better."

She gestured at the empty space on her bench, invitation clear. "Come sit. Ten minutes before I have to run, but I won't complain about the company."

We introduced ourselves. Emma: midwife at Sunderland Royal, grabbing a slice of calm before her shift started. "Been coming here since I was little," she confided, eyes flicking to the lighthouse. "Dad fished off the end of the pier every Sunday. Now I bring my own kids. If I have a day off – and daylight left to use."

"That must be tricky, with hospital shifts like yours," Ryan commented, surfacing from his tea-induced haze.

Emma's laugh was pure British resilience, a sound sharpened by fatigue yet stubbornly cheerful. "Tricky, yes. The NHS rota and single-parent life don't play nicely. My parents help, though they're still working and up in Durham." For a heartbeat, her smile faltered.

Just then, Lars finished his run and joined us, barely out of breath. Stretching, he glanced at Emma. "You're a midwife? In Sweden, midwives are highly regarded. Paid well, too."

Emma's eyebrows rose, like she heard a punchline coming. "We get the 'highly regarded' bit here. But the 'paid well' never quite made it across the North Sea." She yawned, then grinned. "Band 5 NHS wages are what they are. Two kids, childcare, rent... well, it adds up."

I took a moment to explain why we were there: we wanted to capture moments of British life, both in photos and stories, for our Swedish student. I told Emma that, as a midwife and single mum, she basically represented modern Britain. I asked if she'd be comfortable sharing more about her monthly financial challenges. She relaxed, reassured, and didn't hesitate to get specific.

"My base salary's about £27,000. After all the usual deductions, I see maybe £1,800 a month in my account. Rent is £850, and utilities, £300. Childcare for my shifts is £400, even with government help." She shrugged in a way that looked practised. "Doesn't leave much for anything unexpected."

Lars looked genuinely baffled. "In Sweden, someone like you would earn around 42,000 kroner per month – that's about £3,200. Childcare? Maybe £100."

Emma let out a low whistle. "Sounds like paradise. Well, except for the tax, I suppose?"

Lars nodded. "It's higher, yes. Worth it, though, given the security."

Ryan jumped in. "The irony is, most foreigners imagine Britain as this idyllic land of garden parties and quaint villages where everyone lives comfortably in period cottages."

Emma's laugh was unfiltered this time. "Tell that to my food bill. I'm the queen of beans on toast." She glanced at her watch. "I still wouldn't trade my work. Bringing new life into the world is worth it."

Lars grinned. "My sister's a nurse, back home in Stockholm. Says exactly the same."

Emma's reply came with a tired smile. "Universal language of healthcare: exhaustion and strange satisfaction."

She stood up, putting her phone and keys in her pocket. Lars watched her, his face full of respect. "You matter," he said. His few words made the message even stronger. "Society only works because of people like you."

Emma paused, his words landing. "Good to hear, actually. That helps, you know." She walked away, pausing only to snap the lighthouse before disappearing down the promenade.

Lars watched her go, thoughtful. "Britain preserves its old buildings with devotion, but essential workers have to fend for themselves."

I nodded, hands tucked deep into my jacket pockets. "It's a national blind spot. We're brilliant at legacy, occasionally less excellent at caring for the present."

Ryan's grin reappeared. "Textbook Britain. Keep calm, carry on, and don't mention the leaky roof."

We spotted the Angel of the North on the horizon well before we arrived, its rust-coloured shape standing out powerfully against the sky. Even though it's twenty metres tall and its wings stretch wider than a jumbo jet, there was a surprising delicacy in how it seemed to float above the Gateshead hills. After the morning at Roker's Pier, we'd left the seaside and headed inland to see this famous landmark, which had split public opinion as sharply as Marmite when it first went up in 1998.

"There it is," Ryan announced unnecessarily, pointing through the windscreen as if Lars and I might somehow have missed the enormous steel figure looming ahead. Ryan continued, "Proper Northern icon, that. Though locals weren't keen at first – called it a rusty waste of money."

I glanced in the rear-view mirror, expecting to see Lars making notes or readying his camera. Instead, his gaze was fixed on the approaching sculpture, his expression unusually open.

We parked and stepped into the cold wind. It circled us, sharp and restless, as if to remind us that while the South might own wealth in pounds, the North claims its riches in dramatic weather. Lars stood still for a moment, his camera at his side, but he didn't reach for it.

"It is... more powerful than I expected," he said finally, his voice sounding genuinely impressed. "The scale, the positioning on this hill – it has presence."

Ryan shot me a look of amused surprise. Lars's usual response to public art had been polite dismissal or technical critique. This admiration was new territory.

We walked to the sculpture and joined a few visitors at its base. Up close, the steel's worn surface was even more striking, marked by weather in a way that felt almost intentional, as if nature had helped shape it.

"The engineering is remarkably efficient," Lars observed, reaching out but stopping just short of touching the surface. "The shell is only six centimetres thick despite its size. Very economical use of materials."

As Lars circled the giant feet of the Angel, examining its construction, I noticed an elderly man approaching. He wore a flat cap, a buttoned jacket, and carried a walking stick he used as much for emphasis as support. He watched Lars with amusement before getting closer.

"Impressive, isn't she, pet?" the elderly man called out, his Geordie accent thick as treacle. "Our Angel's been watching over us for nearly twenty-five years now, love."

Lars turned, startled both by the sudden address and its unexpected terms. His brow furrowed slightly as he processed the words.

"She stands exactly where the miners worked for two centuries," the man continued, tapping his walking stick against the ground for emphasis. "Coal seams ran right under our feet, you know. Deep under, lads would be hewing away in the dark while we're up here admiring the view, love."

Lars looked even more confused. He glanced at me, clearly feeling he'd missed something important. The old man kept going, gesturing at the Angel.

"Represents the shift, doesn't she? From industrial to information age. From men underground to this angel watching over. That's why she matters so much to folk round here, pet. Not just a pretty face, like."

Lars, taking a careful breath, replied politely, "Excuse me, sir, but I think you may have confused me with someone else. We haven't actually met before. My name is Lars Andersson. I'm a photographer from Sweden." He glanced between us and the elderly man, waiting for a response.

The elderly man paused mid-gesture, his bushy eyebrows rising in evident confusion.

"Are you feeling all right, sir?" Lars added with concerned formality. "Perhaps I remind you of a relative?"

Ryan, who had been watching this exchange with growing delight, stepped forward with a grin that threatened to split his face. "Lars, mate, he's not confused. Those are just Geordie terms of endearment – pet, love, darling. Everyone uses them up here, regardless of age, gender, or prior acquaintance."

The elderly man chuckled, the sound carrying on the wind as he replied, "Aye, that's right, pet. We're just friendly up North. Don't mean nowt by it." His eyes twinkled with good humour as he addressed Lars.

Lars blinked slowly, processing this information with the careful consideration he applied to all cultural anomalies. "So... these words are not indicating confusion about my identity or suggesting familial relationship?"

"Not at all," I confirmed. "Regional dialect, that's all."

Lars nodded, though his expression suggested he was still cataloguing this information for further analysis. "I see. This is interesting."

The elderly man, oblivious to Lars's cultural recalibration, had already launched back into his explanation of the Angel.

"Antony Gormley knew what he was doing, placing her here. She's got her feet in our industrial past, but she's looking toward the future, arms spread like she's embracing whatever comes next."

Lars listened with newfound attention, clearly determined to engage properly now that he understood the conversational parameters. When the man paused for breath, Lars ventured, "The weathering effect on the steel is quite beautiful... pet."

Lars said the word so stiffly I had to look away so he wouldn't see my smile. It sounded as forced as the Queen trying out cockney slang.

The elderly man beamed. "Aye, that's the COR-TEN steel for you, hinny. Designed to rust on the outside, protecting what's underneath. Clever, that."

Lars nodded seriously. "Very practical design choice... love."

His second attempt was even more awkward, spoken with the care of someone handling something delicate. Ryan caught my eye, laughing quietly.

The conversation continued, with the elderly man sharing local perspectives on the Angel while Lars listened attentively, occasionally interjecting with technically precise observations about the sculpture's engineering. He made no further attempts at Geordie endearments, apparently having determined that this particular cultural adaptation exceeded his current capabilities.

When we said our goodbyes, the elderly man departed with a cheerful 'Mind how you go, pets!' and a wave. Lars, still processing, turned to us with mild bewilderment.

"These regional variations in linguistic custom are quite challenging," he observed. "In Sweden, terms of endearment are reserved for actual close relationships or your lover. Using them with strangers would be considered extremely uncomfortable."

"Well, you made a valiant effort," Ryan assured him, clapping Lars on the shoulder. "Though I wouldn't recommend taking that particular aspect of Geordie culture back to Stockholm with you."

Lars shook his head slightly. "No. I believe that would cause significant social confusion at home." He glanced back at the Angel, its wings outstretched against the clouds. "The sculpture, however, that is something I understand. Form following function, material honesty, scale appropriate to purpose. It's amazing."

As we made our way back to the car, I noticed Lars hadn't taken a single photo of the Angel. Pointing this out, I saw a flicker of surprise cross his face, as if he'd briefly forgotten his purpose.

He returned and took one photo. Just one. But his face told us it was the one worth taking.

The road curved through Northumberland, past open moorland and rounded hills. Lars was unusually animated on our journey, studying photos on his phone. He called them "the perfect composition" – the famous Sycamore tree, nestled in a dramatic dip along Hadrian's Wall. "It is iconic," he said. "The solitary tree is perfectly positioned between two rises of the ancient wall. A masterclass in natural framing."

"The tree had stood in the Sycamore Gap for over two hundred years," Ryan observed from the back seat, where he had been reading aloud from a digital guidebook. "Though it became properly famous after featuring in that Robin Hood film with Kevin Costner. Hence the nickname 'the Robin Hood tree.'"

Lars didn't look up. "The best angle is from the east, late morning. The wall's shadows draw the eye in." He kept swiping. "Every shot tells a new story."

I met Ryan's eyes in the rear-view mirror. We both knew what had happened a few years ago. But Lars had evidently missed the headlines (perhaps it hadn't been a thing in Sweden). Now I wasn't sure how to break the truth to him.

Soon, we reached the car park, which was surprisingly full for a weekday morning. As we gathered our equipment, I became aware of a particular quality to the visitors making their way toward the path – a hushed reverence more commonly associated with memorial sites than tourist attractions. Meanwhile, Lars, entirely focused on extracting his tripod from its case, remained oblivious to this subtle atmospheric shift.

"Let's go," he declared, swinging his camera bag over his shoulder. "The light's almost perfect."

The path to Sycamore Gap ran alongside Hadrian's Wall. This ancient stone barrier marked the northern edge of the Roman Empire. The wall undulated across the land, rising and falling with the contours of the hills. Today, though, I couldn't pause to admire the Roman feat. My focus was on the moment of discovery that waited ahead.

As we reached the top of a small hill, something felt different. The famous gap appeared ahead, that unique dip where the wall dropped and climbed again in a perfect 'U' shape. But in the centre, there was nothing. Just a small fenced area around a stump, with a few withered flowers at its base.

Lars stopped so abruptly that Ryan nearly collided with him from behind.

"The tree," he said simply, his voice flat. "It is gone."

"I'm afraid so," I confirmed gently. "It was cut down a while ago. An act of vandalism."

Lars lowered his camera as he processed this. His usual composure gave way briefly to confusion and disbelief.

Distress edged his voice. "Why would someone do this? In Sweden, trees are respected. We have a saying: 'A tree is a poem the earth writes to the sky.' Destroying one needlessly is unthinkable."

The accusation in his voice was clear, as if this act of vandalism showed a deep British disregard for nature. I walked over to him.

"Lars," I began, "this wasn't a reflection of British attitudes toward nature. It was an act of vandalism that shocked the entire nation. When this happened, it was front-page news everywhere. People were genuinely devastated."

Ryan nodded in agreement. "It was practically a day of national mourning. People left flowers, held vigils. The two blokes who did it are universally despised. They've been charged with criminal damage, and there was serious discussion about harsher charges, recognising what the tree meant to us."

Lars's face stayed sceptical, still marked by disbelief. He looked at the fenced stump. Only then did he see what he had missed before. Faded ribbons hung from the fence, and small tokens like carved wooden figures, laminated poems, and painted stones were scattered at the base. A simple plaque told the tree's story in a few sad words. The last line sounded less like a notice and more like a promise: saplings from the original tree's seeds would be planted one day.

"Look around," I suggested quietly.

Lars raised his gaze to take in the other visitors to the site. A family stood several metres away, the parents speaking in hushed tones to their children as they explained what had happened. An elderly couple placed a small posy of wildflowers against the fence with the solemn care usually reserved for grave visitations. Two hikers removed their hats as they approached the stump, a simple gesture of respect that seemed entirely fitting.

"There's a visitors' book," Ryan mentioned, pointing toward a weatherproof container attached to the fence. "People have been leaving messages for months. Some come back repeatedly, documenting their grief as if the tree were a person."

Lars approached the fence slowly, his camera drooping uselessly in his hand.

"I misunderstood," he finally said, straightening up. "I assumed..." He gestured vaguely, uncharacteristically inarticulate. "In Sweden, we sometimes think other countries do not value nature as we do. This was... a prejudice."

Lars' gaze returned to the stump. "The tree was a landmark. A natural monument. Its destruction is like..." He searched for an appropriate comparison. "Like someone attacking one of your cathedrals."

"That's exactly how many people here felt about it," Ryan agreed. "It wasn't just a tree – it was a symbol, something that had become part of our collective identity."

Lars unzipped his camera bag, extracting his camera with newfound purpose. "I will document this," he announced. "Not the composition I planned, but the absence. The loss. The human response to that loss."

The causeway to St. Mary's Lighthouse was covered with seaweed, sand and stones – it is only briefly visible when the tide has retreated. The white tower stood in splendid isolation on its small, rocky island, its glass lantern room catching the late-afternoon sun with particular brilliance. This perfect alignment of sunset and low tide had been carefully planned; we'd studied tide tables with the dedication of medieval astronomers to ensure our arrival coincided with this window of dry passage to the island. The North Sea waited patiently on either side of the exposed causeway, ready to reclaim the path in a few hours' time.

"Mind the seaweed," Ryan cautioned as we stepped onto the causeway. "It's like nature's ice rink when it's wet."

Lars nodded, picking his way across carefully. The lighthouse ahead, bright white against the darkening sky, had captured his full attention.

"The light quality is exceptional," he observed. "The angle of the sun creates strong directional shadows while the sea reflects warmth. Very rare conditions."

We crossed without any trouble, though Ryan performed a brief, unintentional pirouette on a particularly slick patch of seaweed. The small island felt cut off from the mainland by more than just water. The noise of traffic faded away, replaced by the steady sound of waves hitting the rocks and the occasional call of gulls flying overhead.

Lars wasted no time. He assembled his tripod, extending its legs and securing his camera with a series of precise movements. He positioned himself at the end of the causeway, angling his equipment to capture the tower against the sunset sky. For several minutes, he stood motionless, waiting for the exact quality of light he sought.

I wandered toward the rocky edge of the island, where a solitary figure sat perched on an outcrop. A fishing rod was propped against the rocks beside him, its line disappearing into the water below. The man's face was creased and tanned, his hands bearing the marks of countless fishing lines and hooks. He wore a faded blue jumper that had clearly seen better decades and a woollen hat pulled low over greying hair.

He nodded in greeting as I approached. "Quite the view tonight, isn't it? Sea's calm as a mill pond."

"It is beautiful," I agreed. "Perfect timing with the tide."

"Aye, you've timed it right enough." He glanced toward Lars, who remained absorbed in his photography. "Your friend's got himself some serious kit there. Professional, is he?"

"We're all photographers, working on a project about Britain's coastal communities and landscapes."

The man's eyes crinkled with interest. "Well, you've picked a good 'un here. Not just a pretty face, this lighthouse – got proper history."

Ryan had wandered over to join us, drawn by the prospect of conversation. The fisherman, who introduced himself as Gordon with a firm handshake, began sharing his extensive knowledge of the site.

"Few people know there was an 11th-century chapel here long before the lighthouse," he explained, gesturing toward the tower. "Monks kept lanterns burning to warn ships off the rocks. Proper dedicated, they were – praying while keeping those lights going through all sorts of weather."

Gordon shared his local knowledge in the unique accent of the North East. He pointed out different parts of the coastline we could see, naming the various bays and headlands. It was clear he had spent many years watching them from both land and sea.

As the light began to shift, Lars, finally satisfied with his photographs, joined our small gathering. Gordon regarded him with open curiosity.

"Here he comes, a proper Viking with that camera!" Gordon said with a grin. "Are you planning to raid our monastery, lad? You're a bit late, the Danes arrived about a thousand years ago."

Lars blinked, momentarily taken aback by this greeting. "I am Swedish, actually. Not Danish."

"Close enough!" Gordon said with a dismissive wave. "You

lot all came over in the same longboats, didn't you?"

Lars frowned slightly. "Actually, Swedish Vikings predominantly travelled eastward through Russia, while the Danes and Norwegians focused on western Europe, including Britain. The historical distinctions are quite significant."

Gordon chuckled, clearly amused by Lars's serious answer."Listen to him! Is the university of the sea not good enough for you, eh? Think you are cleverer than this old man?" He looked at Lars's technical clothing. "You foreigners always wear the wrong clothes. Where's your proper coat? That thin layer won't keep out a North Sea wind."

Lars's posture stiffened noticeably. His expression shifted from mild confusion to growing discomfort. "My clothing is specifically designed for outdoor photography. The layers are technically advanced and more efficient than traditional heavy coats."

"If you say so, lad," Gordon replied with a wink in my direction. "Though you might want to tell your face it's not a funeral. What's with the serious face? You look like a passport photo!"

This last comment seemed to be too much for Lars. His face became tense, and he stood up straight, his jaw tight.

"I do not understand why you talk to me like that," he said with a careful, clipped voice. "We have just met, and I have done nothing to offend you. I am not actually a Viking, and my clothing is perfectly appropriate for this activity. And I was born with this face. I am sorry if you don't like it. Where is the British politeness everybody talks about? In Sweden, we do not insult strangers upon first meeting."

An uncomfortable silence fell over our little group. Gordon's smile faded, replaced by a look of genuine worry and regret as he realised his comments had been completely misinterpreted.

"Hold on, lad, I didn't mean–" he began, but I gently intervened.

"Lars," I explained, "this is what Britons call 'banter' – it's a form of playful conversation that often includes teasing or mock insults. Particularly in the North of England, it's actually a sign of acceptance and friendliness, not hostility."

Ryan nodded in agreement. "It's counter-intuitive, I know,

but being gently 'insulted' by someone you've just met is often a good sign. It means they're comfortable enough to joke with you."

Lars looked genuinely perplexed, his brow furrowed as he processed this information. "So... these comments about Vikings and my clothing were meant as... friendly communication?"

"Exactly," I confirmed. "Gordon wasn't criticising you – quite the opposite. He was trying to make you feel welcome in his own way."

Gordon, looking slightly abashed, extended a weathered hand toward Lars. "I'm sorry, lad. Didn't mean to cause offence. Sometimes I forget not everyone gets our way of talking. No harm meant, I promise you."

Lars hesitantly accepted the handshake, though his uncertain smile and wary eyes showed he was still trying to reconcile this cultural information with his understanding of polite interaction.

"Let me make it up to you," Gordon offered, reaching for a thermos tucked beside his fishing gear. "Cup of tea? It's proper strong – none of that weak stuff they serve down south."

Lars accepted the offered cup with careful politeness. "Thank you. In Sweden, we also appreciate strong coffee, though perhaps not tea as much."

This simple exchange seemed to restart the conversation. As we sat and watched the sunset colour the lighthouse, Gordon told stories about storms he had faced and changes he had seen along the coast over the years. Lars listened closely and sometimes asked questions.

As darkness began to fall and we prepared to cross the causeway before the tide returned, Gordon packed up his fishing gear. "Well, you've certainly got an eye for photography, Mr Viking. Better than those Instagram types who come here for selfies and nearly get washed away because they don't check the tide times."

Lars, who had been carefully rinsing Gordon's cup with water from his own bottle before returning it, paused. A small smile touched his lips. "Thank you. Though I'm surprised you know about Instagram, given you appear to be from the Viking age yourself."

For a moment, Gordon looked startled. Then he burst into delighted laughter, clapping Lars on the shoulder. "There you go! You'll be a proper Geordie by the time you leave!"

As we walked back across the causeway, now lit by the lighthouse beam moving over the dark water, I saw that Lars looked noticeably more relaxed. "This was... liberating, in a way," he said. "Swedish social interaction can be quite limited by politeness. There is something refreshing about this 'banter', it simply skips formality."

Maybe our Swedish friend was starting to notice something about Britain. Under all these tedious queuing and puzzling traditions, there's a real sense of warmth, humour, and friendliness. This quiet kindness, which sometimes is disguised as sarcasm, felt comforting. It made me think of British weather: not often sunny, sometimes stormy, but always there when life goes wrong. Perhaps Lars was beginning to see not just what made Britain seem odd to visitors, but also what made it feel like home to the people who stayed.

Allendale looked just like any other NorthumRyan village: stone cottages clustered for warmth, a market cross at the centre, and a pub offering shelter from the drizzle. At first, nothing seemed unusual. But soon, in the narrow streets, we noticed hints of a much stranger tradition.

"Is that man filling barrels with sticks?" Ryan asked, pausing mid-stride to observe a middle-aged fellow methodically packing a wooden cask with what appeared to be an assortment of kindling.

"And sawdust, I think," I replied, noticing similar activities taking place in several adjacent gardens. "Though why anyone would need quite so many barrels is beyond me."

Lars lowered his camera. "It's not just him. Several households are doing the same thing."

He was right. As we continued our walk, the evidence continued to mount. A group of women sat in a back garden, sewing what appeared to be elaborate costumes from heavy fabric. Further along, several men wrestled substantial logs onto a growing pile in a field at the edge of the village, the foundation of what would clearly become an impressive bonfire.

"There's a certain efficiency to their method," Lars noted. "They are not doing this for the first time."

Ryan, meanwhile, had diverted from our path to examine one of the barrels more closely. One of the men filling the barrels, a sturdy fellow who clearly was accustomed to manual work, seemed amused by Ryan's interest and started to explain what he was doing.

"Paraffin," Ryan announced upon rejoining us. "They're soaking the wood shavings and sawdust in paraffin. Quite generously, I might add."

"That explains the smell," I said. "Though not the purpose."

Lars's brow had furrowed into the particular configuration that I'd come to recognise as his 'British confusion' expression. "This is concerning. Open flames near old buildings – what about the fire risk?"

We continued toward the village centre, where Allendale's community hall stood with its notice board offering the possibility of enlightenment. Amidst the usual advertisements for yoga classes and parish council meetings, a laminated photograph caught our attention. It showed a line of men walking through the village at night, each with a burning barrel balanced precariously on his head.

"This cannot be real," Lars stated, leaning in to examine the image with the intensity he uses for potential photographic manipulations. "Carrying open fire on one's head would violate every safety protocol I can imagine."

"I don't think it's meant to be taken literally," Ryan suggested, though his voice lacked conviction. "It's probably some sort of artistic representation. A metaphor, perhaps."

Lars shook his head. "The photograph appears unaltered. Those men are literally carrying flaming containers on their craniums."

"We need local insight," I decided, nodding toward the pub. "Let's ask there."

Despite the early hour, several locals occupied the well-worn benches and stools, nursing what appeared to be their first pints of the day. Behind the bar, a man of indeterminate but considerable age polished glasses.

"Afternoon," he greeted us. "What can I get you?"

After ordering tonic water for Ryan and me, and, predictably, water for Lars, I ventured to ask our question.

"We were wondering about the barrels," I began. "And the costumes. And the rather alarming photograph on the community notice board."

The landlord's face broke into a grin of evident pride. "Ah, you've spotted the Tar Bar'l preparations! We are busy all year with making our New Year's Eve celebration perfect."

"Tar Bar'l?" Ryan repeated, testing the phonetics carefully.

"Aye, 'Barrel' in the local dialect," the landlord explained. "One of the oldest fire festivals in Britain, that is. Every New Year's Eve, our guisers carry burning tar barrels through the village on their heads to welcome in the New Year."

Lars, who had been listening with increasing concern, interjected. "On their actual heads? Balanced directly on the skull?"

"Well, they wear special hats padded with damp sacking," the landlord clarified, as if this minor safety precaution rendered the whole enterprise perfectly reasonable. "Been doing it for centuries, we have. The role of guiser is passed down through the families – proper hereditary honour in the Allen Valleys."

He leaned in, clearly enjoying the chance to share a favourite local tradition. "We prepare all year. The barrels you saw need to be seasoned properly. Years ago, we sometimes 'borrowed' them from road works, farms, or anywhere we could find. The police got involved in the 1950s, so we set up a committee to get them the right way. Now we use old whisky barrels from the distilleries."

"But the fire risk," Lars persisted, his Swedish sensibilities clearly offended by this casual approach to combining open flames and human heads. "Surely there are regulations?"

The landlord chuckled. "Been doing it since before regulations were invented, lad. The village knows how to manage. We've never lost a building yet, and only the occasional eyebrow."

This failed to reassure Lars, whose expression suggested he was mentally calculating the insurance implications.

"Here," the landlord continued, pulling a smartphone from his pocket with the particular pride of someone from an older generation who has mastered technology, "my grandson took this last year. Proper spectacle, isn't it?"

The video showed a procession of men in strange, soot-blackened costumes, each balancing a flaming barrel on his head. They paraded through the village streets at midnight. Sparks and flames leapt from the barrels, illuminating faces in the crowd with an otherworldly glow. The procession ended at an enormous bonfire. It roared to life as the barrels' contents fueled it.

"It's absolutely fascinating," Ryan declared, his initial amusement now transformed into genuine enthusiasm. "The pagan roots, the community participation, the element of controlled danger!"

Lars, to my surprise, was watching the video with an expression that had shifted from concern to something almost appreciative. "The collective risk management is actually quite sophisticated," he observed. "Notice how they coordinate their movements, maintain specific distances. There's an implicit safety protocol in their formation."

"Aye, there's method to our madness," the landlord agreed, pleased by this acknowledgement. "Been refining it for generations, we have."

As we finished our drinks and prepared to continue our exploration of the village, I noticed Lars taking voice notes on his phone, summarising what he had learned about this Tar Bar'l festival.

"What are you thinking about it?" I asked as we stepped back into the grey NorthumRyan afternoon.

"It is fascinating," Lars replied. "I reflected on this typical British knack for nurturing traditions that would likely be extinguished elsewhere by regulation."

He was right. There was something admirable in the community's fierce resolve to keep this blazing ritual alive, despite the constraints of modern safety rules. It was a stubbornness that spoke to a deep-rooted belief: some traditions are worth the peril they bear.

The enormous structure appeared through the downpour like a half-remembered dream. Dunstanburgh Castle's massive outline blurred under sheets of rain that swept across the landscape with horizontal determination. What should have been a pleasant coastal walk from Craster had turned into an amphibious expedition. Paths became shallow streams, and fields turned into temporary marshland. The ruins, perched on their windswept headland, seemed to welcome the elemental battering. Their weathered stones had endured far worse over the centuries.

"Perfect conditions." Lars grinned, pulling his camera from its weatherproof bag. Rain cascaded from his hood and formed miniature waterfalls at his elbows, but he looked utterly untroubled by the storm, as if basking in a gentle spring mist rather than enduring a tempest.

Ryan, huddled beneath his supposedly waterproof jacket which had surrendered to the rain twenty minutes earlier, now shivered in defeat. He wiped water from his brow, his efforts futile. "I believe animals have started pairing up and looking for a large wooden vessel," he observed miserably.

I paused to tighten the drawstring on my hood as a fresh gust of wind tugged at every seam in my jacket. A sudden bolt of cold made me flinch; my cheeks stung as I watched Lars stride ahead, his boots sending ripples through a puddle that could more accurately be described as a small Scottish loch. "The forecast did mention 'occasional showers,'" I said, forcing a laugh and hurrying to keep up.

"Yes, and the Titanic experienced 'minor navigational issues,'" Ryan shot back, shaking one foot that had disappeared ankle-deep into unexpected mud.

Lars had positioned himself at the best vantage point, unmoved by rain streaming down his face as he adjusted his camera. His boots stood firmly in a shallow stream crossing the path. He stayed focused on capturing the ruined gatehouse against the stormy sky, pausing often to wipe his lens dry.

"The rain makes the light look amazing," he called over his shoulder, eyes locked on his camera. "The reflections on the wet stone make the colours and shades stand out more. This weather is a gift for serious photography."

A gift? Really? At maximum one of those 'White Elephant' gifts, I thought to myself. But Lars was clearly tougher than we were, maybe because of his Scandinavian roots.

After an hour methodically photographing various viewpoints – during which Ryan's complaints grew from remarks about British weather to philosophical musings on human suffering – Lars finally returned. He joined us beneath the partial shelter of a crumbling wall.

"I have decided," he declared, adopting the air of someone delivering a carefully considered judgment, "to cycle to Bamburgh Castle this afternoon."

There was a moment of stunned silence, broken only by the percussive rhythm of raindrops hitting stone.

"Cycle?" Ryan repeated. "As in, on a bicycle? In this?" He swept his arm at the waterlogged landscape around us.

"Precisely," Lars affirmed. He gave a single, decisive nod, causing a small cascade to fall from his hood. "It is approximately twelve miles via the coastal route. Good for character building."

I studied Lars's expression for any hint that this might be his first attempt at British-style deadpan humour. Finding none, I ventured, "You do realise the forecast suggests this rain will continue all day? It may even intensify this afternoon."

"Weather is just weather," Lars intoned with Scandinavian stoicism. "In Sweden, we have a saying: 'There is no bad weather, only inadequate clothing.'"

"Well, we have the same saying, but..." Ryan exchanged a glance with me. His message was clear. We are Brits. We deal with challenging weather all the time. But we do have our limits.

"While I deeply admire your commitment to character building," I began diplomatically, "I think Ryan and I might opt for the slightly less heroic option of a warm pub and perhaps some background research on the castle's history."

"Very sensible," Ryan chimed in with suspicious enthusiasm. "Someone should document the historical context of these ruins. Academic responsibility and all that."

Lars looked at us, his expression hard to read. Maybe he was disappointed or annoyed. He checked his watch before saying, "I understand. Not everyone has the Nordic ability to handle challenging weather situations." Then he added, "I will meet you at the Jolly Fisherman in Craster at seven o'clock. That should give me enough time to get back, including stops for photos."

Twenty minutes later, Ryan and I sipped tea while watching through the steamy window of the Jolly Fisherman. We saw Lars outside, mounting his rented bicycle. He gripped the handlebars, leaned into the wind, and pedalled away through the rain, water streaming from his waterproof trousers in rivulets.

"Do you think we should be concerned?" Ryan asked, barely sounding concerned as he settled deeper into his chair beside the crackling fire.

"He did grow up in a country where winter darkness lasts for months and children are taught to ice swim before they can walk," I pointed out, spreading out a guidebook on the table between us. "I suspect he'll not only survive but return with high praises about the excellent photography conditions."

The pub was a welcome comfort, a true escape from the storm. Warmth slowly returned to our chilled bones. The firelight glowed softly, and the low hum of conversation matched the steady rain outside. We ordered tea, warmed our hands on the cups, and started reading about the Wars of the Roses and Dunstanburgh's history, with Ryan sharing the most dramatic parts.

"Listen to this." Ryan tapped a paragraph in the guidebook. "'The mighty fortress was built by Earl Thomas of Lancaster, who was executed for rebelling against his cousin, King Edward II. Later, during the Wars of the Roses, it changed hands several times between Yorkist and Lancastrian forces before being largely abandoned and left to decay.' Rather puts our little rainy adventure in perspective, doesn't it?"

The hours passed pleasantly, punctuated by Ryan's increasingly elaborate vegan snack orders – "Do you suppose they could do the chips with a drizzle of truffle oil? No? Perhaps a side of guacamole then?" – and occasional explanations to curious locals about why our Swedish companion had chosen to cycle to Bamburgh in weather that had caused several fishing boats to cancel their outings.

"He's Swedish," became our standard reply, which seemed to satisfy most inquiries, usually accompanied by knowing nods as if this single fact explained everything.

At precisely seven o'clock – Swedish punctuality, undaunted by downpours – the pub door swung open. A sharp gust silenced the room as Lars entered. Water cascaded from every part of him, forming a wide puddle at his feet. His soaked trousers clung miserably to his legs, his jacket heavy and a few shades darker. His hair was plastered to his head in sodden, defeated strands.

Yet despite this thoroughly drenched state, he stood tall, shoulders back, expression containing something that might have been classified as triumph. He looked every bit the wet and proud Viking, as if he'd just navigated a longship through a particularly challenging fjord rather than cycled along the Northumberland coast.

"Mission accomplished," he proclaimed as he strode toward our table, his boots squelching with each step and leaving a winding trail of water on the floor. The landlord gave Lars a resigned glance, watching his soggy progress from across the room.

With no further comment, Lars placed his camera on the table and unlatched its waterproof case. He flipped through the photo gallery, then turned the screen toward us, revealing a series of images that, against all reasonable expectations, were breathtaking.

Bamburgh Castle looked impressive against the dramatic sky. The clouds were dark and heavy, split by golden light. The old stone seemed to glow in this light. Rainwater made pools in front of the castle, reflecting its shape. In one photo, lightning flashed behind the tallest tower. The timing was so perfect it hardly seemed real.

"The weather made things perfect for drama," Lars remarked with his typically understated satisfaction. "The storm coming in changed the light in amazing ways."

"You're sitting in a puddle of your own making," Ryan observed, "but I have to admit, these photographs are extraordinary."

Lars accepted this with a slight inclination of his head, sending a small cascade of droplets onto the table. "The discomfort was temporary," he said. "The images are permanent."

I signalled to the barman for a round of drinks. "I think you've earned a proper British remedy for weather exposure," I suggested. "Hot whisky with lemon and honey."

"An acceptable prescription," Lars conceded, finally permitting himself the luxury of a slight shiver. "Though in Sweden, we would naturally prefer aquavit."

"Of course you would," Ryan muttered, sliding his chair slightly away from the expanding puddle beneath Lars's seat. "Probably served in a cup made of ice while sitting in a snowbank."

Lars considered this with perfect seriousness. "That would be impractical. The ice would melt."

The causeway to Lindisfarne stretched out before us, a narrow road across the seabed. Soon, the North Sea would cover it again. To our left, wooden poles marked the higher path – the Pilgrims' Way, an ancient route generations of the faithful had followed across the sands. To our right, the sea waited with tidal patience, ready to isolate the island once more. The sign at the mainland end was admirably straightforward: "DANGER. Do not proceed when water reaches causeway." Below, a board displayed the day's safe crossing times with the particular authority of information that can mean the difference between convenience and catastrophe.

"Safe crossing until 2:15 p.m.," Ryan read aloud, consulting his watch. "It's just gone eleven. Plenty of time."

Lars, who had been studying the landscape with the focused attention he brought to all potential photographic subjects, nodded. "The light conditions should be optimal around one o'clock. Cloud cover is expected to thin by then."

We drove across the causeway, which curved gently over the exposed seabed. Salt-tolerant plants clung to small patches of higher ground. Now and then, an empty crab shell reminded us that this place belonged more to sea life than to people. I couldn't help thinking how this narrow road would soon vanish under the rising tide, a twice-daily reminder that nature doesn't care about our schedules.

Lindisfarne itself rose before us. Its most famous landmarks were clearly visible, even from a distance. The ruined priory stood with the dignified incompletion that only centuries of weathering can achieve. Nearby, the castle perched atop its rocky outcrop. Restored, yet it still maintained the silhouette that had guided sailors for generations.

"We should start with the priory," Ryan suggested as we parked. His phone was already in his hand, screen displaying a Wikipedia page. "Founded in 635 CE by Saint Aidan, it was where the Lindisfarne Gospels were created. The Vikings raided in 793 – one of the first and most notorious Viking attacks on Britain."

Lars looked up from his camera bag, frowning a little. "It seems like the Vikings always get blamed in British history. While your monks were busy making illuminated manuscripts, my ancestors were just finding creative ways to share resources efficiently."

"Is that what they're calling looting and pillaging in Sweden these days?" Ryan asked with a grin. "Efficient resource sharing?"

"I'm going to photograph the castle from that rise," Lars announced, clearly choosing to ignore Ryan's comment as he assembled his tripod. "The perspective will capture its relationship with the sea and sky. Very minimal. Very pure."

"I'll join you," I decided, leaving Ryan to his historical research. "The light's beginning to work in our favour."

We walked along the shore, feeling the wind pick up as we neared the open sea. The North Sea reached out to the horizon, its surface shaped by sunlight filtering through layers of cloud. The castle stood out against this scene, its simple shape even more impressive than many of the fancier buildings I'd photographed.

Lars worked in silence, adjusting his tripod with millimetre precision, occasionally consulting a light meter despite his camera's sophisticated built-in systems. I watched as he captured a series of images that eliminated all extraneous elements, focusing on the clean lines of the castle against the simplified planes of sea and sky. There was something almost meditative about his process – a careful reduction to essentials that revealed more than it excluded.

After an hour of photography and exploration, I noticed the wind had shifted, now coming from the northeast with increasing strength. Cumulus clouds were building on the horizon, their edges hardening in a way that suggested changing weather. I checked my phone's weather app, then consulted the tide tables I'd downloaded before our visit.

"We should consider leaving earlier than the posted time," I joined Ryan and Lars as they examined a weathered stone cross. "There's a spring tide today, and this wind will push the water in faster than normal."

Lars nodded immediately, already calculating the impact on his remaining photography time. Ryan looked less convinced.

"But the sign said safe until 2:15," he protested. "It's just after one o'clock."

"Those times are based on average conditions," I explained. "This northeast wind could bring the tide in up to thirty minutes earlier. Better safe than stranded."

As we packed our equipment and headed toward the car park, a rental vehicle pulled in – its pristine condition and cautious manoeuvring marking it clearly as a tourist vehicle. Two couples emerged, dressed in the particular urban fashion that looks immediately out of place in coastal settings: designer trainers ill-suited to muddy paths, light jackets insufficient against the strengthening wind, and the unmistakable air of people who check the weather app but don't actually believe it.

"Excuse me," called the taller of the two men, approaching us with the confident stride of someone accustomed to having questions answered promptly. His accent placed him somewhere in the Home Counties. "We've just arrived. Are the priory and castle both open for visiting?"

"They are," I confirmed, "but you might want to keep your visit brief. The tide's coming in faster than the published times suggest."

The man glanced at his watch with the particular smile of someone humouring an overcautious stranger. "It says we've got until 2:15 on the sign. Surely they build in a safety margin?"

His female companion nodded in agreement. "We've come all the way from Guildford. We can't leave without seeing the priory properly."

"The Northeast wind accelerates tidal ingress," Lars stated flatly. "Water physics doesn't respect your travel arrangements."

The second man chuckled, clearly interpreting Lars's sincere warning as some sort of dry joke. "We'll just have a quick look. How long can it take? Half an hour tops."

With polite nods and the particular smile that communicates both farewell and mild disapproval, we left them heading eagerly toward the priory. Ryan glanced back with concern.

"Should we have been more insistent?" he asked as we reached our car.

"You can warn people," I replied, starting the engine, "but you can't make them listen."

We crossed the causeway without incident, though I noticed the water already beginning to encroach on the lowest sections. From the safety of the mainland, we paused at a viewpoint that offered a clear perspective back toward the island. Through the zoom lens of my camera, I tracked the progress of our recent acquaintances. I saw them emerge from the priory and make their unhurried way back to their car.

"They're cutting it very fine," I observed, checking the time. It was 2:10 – still within the official safe period, but the rising water told a different story.

"They're starting to drive across now," Ryan reported, watching through his own telephoto lens. "But look at the causeway – there's already water on the lowest section."

Lars, who had been quietly searching on his phone for potential sunset shots, joined us at the viewpoint. "They should have listened."

We watched as the rental car made its way cautiously onto the causeway. For the first few hundred metres, their progress seemed secure. Then, as they reached a dip in the road, their speed dropped. Even from our distance, it was clear they had encountered water deeper than they had anticipated.

"They're stopping," Ryan announced, his voice rising with that certain photojournalistic excitement. "The water must be up to the axles already."

The car sat still for a few moments. Then it started to slowly reverse, clearly trying to get back to the island. But it was too late. Water now covered the stretch they had just crossed, leaving them stuck on a shrinking patch of road with water rising on both sides.

"There's a refuge box on the causeway," I explained, pointing to a small elevated structure visible about fifty metres from the stranded vehicle. "It's there precisely for people who ignore the crossing times."

Sure enough, we soon saw the car doors open and the four figures make their way carefully through the rising water toward the emergency shelter. They climbed the ladder and disappeared inside the small hut, which now stood as an island in the advancing tide.

"I'm calling the coastguard," I said, already dialling the emergency number. "They'll need to be rescued."

Ryan, meanwhile, had shifted into full documentation mode, recording the scene. Situations that combine human drama with potential social media impact are his treasure troves.

"This is absolute Insta-gold," he murmured, his camera tracking a particularly large wave washing across the now fully submerged causeway. "Hashtag tidal karma."

"That's not helpful, Ryan," I admonished, though I couldn't entirely suppress a smile as I explained the situation to the coastguard dispatcher.

The rescue operation unfolded with the efficiency of people who perform the same task with depressing regularity. A coastguard boat approached from the north side of the causeway, reached the refuge hut without difficulty, and safely extracted its four occupants. Within twenty minutes, all four tourists were back on the mainland, looking simultaneously relieved and embarrassed as they thanked their rescuers.

As they were being provided with warm drinks and foil blankets, one of the coastguard officers approached me.

"Thanks for the prompt call," he said, nodding toward the now completely submerged causeway. "Though I have to say, it's a scenario we're well familiar with."

"I imagine it happens rather frequently," I replied.

"Happens every year several times," he confirmed with a resigned sigh. "Northeast wind like today's can bring the tide in up to thirty minutes ahead of the tables. Then there's barometric pressure, spring tides, and a dozen other factors that don't make it onto the laminated charts. But tourists won't listen to the warnings."

"What happens to the car?" asked Ryan with a certain glee.

"Once the tide goes out, we'll try to recover it," the coastguard answered. "But it is a complete loss. No car loves being drowned in salt water."

He glanced toward the four bedraggled visitors, now looking distinctly less urban-chic with their sodden designer trainers and salt-stained jackets. "They always say the same thing afterwards: 'But the sign said it was safe until 2:15.' As if the tide's obliged to read the noticeboard."

As we left Lindisfarne, I looked in the rear-view mirror. The causeway had disappeared, and the island was once more cut off from the mainland by the steady pull of the tide. No matter how carefully we mark the signs or check the tide tables, nature decides when we can cross and when we must wait.

Our last day with our Swedish companion arrived, and with it came the end of the entire exchange program.

Berwick-upon-Tweed looked just as you'd expect for a town with such a turbulent history. It seemed a bit battered but never broken, always unmistakably Berwick. Massive Elizabethan walls, once England's most expensive project under Queen Elizabeth I, surround the town like a stone hug. To the north, the River Tweed marks the start of Scotland, its border shaping Berwick for centuries. It's not quite English or Scottish, but something unique – a brief pause in the story of Anglo-Scottish relations.

"This is fascinating," Lars announced as we walked along the perfectly preserved ramparts. "Berwick-upon-Tweed changed nationality fourteen times between 1174 and 1482. The town was valued for its strategic position and wealth from the wool trade," Lars continued, warming to his subject. "Edward I of England captured it in 1296, then the Scots reclaimed it in 1318. It changed hands repeatedly during what you call the 'Border Wars'."

"I'm impressed," I admitted, genuinely surprised by this detailed knowledge. "You've clearly done your research."

Lars nodded. "Border territories have always interested me. Places where cultures meet and blend. Sweden has similar examples with Norway and Finland – though with considerably less historical violence."

We walked the walls as Lars occasionally pointed out architectural details. Dramatic shadows were cast by the afternoon light, which he captured with precise photographs.

"Did you know," he announced as we descended toward the old harbour area, "that Berwick-upon-Tweed was technically at war with Russia for over a century?"

Ryan, who prided himself on obscure historical knowledge, looked genuinely intrigued. "I hadn't heard that one."

"During the Crimean War," Lars said, "Queen Victoria signed the declaration of war as 'Victoria, Queen of Great Britain, Ireland, Berwick-upon-Tweed, and all British Dominions.' When the Treaty of Paris was signed in 1856 to end the war, Berwick was not mentioned."

"So technically," I said, following the logic, "Berwick remained at war with Russia?"

Lars nodded, pleased at the oversight. "Precisely. The error wasn't corrected until 1966. During the Cold War, a Soviet official signed a peace treaty with the town council. Some say it was still legally invalid. Berwick might technically remain at war with Russia even now."

By early evening, we had finished our tour of the walls, the lighthouse, and the bridges. As darkness fell, we found ourselves outside the Barrel's Ale House. The pub had probably served thirsty travellers for centuries.

We found a corner table and ordered dinner. Ryan and I chose the vegan pie, while Lars opted for a simple Ploughman's platter. The dish suited his minimalist Scandinavian principles.

"I will have another," Lars announced after finishing his first pint of local ale, prompting Ryan to freeze mid-bite and stare in undisguised surprise. Throughout our journey, Lars had maintained a strictly enforced limit of one alcoholic beverage per evening, usually sipped with such moderation that it lasted the entire meal.

"Another?" I echoed, wondering if I'd misheard.

"Yes," Lars confirmed with a decisive nod. "This 'Export' is quite acceptable. And it is our last evening, we need to celebrate!"

Before I could stop him and explain that Ryan and I couldn't drink because we had to drive back to London overnight, Lars's second drink arrived. It disappeared even faster than the first, and I noticed a change in him. His usual restraint faded, his posture relaxed, and soon his gestures became broader. His voice grew more animated as he compared Swedish and British brewing methods.

By the time he ordered a third pint, the transformation was unmistakable. A flush had appeared across his cheekbones, and his accent was becoming simultaneously more pronounced and somehow more melodic.

"In Sweden," he announced to no one in particular, "we have a proper relationship with alcohol. Most of the time, we don't drink at all. Or perhaps just sip, very cautiously. But if we do drink – well, then we really dive in." He laughed.

Before we could process this philosophical bombshell from the methodical man who had previously lectured us on how to optimally recycle our garbage, a screech of feedback cut through the pub's ambient noise. A small platform in the corner, previously unnoticed, was now occupied by a man setting up what appeared to be karaoke equipment.

"Thursday night is karaoke night at the Barrels," he announced into the microphone. "Sign-up sheet at the bar for anyone brave enough."

Lars's head turned toward this announcement with a sudden interest. His eyes, typically narrowed in critical assessment, had widened with what appeared to be real excitement.

"ABBA," he said, with the gravity of someone pronouncing an essential truth. "Sweden's greatest cultural export."

"Greater than Ikea?" Ryan inquired with a raised eyebrow.

Lars dismissed this with a dramatic wave of his hand. "Furniture is functional. Music is transcendent." He rose from his seat with surprising grace, especially given his recent alcohol consumption. "I must represent my country with honour."

Before either of us could formulate a response to this declaration, Lars had crossed to the bar and was writing his name on the sign-up sheet. He returned to our table with a satisfied expression.

"I picked 'Mamma Mia' for my performance," he told us. "It has a well-known tune and is not too hard to sing."

"I didn't know you were a singer," I remarked, trying to reconcile this new information with the reserved, safety-conscious Swede we had come to know.

"All Swedes can sing ABBA," he replied with absolute conviction. "It is encoded in our DNA. Like tolerance for cold temperatures and appreciation of minimalist design."

Twenty minutes later, Lars's name was called. He stood, straightened his shirt with ceremonial care, and walked to the stage. The opening piano notes of "Mamma Mia" filled the pub, and his reserve vanished. Joy lit his face as if music unlocked a hidden side. His melodic voice, well-suited for ABBA, carried surprising strength and captivated the room.

By the chorus, he had dropped all Swedish reserve. His arms moved in perfect imitation of Anni-Frid and Agnetha's choreography. The pub's patrons watched, at first with the usual British mix of secondhand embarrassment and reluctant admiration. But soon, they joined in, some singing along and others filming on their phones.

"I had no idea," Ryan murmured, watching in fascination as Lars held a sustained note with professional precision. "He's actually good."

"There's clearly more to our Swedish friend than safety protocols and camera settings," I replied, equally astonished by this hidden talent.

As Lars concluded to enthusiastic applause, he acknowledged the crowd with a small bow before announcing, "I will now perform 'Waterloo.' Please join me if you know the words."

I glanced at my watch and nudged Ryan. Our plan was to drive overnight to London, thereby avoiding the worst of the traffic. "We should probably think about getting on the road soon, if we don't want to find ourselves arriving in the middle of London's maniac morning rush."

Ryan nodded reluctantly, clearly torn between the practicalities of travel and the spectacle unfolding before them. "Should we wait until he finishes this song?"

Two songs later, Lars still showed no sign of ending his ABBA concert. He had gathered a group of enthusiastic locals by the small stage. Now he was teaching them the choreography to "Dancing Queen."

"I don't think he's finishing anytime soon," I observed as Lars launched into what appeared to be a medley of lesser-known ABBA tracks. "He seems to have made some new friends."

Several attempts to catch Lars's attention proved futile. We waved, shouted, and pointed at our watches, but he was completely absorbed in his performance.

"Maybe we should just leave him to it?" Ryan finally said. "He did mention earlier that he's booked in at the local B&B tonight anyway. Tomorrow morning, he wants to head off in the direction of the Scottish Highlands. We could leave a note to say we had to get back."

This seemed the most practical solution. Ahead lay a seven-hour drive to London, with charging stops. We couldn't wait any longer. I rummaged in my bag, found a pen and paper, and wrote a quick message to Lars. I told him how much we enjoyed travelling with him, wished him well, and tucked the note into the side pocket of his rucksack.

We slipped out of the pub into the fresh evening air, Lars's exuberant singing following us down the street. The contrast between this performer and the earnest photographer we'd known was striking.

"Who'd have thought," Ryan mused as we walked toward our car, "that beneath all that Swedish stoicism lurked an ABBA tribute act waiting to break free?"

"I suspect that's true of many people," I replied, glancing back toward the warm glow of the pub windows. "We all contain unexpected dimensions, waiting for the right circumstances to reveal themselves."

My last look through the pub window showed Lars standing on a chair, microphone in hand, leading a swaying, arm-waving chorus. The introverted Scandinavian had become a joyful celebration of his country's most famous musical export. It felt like the perfect finale for our exchange – a reminder that travel's greatest gift isn't just seeing new places, but revealing the hidden depths in those we meet along the way.

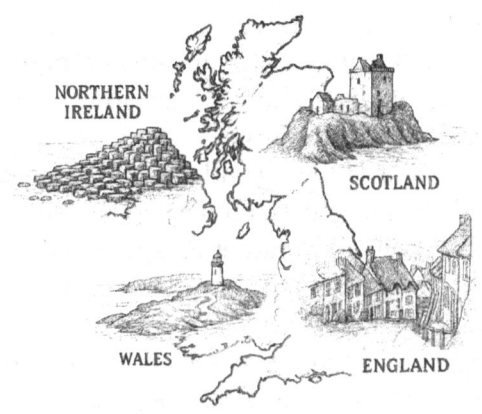

BRITISH OR ENGLISH?

The electric car moved quietly along the moonlit A1, its soft hum lost in the stillness of the night. Behind us, Berwick-upon-Tweed faded into the darkness, and the Northumberland coast appeared as a deep blue outline. Ryan sat in silence, watching the scenery change from the rough, dramatic north to softer hills.

He gave a small grunt, which meant his mind had at last reeled in a thought worth sharing. "Do you think Lars will recover from his ABBA tribute act?"

"I suspect he will be nursing both a hangover and a profound sense of Swedish embarrassment," I replied, adjusting the climate control. "Though I'm rather disappointed we didn't capture his performance for posterity. Marco would have paid good money to see that footage."

Mentioning Marco reminded me of our photography students who had just left. After weeks of guiding five lively travellers around Britain, the sudden quiet felt strange, like sunlight exposing where favourite furniture used to be.

Ryan chuckled as he reached for his thermos of tea. "Poor Marco. I'll never forget his face when he tried to put brown sauce on his chips. You'd have thought that's committing an act of culinary terrorism."

"It wasn't just the brown sauce," I reminded him. "It was the entire concept of English food that horrified him. He kept muttering about 'I need real pasta' and that a dinner should last at least three hours."

Ryan nodded, his face lighting up as he remembered. He grinned and said, "And then there was the Great Cream Tea Debate in Devon..."

"He looked as if he'd accidentally triggered an ancient blood feud," I finished. "Which, to be fair, he sort of had."

As we drove further south, the hedgerows became neat green fences, and the fields spread out like a patchwork under the moonlight.

Ryan watched the landscape change and observed, "Katrin was the opposite, wasn't she? The British way of thinking really surprised her. She documented everything. Remember how she started categorising all the British eccentricities she observed?"

"Absolutely, her field notes were amazing. She even had a whole section called 'The British Relationship With Home Repairs,' with photos of shaky shelves and pipes held together by duct tape and hope."

Ryan laughed, recalling a specific moment. "And she was so puzzled by how often we apologise. One day in the Cotswolds, she counted fourteen times Brits said sorry for things that weren't their fault. She thought it was a new kind of mental condition."

"She called it 'pathological politeness disorder, PPD'," I recalled. "And suggested it might qualify as a uniquely British mental health condition."

The motorway widened while we approached the more populous Midlands, traffic thickening around us. I checked the battery level – still comfortable, though we'd need to stop at a charging station before too long.

"Fleur was my favourite," Ryan admitted, scrolling through the photos on his phone. "Her perpetual war with our weather was like watching someone fight the ocean with a teaspoon."

"It wasn't just the weather that surprised her; she was also shocked by our bread," I said. "Remember that village shop in Kent? She held up a perfectly innocent pre-packed sandwich like it was evidence in a crime and called it 'an insult to the concept of boulangerie.'"

"And yet," Ryan noted, "by the end, she was drinking tea with milk and defending our cheese to that American couple we met in the New Forest. She'd gone partially native without realising it."

"Unlike Chuck," I said, signalling to exit the motorway. "Who was trying so desperately to go native that he missed all the nuances."

Ryan snorted. "Chuck, with his catastrophic approach to vocabulary. That time in Aldeburgh, when this gentleman politely asked if he could borrow a 'rubber', and Chuck was genuinely, utterly scandalised." He chuckled at the memory.

"And his battle with British plumbing," I added as we pulled into the service station. "The look on his face when he couldn't figure out the power shower in that B&B."

The service station looked like every other one in Britain, with a mix of tired shops and weary travellers. We plugged in the car and went inside, where the smell of coffee mixed with that unique scent you only find at motorway services in the middle of the night.

As we queued for coffee, Ryan turned to me and asked, "What about Lars? Our stoic Swede. I still can't reconcile his ABBA performance with the man who lectured us for twenty minutes on the optimal way to avoid Microplastic."

"I think Lars understood the British landscape better than any of them," I reflected. "He was also closer by nature to our reservedness. Just our humour he took way too literally."

"True," Ryan agreed, paying for his coffee and my green tea. "Though I maintain his confusion about pub etiquette was the highlight of the trip. The genuine bewilderment when he realised he was expected to carry multiple drinks through a crowded space without a tray."

We found a table by the window and watched as other travellers passed by. In the distance, our car stood connected to the charging point – silently replenishing itself for the journey ahead.

"It's odd, isn't it?" Ryan stirred his coffee with uncharacteristic thoughtfulness. "Seeing your own country through foreign eyes makes you notice things you've always taken for granted. Things that seem perfectly normal until someone from elsewhere points at them with confusion."

"Exactly." I nodded. "I've lived here my entire life, but somehow watching five foreigners navigate our cultural quirks has made Britain seem both more familiar and more strange."

Outside, the battery indicator showed we had enough charge to reach London. We picked up our things and started talking about practical stuff like traffic and timing as we walked back to the car. As we drove again on the motorway, I felt a quiet nostalgia for our absent companions. Their different views on Britain had taught us as much about ourselves as about them.

The projector hummed quietly as Ryan advanced through our carefully curated slideshow. The darkened room of the London Photography Club fell silent as an image of Holy Island appeared – the priory ruins silhouetted against a dramatic sky, tide waters beginning their ancient reclamation of the causeway. From my position near the laptop, I could see the audience leaning forward slightly, that subtle shift in posture that signals genuine engagement rather than polite attention. Twenty-five faces illuminated by the reflected light of someone else's journey.

"This series was captured by our Swedish student, Lars," Ryan said. "Note how he's composed the shot to emphasise the island's isolation – the causeway partially submerged, the ruins standing against the elements."

I advanced to the next slide – a close-up of Chuck's bewildered face as he attempted to comprehend the complexity of the British class system. "While Lars focused on landscape, our American student, Chuck, provided us with rather more... spontaneous cultural documentation."

A ripple of appreciative laughter moved through the room.

"What Chuck lacked in subtlety, he made up for in enthusiasm," I said. "Every British tradition got the same reaction from him: pure excitement, followed by lots of photos, usually with himself in the shot."

The slideshow continued with Katrin's careful photos of Cotswolds cottages, then Fleur's moody lighthouses, and Marco's touching British tea series. Each picture came with a story that told us as much about the photographer as about what was in the photo.

When the last slide faded, the lights came up, drawing the audience back from our journey. Technical questions followed, and soon the chairperson invited us all for further discussions next door at The Shutter, the club's unofficial headquarters. We gathered at a corner table with several engaged club members.

"Fascinating project," said a woman whose silver-streaked hair was gathered in a practical bun secured by what appeared to be a repurposed lens cap. "Especially seeing how differently each nationality interpreted our little island."

Ryan nodded, returning from the bar with a tray of drinks. "It was rather like having five different translations of the same text – all accurate in their way, but each emphasising different aspects."

A tall man with a russet beard and that particular complexion which marked him as unmistakably Scottish, leaned forward. "I couldn't help but notice," he began, his voice carrying the distinctive rhythms of Edinburgh, "that most of what you were describing as 'British' quirks were actually English ones."

He extended a hand across the table. "Hamish MacGregor. Edinburgh originally, though I've been photographing London architecture for the past decade."

"Fair point," I acknowledged, shaking his offered hand. "I suppose we're guilty of that typical English sin – using 'British' and 'English' interchangeably."

"Everyone does it," Hamish shrugged, though his tone suggested this universal error didn't make it any less irritating. "I'm just wondering – do you think your students even knew the UK isn't just England?"

He slid from his seat and approached the bar, bypassing the orderly queue with the casual confidence of someone who knows exactly where and how to stand to catch the bartender's eye without appearing to push in.

"That right there," Ryan said, nodding toward Hamish's queue-circumventing manoeuvre, "is cultural difference in action. An Englishman would rather die of thirst than skip the sacred queue."

Hamish returned with a fresh pint, settling back into our conversation. "It's genuinely confusing for foreigners," he admitted. "The terminology is a proper muddle – United Kingdom, Great Britain, British Isles. Even the sports teams can't agree – sometimes we're Team GB, Team UK, sometimes England, Scotland, Wales and Northern Ireland compete separately."

"I spent an entire afternoon explaining to Marco that Scotland is a country, not a region of England," I recalled. "He kept referring to it as 'the north part with the special costumes.'"

"Ah yes, our 'special costumes,'" Hamish rolled his eyes.

"Did you clarify that we don't all wander about in kilts playing bagpipes, or did you leave him with that delightful stereotype intact?"

"Actually, our Swedish student Lars was surprisingly well-informed about the distinctions," Ryan interjected. "He gave us quite a lecture about the etymological differences between 'England,' 'Britain,' and 'UK' while we were driving through Northumberland."

"Of course he did," Hamish laughed. "Scandinavians understand the importance of regional identity. They've spent centuries trying to convince the world they're not all the same frozen country."

A woman with dark hair and striking green eyes, who had been listening quietly, leaned into the conversation. "It's not just geography people get confused about – it's temperament too. I'm Siobhan, from Belfast," she added with a quick smile. "And I've lost count of how many people have been shocked that I'm not terribly reserved or indirect. The classic 'British' restraint isn't universal across these islands."

"True enough," Hamish said, with a brisk nod, "we Scots don't go in for all that English roundabout talk. We'd just spit out what we mean and have it done. A bit of sharp humour is the warmest handshake you'll get; we'd rather toss an insult across the table than fidget with polite nothings."

He grinned at Ryan. "Nice jumper. Did they not have it in your size?" Then added, "An Englishman would say: 'Brave of you to wear this jumper – it has a very tailored fit.' Both mean: 'That jumper's the wrong size, or you've had too many biscuits lately!'"

Siobhan laughed. "We've got a similar approach in Northern Ireland, but with a dual nature. We call it 'good craic' – warm, direct, and performative with friends, but cautious and indirect with strangers. We code-switch depending on who we're with. Necessity, really, given our history."

"And what about Wales?" I asked, glancing toward a woman with copper-coloured curls who'd been nodding in recognition throughout this cultural cartography.

"I'm Rhiannon," she offered. "North Wales born and raised.

We tend toward politeness and indirectness similar to Southern English styles, but we've got a storytelling tradition that produces a more surreal humour." She took a sip of her drink before continuing. "Rhod Gilbert – he's a Welsh comedian – describes Welsh humour as 'weirder and darker than English humour.'"

Her eyes brightened. "In the case of the jumper, we would probably invent a story where a man got strangled by a too-tight jumper after eating one more biscuit."

She grinned. "A farmer in my village once convinced American tourists he spoke to his sheep in a special whistle language. For hours, they repeated random noises, sure they were chatting to the flock."

The table erupted in laughter, not only at the story but at Rhiannon's distinct Welsh English delivery, which made it even more delightful.

"Or the modern pest of campervans blocking our tiny rural roads!" Hamish added. "An Englishman would seethe quietly and then write a strongly worded letter to the parish council about how campers should be banned from small roads. A Scot would tell them exactly where to park and how to do it with rather harsh words. A Welshman would create an elaborate fiction about ancient parking rituals, and a Northern Irish person would be incredibly helpful but with a completely stone-faced."

That, I had to admit, was the best summary of British diversity I had ever heard.

As the evening continued, I realised how special it was to sit with people from all four UK nations. Each took pride in their background, but we still felt like one complicated family. It reminded me that real divisions owe as much to landscape as to politics.

"For all our differences, though," Hamish observed, signalling for another round, "certain things unite the whole bloody lot of us, don't they?"

"The weather," Siobhan and Rhiannon replied in perfect unison, then glanced at each other with surprised laughter.

"Precisely," Hamish nodded, accepting his fresh pint from

the bartender with a grateful nod. "The weather – unpredictable, unreliable, and absolutely central to every conversation in these islands. I still check three different forecasts before deciding whether it is worth starting the barbecue or not."

"And it doesn't matter which forecast you believe," Ryan added, "because they'll all be wrong in slightly different ways."

I nodded in agreement. "Our photography students found that particularly baffling. Lars kept insisting there must be a more reliable system for prediction, while Chuck thought we were exaggerating for dramatic effect. Then they all experienced four distinct seasons in a single afternoon."

"That's the thing," Rhiannon said, leaning forward. "Our weather isn't extreme by global standards – we don't have devastating hurricanes, super hot summers, or months of -40 degree temperatures – it's just persistently inconsistent. You can never quite trust it."

"Like our politics," Hamish muttered into his beer.

"I think it's the island mentality as well," Siobhan suggested, redirecting the conversation. "There's a particular outlook that comes from living on islands, isn't there? A sense of both isolation and connection. We're separate from the continent but have absorbed influences from everywhere."

"We're simultaneously insular and outward-looking," I agreed. "Protective of our traditions but constantly adopting and adapting outside influences. Think about our food – fish and chips originated with Jewish refugees, tea came from our colonial past, curry is now as British as roast beef."

"And we all share that peculiar pride in being slightly odd," Ryan observed. "Every corner of these islands has its eccentric traditions that make absolutely no sense to outsiders but are defended with passionate intensity by locals."

"Like the Kirkwall Ba' Game," Hamish offered. "Hundreds of men fighting over a leather ball through the streets of Orkney. Been going since the 1600s. Health and safety nightmare, but suggest cancelling it and you'd have a proper rebellion on your hands."

"Or the Padstow 'Obby 'Oss in Cornwall," I added. "Where grown adults dress up as hobby horses and dance through the town while locals sing songs nobody can understand the words to."

"And bog snorkelling in Wales," Rhiannon chimed in. "Where people swim through muddy peat bogs wearing snorkels and flippers. Complete madness, but we're inordinately proud of it."

"Don't forget our Belfast Telegraph Sit-Out," Siobhan laughed. "Where our former Lord Mayor sits in a glass box on Donegall Square before Christmas, collecting for charity. Absolutely freezing, completely daft, but a beloved tradition."

"But most importantly," Hamish said, raising his glass slightly, "we all share that particularly British approach to humour. Different flavours across the regions, certainly, but humour remains our shared language – our way of dealing with everything from minor inconveniences to national disasters."

"It's our coping mechanism," Rhiannon agreed. "When the weather turns foul, the trains stop running, or the government collapses, we default to jokes. It's practically a national defence strategy."

"And largely incomprehensible to outsiders," Ryan added. "Poor Marco never quite grasped why we found it funny when things went wrong rather than getting properly upset. He kept waiting for the appropriate emotional and Italian-like dramatic response, and instead got deadpan understatement."

"To be fair," I countered, "he did eventually catch on. By the end of the trip, when that seagull stole half his sandwich in St Ives, his first response was 'Well, I suppose he needed it more than I did.' Pure British resignation."

Ryan lifted his glass. "To seeing ourselves as others see us," he proposed, "and learning we're even odder than we thought."

"Hear, hear," came the chorus of responses as glasses clinked around the table.

As the evening began its gentle dissolution and conversations fragmented into smaller groups, with people finishing their drinks and gathering belongings, I found myself in that liminal space between the warmth of the pub and the London night, reflecting on our journey.

"You know," I said to Ryan as we collected our coats, "when

we started this project, I thought we were teaching our international students about British culture. But I'm not sure that's what happened at all."

"No," he agreed, helping me into my jacket. "In many ways, they taught us more about ourselves than we taught them about Britain."

We said our goodbyes and swapped contact details, promising to work together again – a mix of genuine interest and the usual British sense of duty. Then we stepped outside into the gentle London rain. It wasn't heavy enough for an umbrella, but just enough to make you wish you had one.

The wet streets shone under the streetlights as taxis splashed through puddles. We had both decided to walk instead of taking the Tube, not quite ready for the day to end.

There was no need for words between Ryan and me. It was the sort of comfortable silence that only a long-standing friendship can produce. As we walked, I found myself reflecting on just how much this international exchange had altered my perspective on things. It wasn't about defining the best country or culture, but about recognising that our shared quirks and differences weave together something richer. Without these contrasts, the world is less vibrant. English, Scottish, Italian – it's the mix that matters most.

ABOUT THE AUTHOR

Ask Joana about her nationality and watch her pause, considering which answer to give you today. "European" might slip out first – a diplomatic compromise. Her German passport sits in a drawer; memories of Swiss mountains and Italian olive groves colour her past. Then, after moving to Britain, she learned to feel "utterly British," gesturing toward the windswept landscape she now calls home.

Becoming an islander wasn't always easy. She mastered the art of queuing, tried to lower her voice and tame her Italian gestures (both still work in progress), and discusses the weather with increasing skill - all while quietly enjoying every new British quirk she discovers.

Through her Canon camera, Joana collects more than images; she gathers memories. For over twenty years, her camera has been glued to her hand, accompanying her from her home on Scotland's windswept northeast coast to continents around the world. Her photo agency's portfolio, which boasts 30,000 images and counting, tells this story.

When not travelling or editing photos, Joana writes – a natural extension of her storytelling through images. Her name appears on travel guides and coffee table books, and now this book joins them. It is both a love letter to Britain and a way to process the culture shock she once felt, such as the time she stood confused in Tesco's baking aisle, faced with about 20 types of sugar – far more than the two she knew in Switzerland – and had no idea which one to choose.

When she feels the urge to travel, her electric Fiat 500e carries her across Europe, its small size perfect for winding country roads. At home, she puts down her camera and picks up kitchen knives, making vegan dishes that even meat lovers enjoy (so she hopes). Some of her recipes are featured in calendars and cookbooks, but for her, cooking is mostly a break from editing photos.

THE TRAVEL SPARKS SERIES BY JOANA

www.ingramcontent.com/pod-product-compliance
Lightning Source LLC
Chambersburg PA
CBHW011420070526
44584CB00026BA/3772